Facing the Wild:
Ecotourism, Conservation
and Animal Encounters

For Sandra, my ffStb.

Facing the Wild:
Ecotourism, Conservation
and Animal Encounters

Chilla Bulbeck

London • Sterling, VA

First published by Earthscan in the UK and USA in 2005

ISBN: 1-84407-138-3   paperback
        1-84407-137-5   hardback

Typesetting by FISH Books, London
Printed and bound in the UK by Bath Press, Bath
Cover design by Suzanne Harris

For a full list of publications please contact:

Earthscan
8–12 Camden High Street
London, NW1 0JH, UK
Tel: +44 (0)20 7387 8558
Fax: +44 (0)20 7387 8998
Email: earthinfo@earthscan.co.uk
Web: **www.earthscan.co.uk**

22883 Quicksilver Drive, Sterling, VA 20166-2012, USA

Earthscan is an imprint of James & James (Science Publishers) Ltd and publishes in association
with the International Institute for Environment and Development

A catalogue record for this book is available from the British Library

Library of Congress Cataloging-in-Publication Data
Bulbeck, Chilla, 1951–
        Facing the wild: ecotourism, conservation and animal encounters/Chilla Bulbeck.
            p. cm.
        Includes bibliographical references and index.
        ISBN 1-84407-138-3 (pbk.) – ISBN 1-84407-137-5 (hardback)
        1. Ecotourism. 2. Nature conservation. I. Title.

        G156.5.E26B85 2005
        338.4'791–dc22

                                                                2004019976

Contents

List of Figures and Tables

Figures

Tables

List of Acronyms and Abbreviations

ABC	Australian Broadcasting Corporation
ACF	Australian Conservation Foundation
ADRF	Australian Dolphin Research Foundation
AQWA	the Aquarium of Western Australia
CALM	Western Australian Department of Conservation and Land Management
CAMPFIRE	Communal Areas Program for Indigenous Resources (Zimbabwe)
CBD	Central Business District
EPA	Environment Protection Authority
FITs	free independent travellers
GITs	group inclusive tourists
GNP	gross national product
IAATO	International Association of Antarctic Tour Operators
ISIS	International Species Information System
IWC	International Whaling Commission
NHT	Natural Heritage Trust
PCBs	polychlorinated biphenyls
RZSSA	Royal Zoological Society of South Australia
SAMs	sub-adult males
SHEL	Southern Heritage Expeditions Limited
TAFE	Technical and Further Education College
WALHI	Wahana Lingkungan Hidup Indonesia (Friends of the Earth, Indonesia)
WTO	World Trade Organization
YUMIES	young urban males into extreme sports

Acknowledgements

In a project of almost 15 years' gestation, I owe a debt of gratitude to several institutions and many people, whose appearance here, of course, absolves them from any errors in the book. I received financial support with university research grants from Griffith and Adelaide Universities. More important were my periods away from teaching and administration, a secondment to the Australian National University in 1995, study leave in 1988, 1992, 2001 and an appointment to Tokyo University in 2002–2003. I thank my colleagues who carried the burden of my teaching during these absences, particularly those at Adelaide University in 2001 and 2002–2003, Margaret Allen, Kathie Muir, Barbara Pocock, Susan Oakley and especially Margie Ripper for offering my large first/second year social sciences class in its new flexible delivery mode for the first time in 2001 and acting as head of discipline in 2002–2003. I would also like to acknowledge the support of Women's Studies, English Department, University of Western Australia in providing a visiting appointment during the penultimate writing up of this manuscript in 2001. This project has always stimulated interest amongst my colleagues and friends and I am grateful for their enthusiasm over the years.

My sincere thanks go to all those who supported the research at the animal encounter sites analysed in this book, either by completing questionnaires, distributing and retrieving questionnaires or generously sharing their philosophies, knowledge and experiences with me. A number of these people shaped the project in significant ways, as can be seen by reference to their thoughts in the book: David Langdon (Monarto Zoological Park); John Wamsley (Warrawong Sanctuary); Dominic Farnworth, Helen Irwin and Kerry (Currumbin Sanctuary); Ron Shepherd (Department of Conservation and Land Management WA: Monkey Mia); Peter Martinson, Paul Tulloch and Ron Ballantyne (Cleland Conservation Park); Terry Dennis (National Parks and Wildlife Service SA: Seal Bay); Richard Jakob-Hoff (Auckland Zoological Park); Rodney Russ (Southern Heritage Expeditions: Macquarie Island and Antarctica); Mike Bossley (Australian Dolphin Research Foundation: Port River dolphins); Iain Greenwood and Tim Bickmore (Osprey Expeditions: Great Australian Bight). I especially thank Iain Greenwood for allowing me to accompany an expedition to the Great Australian Bight free of charge. A number of managers, guides and education officers at the sites generously granted me interviews, including Simon Heppelthwaite and Jeni of Southern Heritage Expeditions; Jim Grant of Buckeringa Sanctuary; Ed Macalister of

Adelaide Zoological Gardens; and Meredyth Hope of Warrawong. Raymond Soneff, Patricia Irvine, David Nathansan, Peter Shenstone, William McDougall, Olivia De Bergerac, Heather Aslin and Jill Whitehouse also kindly shared their ideas with me.

Chris Sauer accompanied me on this book's road to Damascus, Monkey Mia, and kept me posted concerning changes at the resort. Barbara Baird alerted me to Port Adelaide residents' affection for their dolphins. Professor Kellert provided me with his wildlife issues scale. Bill Faulkner, then of the Bureau of Tourism Research, assisted with tourism data. Andy Russell granted me an interview and Ralph Buckley made me think about which 'animals' I meant. Sue Doye administered my questionnaire at Monkey Mia and shared her interview results and insights with me. Mayumi Kamada, knowing my interest in animal encounters, took me to the Zoo at Nagoya and translated the many signs for me. Lenore Layman gave me invaluable feedback, including the insight that many visitors understand Antarctica in a romantic register. Adrian Franklin has shared his research on, insights concerning and enthusiasm for the social meanings of animals with me, particularly offering useful suggestions as a reader of an earlier manuscript.

Finally, my love and thanks go to my mother, Paquita Bulbeck, who accompanied me to many of the encounter sites discussed in this book: Warrawong, Yookamurra, the Galapagos Islands and Antarctica, although she drew the line at the orangutans of Borneo. She, like me, yearns pessimistically for a saved world. Indeed, her love of wild Australia goes back many years and shaped my own interest in this project long before I imagined it.

Introduction

Imagining animals

humans need animals in order to be human

(Erica Fudge, 2000, p2)

The amount of money spent by pet owners on their animals exceeds that spent by parents on baby food (Arluke, 1993, p5). Wildlife programmes attract higher audience ratings than soap operas (Davies, 1990, p74). Attendance at zoos is far greater than at professional sporting events (Franklin, 1999, p175). Between the living (pets and pests), the dead (beef and lamb) and the virtual (wildlife films and television series), even inner-city human worlds are full of animals. We are intimate with their soap opera lives (Skippy, Flipper), read about them in novels (from *Moby Dick* to *Watership Down*), constantly call on them in language (the faithful dog, the dirty rat) and in jokes. We represent them in advertising, greeting cards, children's stuffed toys, as brand names (for example the rosella eating Arnott's biscuits or Kiwi shoe polish) and as mascots (the West Coast Eagles, the Socceroos) (Berger, 1980, pp20–21; Ammer, 1989, pp96, 102, 108, 125; Brabant and Mooney, 1989; Baker, 1993, p6; Sax, 1998, pp217–218). Animals are rendered in concrete, including Australia's flock of 'big' sheep, cattle, lobsters and so on. In these multiple relationships, animals are eaten, abused, pampered, hunted, preserved; they provide labour and entertainment, from dogfighting to zoos; they are pets, pests, meat and laboratory animals (Benton, 1993, pp60–64; Birke, 1994, p21; Eder, 1996, p149).

Almost every day, suburban newspapers run 'nature' stories. Oil spills threaten penguins and seals; orphaned zoo animals are cared for by human foster parents; endangered species are snatched back from human decimation; mining or forestry threatens coral reefs or rainforests; environmental activists chain themselves to trees or sail their ships of green peace into the path of nuclear-powered vessels. Newspapers are peppered with gratuitous pictures of cute animals or splendid scenery, proliferating in advertisements and the travel section.

Patrolling our constructed borderlands between the human and the natural world, animals are dense with the symbolic meanings attributed to otherness. As Claude Lévi-Strauss famously said, specifically of totemic animal species, animals are 'goods to think' (*bonnes à penser*). Edmund Leach (1970, p34) translated this as 'goods to think with it' (Mullin, 1999, p208), while most

Note: (top) A pictorial souvenir of the 2000 Sydney Olympics includes an image of one of the torch carriers, John Bertrand, running past an elephant at Taronga Zoo in Sydney, before arriving at the Olympic stadium. (middle) The big lobster in Kingston, South Australia, encourages visitors to the restaurant and souvenir shop. The Big Sheep is near Goulburn, New South Wales; the main roads entering Rockhampton are guarded by big cattle of different breeds. (bottom) Bronze pigs in the city's shopping mall, Adelaide, their noses and backs rubbed to a golden lustre by children stroking and riding them.

Sources: (top) *The Australian*, 2000, p11, photography by Nathan Edwards and courtesy of Newspix

Figure I.1 *The Ubiquity of Animals*

contemporary commentators render the comment as 'good to think with'.[1] Edmund Leach (in Tapper, 1988, p47) suggests that animals 'carry not only loads but also principles', offering an 'almost inexhaustible fund of symbolic meaning'.

What is the outcome for urbanites of this widespread deployment of animals as 'good to think with' rather than as goods to trade or eat? As opposed to hunters and gatherers, pastoralists even, people living in big cities often do not register on a daily basis that we rely on animals for much besides entertainment. Some commentators suggest that, as we no longer recognize the material importance of animals in our lives, animals and the wild are trivialized. Children's stories – such as Beatrix Potter's *Peter Rabbit*, Kenneth Grahame's *The Wind in the Willows*, Rudyard Kipling's *The Jungle Book*, Michael Bond's *Paddington Bear* and E. B. White's *Charlotte's Web* – reproduce the 'bambi complex' or the 'Disnification' of animals, for which Walt Disney is blamed as the primary progenitor. Wild animals are reduced and marginalized: 'The animal is the sign of all that is taken not-very-seriously in contemporary culture: The sign of that which doesn't really matter' (Baker, 1993, p174).

Another issue that influences our experience of nature concerns the vast imbalance between representations of animals and the presence of material or concrete animals in our lives. Most urbanites have seen many pictures of lions, dolphins, elephants, but it is far more rare that we have smelled, heard or touched actual lions, dolphins and elephants. The mass media and the Internet saturate daily life with 'commerce and commodification' (Seidman, 1997, p45), with images. Is the 'real' thing treated as no more valuable than its representation, perhaps even less so if it is visually less striking due to its distance, as Umberto Eco (1986; see also Wilson 1992, p122) argues? Is the 'real' elephant just another signifier, part of the set of elephant signifiers (Kinder, 1991, p35)? Given that horses like Black Beauty write their biographies, Peter Rabbit dresses in clothes and Toad drives a car, does this make ordinary horses and rabbits seem inferior? Can animals lacking in these human capacities be killed and eaten with impunity and dissected in biology class (Lansbury, 1985, pp182–183, 188)? As discussed in Chapter 3, my research at dolphin encounter sites reveals the significance of preconceptions in framing animal encounters. For example, many visitors to Monkey Mia seemed overwhelmed by the perceived privilege of inter-species communication, imagining an animal closer to 'Flipper' than an animal whose 'behaviour is unpredictable', as signs at the site warn us.

John Berger (1980, p9) suggests that 'today we live without them [animals]'. Because independent animals no longer populate most human environments, the 'look between animal and man' has been extinguished (Berger, 1980, p26). There are no animals sufficiently autonomous from humans to decentre us with their stare, to make us see ourselves from somewhere else. Animals are no longer their authentic wild selves, but reduced to pets, impoverished spectacles in zoos and objects of wildlife photography (Baker, 1993, pp13–14).[2] Pets cannot look at us independently, because we treat them like humans. Nor can animals in zoos give us a self-sufficient gaze; they are prisoners, 'something that has been rendered absolutely marginal' (Berger, 1980, p22). In like vein, Jack Turner (1996, pxv) suggests that the greatest threat to the environment is what he calls 'abstract nature'. This is the kind of nature sold by Nature Company (Price, 1999), experienced in national parks or watched on television. Ironically, city-dwellers, who are usually the most strident advocates of nature, fail to preserve nature because they do not really know what they are trying to save.

I am more hopeful than Berger and Turner. There are ways in which animals have come close to humans again, both in some city zoos seeking to impart a conservation message and at less-caged animal encounter sites. Berger does not reflect on dolphins and other animals encountered in the wild or in nearly wild environments. This book explores the closeness and inexplicable pleasure many tourists experience in their animal encounters at wildlife destinations, their sense of 'I' contact through 'eye' contact with a wild animal, an animal that visitors perceive as equal and independent. This book ponders whether Bambi and Flipper always get in the way of this contact or whether some visitors take the opportunity to give real material animals more weight in their lives, and so become environmentalists, acting to save water or wild habitats and forgoing some of their creature comforts such as meat-eating. Indeed, some research suggests that 'really being there' is more likely to produce changed behaviour in relation to animals than mere knowledge offered by science or entertainment offered by films.

I/eye contact: Things best left unsaid

This journey into the dolphin's world taught me not only about them, but about myself and my fellow humans. It is as if, having for so long strained to see dolphins moving below the reflective surface of the water, my eyes suddenly shifted their depth of focus and I realized that I was all along staring through my own reflection.

(Rachel Smolker, 2001, p15)

he never knew I was there. I never knew I was there, either. For that forty minutes last night I was purely sensitive and mute as a photographic plate; I received impressions, but I did not print out captions... (E)ven a few moments of this self-forgetfulness is tremendously invigorating. I wonder if we do not waste most of our energy just spending every waking minute saying hello to ourselves.

(Annie Dillard, 1988, pp116–117, on watching a muskrat)

The notion of eye contact as 'I' contact comes from a much quoted extract from

John Berger's 1977 essay 'Why look at animals?' (Berger, 1980).[3] Berger claims that the animal's gaze decentres us, makes us see ourselves from the perspective of another creature: 'The animal scrutinizes him across a narrow abyss of non-comprehension' (Berger, 1980, p3), a gap that is both narrow yet impassably deep. Vicki Hearne (1987, p264) elaborates by noting that 'Everything in the universe is ... Other, but animals are the only non-human Others who answer us' without the intermediary of a guru. Thus I/eye contact is neither a mirror that merely reflects back our unchanged 'selves', nor is it so alien that we cannot write into the animal's eyes at least some of the messages we wish to read.

The preferred animals for I/eye contact, according to Konrad Lorenz (1954, p12), are not sharks or lions but 'baby releasers', animals with similar morphology to human babies. We respond to animal babies because of their triggering features of short chubby limbs, big eyes and relatively big heads. They are soft and round like helpless human infants.[4] Companion animals adapt their own facial expressions to those of their human family. A puppy reared in a family who smile a great deal learns to produce a sideways grin with its lips, a facial expression never seen in wild wolves (Clutton-Brock, 1999, p50).

However, where eye contact with pets returns the gaze of the complacent master or mistress, eye contact with wild animals seeks something else. Wild animals, according to some observers, have an 'inwardness', a mysterious inner side, a self. 'The animal is really nature glancing back at us' (Noske, 1989, p62). The three famous female primatologists who walked with apes – Jane Goodall, Dian Fossey and Biruté Galdikas – all comment on the abyss between animals and humans, and their painful attempt to cross it through eye contact. Fossey cabled Leakey when the gorilla Peanuts:

> suddenly stopped and turned to stare directly at me. The expression in his eyes was unfathomable. Spellbound, I returned his gaze – a gaze that seemed to combine elements of inquiry and acceptance.
>
> (Fossey, 1985, p141)

Galdikas writes:

> Looking into the calm, unblinking eyes of an orangutan we see, as through a series of mirrors, not only the image of our own creation but also a reflection of our own souls and an Eden that once was ours. And on occasion, fleetingly, just for a nanosecond, but with an intensity that is shocking in its profoundness, we recognize that there is no separation between ourselves and nature. We are allowed to see the eyes of God.
>
> (Galdikas, 1995, p403)

'One is never the same again' (Galdikas, 1995, p390). Goodall (in Fouts, 1997, px) claims that we must bridge this inter-species chasm for the sake of the planet. While we might aim to 'dissolve the oppositional gap between ourselves and nature', we can never close it, can never merge with nature. But the desire to do so is unrelenting. That widespread hunger fuels the popularity of these female primatologists, enthusiasm for New Age philosophies and visitation rates to wild animal encounter destinations.

Running counter to the fact that the vast bulk of 'embodied thought is non-cognitive', academic thought focuses on 'the cognitive dimension of the conscious "I"' (Thrift, 2000, p36). Is this because bodily experiences can barely be analysed, written or spoken? Must they always remain on the edge of speech, as in Isadora Duncan's dancing: 'If I could tell you what it meant, there would be no point in dancing it' (Bateson, 1972, pp137–138)? Similarly Hélène Cixous (1994, pp44, 59) describes *écriture féminine* as that which 'has never ceased to hear what-comes-before-language', as woman's 'art of living her abysses, of loving them, of making them sing, change, resounding the air with the rhythms of her earth's tongues, regardless of the littoral and acoustic delimitations of their syllables'.

According to Donna Haraway (1992, p3), fact–science–truth and fiction–literature–romance are the two competing discourses by which we know the world, although the division is itself a romantic fiction. In science, there should be no room for the unknowable, the inexplicable, the ineffable. Among the discourses that seek a truth-effect are anthropology, the natural sciences, psychology and sociology. Fiction, including advertising, cares little for brute and boring facts and weaves its spells from our subconscious desires. Science's animals are not in the same world as fabled beasts. Some understandings are hard to read through the prism of Western science's archaeology of knowledge, for example, traditional ritual performance, personal epiphanies at animal encounter sites, representations of animals in former times or at other places such as medieval bestiaries, or Shinto, Hindu and Buddhist constructions of animals. Some discourses are self-consciously political, like the conservation movement or indigenous peoples' and women's claims in the political arena. The law's animals do not exist in the same domain as psychology's companion animals or pets, which inhabit a different world from animals raised to be eaten or which are hunted.

This book had its genesis in a personal epiphany. At Monkey Mia in north-western Australia, dolphins swim into the beach to be stroked (and fed) by humans. The experience is indescribable, not a situation in which a social scientist likes to find herself. That sun-drenched dolphin-touched day was the first step on a journey of a thousand citations. It seemed that to understand Monkey Mia I had to understand human relations with animals, the lure of wildness and the development of ecotourism. I needed to explore these across time and space, looking for historical and cultural patterns. I wanted to know why humans in the West, despite (or perhaps because of) their animal-deficient environment, went in search of communication with dolphins, eye contact with big cats and the vistas of apparently untouched nature. After writing this book, I have come to the conclusion that some things about contact with animals cannot be said: those things which are not about the 'I' reflected in their 'eyes', but which are indeed about an indescribable, mysterious, deliriously pleasurable other.

Rather than bemoan this deficiency, I argue that we must value our emotional response to animals, and that animal encounter sites should do more to bend these emotions towards a new kind of environmental conservation, which I call respectful stewardship of a hybrid nature. The enormous popularity of indigenous and New Age spirituality and of the search for 'authentic' tourism testifies to many contemporary Westerners' need for meaning, for a sense of the spiritual. If social 'science', as in this book, does not grapple with this need, it will be left to those we decry as New Age 'loonies'. In this search for hybridization, we can neither go back to the premodern past nor stay safely in the disgodded present (Berman, 1981, p69).[5] We are neither completely separate from nor completely merged with the world around us. We need the 'double perspective' of both critical distance and of wonder and amazement (Bryld and Lykke, 2000, pp69–70). Some writers who seek to combine intellect and emotion, fact with value, in a new understanding of the wild world are discussed in Chapter 6. I attempt a similar hybridization in this book, seeking to bring the full rigour and exposure of the social sciences to my task without destroying the unbearable lightness of the encounters I, and others, have had with wild animals.

Related to my claim that we need to combine science and emotion is the suggestion that our understanding of and engagement with nature may arise much more strongly out of tactile embodied experiences with actual animals than intellectual engagement with ideas (Aslin, 1996, p321).[6] Our rehabilitation of animals injured on roads or building frog ponds in our back garden may be far more persuasive than reading books about 'the abstract wild' (Turner, 1996). Some, at least, of the animal encounter sites in my study allow visitors to feel animals in both ways: physically and emotionally.

My concept of 'respectful stewardship' seeks to explore this combination of an emotive and intellectual approach to wildlife understanding and management. Furthermore, it will be a respectful stewardship of a 'hybrid nature'. There are no wilderness areas left in the world; all is touched in some way by human intervention. This means that the so-called natural world must be managed. This is a grievous burden for humans to shoulder, and not one we are likely to undertake successfully, given humanity's accelerating 'rape of the wild' (Collard, 1989, p1). But I can see no other option. The idea of stewardship is expressed by Franklin et al (2000, p22) as 'second nature' or 'assisted nature', denoting the way that a second assists someone or endorses a proposition. In Western people's desire for the authentic, nature 'seconds' culture, as a legitimizing 'vote'. By contrast, paradoxically, 'wilderness management' means extending, building upon or seconding nature.

As little pieces of hybrid nature, there is a role for managers of nature destinations in extending 'respectful stewardship', not only to the animals in their care but also proselytizing to the visitors to those sites. To enhance human success in our obligation, those concerned with environmental issues or preserving the wild world must supplement the scientific discourses concerning animal extinction, global warming and so on with an understanding that humans need to feel and want, as well as to know, if we are going to act to change. Indeed, as the following chapters reveal, many animal encounter site managers are fully aware of the emotional power of the animals in their charge. This is one of the promises made by animal encounter sites and the half-articulated experiences of many who visit them with such pleasure. The book concludes by asking how people's experiences at animal encounter sites can be understood, used and deployed as part of respectful stewardship.

Encountering animals: Outline of the book

The research undertaken for this book concerns how people experience and understand encounters with wild animals at specific animal encounter destinations. The explosion in ecotourism and nature documentaries, so that one cable television channel offers 'all animals, all the time' (Mullin, 1999, p212), reveals that, for people living in big cities, wilderness is a site of leisure, not work. We 'escape' our daily existence and work demands to a space where time is our own. Wild animals symbolize that leisure and pleasure – particularly those animals whose lives appear effortless and fun-filled, such as dolphins. Generally we imagine wild animals not as the ants, birds and frogs in our backyards, but as lions on the savannah, penguins in Antarctica, whales and dolphins in the Southern Ocean. We imagine them in a non-urban remote setting. Even so, and akin to pets, many wild animals are imagined as 'emotional partners' (Eder, 1996, p97), but emotional partners of a different stripe to pets, as is particularly obvious in the case of dolphins.

I chose sites that represented a continuum from staged to authentic or wild, using MacCannell's (1976) notion of 'authentic tourism'. At one end is the urban zoo, Auckland Zoological Park; at the other end are the sea lions of Seal Bay, the whales of the Great Australian Bight, the penguins of Antarctica. Intermediate experiences include open plains zoos, such as Monarto, and wildlife sanctuaries, such as Warrawong, Currumbin and Monkey Mia, where the animals are at least partly provisioned (fed). Given my interest in tactile experiences, sites were also selected to include several where visitors can touch the animals: the lorikeets at Currumbin, the koalas at Cleland and the dolphins at Monkey Mia. Finally, the sites were chosen to represent a variety of animals encountered and philosophies promoted by site managers. Each site was visited, site personnel interviewed and material about the site collected and analysed. However, the crucial instrument of data collection was a survey of visitors to the chosen sites. The research methods are explained in detail in Appendix 1.

Tourism is possibly the largest global industry; within it ecotourism is a rapidly expanding sector. The introduction to Part 1 provides a discussion of site management issues, in particular the dilemma of guaranteeing an 'authentic' experience while also ensuring a close encounter. Authenticity and the wellbeing of animals are challenged as sites become popular and ecotourists destroy the very thing they love to see. Donald Horne (1992, pix) notes 'how intimately [sightseeing] is connected with the crisis of authenticity in modern societies'. Ecotourists want to see alligators in the Everglades, sea lions on Kangaroo Island, toucans in the Amazon. Seeing these animals in cages in zoos is not the 'real' thing. Ecotourists come to animal encounter sites to contemplate and be rejuvenated by pristine authentic nature. Animal lovers seek to communicate with wild and free animals across the 'narrow abyss of non-comprehension' (Berger, 1980, p3). On the other hand, not all are in search of authenticity. 'Happy snappers' are merely notching up another 'must-see' site. Even a few apparently purposeless visitors fetch up at animal encounter sites on their way to fishing or other pursuits. For these latter kinds of tourists, authenticity is often not desired.

Chapters 1 to 3 discuss the experiences of visitors to the nine surveyed animal encounter sites. Chapter 1 discusses the shift in the purpose of zoos from entertainment to education (for conservation), from fanciful displays of single examples of exotic megafauna to a focus on endemic but endangered animals, and displays more closely approaching complete ecosystems. Auckland Zoo provides the example of a city zoo. Many ecotourists wish both to 'touch' animals and see animals 'untouched' by humans. The responses of visitors to Cleland Nature Reserve and Currumbin sanctuary are discussed, to introduce discussion of the role of touch in wildlife conservation. When animals are fed, this can lead to behavioural problems that endanger visitor safety and the very lives of misbehaving animals.

Chapter 2 discusses semi-authentic and authentic animal encounters in which the overriding message is one of conservation, although expressed in different keys at different sites. The sites described in this chapter include Monarto Zoological Park, an example of a plains zoo, and Warrawong Sanctuary, founded by the iconoclastic John Wamsley with his attempts to save Australia's small marsupials. Given their previous role in resource exploitation and their current role as wildlife to be watched, the cases of sea lions (Seal Bay, South Australia), whales (Southern Right Whales in the Great Australian Bight) and penguins (particularly Southern Heritage Expeditions' tour of Antarctica and the sub-Antarctic Islands) are also considered. All these sites use the animals as ambassadors for their conservation messages.

The visitor surveys revealed that visitors to the dolphins at Monkey Mia registered distinct responses to the animals when compared with visitors to other 'authentic' animal encounter sites. A significant number of visitors to Monkey Mia construed a close connection or communion with the dolphins. These findings support claims for the ubiquity and particularity of dolphins as sign-bearers in contemporary Western society, for example, in the environmental movement, New Age spiritualism, science and science fiction.

Chapter 3 asks why dolphins are such splendid bearers of our fantasies, exploring the recent eruption of dolphins into Western consciousness. We visit a number of dolphin encounter sites, including two places in Australia where dolphins are fed: Monkey Mia and Tangalooma. The chapter explores interactions between dolphins and human communities, with a focus on the dolphin pods who live in the river at Port Adelaide. Many who experience dolphins in these locations speak of the 'privilege' of being able to 'touch' 'wild' dolphins, of being 'uplifted by the presence of dolphins'. The chapter concludes by musing whether the discovery of (male) dolphins' aggression and sexual obsession will undermine these popular constructions of the spiritual, peace loving friendly dolphin.

The second part of the book explores how the experiences of visitors to animal encounter sites might extend our understanding of conservation issues. I claim that we can no longer sustain a series of dualisms by which we construct the natural world. For example, the opposition 'wilderness' and 'managed' is challenged by the example of 'feral animals', both wild animals that become a nuisance and domesticated animals that become wild. Nevertheless, (some Western) humans have and yearn for 'authentic' experiences, for encounters with a romantic wild, for a spiritual or religious experience of nature. Instead of decrying this as impossible and inaccurate, conservation managers should build on these dreams and desires in the messages they offer at animal encounter sites. (Male) scientists and environmentalists often demean (female) humanistic approaches to animals, the former based on knowledge of the need to save ecosystems and the latter seeking the wellbeing of individual animals, often in an extension of love for pets. Again, however, the two ways of knowing nature must be given their due. Tactile connection in hunting is celebrated by some men; why should not tactile connection in saving orphaned marsupials be similarly recognized?

The introduction to Part 2 explores these issues by challenging the nature–culture dichotomy and outlining my adaptation of Stephen Kellert's (1978a, 1983, 1989) animal orientations to describe the main attitudes to nature found in my sample: humanistic, moralistic and conservationist. The lack of a spiritualistic orientation in Kellert's schema is surprising, particularly in the light of survey responses at Monkey Mia and given the search for meaning by many (white and middle class) members of Western society. As explored in Chapter 4, this search for meaning operates through the search for the 'authentic' and the 'primitive' in constructions of the 'other'. The 'self' stands for civilization, rationality, individualism, while the other stands for naturalness, emotion and connection. The quest to fill the emptiness of the self with the other is variously expressed in New Age spirituality, the bodily practices of hunting and constructing Fourth World peoples as 'original' ecologists and tourist guides. There are surprising resonances between hunting as a masculine engagement with the wilderness and the romantic quests of tourists, explored with the example of Antarctica as perhaps the most romantic contemporary tourist destination.

Chapter 5 returns to worry at the impossibility of dividing the world into nature and culture, wild and tame, good and bad. Science, for example with the development of ethology, ecology and environmentalism, is finally following tardily in the footsteps of everyday understandings, and moving away from a dualistic opposition between humanity and all other animals, between knowledge and passion. Passion is likely to come as much through physical experience of the wild world (the 'concrete' wild) as from knowledge of the wild world (the 'abstract' wild). While tactile animal encounters can be dangerous for humans and animals, my survey demonstrates the enormous desire for these among many humans. This desire can, I argue, be bent to conservation purposes. There are different kinds of animals in the world and we respond to them in kind, in the different kinds by which we have classified them. The effect of classifying animals as 'wild' is pursued through analysis of the distinction between feral and wild animals, and the treatment of animals in these two categories.

Chapter 6 opens by identifying some of the hurdles to establishing successful 'respectful stewardship', humanity's honest admission that we can destroy the planet, and most likely will if we do not change. This understanding obliges us to treat the rest of life empathetically, on the basis of the needs of other creatures rather than just our own desires. Despite ecotourist dreams, I argue that there are no authentic animal encounter sites. Instead sites are classrooms or cathedrals. Curators of zoos and sanctuaries provide Noah's arks; ecotourist operators seek to instil their love of wild things in visitors; tourists at animal encounter sites act elsewhere in response to the moral and ecological issues posed by their very presence at animal encounter destinations.

I am not optimistic that humanity can embrace respectful stewardship in the short time we apparently have left to us. A substantial minority of people is in fact indifferent to animals. Many more adopt a utilitarian approach in their nature dispositions, seeking the preservation of only that which does not threaten their own self-interest. The humane movement that arose with industrialization did not oppose meat eating or fox hunting. Most visitors to animal encounter sites are also unreflective meat eaters. On the other hand, as Adrian Franklin (1999, 2002) has argued, animals and nature are strong magnets for political intervention and as bearers of meaning, even if many of us now understand this nature as 'second nature', as constructed by human understanding. This is all to the good if we are going to displace the desire for authentic animals and untouched wilderness with an honest obligation for management and self-imposed limitation of human desires. Before the end of the day, the distinction between 'us' and 'them', between humanity and the rest of nature, must be challenged, and the dependence, not only of nature on humans but of humans on the rest of the world, must be expressed in our nature politics.

PART 1

Back to Nature Tourism

Introduction – Part 1

The world is a book; he who stays at home reads only one page.

(Augustine in the 2nd century AD in Sofield, 1991, p56)

Authentic tourism

The tourism industry is a favoured child of globalization, feeding and feeding off the information superhighway, shipping lanes and airport terminals (Weston, 1989, p43). Indeed, the last frontier of tourism is not Antarctica or the floor of the Atlantic Ocean, but outer space.[1] Studies breathlessly recount the phenomenal growth of the tourism industry, 'the greatest continuing mass movement of peoples in human history' (Horne, 1992, pix). The oft-cited prediction that tourism would be the largest industry in the world at the millennium (Urry, 1992, p1; Rojek, 1997, p70) is indicated by the facts that tourism accounts for 7.5 per cent of world trade (Rojek, 1997, p70) and that there are over 670 million arrivals at international ports (Addley, 2001, p22).[2] Tourism employs more people than any other industrial sector – over 112 million people, one of every 15 workers in the world. Travel is the major foreign exchange earner for the US and for many developing countries (McLaren, 1998, p13).[3] Or, as Deborah McLaren (1998, p13), in an attack on the economic and environmental degradation caused by tourism, puts it: 'With annual revenues of almost $3 trillion, its economic impact is second only to that of the weapons industry'. In 1988, tourism contributed 6 per cent to Australia's Gross Domestic Product (GDP), almost equivalent to the contribution of the rural sector (Carroll, 1991a, p18). In 1992, Australia had to export 50 tonnes of coal to generate the same earnings as two Japanese honeymooners spending a week in Australia (Rowe, 1993, p7).[4]

The earliest travellers are often imagined as pilgrims on their journey to the Holy Land, whether Jerusalem or Mecca.[5] It is common, also, to posit tourism as the contemporary version of a religious calling (Pearson, 1991, p126) 'in its concern with pilgrimages, with authentic relics and with regeneration through communion with Nature, Art, the Authentic, the Past and other forms of spiritual refreshment' (Horne, 1992, p76), a quest lampooned by David Lodge (1992, p75) in his novel *Paradise News*. Even the word 'holiday' echoes 'holy-day' (Davidson and Spearritt, 2000, pxviii).

The industry of tourism is premised on a 'vacationing infrastructure': a financially comfortable population who have won vacations as part of their working conditions,[6] which they could experience in resorts, holiday camps or hotels and to which they could travel by way of railways, steamers or other transportation. The infrastructure of transportation and vacation destinations was assembled in the US during the last half of the 19th century (Aron, 1999, p167). To this material infrastructure, Patricia Jasen (1995, p10) adds the symbolic infrastructure of guidebooks describing itineraries all could follow. For example, *Walkabout* was founded by the Australian National Travel Association in 1934 (Davidson and Spearritt, 2000, p80). Guidebooks and the guided tour left and leave most of the country blank, directing the tourist towards predetermined ways of seeing the landscapes (Horne, 1992, p24).

Frederick Billings, president of the Northern Pacific Railroad, was involved in the creation of Yosemite and Yellowstone National Parks (Spence, 1999, p36). Billings believed 'commerce could serve the cause of conservation by bringing visitors to a site worthy of preservation', where nature worship replaced other forms of religion (Spence, 1999, p37). In Canada, friendly societies, mechanics' institutes, Sunday schools, temperance societies and many employers organized outings by steamer and rail (Jasen, 1995, p127). In Australia, the opening of the Blue Mountains to tourism was an unintended side effect of the railway line to Bathurst (Davidson and Spearritt, 2000, p15). A paddle steamer especially fitted for 'excursionists' or day-trippers encouraged the development of Queenscliff and Sorrento (Sydney suburbs) from 1872. In 1896, the first road map of Victoria was produced, an increasing number being produced from the 1920s (Davidson and Spearritt, 2000, pp163–164). After World War II, the motorcar became the major means of transportation in Australia and North America (Davidson and Spearritt, 2000, pp34–35).

Dean MacCannell (1976, p41) has famously argued that 'Modern man has been condemned to look elsewhere, everywhere, for his authenticity, to see if he can catch a glimpse of it reflected in the simplicity, poverty, chastity or purity of others'. This 'elsewhere' might be another time (heritage tourism), another place (ethnic tourism) or another species (ecotourism) (see Horne, 1992, p105). 'The tourist hopes to find enlightenment in the "real lives" of other species, people and places' (Jarvis, 2000, p38). Tourism rhetoric is full of claims to authenticity: 'the very place where...', 'a real piece of the true Crown of Thorns', 'original', 'actual' (MacCannell, 1976, p14). However, the tourist is forever deprived of this goal, his or her very presence declaring the staged nature of the experience. Tourists desire that wilderness areas be 'pristine and unaltered by humans' (Ross, 1988, p317), but the destination cannot be so far off the beaten track as to deny access. The best a privileged few might achieve is access to a staged back region, usually sanitized, for example when zoo friends are given a behind the scenes tour (MacCannell, 1976, pp94, 99, using Erving Goffman's notion of front and back regions).

Where some forms of tourism merely require the infrastructure of transportation and accommodation, special interest tourism must also provide an *experience*, a transformation of the self. Special interest tourists are more likely to be free independent travellers (FITs) than group inclusive tourists (GITs) who are members of a package tour. The acronyms FITs and GITs suggest a hierarchy of tourist types and of class differences. As with other displays of taste, Pierre Bourdieu (1984, pp50, 55) suggests that an 'aesthetic disposition' can be expressed in tourism. Teachers and intellectuals choose 'walking, camping, mountain or country holidays' while the old bourgeoisie choose hotel holidays in spa towns (Bourdieu, 1984, p28). The working class enjoy participatory entertainment (Bourdieu, 1984, p34) in casinos rather than in culture contact, preferring the sights at Blackpool to those of beaching whales (Crick, 1989, p327; Urry, 1990, p10; see also Savage et al, 1992, pp109–110; New South Wales Tourism Commission, 1989a, pp65–67). Some special interest tours, as with the Grand Tour in the late 17th century, also require intellectual capital. The experience may require knowledge of the poetic heritage of the Lake District (Urry, 1990, p86), an ability to differentiate a complex ecosystem and a stand of conifers (Urry, 1990, p99) or apprehension that wildlife is in its natural setting with minimum disturbance (Varcoe, 1988, p27). A study tour requires preparatory homework to appreciate the experience (Varcoe, 1988, p27).

Ecotourism

The term ecotourism overlaps with other terms like adventure tourism, nature-oriented tourism, alternative tourism, appropriate tourism, soft tourism (*tourisme doux*), responsible tourism, ethical tourism, environment-friendly travel, green tourism, sustainable tourism and nature tourism (Miller and Kaae, 1993, p39). Ecotourism, as a concept, dates from at least 1965, when Nicholas Hetzer called for a rethinking of culture, education and tourism and promoted an 'ecological tourism'. For Hetzer, ecotourism attempts minimum environmental impact, maximum respect for host cultures, maximum economic benefits to the host country's grass roots and maximum 'recreational' satisfaction for participating tourists (Miller and Kaae, 1993, p39). Over time the significance of 'relatively undisturbed or uncontaminated natural areas' (Boo, 1990, pxiv) has lost ground to a greater prominence for learning, ecological sustainability and the wellbeing of local people. Indeed Janet Richardson (1993, pp9, 11–14) suggests that areas of disturbance may yield the greatest learning potential, noting the goal of fostering understanding, participation and conservation, through activities like tree planting and turtle tagging (similarly, see the Commonwealth Department of Tourism's 1994 definition of ecotourism in Jarvis, 2000, p43).

Claims concerning the weight of ecotourism within Australian tourism as a whole vary from only 1 per cent (Davidson and Spearritt, 2000, p245)[7] up to one-third or more (Hodge, 2002, p40; Ralph Buckley in Chryssides, 2001, p42).[8] A 1989 survey revealed that 70 per cent of the Australian travel market considered themselves to be environmentally conscious (Kangaroo Island Tourism Working Party, 1991, p4), suggesting the increasing popularity of the term as much as the green orientation of the tourism industry.[9] Janet Richardson's (1993) guide of Australian ecotours and nature-based holidays identified 18 that mentioned specific animals, such as 'little penguins' or 'soaring eagles', while half noted unspecified wildlife, fauna and flora, or activities such as bird watching, snorkelling or scuba diving.

It sometimes appears that 'ecotourism is really just niche tourism for the rich' or 'less about the environment than about reducing the guilt of wealthy travellers and feeding the human ego' – 'egotourism' (Jarvis, 2000, p44). David Brooks (2000, pp10–11), in his tongue-in-cheek *Bobos in Paradise*, suggests that the new elite of bobos, bourgeois bohemians, have combined economic success with free spirit rebellion, largely through their consumption choices. Holidays become 'dial-an-ordeal' (Brooks, 2000, p210) or 'useful vacations' (Brooks, 2000, p203) in which bobos learn, or achieve spiritual or emotional breakthroughs: 'we don't just want to see famous sights; we want to pierce into other cultures. We want to try on other lives' (Brooks, 2000, p206; see also Eagles, 1992 for Canada). An article in a magazine directed at young Singaporean women advocated 'ecotourism': 'Feed wild dolphins, hug a koala or admire the birds', 'getting away from it all – without of course being too far from the comforts of home such as air conditioning in summer or TV in the evenings'. Along with watching dolphins and birds, the article noted that in December and January Australian swimming pools and beaches 'fill up with hunks and other watchable bodies' (Lee, 1994, pp258, 259). Indeed the ecotourist tag has become so valuable and abused that an accreditation process has been established in Australia, accrediting some 300 tours (Ralph Buckley in Chryssides, 2001, p45).

Ecotourism and cultural tourism draw on the market of 'bobos', middle class, educated urbanites from North America, Europe and increasingly Japan (Ryel and Grasse 1991, p171; Whelan 1991, p5; see also Kierchhoff 1986, p8 for Germany). The survey of visitors to animal encounter sites in Australasia offers some support for the claim that special interest tourists belong to the better educated and/or higher income segments of society. Table A3.11 (in Appendix 3) reveals that the tertiary educated were less worried about good transportation and good eating and rest facilities. The results for important factors when planning a trip overseas generally support the contention that people with higher socioeconomic status focus on self-actualizing needs and those with lower socioeconomic status focus on more physiological needs (see Table A3.22 which uses the factors corresponding to Maslow's hierarchy of needs, as adapted to the tourist experience by Pearce and Caltabiano, 1983, p18). With the exception of the chance to see animals, the tertiary educated tend to choose the experience factors (at the top of Table A3.22) and the less well educated the security factors (at the bottom of the table), although the chance to relax was the most important consideration across the range (chosen by 52 per cent of respondents: the understanding of 'chance to relax' may vary across the socioeconomic range mirroring a desire for experience among the higher socioeconomic groups and representing lazing around for other groups – I am indebted to Kim Allen for this insight). However, blue collar workers chose the chance to be alone in the environment at a higher rate than the other categories of employment, while the chance to shop is more appealing to managers and professionals, suggesting, as Brooks (2000) does, that higher socioeconomic background tourists have more cultural and financial capital.

Managing authenticity

Given that there is normally an entry fee, animal encounter sites must improve on the unanticipated experience (Mullan and Marvin, 1987, pp80–82). A pragmatic problem thus presents itself for the managers of 'authentic' encounters. If the notion of 'authenticity' depends upon the animal being in its 'natural habitat' and thus free to 'choose' the encounter, the tour promoters may not be able to guarantee an 'encounter'. The dilemma is addressed in various ways in encounter site publicity: by (almost) guaranteeing an animal contact, by proclaiming the very closest of encounters, by noting the diversity of experiences to be had, by emphasizing the authentic nature of the experience. Sometimes, especially if the scenery is powerful in its own right, visitors respond to the beauty of even distant animals. Sometimes, too, visitors are promised an education or that they will feel good by participating in conservation. If interpretation is appropriate, visitors can learn about the animals in their natural environment, going about their everyday business. Visitors deploy the narratives structured around the animals to give meaning to what they witness. However, education can produce its own contradiction: the tension between proclaiming the values of a natural environment and staging an interaction.

Another tension with the proclaimed authenticity of the encounter is the desire of visitors for interaction with the animals. Interaction is capable of many meanings, but my survey results suggest that visitors to animal encounter sites did not consider they had an 'interaction' when they observed animals that ignored them. On the other hand, petting or holding an indifferent animal did constitute an interaction. The desire for interaction seems to be a major reason why visitors to animal encounter sites feed animals, even when told not to. Animal feeding produces considerable problems for wildlife management, even signing the death warrants of some human provisioned animals. For some visitors, interaction with dolphins provokes almost mystical responses, with some visitors saying the dolphins 'chose me'.

The 'resort cycle' denotes another management issue impacting on the meaning of the experience. As visitor numbers grow, the encounter is changed from a private communion in the wild bestowed on the privileged few to a routinized and regulated moment with the animals. Between 1988, when I first visited Monkey Mia, and 1999, when I returned to find a resort, the gap between Monkey Mia and Sea World had narrowed. David Attenborough (1990, p11) made the march of the scarlet land crabs on Christmas Island so famous that a resort is being built to lure an estimated 40,000 tourists each year to the little island (Dunn, 1989, p5). The resort cycle does not necessarily mean that those visiting a busier site with manifest infrastructure do not have an 'authentic' encounter, as some of the responses at Monkey Mia reveal. Especially if they know the site in no other guise, some still commune with the dolphins. However, as Table A3.9 in Appendix 3 reveals, the major reason for not enjoying the dolphins at Monkey Mia was too many other people.

Zoos provide a convenient, diverse and staged animal encounter experience. Belle Benchley, Director of San Diego Zoo for almost 30 years from 1953, asks: 'Where could they go and in the course of the morning watch a snake shed its skin, a young parrot learn to fly, and a newborn fawn "freeze" at the command of its young mother? Have they ever seen even one of those things happen in the wild? Probably not' (in Fackham, 1978, p26). Similarly, claims the New York Zoological Society (c1991) of 'Bronx Zoo', instead of travelling '31,000 miles' to see the animals, you can 'journey to the Himalayas', 'safari to wild Asia', 'enter the world of darkness' and finally 'go wild' without leaving New York.

At the other end of the 'authenticity' spectrum from the city zoo is the unexpected totally unmediated experience of seeing an animal on a bush walk or while camping. Authentic animal encounters, as destinations, develop out of formerly unmediated experiences of animals (Franklin, 1999, p81). Tourists can watch turtles lay their eggs, spot crocodiles, watch bears catching salmon (Dawson, 1992, p3; Duffus and Dearden, 1990, p220). Bizarre experiences play with people's love of fear, for example watching masses of intermingling garter snakes mate near Winnipeg (Winnipeg Tourist Brochure, 2001, p7), Tasmanian devils tear wallaby carcasses to pieces (Bell, 2001, ppR30–R31), or wolves in Canada consume a beaver carcass (Dexter, 2001, pL12). Rodney Fox, once a shark hunter, was part of the successful 1997 campaign for federal protection of white pointer sharks. He has turned to cage diving, reputedly becoming a millionaire.[10] There are seven cage dive operators in South Australian waters alone, offering close encounters with great white pointers.[11]

After visiting a number of sites, I chose eight for further study: Auckland Zoological Park, Cleland Wildlife Park, Currumbin Sanctuary, Monarto Zoological Park, Monkey Mia, Seal Bay, Warrawong Sanctuary and the Whales in the Great Australian Bight. The Sub-Antarctic Islands and Antarctica were subsequently added to the sample. Appendix 1 describes the survey methods at each encounter site and Appendix 2 reproduces the questionnaire. Appendix 3 summarizes the results. The sites range from traditional zoos and sanctuaries through open plains-type zoos to 'authentic' sites, where animals can be viewed in their natural environment but under the regulation of authorities, such as the Department of Conservation and Land Management at Monkey Mia.

Staged or zoo-like sites were represented by Auckland Zoo in New Zealand, Cleland Wildlife Park in the Adelaide hills and Currumbin Bird Sanctuary on Queensland's Gold Coast. As 'semi-authentic' sites that sought to give visitors an impression of uncaged animals, Warrawong Sanctuary in the Adelaide hills and Monarto Zoological Park, an open plains zoo near Adelaide, were selected. Although authentic in the sense that humans went to see the animals, there was some infrastructure associated with the sea lion colony on Kangaroo Island off South Australia and the dolphins at Monkey Mia in north-west Western Australia. The least developed sites in terms of infrastructure were Antarctica and Osprey's whale watching expeditions in the Great Australian Bight. Three sites were also chosen because the animals can be touched: bird feeding, koala cuddling and dolphin stroking. Four of the sites are in South Australia, which has been described as the nation's 'Wildlife Capital' (Wamsley, 1995, p1).

Different ways of conceptualizing this continuum offered by different authors and some of the characteristics of each type of site are shown in Table P1.1, which also locates the surveyed encounter sites on the staged–authentic continuum. David Duffus and Philip Dearden (1990, pp215–216) distinguish between a non-consumptive experience of wildlife, allowing repeat 'use' of the product, and a consumptive experience. Mark Orams (1995, pp59–61) uses a wild–captive continuum, from a natural environment through to a human made location. Christina Jarvis (2000, p9) suggests a classification based on the degree of mediation of the animal encounter. Some commentators and ecotourist operators claim that not only should ecotourism be non-damaging to the environment, it should also make a direct contribution to 'continued protection and management of the protected areas used' (Valentine, 1992, p5), a point expressed in Table P1.2. Table A3.12 reveals that visitors often reflect the messages of conservation site managers: visitors to Warrawong focused on conservation and breeding of animals, visitors to Auckland on education and entertainment, and visitors to Monkey Mia and Cleland on interaction with the animals.

While animal encounters at natural destinations may seek non-consumptive wildlife viewing, this is not always the effect, as discovered in a survey of national park superintendents in the US (Wang and Miko, 1997). Visitors in sufficient numbers insufficiently regulated can interrupt mating or hatching,[12] or separate baby animals from their mothers (Edington and Edington, 1986, pp38–39, 42, 345; Burger and Gochfield, 1993, pp256, 258). Since 1994, dugong numbers on the Great Barrier Reef have declined by 80 per cent, with reductions in the numbers of other species. Some environmentalists claim there is too much focus on tourism (worth AUS$1.3 billion each year, or about US$750 million) and fishing (worth AUS$500 million, or about US$300 million each year) (Kennedy, 1997, p4). Even in the 'last wilderness', Antarctica, improperly disposed waste carrying a potentially fatal domestic poultry disease has spread to wild flocks of Antarctic Adelie and Emperor penguins (Williams, 1997, p5).

Table P1.1 *Classification of Animal Encounter Sites*

AUTHENTIC	SIMULATED NATURAL	STAGED
Duffus and Deardon:		
non-consumptive	somewhat consumptive	consumptive
animals as subjects, with their own needs and life forms	subject/object	objects for the gratification of humans
Orams:		
wild	semi-captive	captive
national parks, migratory routes, breeding sites, feeding/drinking sites, such as Philip Island penguins, Hervey Bay whale watching, Mon Repos turtle breeding site in central Queensland	wildlife parks, rehabilitation centres and programmes, dolphin pens; feeding wildlife, e.g. at Tangalooma, Monkey Mia, Bunbury, Potato Cod Hole Great Barrier Reef, lorikeets at Currumbin Bird Sanctuary.	aquaria, oceanaria, zoos, aviaries
Jarvis:		
minimum mediation	moderate mediation	extreme mediation
animals in own habitat	natural habitat or facsimile	removed from habitat
emphasis on natural behaviour	rarely trained	may be trained to perform
physical barriers between humans and animals minimal or absent; close proximity seemingly at discretion of animal	close proximity but physical barriers; visual may be supplemented with other interaction such as feeding, touching	emphasis on spectacle with little other interaction; visitors marshalled in specific ways
[likely ecotourism message]	interpretation possible, e.g. visitor centre	minimal interpretation
boat tours to observe marine animals; Antarctica wildlife tours	some safari tours, wildlife parks	traditional zoological gardens, nature theme (e.g. Sea World)

Note: I do not agree with all Jarvis' distinctions. Staged encounter sites also offer touch or feeding, e.g. 'touch pools' and lorikeet feeding at Currumbin. Visitors are also 'marshalled' at minimum mediation encounter sites, for example, dolphin or whale watching cruises, in terms of proximity to mammals, time in the water and so on.

Sources: Duffus and Dearden, 1990, pp215–216; Orams, 1995, pp59–61; Bulbeck, 1999; Jarvis, 2000, p9

Table P1.2 *Nine Animal Encounter Sites Ranked by Nature of Animal Encounter and Conservation Orientation*

nature of animal encounter

AUTHENTIC ‹———› STAGED

Antarctica	Osprey	Seal Bay	Monkey Mia	Warrawong	Monarto	Cleland	Currumbin	Auckland
penguins	whales	sea lions	dolphins	endangered Australian marsupials	African plains animals	South Australian animals and birds	Australian animals and birds	exotic, indigenous animals and birds

Conservation orientation and major activities of animal encounter site

ECOTOURISTIC ORIENTATION ‹———————————————————————————————————————› EDUCATION OF VISITORS

Antarctica	Osprey	Seal Bay	Monkey Mia	Warrawong	Monarto	Auckland	Currumbin	Celand
resource expenditure; education	education; involvement indigenous people	habitat preservation; education	habitat preservation; education	resource expenditure; behaviour change; education	education; endangered species breeding and rehabilitation	education; endangered species breeding and rehabilitation	education; care for local injured animals	education

Visitor numbers – latest available data

500[1]	50,000[2]	15,000[3]	109,380[3]	106,364[4]	65,045[5]	625,500[6]	351,014[7]	91,230[3]

Note: 1 About 500 people each season visit the Ross Sea Area (New Zealand Antarctic Institute 2000; Gateway Antarctica, c 2000); 2 an estimate of 40,000 public visitors plus 10,000 school children in 2003 (information kindly supplied by Mark Edwards, Earth Sanctuaries Ltd, 29 March 2004); 3 data kindly supplied by Michelle McPherson, the Department of Heritage and Environment, South Australia. In relation to the Great Australian Bight Marine Park (Osprey), the visitor figures were 16,000 (2001–2002), 12,000 (2002–2003) and 14,000 (by the end of May 2003–2004); 4 data supplied by Monkey Mia Visitor Centre for 2003 (personal communication, 25 March 2004); 5 data for financial year 2002–2003, kindly supplied by Monarto Zoological Park, 25 March 2004; 6 IA 2002, 'a record 625,000 visitors went to the zoo' (Auckland City, 2003); 7 2003 data, kindly supplied by Darren Larkin, Financial Controller, Currumbin Sanctuary, 5 April 2004

The major strategies for minimizing human impact can be classified as education, physical restraint (such as cages and boardwalks), legal control (such as zoning and permits) and economic regulation (such as the costs of entry to the site, particularly at sensitive times for the animals, such as the breeding season) (Orams, 1995, piv).

Appropriate education is a challenge due to the diversity of visitors, and lack of knowledge concerning wildlife and limited personnel (Orams 1995, pp27–32). It is well known that the gap between professed attitudes based on knowledge (for example of impending environmental catastrophe) and everyday behaviour can be very wide (Traynor, 1992, pp23–24). Education is more than conveying knowledge; it involves emotional engagement and a sense of empowerment. Indeed a stronger emotional experience may encourage greater commitment to following the requirements of the programme (Orams, 1995, pp54, 56), a point strongly emphasized in later chapters.

One of the guides at the sea lion colony at Seal Bay, Tim (interviewed on 30 December 1992), suggested that visitors from Europe 'appreciate' Seal Bay more than locals. Europeans say: 'this is fantastic; you must not let this be destroyed', even remonstrating with Australian visitors who complain about the heat or the entry charges. Tim Bickmore, guide leader for the whale watching tour of the Great Australian Bight, said that international visitors tended to be 'wrapped' in the experience while Australians were more likely to complain about the wet tents or other hardships. A similar comment was made to me by an Ecuadorian guide when I visited the Galapagos Islands in 1989, although now the 'good' foreign tourists were Australians while the unappreciative tourists were Ecuadorians. Of course, foreign visitors are sifted by the greater distance and cost of travelling. Following this line of argument, one would expect that visitors to Antarctica would be more dedicated ecotourists than visitors to Auckland Zoo, even if both sites provided similarly authentic experiences. The staged and more readily accessible sites attract a greater percentage of 'mainstream' tourists, perhaps seeking a variation on their usual experiences, or 'casual' tourists, who partake in an ecotourist experience as part of a broader trip (Hvenegaard, 1994, p28, citing Lindberg's categories).

All the sites in this study claim to propound a conservation message. The message does not, however, reach visitors in equal measure. Tables A3.3, A3.5, A3.7 and A3.9 show a largely predictable set of results, with visitors to the more 'authentic' animal encounter sites enjoying the fact that animals were in their own environment. With the exception of Monkey Mia, authentic animal encounters were also more likely to be described as a learning experience and as a unique experience. At Monarto, Warrawong and Seal Bay, 'learning about the animals' and 'felt good these animals were being preserved' were items chosen by respondents at a significantly higher rate. At the sites of Currumbin, Cleland and Monkey Mia, visitors were more likely to dwell on factors concerning interaction with animals than on conservation issues. The conservation message sites are explored in Chapter 2, while dolphin encounters are the subject of Chapter 3. At the more staged end of the continuum, visitors appreciated the chance to interact with animals without a guide (not always possible), to touch or feed the animals where this was possible, and even to smell the animals. They were more likely to feel that the animals wanted to interact with them. As will be explored further in Chapter 1, Cleland's koalas and kangaroos elicit 'cute and cuddly' responses. Warrawong's marsupials, although just as cute and cuddly to look at, have been transformed into bearers of conservation messages. Monkey Mia's dolphins bequeath the gift of their presence and interaction, as explored in Chapter 3.

1
Zoos and Circuses

I find zoos a terrible challenge. They reveal the best and the worst in us and are stark portrayals of our confused relationship with the other animals with which we share this planet.

(former director of Werribee Zoo, in David Hancocks, 2001, pxvii)

Homo Sapiens, a dangerous predatorial tool- and weapon-making primate.

(actor Michael J. Fox, remembering the caption for an exhibit of a large mirror behind bars, in Jasper and Nelkin, 1992, p164)

Natural history

With shifts in the weight of animals against humans, or of nature against culture, the scales of nature meanings and politics also tip, towards either 'them' or 'us', a different balance in each society and at each place, but a precarious imbalance for the planet as a whole. The romantic movement of the 19th century, rebelling against the ugliness of the Industrial Revolution, reconfigured the increasingly depopulated countryside as a site of spiritual renewal rather than of farming. Similarly, in our own epoch, animal welfare becomes animal liberation and conservation becomes environmentalism. The history of the representation of animals, first in zoos that resembled circuses or pleasure parks, but increasingly in naturalized settings, is another aspect of humanity's natural history to be explored before we examine the first set of animal encounter sites.

It is generally accepted that animals were once near to humans, in their role as hunted game. Humans felt themselves barely superior to wild animals, and so sought to 'magic' them into submission. For more than 100,000 years, that is for all but 1 per cent of human history, we have been hunter-gatherers. From about 10,000 years ago, at the end of the Ice Age, some people, 'instead of bending their own activity towards that of their prey, learned how to manipulate or tame the behaviour of some of the animals that they could communicate with, and so began the process of domestication' (Clutton-Brock, 1999, p1).[1] The domestication of animals has contributed to the human population explosion over the last 10,000 years (Clutton-Brock, 1999, p62). By 5000 years ago, the majority of people in the most densely settled areas were farmers. With urbanization and industrialization, attitudes to animals split, so that urban dwellers developed a new closeness to animals, but also to a new kind of animal – pets or companion animals – rather than stock animals or game animals.

These changes are indicated by the history of the legal treatment of animals. In the Middle Ages, animals were treated like humans in that they were responsible for their crimes and punishable by law. Animals were tried and punished as early as AD 824 when moles were excommunicated (Evans, 1906, p34),[2] although most of the reported trials occurred from the 15th to the 17th centuries (Beirnes, 1994, pp32–33). Episcopal tribunals convicted animals of damage to crops, of infanticide of baby humans, of being witches' familiars or of witchcraft (Eder, 1996, pp102–103; Beirnes, 1994, p39; Evans, 1906, pp157, 167) as well as of bestiality (Salisbury, 1994, p91).[3] In the 17th century, especially, beasts were put on the rack to extract a confession (Evans, 1906, p139). Nevertheless, people, not animals, attended the trials (Fudge, 2000, p122), suggesting that the trials were for the instruction of people rather than the edification of animals.

Once no longer put on trial, animals came to be treated as mere property (Fudge, 2000, p116; Ritvo, 1987, p2). Recent years have seen a growing debate that animals, indeed even trees,[4] should have at least some legal rights. The claim that animals might have access to rights marks a renewed human closeness to the natural world, although now extended by a clearly superior species (Tester, 1991, p77). Writing at the end of the 18th century, Henry Salt argued that animal rights were an extension of human rights (Franklin, 1999, p180). In 1997, the European Union redefined farm animals as 'sentient beings' rather than as 'agricultural produce' (Clutton-Brock, 1999, p39). In Sri Lanka a court ruled that elephants kept as pets have 'the right to happiness' (Melba, 1999, p2). Sumatran elephants and tigers were named among the plaintiffs by the Indonesian environmental protection group, Wahana Lingkungan Hidup Indonesia (WALHI – Friends of the Earth Indonesia), when demanding compensation in the Tokyo District Court from the Japanese government for a dam it funded in Sumatra, thus destroying the animals' habitat (Wijers-Hasegawa, 2003, p3). In line with popular perceptions,[5] in November 1999, with its *Animal Welfare Act*, New Zealand became the first jurisdiction to grant animals – in this case great apes – 'basic rights to freedom from imprisonment and torture ... recognizing their advanced cognitive and emotional capacity' (Mee, 2000, pp4, 6).

Judaism, Christianity and Islam are still called on to justify human dominion over the rest of nature. Thus St Thomas Aquinas' approach was that humans were 'chosen' by the Creator and 'all animals are for man' (in Singer, 1977, p201; Walker, 1983, p4; Ryder, 1989, pp32–34). However, the Bible can also be read as demanding stewardship of animals (Thomas, 1983, p24).[6] There has been a long-running tension in the Christian Church between the anthropocentric Thomas Aquinas and 'animal loving' St Francis of Assisi, born 32 years later (Armstrong, 1973, pp56–59,164–167; Walker, 1983, p4; Ryder, 1989), as well as other saints who had animal companions, such as St Milburga, St Thecla and Blessed Viridiana (Greer, 1991, p406). Over time, in the stories of the saints, animals achieve increasing equality with the saints. Animals first assisted saints, saints then saved animals, and finally a dog was sanctified to become Saint Guinefort when it killed a serpent attacking his master's baby (Salisbury, 1994, pp172–175).

A question receiving less attention in this natural history concerns the role of wild animals in the modern, and then perhaps postmodern, imaginary. Over the last 100 years or so, the almost lost wilderness and its wild animals again became desirable and desired, but no longer as our equals, no longer feared. Like the hunter-gatherers, humans are again enjoined to treat wild animals as neighbours, as kin. But now we are superior in the relationship: we owe them protection of their environment, assistance even in their own species survival. The changing messages of zoos reflect this narrative.

Zoos: From circus spectacles to Noah's arks

VISIT THE RELLIES XMAS DAY

(Royal Zoological Society of South Australia, poster of the Adelaide Zoo's apes, to advertise opening on Christmas Day, 1992)

The archbishop takes his flock to the zoo.

(King, 2000, p15, reporting that the 'Anglican archbishop of Adelaide takes his family to the zoo as part of National Family Day where he will bless the animals at the zoo')

Introduction

For many years, zoological gardens or menageries were associated in the public mind more with circuses than with science. Hence P. T. Barnum's 'Great Museum, Menagerie, Circus and Travelling World's Fair' (Goodman, 1990, p29). Zoos have their predecessors in the menageries of ancient kingdoms, apparently an expression of imperial power and for the entertainment of their owners, with the display of animals possibly dating to 2500 BC (Tuan, 1984, p76).[7] However, many commentators distinguish the zoo, which emerges with European industrialization, as being part of the bourgeoisie's civilizing process and scientific goals. Zoos were established for the moral improvement and education of the populace, a purpose shared by museums and city parks (Berger, 1980, p19; Franklin 1999, p67). There is debate concerning whether the first modern zoo is in London, Paris or even Vienna.[8] It has been claimed that London Zoo is 'regarded as the first to actively integrate recreation into what had to date been a largely scientific venture' (Jarvis, 2000, p78). Whipsnade Zoo, founded in 1931, heralded the era of conservation in zoo philosophies.[9] There are an estimated 10,000 zoos worldwide (Jarvis, 2000, p77).

Nigel Rothfels (2002, pp22–24, 31, 37–38) disputes this teleological narrative. For many years after the zoo came to represent the 'optimism, power and ambitions of a new bourgeois elite', it continued to offer spectacles such as the bear pit, in which dangerous animals were made to perform for children (for example catch buns thrown to them). Thus education, conservation and science were not the main purposes of the modern zoo. By contrast, some early menageries were collected for research purposes, for example Aristotle's experimental zoo; his pupil Alexander later founding the first public zoo in Alexandria. Kay Anderson (1998, pp36, 42) suggests that, between 1878 and 1930, the Adelaide Zoo was a menagerie or pleasure garden, while from 1930 to 1963, the zoo was more like a fairground.

Akin to the royal menageries, 'public zoos were an endorsement of modern colonial power'. Victorian zoos expressed dominion in a racial register (Ritvo, 1987, p219). Settler societies participated in this process by defining nature as elsewhere, focusing on Asian or African exhibits. Indeed, Adelaide Zoo did not open its first Australian exhibit until 1972, responding to a period of nationalism (Anderson, 1998, p39).

Representing nature

> Despite the enormous variety in responses to and attitudes towards animals in different cultures this does not seem to be reflected in zoo philosophies throughout the world.
>
> (Mullan and Marvin, 1987, p127)

A public increasingly educated by wildlife films and safari experiences (Davallon and Davallon, 1987, p33) has produced a strain in zoos towards a more 'naturalistic' representation of animals, in terms of zoo architecture, animal displays and animal behaviour. The move to more naturalistic enclosures is associated with Carl Hagenbeck,[10] who in 1907, at his Stellingen Zoo near Hamburg, attempted to create the impression of viewing animals in their wild state (Mullan and Marvin, 1987, pp50–51). When Hagenbeck, an animal trainer, discovered that an animal's maximum leap could determine the width of ditches or height of fences, bars could be removed from enclosures (Hahn, 1990, pp142–3). In this way, Hagenbeck is often made the hero of the modern zoo exhibit, an animal saviour, a Noah figure (his own self-promotion from 1908: Rothfels, 2002, p176). By contrast, Nigel Rothfels (2002, p199) suggests that many zookeepers at the turn of the century, before Hagenbeck's intervention and knowing that their viewing public was uncomfortable with cages, were experimenting with alternatives. However, Hagenbeck offered

Note: In Calgary, the sign 'history behind bars' tells visitors they 'are looking at the last of the old-style barred exhibits', once enclosing Asiatic black bears. The Bear Castle at Berlin Zoo was demolished in 1968 when the 'free range bear sanctuary' was completed. Visitors are told that the Castle's arches and turrets gave 'the spectator a feeling of security', and offered a view akin to that of 'the bear pits devised by our ancestors' (thanks to Martin Travers, Griffith University, for translation of *Bärenburg, eröffnet 1870: The Bears Castle, opened in 1870*, a sign in Berlin Zoo).

Figure 1.1 *Replacing the Bars*

'narratives of freedom and happiness' for animals in zoos, suggesting that they were better off in captivity than in the wild (Rothfels, 2002, p199). Whereas earlier animal trainers represented themselves as lashing wild animals into submission, Hagenbeck sought to present the 'power of human kindness', that animals 'respect, love, admire' their keepers who can make animals lie down with their animal enemies (the lion with the lamb) and with humans (Rothfels, 2002, pp160–161).

Rothfels (2002, pp171, 174–175, 200) argues that Hagenbeck's early 1900s displays of animals in 'panoramas' changed little over time: it was their *interpretation* that shifted. Originating as Biblical scenes, they came to be understood as replicas of natural habitats, designed with the interests of animals in mind. This explains why there is no clear historical trend towards naturalistic exhibits (Rothfels, 2002, p200), and the associated replacement of exotic animal houses or barred enclosures with more naturalistic exhibits. Even in the 1920s and 1930s, Australian zoos were still building elaborate stucco buildings, often reflecting the architecture of the place from which the animal ostensibly came (McGrath, 1978, p11). Contrariwise, it is claimed that Taronga was influenced by Hagenbeck's ideas from its inception in 1916 (Davidson and Spearritt, 2000, p234). Elsewhere, Hagenbeck's naturalism, which allowed shy animals to hide themselves from the public gaze, was rejected for 'clean, open, bright, and streamlined' modernism (Hancocks, 2001, p74), or for 'antiseptic bathroom style primate houses', as at London Zoo in the 1950s (Rothfels, 2002, p200). Towards the end of the 20th century, however, low buildings in muted tones, landscaped paths, staged eye level views of animals in their natural surroundings, naturalistic immersion exhibits for the pleasure of the public and not the animals, did become increasingly popular. But they are not nature, nor replicas of nature, but 'fantasies now reinforced by nature television' (Rothfels, 2002, pp200–202). They have been reduced to a monotony of narrow isolated cement-rendered canyons featuring a lip overhang and a series of similar sized grottos, 'a combination that probably does not exist anywhere in nature, yet is ubiquitous in zoos' (Hancocks, 2001, p73).

Another step taken towards naturalistic displays is a move from 'serried rows of cages of cats, dogs and monkeys' (Ed McAlister, Director of the Adelaide Zoological Gardens, interviewed on 7 January 1993) to the representation of ecosystems in regional displays, both in city-bound zoos and their safari park offshoots. Linked with this is the suggestion that animals should live in their natural social groups, rather than in ubiquitous pairs or solitary isolation (Packard et al, 1990). It is claimed that Bronx Zoo pioneered the 'ecological' exhibit with their African Plains area (Hahn, 1990, p259). Adelaide Zoo in 1963 commenced the process of landscaping and naturalizing exhibits (Anderson, 1994, p231). The multimillion dollar expense[11] of these new-style enclosures often requires fundraising from corporations such as Telstra or McDonald's, or, on a lesser scale, Haigh's, which sponsored the bilby enclosure at Adelaide Zoo.[12] According to Hancocks (2001, pp127–134), in 1978 Seattle's Woodland Park Zoo pioneered the immersion exhibit with its gorilla exhibit. Due to Dian Fossey's and George Schaller's research, it was established that gorillas were family oriented and peaceful rather than violent and murderous. These primatologists assisted with the design of the new exhibit:

> Zoo visitors who once had stood in the grimy corridor of the old ape house, passively gawking at or mocking the animals with whoops and shuffling jumps, now stood in small clearings amid dense vegetation and did not shout or howl or, often, even talk, but occasionally whispered to each other, with wonder in their eyes.
>
> (Hancocks, 2001, p134)

Umberto Eco (1986, p44) suggests that zoos are an example of the hyper-real. They promise a natural reality but their 'authenticity is staged'. Thus the signage at zoos locates an animal's origins on a map of the world, yet many of the animals are supplied by other zoos (Anderson, 1998, p40). Indeed, some animals bred in captivity must be taught to 'act naturally'; for example rhesus monkeys view videotapes of wild animals to learn appropriate behaviour (Snowdon, 1989, p155). The desire for 'natural behaviours' has displaced the former carnival aspects of zoo entertainment, for example elephant rides and chimpanzee tea parties, which persisted into the 1960s in many zoos. In Auckland Zoo, a chimpanzee tea party, introduced in 1956, was only abandoned in 1964 due to the lack of replacement chimpanzees (Wood, 1992, pp67, 73, 92–93). At the Adelaide Zoo, between 1935 and 1942, Lillian the elephant walked from the zoo through the city to be weighed at the Central Markets, the practice only discontinued when she expressed nervousness at leaving the zoo (Anderson, 1998, p43).[13] Samorn, another elephant at the Adelaide Zoo, only stopped giving elephant rides in 1982: 'it is not what elephants were put on the earth for' (interview with David Langdon, Assistant Director Collections at the Adelaide Zoo in 1992, and Director of Monarto Zoological Park, when interviewed on 7 January 1993).

In Bombay crocodiles have been stoned to death to elicit a response and in US zoos listless animals have been lamed and maimed (Mullan and Marvin, 1987, p135). However, zoo visitors now also express distress at seeing what they read as animal unhappiness, for example restless pacing or head-bobbing. Zoo curators and staff discourage such practices with ingenious forms of behavioural enrichment, advocated first in 1950, as 'the importance of play', by Heini Hediger, then director of Basel Zoo in Switzerland (Hancocks, 2001, p78; Mazur, 2001, pp80–81). At Adelaide Zoo, the volunteer group 'Animal Activists' spend Sunday afternoons making behavioural enrichment devices which the 'animals destroy in a couple of minutes' (Harper and Allen, 1999, p4).

One response to *human* disquiet has been to repackage spectacles as examples of animals' natural behaviours (Franklin, 1999, p78). Adelaide Zoo has introduced a pulley system to feed the Cape hunting dogs and the caracel, a smaller member of the cat family. The animal stalks the food, 'pounces with frightening speed and accuracy, ripping its prey from the pulley'. The marketing manager, Graeme Craske, points out that such behaviour is as spectacular as tricks but superior because the caracels use their 'natural skills as they would in the wild' (Savage, 1997, p59). Over the years, 'Shamu', the orca at San Diego Sea World, has discarded the costumes and the 'tricks' that might humiliate him and there has been gradual refocusing on the killer whale's 'body and strength, the trainer's skill and the theme park's commitment to science' (Davis, 1997, p178). Partly to displace the public horror when a trainer was killed by an orca, San Diego Sea World even developed a 'killer' whale demonstration, including a 'mouth-open swim' revealing large teeth and a mock attack on a trainer (Davis, 1997, pp178, 184–185).

There is some debate concerning whether training and performance diminish all involved or provide behavioural enrichment for those animals that[14] find captivity boring.[15] However, rather than being seen as prison guards, handlers

Note: In the Miya Jima Aquarium in Japan (top) the seals catch quoits around their necks, wear hats, dance in unison with the trainer and play the piano. At Currumbin in the 1990s, three keepers were full time animal presenters in shows of animals 'conditioned' to display natural behaviours, including a lizard, cockatoo, lorikeet and tawny frogmouth (interview with Helen Irwin, Education Officer, 15 June 1993). The keepers use their knowledge to add to the performance effect of the presentation. In 1993, Currumbin's Wildlife Presentations included: (middle) a lizard is put down with the command 'off you go', the keeper pointing the direction. The lizard appears to be following instructions but is, in fact, running to the nearest log.

(bottom) At Adelaide Zoo, two South American blue and gold macaws will be used to 'teach children about this endangered species and its natural habitat, the Amazon rainforest in South America', according to the bird keeper, Ryan Watson (Osborne, 2000, p15). Six months later, in another article featuring the macaws, potential visitors are assured that their entrance fees are 'contributing to research into the [rare] birds, and in the end their overall welfare' (Rice, 2000, p10).

Source: (bottom) Photography by Cameron Richardson, and image courtesy of *The Advertiser*

Figure 1.2 *Behavioural Enrichment, Entertainment or Education?*

and trainers might be viewed as translators between the animal and human worlds, bequeathing on animals increased freedom of movement (Hearne, 1987, p215).

Some improvements are clearly for sensitive visitors rather than the animals. When glass replaces iron bars, animals do not feel relieved of a prison image; rather they lose bars to swing on and free flowing air (Mullan and Marvin, 1987, p28). Shy animals, preferring to be elsewhere, might be lured to a viewing area by heated sand (Wilson, 1992, p253). Concrete, which does not look 'homely' as one of my focus group respondents said, can be washed of animal excrement that would otherwise accumulate parasites (Hahn, 1990, p182). The greenery in Taronga's McDonald's Gorilla Forest is protected from gorilla marauding by an electrified fence (Powell, 2003, p31). The dolphin pool at Sea World San Diego was redesigned to make it clear to human visitors that the dolphins could escape human interaction: the dolphins already knew that they had sanctuary in the centre of their featureless pool (Davis, 1997, p108). Backstage areas are still often unhomely cages, although visitors are increasingly trained to see them as animals might.[16]

From entertainment to education and conservation

> [pandas are] priceless. There are more Rembrandts in the world than there are pandas.
>
> (Metro Toronto Zoo advertising its visiting pandas from China,
> in Wilson, 1992, p249)[17]

In an attempt to raise the status of their exhibits, zoos have been redefining themselves as cultural institutions.[18] David Langdon claims:

> Animals and plants are like living art: they're a cultural heritage, as well as a biological inheritance. ... Isn't the giant panda part of the natural heritage of the Chinese people? ... It would be a tragedy if the only living creatures on the planet that remained in a decade or two were dogs and cats, horses and rats.
>
> (in Ward, 1992, p3)

As evidence that zoos are cultural artifacts, the 'wild' animals found in zoos vary across the world, the beagles on display at Beijing Zoo surprising me to this fact.[19] Keeping animals in heterosexual pairs imposes Western notions of appropriate relationships onto animals, especially as many species exhibit homosexuality or homosociality. In October and November 2000, as part of the gay and lesbian Adelaide Feast Festival, a tour of Adelaide Zoo, 'All creatures great and small – an outing at the zoo', led by Dr Gertrude Glossip, alias for Will Sergeant, made this abundantly clear. Using Bruce Bagemihl's (1999) examples, cage upon cage of heterosexual pairs were deconstructed with their preference: for male pair bonds, for example black swans; or female pair bonds, for example black wing stilts; or homosocial groups, for example lions.

As cultural institutions, the messages zoos offer are not immanent in the animals, but are open to human manipulation. Victorian zoos may have demonstrated culture's control of nature and Britain's control of its colonies. The humanistic messages expressed in animal entertainment are now replaced by more scientific approaches. A content analysis of photographs in the Royal Zoological Society of South Australia's Annual Reports over the last 20 years suggests a trend away from images of baby animals and animals cuddled by humans (see Figure 1.3). Furthermore, in the 1990s, there is a growing tendency to caption images of young animals as examples of the successful breeding of endangered species. Perth Zoo decided not to name its animals, instead presenting them 'as ambassadors for their wild cousins' (director John DeJose in Bell, 1990, p47). Increasingly, modern zoos justify their existence with a focus on education, even conservation, rather than the entertainment of previous times. Zoo animals serve as either sacrificial ambassadors for their kin in the wild or as the last hope for endangered species.

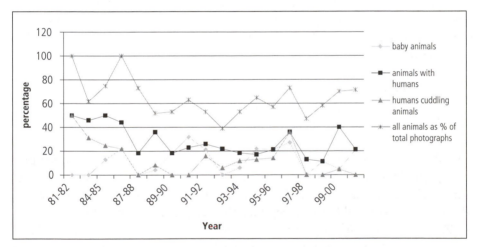

Source: My thanks to Silvia, the Adelaide Zoo librarian, for providing access to the Annual Reports

Figure 1.3 *Royal Zoological Society of South Australia's Annual Reports 1981–1982 to 2000–2001: Percentage of Photographs in Different Categories*

My research results suggest that the role of advertising and interpretation in making sense of animal encounter sites is important, there being a strong correlation between visitors' perceptions of a site and the way it is presented by the site managers. Of course, this may reflect self-selection by visitors in their chosen destination as much as attitudes changed by their experience at the site. Parks and wildlife managers must define an area (zone it, determine access), interpret the experience and then manage the animal colonies and the people's interactions with them (Terry Dennis, District Ranger, interviewed 30 December 1992). In the 1950s, Freeman Tilden (1977, p38), the US heritage and conservation advocate, noted the following template for tourist education in a Park Service Administrative manual: 'Through interpretation, under-standing; through understanding, appreciation; through appreciation, protection'. Interpretation, Tilden (1977, p8) defined as 'An educational activity which aims to reveal meanings and relationships through the use of original objects, by firsthand experience, and by illustrative media, rather than simply to communicate factual information'.[20] Tilden recommends a light touch in interpretation: 'The chief aim of interpretation is not instruction, but provocation' (Tilden, 1977, p9).

However, zoo self-publicity often involves a kind of schizophrenia, proclaiming that zoos can be both fun and good for you (and the world) too. Adelaide Zoo's slogan from 1961 to 1963 was 'Visit the zoo: laugh and learn' (Anderson, 1998, p45), a slogan built on the assumption that learning occurred merely by observation (Anderson, 1998, p27). The London Zoo, where the use of the name 'Zoo' originated, in a pamphlet from the 1990s promised its visitors 'KNOWLEDGE', 'CONSERVE', but also 'SOMETHING SPECIAL' and a 'GREAT DAY OUT'. Auckland Zoo publicizes its Friends of the Zoo scheme with:

> Friends to have fun with, friends to support, friends who care.
> Auckland Zoo can offer you a great friendship. It's fun, it supports our animals and it cares about our future.

An Auckland Zoo friend will feed and care for animals and birds, support programmes to save endangered species, contribute to research that conserves the environment, and foster the educational role of the zoo. All the while, however, in bold and bigger type, the friend is '**going to have a lot of fun**'.

Zoos also proudly publicize their breeding programmes for endangered species, including the additional benefit of breeding replacement animals for other zoos rather than capturing them from the wild.[21] Frankfurt Zoo notes our obligations, as 'rulers of the earth', to protect the right to life of all animal species. Its booklet claims the species snatched from extinction include the European bison, the Hawaiian goose and the Oryx antelope, 'to name but a few' (Frankfurt Zoological Gardens, no date, pp3–4), to which can be added the Bengal tiger, Przewalski's horse and Père David's deer (Huxley, 1981, p58). This combined list is larger than the 'fewer than five species...saved from extinction by zoos' that Hancocks (2001, pxvii) suggests, indicating differences of opinion concerning the efficacy of zoos as Noah's arks.

In Calgary, the sign 'history behind bars' notes that the disappearance of habitat is the 'most serious problem wild animals face today' and that zoos are 'the last refuge' for breeding and reintroduction programmes. Zoos have

Source: Auckland Zoo's 'Friends of the Zoo' brochure, permission to reproduce kindly supplied by Glen Holland, Director, Auckland Zoological Park.

Figure 1.4 *We All Need Friends – Of the Zoo*

become arks, filled against the rising tide of *homo sapiens*. The ark metaphor was first suggested by Gerald Durrell (1976), when he described his Jersey Zoo as *The Stationary Ark*. In Japan, the Miya Jima public aquarium in 2003 offered the following somewhat ambivalent conservation message in relation to the Stellar sea lion:

> Found in the North Pacific including Hokkaido. Pests to fishermen, they were once called the 'gangs of the northern seas' and were systematically exterminated, but recently people want these rare animals protected.

Many zoos combine conservation with education and entertainment in their goals, for example Adelaide and Taronga Park in Australia (McGrath, 1978, p11; Royal Zoological Society of South Australia, 1992, p1). Adelaide Zoo is participating in the project to save Asiatic or Moon bears.[22]

Overcoming the imperialist frame, zoos in Australasia have increasingly turned their attention away from breeding exotic endangered animals to saving those closer to home. Adelaide Zoo is involved in a number of indigenous breeding and release programmes, including the Mallee Fowl Recovery Plan, in which the 'four main zoos in Australia – Adelaide, Perth, Melbourne and Taronga Zoo' – are involved (Plane, 2000, p7). Monarto's captive breeding programme for bilbies has bred 52 bilbies since 1994 (Loechel, 2001, p10), nine of which, to coincide with Easter 2000, were released near Roxby Downs in the far north of South Australia (Wakelin, 2000a, p3). Auckland Zoological Park is working with government parks and conservation agencies to breed and reintroduce kakapo into the wild.[23]

Note: At Auckland Zoo, old style exhibits, such as the polar bears, are gradually being replaced by naturalistic exhibits, such as the New Zealand birds aviary and Telecom's meerkat exhibit, opened in 1992 (Wood, 1992, p156).

Figure 1.5 *Auckland Zoo: Conservation Close to Home*

However, such breeding programmes may not be the visitor draw-cards provided by 'charismatic megafauna', such as elephants, tigers and lions. Zoos must attract visitors, even if to then educate them. This tension was discussed when an elephant killed the senior keeper at London Zoo in 2001, suggesting this 'tragic event' could spark the end of 'all Britain's urban zoos', if zoos were no longer allowed to display magnetic megafauna and so were unable to attract sufficient crowds (Moss and Mills, 2001, p21). Gerald Durrell, among others, recommends that zoos, in pursuing their conservation role, turn away from megafauna to 'unfashionable brown jobs' (neglected toads, snakes, newts and lizards). Indeed, the endangered Regent honeyeater and green and golden bellfrog are bred off display at Taronga (Powell, 2003, p31).

In zoos, population management is required, not only in breeding endangered species but also in culling or sterilizing those which breed prolifically. The silences and complicated dancing around these issues indicate that not all zoo visitors are happy to learn that animals are managed.[24] City newspapers focus their frequent stories of happenings at the local zoo on births and new acquisitions (e.g. see Hahn, 1990, p98). A favourite theme concerns animals raised by humans because their own mothers reject them, offering the message that humans make better mothers than even the biological ones. Free-hopping kangaroos, which delight visitors to Western Plains Zoo, must be regularly culled to prevent overpopulation. In 1992 Richard Jakob-Hoff, Senior Curator at Auckland Zoological Park, made a decision to kill a newborn hippopotamus to prevent it being mauled to death by the adult animals, the fate of the previous hippo infant, witnessed by visitors and attracting negative publicity. To my suggestion that the zoo should educate the public in population management, Richard replied that this would meet with resistance, particularly from political supporters of the zoo (Jakob-Hoff personal communication; see also Mazur, 2001, p161 on the impact of powerful players on zoo operations).

However, at one animal encounter site in my sample, visitors are told about animal management, the requirement to control populations with birth control, culling, even feeding some animals to others. In August 2002, the tour group I joined at Monarto was told matter-of-factly by the male guide that 'We've got too many kangaroos so we feed them to the other animals. We get a permit to shoot them after an assessment of the numbers is completed. Otherwise they destroy the habitat'. In the 1970s, Woodland Park Zoo in Seattle started feeding whole sheep and goats to the big cats, although not without complaints from 'concerned citizens' who preferred to see only 'nice chunks of meat' (Hancocks, 2001, p249).

To what extent, then, do visitors to the staged animal encounter sites expand their understanding of conservation issues, learn about animals and their behaviour, or simply have an enjoyable experience?

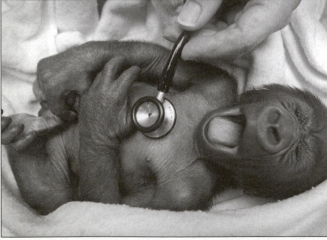

Figure 1.6 *Zoo Babies*

Note: (top) Babies are commonly featured in newspaper stories concerning zoos, for example 'Zambesi junior earns his stripes' discusses a week-old zebra born at Monarto Zoological Park (O'Brien, 2000a, p3, photograph courtesy of *The Advertiser*).

(bottom) Even better, when saving the baby requires human intervention. This baby male Western Lowland gorilla, Yakini (Swahili for 'truth' or 'certainty'), was resuscitated by a team of medical specialists and placed in a humidicrib in 1999. In these stories, baby gorillas are just like us, hating the coldness of a stethoscope or responding to the stimulation of colour; gorilla mothers are as overjoyed as human ones finally to be reunited with their babies after a period in intensive care (e.g. see Clery, 2001, p4; Poutney, 1999a, p3). A front page 'photo opportunity' in The Advertiser was captioned 'the touching moment when mother Yuska kissed her baby for the first time since the gorilla was born 11 days ago at Melbourne Zoo' (9 December 1999: 1 – 'Mum's first kiss for her baby'). The story elbowed out images of the devastation caused by a 'wild storm' in central Australia the previous day. In successive editions, the growth of the gorilla was charted, for example a large colour photograph of Yakini, touching its 'new nursery mural', created to stimulate Yakini's visual development (Mulligan, 2000, p3).

Auckland Zoo

> These animals aren't happy. They look like mental patients. I won't be
> coming back: zoo visitor, mother with children (in Swart, 1993, p295).
> At the beginning of her visit, she responded to the inquiry as to
> whether the animals were happy with, 'What kind of question is that?
> They're only animals'.
>
> (Swart, 1993, p291)

Almost everyone in Australia's capital cities has visited a zoo at some stage in
their lives (Hyde and King, 1987, p8 for Melbourne; Mazur, 1994, pp3, 7 for
Adelaide; see also Kellert 1978b, pp50, 52 for the US). In most cities, about 20
per cent of the population visits the zoo annually (in terms of crude numbers)
(Mullan and Marvin, 1987, pp132–133), although there is evidence that other
leisure destinations are more popular, such as casinos, botanical gardens and
museums. In Adelaide, however, these sites do not have entrance fees (figures
provided by Tourism South Australia to David Langdon, personal
communication).

Auckland Zoo was established in 1922, following a decisive electoral poll
(Wood, 1992, p15). It commenced life as a mixed bag of animals from a defunct
private collection, including a fox, ducks, swans and a Shackleton Antarctic
Expedition dog (Wood, 1992, p24). At Auckland Zoo, as at other Western city
zoos I have visited, a conservation-oriented management grapples with an
inheritance of barred cages and exotic megafauna as well as community
memories of elephant rides and personable apes. In 1987, a new orangutan
exhibit was opened with behavioural enrichment aspects (Wood, 1992, p112).
In 1991, Auckland Council proposed that exhibits be 'habitat-oriented',
exhibiting animals in thematic zones (Wood, 1992, p157) or in complete
ecosystems. Naturalistic exhibits have been built for the giraffes (rather like a
football oval but with a steep incline rather than fences to prevent giraffe
escape), the elephants, the meerkats, and a New Zealand bird aviary. Some
visitors commented favourably on these initiatives, for example commending the
aviary, which gave greater space for the birds and featured '*native* birds in a near
natural environment' (female professional visiting from Australia, aged 20–29).

On safari, because visitors feel they are encountering animals in the wild,
they will spend time watching a lion drink, 'real behaviour' that one has been
lucky to see. By contrast, at zoos, unless there is activity in the cage, or the
animal is a special favourite, watching it usually consists of walking past and
observing the animal in the process (Mullan and Marvin, 1987, p133). Given
this, besides the exotic megafauna, the most popular exhibits at zoos are often
new exhibits, those where the animals are active, or where one can interact with
the animals (Moar, 1987, pp39–42; Townsend, 1988, p34; Hyde and King,
1987, p8). At the time of my survey at Auckland Zoological Park, the aviary
was relatively new and was singled out for mention. The children's zoo was

commended because it allowed interaction between children and animals or keeper and animals. Auckland Zoo visitors enjoyed animals swimming, playing or being fed, including the elephants, hippos, sea lions, chimpanzees, otters, polar bears and meerkats:

> The meerkats were the most enjoyable part. Watching their interaction
> was wonderful. It seemed they all had very individual personalities.
>
> (no personal data given)

Two respondents noted the pleasure of being close to animals, seeing lions out of their cage and watching chimps playing very close to the glass.

Visitors' relations with animals tended to be anthropomorphic: feeling affection and communication (or control of the situation) (see Table A3.7 in Appendix 3), for example the enthusiasm of three respondents who 'met' the wallabies. This might reflect the tendency for people living in a city to come to view animals in 'their' zoo as 'friends'.

Educational activities are featured at Auckland Zoo: for example explication of the kakapo breeding programme includes activities and displays with an educational and environmental message. Yet nobody spontaneously mentioned how much he or she had learned about either animals or conservation as a result of their visit. The closest approximations were three visitors who commended the helpful and informative attitude of volunteers, the 'behind-the-scenes' activities and the educational signs.

A significant percentage commented on the good enclosures and a well-managed site: the 'peace, quiet and cleanliness', 'awe and enjoyment for the children and us'. However, and not surprisingly given that this was the most managed site in my sample, with its many enclosures, Auckland visitors were more likely than visitors to other sites to express concern that the animals were in enclosures,[25] inactive, non-interactive and seemingly unhappy, like the polar bear, or in pain, like the elephant (see Table A3.9 in Appendix 3). As one respondent wrote:

> I felt sorry for the animals. The areas where some animals are placed
> are not large enough, e.g. monkeys. ... The elephant looked like it had
> an infected eye. People have no respect for animals. I'd rather watch
> them on T.V. in their natural environment
>
> (Maori/Pacific Islander female, home duties, aged 20–29)

While wildlife films are popular, viewers commonly note something is missing: being there. Are they referring to the loss of the other senses, smell, touch, taste, sound? Visitors to Auckland Zoo commented positively on smelling the animals as well as touching the animals in the children's zoo (Table A3.5). Paul Carter (1992, p9) identifies the haptic experience, sensing place through 'your body rather than by simply looking at it through a car

Note: Sanctuaries are advertised as places where visitors can 'talk to' animals, 'see goannas eye to eye', have a sulphur-crested cockatoo perched on their wrist, 'feed our kangaroos' and, until New South Wales legislation banned tourists handling them, 'cuddle a koala' (Featherdale Wildlife Park, c1988).

(top) At the aquarium in Miya Jima, Japan, a daily 'penguin parade' allows visitors to touch the penguin, parading in a diamond necklace; (middle) touch pool in AQWA aquarium, Perth. At Oceanworld in Sydney 'you can literally touch, hold and get to know dozens of sea creatures in our special touch pool' (advertising pamphlet); (bottom) at Monarto, a single touch table in 1993 had grown to three large tables by 2002, displaying hides, horns, eggs, feathers and skulls, and signs: 'please handle us – gently'.

Figure 1.7 *The Desire to Touch*

windscreen'. Three animal encounter sites offered tactile interactions; two of these are discussed below, while stroking dolphins is addressed in Chapter 3.

Animal interactions: Touching and feeding

> [the attraction of the zoo is] direct, almost touch, contact on a regular basis with a diverse collection of animals.
>
> (David Langdon, Assistant Director Collections at the Adelaide Zoo,
> interview on 18 December 1992)

My focus group respondents claimed that the desire to touch was a natural human wish, enabling learning as well as a more complete experience of the animal. Carolyn said, 'think of a baby, the first thing is touch and taste, we've never grown out of it'. When an animal is close to the front bars of its cage, people reach in an attempt to touch it (Townsend, 1988, p55 discussing the siamang at Adelaide Zoo; Jarvis, 2000, p139 on the penguins at Port Phillip Island; see also Kellert and Dunlap, 1989, no page numbers).

In zoos, the possibility of touch is usually limited to the children's farm area (Davallon and Davallon, 1987, p26), but may encompass marsupials and reptiles in sanctuaries. Loxton High School students, surveyed after their 1993 visit to Monarto Zoological Park, said they would like to 'get out and pat the animals'. David Langdon (interviewed on 27 July 1993) replied that the 'typical contact syndrome is extremely labour-intensive and reinforces the wrong attitude to animals, that they're good'. He attempted to deflect this desire into what he considered more appropriate channels with 'touch table' exhibits like ostrich eggs and feathers. Many aquaria, such as the New York Aquarium and Melbourne Aquarium (Jarvis, 2000, p108), have a touch pool.

Related to the desire to touch is the almost as insistent impulse to feed animals. Visitors to London Zoo were once allowed to bring their pets to feed to the lions (Ritvo, 1987, p207). Now few zoos allow such haphazard animal feeding by visitors. This has certainly changed the relationship between human visitors and zoo animals, as is made clear by the astonishing attentiveness to the arrival of visitors and subsequent interaction with them on the part of bears, elephants and hippopotamus at Chiang Mai Zoo in Thailand. Visitors can buy plastic bags of food to feed to these animals.

Some commentators suggest people wish to feed animals to express our dominion over them, while others suggest it is more a nurturing or intimacy-driven behaviour (Ritvo, 1987, p220; Tuan, 1984, p80; Levinson, 1972, p94; Lott, 1988, pp255–256; Steinhart 1980, p127). Table A3.10 in Appendix 3 divides the reasons given for feeding the animals into 'domination' and 'intimacy' categories for the 108 respondents in my sample who were able to feed animals. Most were visitors to Cleland or Monkey Mia. Men were more likely to choose 'domination' reasons (touch and feel, get close) and women 'intimacy' reasons (animals show trust or affection, enter the world of the

Note: (top) The bears stand on their hind legs when visitors appear, begging for food; (middle) the hippopotami open their large mouths in entreaty; (bottom) food for 'bear – serow – hippoptemus – deef' (sic).

Figure 1.8 *The Need to Feed: Chiang Mai Zoo*

animals). Those with no religion were more likely to choose domination and those with a religion chose intimacy, challenging the common arguments about Judaeo-Christian attitudes concerning the domination of animals. As expressed by one Jehovah's Witness – who included a religious tract with the completed questionnaire – when visiting Seal Bay: 'The beauty of the animals is a gift from our Creator'. Visitors to Monkey Mia chose intimacy reasons. Visitors to Cleland, Currumbin and to a lesser extent Auckland, chose domination reasons.

Table A3.5 in Appendix 3 shows the high response rates for enjoying the animal encounter because animals were touched in the case of Monkey Mia, Auckland, Currumbin and Cleland, although only the last shows a statistically significant relationship. We will encounter the Monkey Mia dolphins in Chapter 3, and turn now to the tactile experiences at Cleland and Currumbin.

Cuddling koalas at Cleland Nature Reserve

Although the koala is a baby releaser, 'This of course has not prevented it from being slaughtered before 1903 for the commercial value of its fur' (Walker, 1991, p27). Today things are different, the Brisbane City Council proclaiming 'Brisbane – koala capital' in its policy to purchase koala habitat and thus draw tourists to the city.[26] As early as 1927, a tiny piece of koala land already existed in Brisbane. Lone Pine Koala Sanctuary is the oldest and largest koala sanctuary in the world. It now houses over 140 koalas and 50 types of native marsupials. The koalas require 140,000 eucalyptus leaves to feed them. As there are only 40,000 trees at the Sanctuary, about $100,000 is spent annually on wages for truck drivers to search Brisbane, trimming suitable trees and locating trees that have been cleared for urban development (Dominic Farnworth, Currumbin education officer, personal communication).

Focus group members who had visited Lone Pine bemoaned the small cages enclosed in chicken wire and the excessive number of Japanese visitors, one who took a Japanese friend to the site even making this complaint![27] At Lone Pine, visitors can feed the kangaroos in a wash trough, thoughtfully provided at the exit to the enclosure. Visitors can also hold a koala, but only as long as it takes to snap a photograph.

The koala cuddling experience is a little longer at Cleland Wildlife Park, in the Mount Lofty Ranges, about half an hour's drive from Adelaide. Cleland feels less like a zoo than does Lone Pine: 'The openness of the displays means that people are able to mingle with the animals in a sensitive way without feeling hemmed in by high wire fences' (Martinsen, 1985, p9). Cleland Wildlife Park was initiated in 1964, in response to the blossoming of conservation philosophy in the 1960s (Department of Environment and Planning, 1985, p74). The first curator, W. R. Gasking (1964–1978), developed the philosophy 'to create a native wildlife display in a near natural situation where visitors were able to relate directly to the animal', thus providing a good introduction

Note: (top) Koalas at Lone Pine; (middle) cuddling a koala at Lone Pine. Du Xuezeng, a visitor from Beijing, still talked about the experience some five years later. (bottom) In one of its brochures, Cleland suggests 'See and Touch Native Animals in a Natural Bushland Setting', a promise kept with this photo opportunity in the koala enclosure.

Figure 1.9 *Lone Pine Sanctuary and Cleland's Koala Encounter*

to wildlife management (Martinsen, 1985, p9). A further naturalistic aspect was the decision to only display animals endemic to South Australia (Martinsen, 1985, p9).[28] Cleland was envisaged as an accessible microcosm of the surrounding National Park, for the 'many people who like animals [but] have neither time nor patience to walk quietly through the bush for hours, hoping for a glimpse of some self-effacing creature who would rather not be seen' (Department of Environment and Planning, 1985, p74).

In its early years, Cleland suffered a number of mishaps, including overgrazing and serious erosion, hairy-nosed wombats burrowing out of their enclosures, and birds killed by visitors' pantyhose caught in their beaks. Plastic bags and the backing sheets of instant photographs killed 'a number of kangaroos', while children 'willfully harassed and injured animals' and 'stoned a pelican to death'. Demands for parental supervision and several media articles improved the situation (Department of Environment and Planning, 1983, p35).

Today the Park consists of 30 hectares. Cleland's visitor numbers have varied between about 78,000 at its inception in 1973 to over 130,000 visitors in 1991 and 91,000 in 2003 (Tourism South Australia, 1991, pp2, 10; see Table P1.2). Most of the visitors are local or come with friends or relatives, although, as with Lone Pine, Cleland is often shown to interstate or international visiting friends (see also Mitchell, 1992, p3). In 1983, half of Adelaide's residents had visited Cleland, almost half of these in the previous 12 months (Department of Environment and Planning, 1983, p39).

Peter Martinsen (1985, p2) was appointed as Ranger in Charge in 1978. In 1985, when he outlined the purposes of the Park, he included contributions to recreation and tourism, endangered species breeding and 'environmental education and interpretation'. Ron Ballantyne (interviewed on 2 April 1994), the Education Officer, feels the educational element has to be really low-key 'chat and pat' rather than slides and lectures. Indeed, this might be a suitable approach, given that Cleland's visitors were among the least likely site visitors to have tertiary qualifications (33 per cent compared with 41 per cent for the total: see Table A3.1 in Appendix 3).

Cleland, according to its literature, offers the most extensive koala fondling experience available. Peter Martinsen (interviewed on 29 December 1992) claims visitors 'go ape' over the koala handling. Between 10 am and 12 noon in the morning, groups of three visitors at a time can enter the koala area with a keeper. They can stroke a koala's back and thus interact for at least 30 seconds (I was probably there for about 5 minutes as no one was waiting). Between 2 and 4 pm, for a fee, visitors can hold a koala for 2 minutes and have a photograph taken. The emphasis is on 'quality of experience, quality of service, quality of photograph' (interview with Peter Martinsen, 29 December 1992). One of the personnel at Cleland suggested that, in contrast with the 'exploitation' of a setup such as Lone Pine, we 'can provide an enormous experience for people which has conservation potential' (telephone interview, 21 July 1993).

In Mitchell's survey in 1992 (p3), 32 per cent said the 'best thing' about Cleland was getting close to the animals. A further 18 respondents (about 15 per cent) mentioned aspects of touching the animals, either koalas or kangaroos. Only about 5 per cent mentioned a purely visual experience, such as seeing the reptiles (Mitchell, 1992, p5). My survey produced similar results. As enjoyable aspects of their animal encounter, respondents mentioned touching the animals, feeding the animals and interacting with the animals at a significantly higher rate than for the total sample (see Table A3.5 in Appendix 3).

The animals that provided this intimacy, which were cute and cuddly, were most often the koalas and the kangaroos,[29] both species allowing close encounters. Respondents mentioned meeting, patting or feeding the kangaroos; patting, holding, cuddling or being photographed with a koala. Several commented on the pleasure of seeing others' pleasure: a 'close encounter and feeding animals with the children'; 'seeing my Indonesian friend patting our animals'.

Currumbin Wildlife Sanctuary

It would be around 30 years since I've been to Currumbin Sanctuary, but I think of it as being unique. I can't remember any other place where you could hold a plate and all the parrots would come and sit all over you.

(lapsed visitor in McNair, 1990, p68)

What I remember is a bird doing a job on my head.

(lapsed visitor in McNair, 1990, p68)

In a Brisbane telephone survey of Gold Coast tourist destinations, those who preferred Currumbin made ready use of a discourse of authenticity to justify their choice. Currumbin is not 'nasty and commercial' like Dreamworld, where 'It's all stress, queues and people'; 'mindless'. 'You walk along, looking vacant, all the entertainment is planned. You watch a show, clap, move to the next show, clap.' Sometimes Seaworld was included in this category of mindless, inauthentic entertainment, as was Lone Pine Koala Sanctuary: 'Currumbin Sanctuary is more natural. ...Lone Pine is like a souvenir shop' (McNair, 1990, p63).

Currumbin, on Queensland's Gold Coast, houses fauna in:

24 hectares of beautifully landscaped parkland and natural forest. Famous worldwide for its wild lorikeet feedings,[30] it boasts a wide variety of Australian native fauna, much of which roams freely around the park.

(McNaught, 1991, p20)

In June 1993, brochures were available in Japanese, Chinese and English.[31] In my survey, Currumbin was often visited with the family; visitors were more likely to be female and engaged in home duties, and less likely to have a tertiary education. There were no respondents from overseas (see Table A3.1 in Appendix 3).

In a telephone survey in 1990, respondents saw Currumbin as educational rather than entertaining, as relaxing rather than stimulating. A number mentioned the appeal of seeing free non-captive animals in their 'natural environment' 'where they look comfortable and happy'. Indeed one respondent said that 'cages would be out of the spirit of Currumbin' (McNair, 1990, p77). Another produced an origin story that matched this naturalistic image:

> As I recall, Currumbin Sanctuary just happened, they didn't set out to make it like that … the birds were already there… It's real as opposed to manufactured.
>
> (McNair, 1990, p76)

My focus group respondents echoed other visitors to Currumbin, referring to the natural surroundings and the freedom of the animals in their open range situation: 'birds doing what they naturally do', which encourages the visitor to relax 'a little bit'. It is 'nice to hand feed an animal rather than have it run away from you'.

Where the McNair survey unearthed criticisms, they echoed those for all zoos and sanctuaries: insufficient, hiding or immobile animals. The bats merely 'hang upside down and sleep, and the dingoes looked like house dogs – I expected them to be wild'. 'You couldn't see the wombat.' 'It was boring' (McNair, 1990, p66). Those aged in their teens to mid-20s particularly described Currumbin as dull and unchanging: 'I get used to being entertained' (McNair, 1990, p59). As at Auckland, several visitors in my Currumbin sample were concerned about the small size of some of the enclosures or noted that the animals 'were very inactive'. Two made fairly extensive comments:

> As soon as people start learning that animals and plants are not here on earth solely for the purpose of man the world would be a much better place.
>
> (housewife, aged 20–29)

> The owls were forced by their enclosure to be awake and visible during the day. Very sad. Darkened enclosures could be used. If goannas etc. are going to be kept in enclosures then the enclosure should be made to meet the animals' needs not just to make it easy to see or look after; the enclosure needs to be larger with the trees centrally located so that it can climb the tree.
>
> (female, aged 30–44)

It is hard to imagine even jaded teenagers being bored by the lorikeet feeding, as hundreds of iridescent birds wheel in for the trays of 'a sloppy mixture of

Note: 'That would have to be it for me – the parrots sitting on your head. You don't forget, the claws were sharp' (visitor, McNair, 1990, p68).

Figure 1.10 *Lorikeet Feeding at Currumbin*

water and honey' held out by visitors. 'The result is a curious sensation of being an especially attractive tree, with lorikeets all over you' (Cherfas, 1984, p214). The birds are so dense in the air that we are warned not to move lest we be hit by a lorikeet following its flight path. If frightened, the birds take flight, but soon resettle, the air resounding with chattering squeaks and whirring wings.

The large number of lorikeets provide a vivid spectacle, although they can be a little daunting at first. Remembered tactile experiences included 'sharp' claws and the bird droppings, 'all part of the fun' according to one focus group member, but unpleasant according to another. The group was divided concerning the authenticity of the encounter. One claimed the birds are conditioned to come in for the feeding but another said that one year, when there was a great deal of blossom around, fewer birds came into Currumbin.

Given the visual and tactile impact of the lorikeet feeding, it is interesting that in a telephone survey in 1990, this was not the most commonly recalled aspect of visiting, although feeding the lorikeets came second (McNair, 1990, p95). An unprompted exit interview in 1989 placed the wallabies or kangaroos first, although when given a list of attractions, one-quarter of the adults chose feeding the lorikeets, well ahead of the next choice (wallabies and kangaroos at 15 per cent) (McNair, 1990, p31). It may be that many of the respondents did not experience the lorikeet feed, which comes at the end of the day. Furthermore, children are ambivalent, as can be seen on their faces, which vary between wide-eyed and scrunched up when confronted by the coloured whirlpool of birds.

My respondents to Currumbin generally noted their enjoyment of interactions with the animals: 'best of all was the *new* animal enclosure – being able to walk amongst the kangaroos and feed them'. As many as 3000 injured or ill animals annually are brought into the sanctuary for free veterinary care (interview with Helen Irwin, Education Officer, on 15 June 1993), and this was popular: 'orphans – very small wallaby sought my attention' (male, aged 45–60, ex-RAAF). An educational programme 'humanizes' the fostering programme for animals (Education Manager, Kerry Kitzelman, interviewed on 15 June 1993).

One respondent desired more information and education:

> after spending time in other similar places I think it could be greatly improved by the addition of a 3D theatre featuring the animals in the park. It would have been good to have had a commentary and history on features of the park and some information on some of the individuals in the park whilst on the train. Also it was disappointing not being able to interact with the animals more. Would have been good to have been able to have a guided tour of the 'hospital' and to be given an insight into the work being done.
>
> (female, payroll administrator, aged 30–44)

Conclusion: Cute, cuddly or wild?

> I really like animals too. I have fed a little chicken before, but I was really sad, because the chicken was dropped down from fifteenth floor (I lived on fifteenth floor) and died. I cried for a long time. ...Now, I want to feed some other kinds of animals such as cats, dogs or ducks. But my parents don't allow me feeding them, because it will make everywhere dirty and smelly.
>
> (letter to the author from Xu Jie, a high school student in Beijing, July 1996)

The 1933 ban on koala exports from Australia was lifted in 1980, and within seven years Japanese zoos at Nagoya, Kagoshima, Saitama, Yokohama, Awaji and Tokyo had koalas, growing the required eucalypts in glass houses (Hume, 1987, p34; Canfield, 1987b, p36). It was estimated that half the Japanese who travelled to Australia in the 1980s booked their journey because they were 'inspired by koalas' (Harding, 1990, p495):

Note: (top) The entrance to Chiang Mai Zoo features cartoon animal characters and topiary elephants (September 2001); (bottom) Adelaide Zoo's welcoming animals are not dissimilar.

Figure 1.11 *Cute/Kawaii*

'Don't ask me to explain this god-like worship Japanese people have for koalas,' says tour guide Yuki Nishizawa. 'They buy books and videos and all kinds of koala souvenirs, turning their interest into a major industry. Yes, I love them, too. They're so cuddly and ... cute'.

(Shears, 1993, p58)

In 2002 Tama-chan, a seal who resides in the rivers of Yokohama, created a craze, particularly among local female residents and school girls, who turned up in their thousands in the hope of sighting Tama-chan. By the end of 2002, he featured among the ten most popular and commonly used terms of the year. While some complain that the craze is only about *kawaii*, 'cute', animals and has supported vendors of Tama-chan t-shirts and such like, others suggest that environmental issues, such as global warming and polluted rivers, are now discussed more widely in Yokohama. There are claims that people have been cured of depression or *hikikomori*, voluntary isolation from family and society, which affects more than one million Japanese. In February 2003, Tama-chan was issued with a certificate of residence, which is denied foreign nationals and Korean and Chinese ethnic groups within Japan. As one foreign rights campaigner suggested, 'they seem to be saying that foreigners aren't even mammals' (Kadri, 2003, p2).

Despite this Japanese enthusiasm for *kawaii* animals, which echoes a Western desire for the 'cute and cuddly', one should not assume that all humans share the contemporary Western preoccupation (or the preoccupation of some Westerners) with touching animals. A dolphin being transported from the US to Italy was put in the swimming pool on the ship when its own pool collapsed. The captain invited passengers to swim with the dolphin. Only one woman and her son took up the offer, staying in the pool for 'about a quarter of a minute', according to Captain Gray (Hahn, 1990, p322). In my own travels to animal encounter destinations, I witnessed occasional reluctance among Asian tourists in handling animals. At Lone Pine on 4 May 1993, among the kangaroos, a timid young woman appeared to be asking her escort to take the picture quickly so that she wouldn't be pestered by the kangaroos. At the Edward River Crocodile Farm, there was much giggling and some awe as we gathered round to handle a small crocodile. While most managed without difficulty, two Japanese English-language students in Cairns almost dropped the crocodile. On one visit to Currumbin, I noticed an anguished Japanese woman holding her trays just long enough for her husband to take the photograph before she flung them to the ground. I asked the Australian Japanese-speaking guide for the dolphin-feeding group at Tangalooma (interviewed 17 April 1997) whether the Japanese were occasionally reluctant to feed the dolphins. He replied, 'They see so few animals, they probably find it more exciting than we do. You see them gather round a possum or a sugar glider. I get excited to see them [the animals] but they really get excited.'

However, I have also seen European background visitors to Currumbin looking fearful as birds settle all over them. My colleague from Beijing, Du Xuezeng, reacted to the animals much as I did at Lone Pine in May 1993. On reflection, I think that we often react to animals differently, not so much because of our cultural backgrounds, but because of how we come to be in the animal contact zone. In a foreign country as a tourist, one's perceptions are heightened, which can cause both increased pleasure and greater anxiety. The happiness of being on holiday may collide with the strangeness of the environment and animals in a foreign land. In December 2002, I visited the Higashiyama Park Zoo in Nagoya. The Japanese responded to the reptile handling much the same way as any group of Westerners I have seen, with a mixture of awe, excitement, of fear for some and delight for others. Where I balked at having a python draped around my shoulders, small children happily embraced the experience.

Figure 1.12 *Handling Reptiles*

Feeding animals in national parks is often tantamount to signing their death warrants. In the early 1920s, newspapers reported thrilled visitors at Yosemite who had bears eating out of their hands. A decade later came reports of injuries from bears. Injuries fell to about two a year in the 1950s, following a publicity programme to discourage feeding, although injury rates rose again as people began flooding to the parks in the 1960s (Rowell, 1976, p24). A range of deterrents are now urged on visitors to avoid being attacked by a bear and to prevent bears foraging for human food. These include hiking in groups, wearing bear bells, securing food in elaborate containers, using bear-proof rubbish bins (Rowell, 1976, p27; Jope, 1985, p35; Albert and Bowyer 1991, pp340, 344). 'Bears Behaving Badly' was the subject of a documentary by David Attenborough, screened on ABC Television in 2000.

North of Calgary is one of the most glorious stretches of scenery imaginable. Sharp snow-clad mountains rise almost from the road's verge while the valleys are peppered with elk, black bears and moose. Here, too, the bear problem means that, on entering national parks, visitors are given a brochure sternly warning of the danger and illegality of feeding bears:

> It is unlawful to entice, or feed bears in national parks – this is to protect both you and the animals. ... Women should be extra careful – bears may be attracted to women during their menstrual period.
>
> (Environment Canada Parks Service, 1989, pp2–3)

'Deer bums', fed because they are 'cute', lose their fear of cars, becoming road accident statistics, or aggressive towards humans,[32] a problem also confronted in Miya Jima in Japan. Miya Jima, an island in the Inland Sea of Japan, is famous for its 'floating' red *torii* (shrine gate). The deer have been so regularly fed by tourists that signs warn: 'Stay away from deers with antlers'. Around the town in January 2003, I saw no deer with antlers, although there were several whose antlers appeared to be sawn off.

Macaques have become aggressive beggars in Malaysia, Singapore and Hong Kong (Edington and Edington, 1986, p36). In Thailand, one response is to administer amphetamines to gibbons and monkeys to keep them awake and active during the day when the tourists visit, and to file their teeth so that tourists are safe. However, teeth filing can lead to infection and death for the monkeys (Corben, 1994, p14). In Amboseli National Park in Kenya, vervet monkeys raiding the lodge for food find themselves in uncomfortable proximity with each other, causing internecine fights, and sometimes attacks on tourists (Brennan et al, 1985). Elephants fed with bananas have overturned and rattled cars in Uganda (Edington and Edington, 1986, p37). Iguanas on Galapagos leave their territories to beg from tourists (Edington and Edington, 1986, p41). From 1993, feeding dolphins was prohibited in US waters under the Marine Mammal Protection Act, when it was found that provisioned dolphins stole baits from fishing lines and crabnets, thus increasing complaints from people fishing as well as threats against dolphins (Orams, 1995, pp99–100).

Every time animals are shot because they attack humans, a debate erupts in Australia concerning who is at fault and who should pay the price. The debate occurred when pelicans were shot in 1998[33] and again in 2001 when 31 dingoes were culled on Fraser Island, following a fatal attack on a small boy by increasingly aggressive dingoes (Pearce, 2001). Because of the desire to feed, some national parks accept the existence of 'sacrifice animals', which are fed by tourists (Richardson, 1993, p22).

None of my survey respondents appeared to have perceived any dangers from feeding or handling the animals at Cleland and Currumbin, perhaps trusting the site managers to look out for the animals' welfare. However, there is debate concerning whether cuddling koalas causes them stress.[34] At Cleland, most koalas are rested for a day before they are handled again, although one keeper claimed that some of the koalas enjoy the handling and climb onto the keepers when the time comes for their photo opportunity (interview with a keeper on 29 December 1992). While visitors' failure to discuss the problems of feeding and touching animals might suggest a lack of scientific knowledge concerning animal welfare, the desire to touch and feed, to care for, can also be an important resource for conservation. This argument is canvassed in Chapter 6, which explores new ways for humans to apprehend their relations with nature.

In animal sanctuaries and zoos close to major urban areas, visitors grapple with the conflict between a close encounter and an authentic one, between their desire to see animals free and happy and their desire to see animals being active, or merely to see animals at all. They respond with pleasure to babies, to the chance to pet and feed animals. They occasionally mention the importance of education, preservation of animals, sometimes even conservation of the environment. However, while the public realize they ought to go to the zoo for an education, they admit they go primarily to view the animals or show the animals to their children (Mullan and Marvin, 1987, p135; Townsend, 1988; Davallon and Davallon, 1987, pp26–7 for France; Kellert, 1978a, p58 for the US; Moar, 1987, p38 for Adelaide Zoo; McNair, 1990, p90 for Currumbin). Indeed some studies reveal that knowledge about animals increases only minimally following a visit to the zoo, and sometimes decreases, although not all research findings are as gloomy (e.g. see Table A3.12 in Appendix 3: visitors to Auckland Zoo understand education to be a major purpose of the site, although they identified the importance of entertainment at a significantly greater rate than visitors to other sites).[35]

Today, in Western cities, a good proportion of zoo visitors do not come with innocent or untroubled eyes. For many, the only justification is conservation, whether directly through endangered species breeding or indirectly through educating the conservationists of the future. As one visitor to Auckland Zoo said, 'Still not sure about the ethical side of zoos – conservation aside – birds in cages a no-no'. Monarto recorded the highest percentage of respondents who saw the major purpose of the site as conservation, followed by Warrawong and the Great Australian Bight (Table A3.12 in Appendix 3). It is to these sites, among others dedicated to conservation, that we turn in the next chapter.

2
Animals as Ambassadors for Conservation

the city is not a concrete jungle, it is a human zoo.

(Desmond Morris in *The Human Zoo* in 1969, text in 'Western Australia: Land and
People', Exhibition of Western Australian Museum, opened 2001)

4800 million years of research and development went into the creation
of the Australian landscape. The result is an absolutely unique and
incredibly diverse place.

(Terry de Gryse, 1989, p60)

There were always some settlers who loved Australia as it was –
unreconstructed.

(William Lines, 1991, p273)

Turning wilderness into national parks

Nature destinations became imagined as sites of leisure during the Industrial
Revolution, when the romantic movement revolted against the ugliness of
industrialization and urbanization. Prior to this, statutes 'protecting' the forests
actually protected hunting grounds (Coates, 1998, p46). From the Middle Ages
to the 18th century, wildness and insanity were interchangeable concepts; both
could be cured by acculturation (Colin, 1987, p7). However, once there was
little enough of it, wilderness took on a more positive gloss, something remote
and untouched, offering ecological variety (Davis, 1989, p11). A growing
wilderness movement emerged in tandem with the receding wilderness, pushed
to the margins by urban living, safely distant from the brute realities of farming
livestock or the threats of wild animals (Jasper and Nelkin, 1992, p4; Tuan,
1984, p112; Walker, 1991, p27).

To the colonists who 'settled' places like North America and Australia, out
on the edge of empire, wilderness abounded and was not initially valued.
Booster literature for Canada in the 1880s saw the 'environment in its raw,
alien, undisciplined state' (Osburne, 1988, p166). 'Australia stood in need of

redemption' (Lines, 1991, p48), 'imaginative possession' through the signs of European activity: downs, meadows, stockmen, smoke rising from chimneys (Lines, 1991, p49). Colonists faced the 'subtle terror' of succumbing to 'wilderness temptations', behaving in a 'savage or bestial manner' (Nash, 1973, p29 for the US; see also Lines, 1991, p69 for Australia). However, between the beginning of the 19th century and the beginning of the 20th, attitudes also changed in the settler societies. In 1864, a grant of Yellowstone Valley was made as a park (Nash, 1973, p106). In 1872, this became the first large-scale wilderness preservation area, declared a national park by President Ulysses S. Grant. The desire for tourist attractions drove Canada and New Zealand[1] to declare areas as national parks. The first urban park in Australia, set aside in 1879, was the Royal National Park at Port Hacking, south of Sydney (Hamilton-Smith, 1988, p31; Dunlap, 1999, p122).[2] The Park was planted with exotic flora and stocked with exotic fish and deer (Walker, 1991, p25–26; see also Hamilton-Smith, 1988, p31). Belair National Park near Adelaide, the second in Australia, was set aside in 1891, also as a 'recreational and pleasure ground' rather than for conservation (Davidson and Spearritt, 2000, p227; see also Hutton and Connors, 1999, pp32–33, 37–38). By 1915, all Australian states had at least one national park, with an emphasis on recreation (Clark, 1990, p234).

The idea of national parks as wilderness, even if imperfectly realized, is peculiar to settler societies. Pristine untouched environments are not even attempted in densely settled countries like Britain (Bosselman, 1978, p233) or Japan, with its famous 'foot binding applied to nature', dwarfed bonsai trees (Kalland and Asquith, 1997, p25) and 'trimmed' views of borrowed scenery, backdropping manicured Japanese gardens (Hendry, 1997, p88). Wilderness may be disdained, as are 'uncultivated' people, nature usually being amenable to improvement so it can 'express itself in a louder voice and in plainer terms' through reductionism, limited diversity, pruning for the pure line (Kalland and Asquith, 1997, pp16–17). 'Nature in Japan is a *work* of art' (Haraway, 1992, p248) just as rice paddies are superior to the unfarmed land they displaced. Intrinsic to the origin myth of rice is its role in transforming the wilderness into rice paddies to create 'Japanese land' (Ohnuki-Tierney, 1993, p132). While Mike Bossley (interviewed on 19 December 2000), Australian environmental scientist and psychologist, might find it 'very depressing' that the Japanese 'can't let a poor bloody tree or plant just grow', many Chinese and Japanese might find Western tourists' photographs of breathtaking scenery empty of all humans just as depressing (Thubron, 1987, p63).[3] However, in Japan, as in settler societies, rapid urbanization of the postwar generations has meant that 'nature tourism' has become a solace for many (Moon, 1997, p226) and 'eco-tourism has brought about a new environmental consciousness' (Kalland and Asquith, 1997, p27).

In the US, Stephen Mather, first director of the Park Service, proclaimed that 'scenery is a hollow enjoyment' after bad food and an impossible bed. He set about making national parks a leisure/pleasure destination, abetted by the spread of the automobile and the improved accessibility of many parks (Rothman, 1989, pp90–91). In 1926, the National Parks Act in South Africa identified tourism as one justification for parks. In the 1950s in Australia, many still saw national parks as largely for recreational rather than conservation purposes, recommending the erection of hotels and leisure amenities (Davidson and Spearritt, 2000, p240). Even so, the national parks in Australia had their protectors among groups like the Mountain Trails Club and the Sydney Bushwalkers (Walker, 1991, p24; Hutton and Connors, 1999, pp23, 61). In 1988, the Wilderness Act in New South Wales sought to protect the 4 per cent of the State that was still in a wilderness-like state (Papps, 1988, p9). In 1996, of the 469 properties in the world on the World Heritage list, 11 were in Australia (World Heritage Unit, 1996, p1).[4] While not all are on the scale of World Heritage sites, this chapter explores a number of nature destinations where conservation is an important part of the message. These range from 'manufactured' sites, Monarto and Warrawong, to more 'authentic' or pre-existing animal encounter sites, such as Seal Bay, the Great Australian Bight and Macquarie Island.

Saving the wild world

they want to see an environmentally friendly place. They want to feel comfortable about where they stay. They want to have a good time.

(Janet Oliver, 1992, p54)

After it had gone from view, the silence on board remained. The crew and the women went to the upper deck. The [corporate] headhunter and I remained below, not speaking, not looking at each other, foreheads pressed against the glass. We were both weeping.

(Andrew Masterson, 1994, p75, speaking of seeing a manta ray on a semi-submersible craft exploring a reef)

I asked the focus group members about their experiences of animals in the wild. For some it was 'the unexpected'; for others seeing something nobody else has seen. Animals in the wild were often surprisingly and pleasingly large, swift or numerous compared with their apparent small size and numbers in the confined space of a sanctuary. John says of Seal Bay, 'my only recollection was "Boy they're big"' and not 'just see[ing] one or two, you see stacks of them'. On a fishing trip, Alison 'counted 25 sharks one morning' and remembers 'literally tens of thousands of these fish [Johnny Ruffs] around the boat'.

Little wonder, perhaps, that some animal encounter sites strive for these experiences by appearing as naturalistic as possible, such as Monarto Zoological Park, an offshoot of Adelaide Zoo, and Warrawong Sanctuary, dedicated to the preservation of small marsupials. The sites in this chapter share two things in common: they attempt a natural presentation and they propose a more insistent conservation message than do the sanctuaries and zoos discussed in Chapter 1. Table A3.5 in Appendix 3 reveals that, for the whole sample, the most common reason for enjoying the animal encounter was learning something about the animals. This response rate was highest for Monarto, Seal Bay and Warrawong, although only statistically significant for the last site. From Table A3.7, it can be seen that the main emotional or affective response of visitors at these three sites was a good feeling that the animals were preserved.

While neither Osprey Tours, with its whale watching in the Great Australian Bight, nor Southern Heritage Expeditions trips to Macquarie Island and Antarctica scored particularly high on either of these score, I include analysis of these sites in this chapter. Whales and seals were major export industries in colonial Australia. Both have been reconstructed for Australian audiences as symbols of conservation. The Macquarie Island penguins were also once boiled down for oil but now serve as a tourist attraction. The chapter concludes by addressing the potential conflict between the goals of conservation-oriented encounter site managers and their visitors. But first let us journey to Africa, an hour's drive from Adelaide.

Monarto Zoological Park

> it was the giraffes. See[ing] such large animals up so close, and in their own environment. With two small children who won't walk far, it was wonderful to go on the bus and still get so close to the animals. And for the children to see animals that they wouldn't normally see, except in books, or on TV, or in a cage.
>
> (female, home duties, aged 30–44)

A number of city zoos have developed safari park-like offshoots, often with names to suit their naturalistic approach. Taronga pioneered open space zoos in Australia in the mid-1970s with the Western *Plains* Zoo, near Dubbo in central New South Wales (Milling, 1987, p18). Western Plains Zoo promises a 'safari around the world in just one day' (Western Plains Zoo promotional booklet, 1986). Victoria's Open Range Zoo is at Werribee. Monarto Zoological Park, Adelaide Zoological Association's safari offshoot, is near Murray Bridge in South Australia, about an hour's drive from Adelaide. The South Australian State government had acquired farming land for its planned satellite city of Monarto, which did not eventuate. In 1963, part of the 200,000-odd hectares became an adjistment area for Adelaide Zoo. From a place where surplus stock and breeding herds, especially of endangered species, could be kept, development of a plains-type zoo was announced in 1982. Rapid development commenced in 1993, when Dr David Langdon was appointed the first director. Monarto was enclosed in 12.5 kilometres of vermin-proof fence to keep out foxes, cats and rabbits; half a million trees and shrubs were planted (David Langdon, interviewed on 7 January 1993). Monarto has been described as 'the third international-standard, open-range zoo in Australia ... part of a worldwide coordinated attempt to maintain global biological diversity in Australia' (Snowdon, 1989, p149). As with Western Plains Zoo, the aim is a 'near-nature experience' (interview with David Langdon on 7 January 1993).

Monarto echoes the surrounding mallee environment with arid and semi-arid habitats (interview with David Langdon on 7 January 1993). Ultimately there are to be four public presentation geo-environments: Africa, Asia, North Africa and Australia (Royal Zoological Society of South Australia, 1992, p1). By 2002, the exhibits open to the public were 'Asian steppes', 'Asian grasslands', 'African plains', 'Cheetah', '[another] African plains', and 'Arid North Africa'. A white rhinoceros[5] exhibit was under development, while the map identified 'future elephant', 'future African plains', 'future African lion', 'future Australian' and 'future South American' exhibits. A major complaint of surveyed visitors in the early 1990s was the lack of facilities. By 2002, a corrugated iron and timber pavilion housed a bistro, toilet facilities, tour desk and gift shop. Nearby were the popular bilbies (asleep in August under a heat lamp) and the meerkats (always on the move like running water, as one of our guides said).

Originally, there were plans to restore one of the old sandstone farmhouses, perhaps as a bilby exhibit, allowing people to leave the bus, go for a stroll and catch the next bus. In 2002, however, the tour was undertaken entirely in the bus, although there were several botanical walking paths near the visitor centre. According to David Langdon (interviewed on 7 January 1993), the safari bus meant people left the familiarity of their motor vehicles for a bus ride. Another proclaimed advantage of Monarto is sufficiently large enclosures to allow natural sized herds of various species to share a single enclosure in imitation of species' coexistence in the wild (David Langdon, interviewed on 27 July 1993). The aim was that, as far as possible, animals at Monarto would be left to their natural devices: to forage for food (although supplements would be provided), to mate, and to die if weak or disabled (although rare species would be handled with more intervention). Distance management was the aim, just enough control of animal behaviour to allow herding for inspection and so on when necessary.[6]

The breeding programme aims to breed species that are 'extinct or rare in the wild', 'as well as those species that are rare within Australian zoos' (Royal Zoological Society of South Australia, 1992, p4). David Langdon described Monarto as 'the golden opportunity to change awareness levels in the community of tomorrow' (David Langdon, interviewed on 27 July 1993). Surveys conducted by Monarto in 1994 reveal that the conservation message is being heard. In one survey, the major thing Monarto offered the community was 'a place to protect endangered animals', followed by an opportunity to learn about animals, and third the chance to see conservation at work ('Monarto Zoological Park Questionnaire', Langdon, personal communication

Note: (top) Early days at Monarto: David Langdon discussing development plans on 27 July 1993; the Asian grasslands exhibit in 2002 included a group of about 50 ungulates, some of them 'excellent' sized herds, according to our guide. Antelope, Nilgai, the Indian black buck and hog deer share an enclosure; (bottom) failures of distance management: the giraffes stripped the trees in their habitat, requiring a feeding device in the barren area. This provoked one member in my tour group to ask if Monarto would grow more trees so that the giraffes 'can eat from the trees', obviously preferring a 'natural experience' for the giraffes (tour, 5 August 2002). Two species of African ungulates, the Addax and Scimitar Horned Oryx, constantly broke down their intervening fences, fighting so much that they required hospitalization, a problem only resolved when they were moved beyond mutual eyesight.

Figure 2.1 *Monarto Rings the Changes*

May, 1994). Similarly my respondents focused on learning about the animals (Table A3.5 in Appendix 3) and their preservation (Table A3.7).

In a 1994 survey, the main thing visitors enjoyed was the guided tour (38 per cent) followed by the animals' freedom (27 per cent) ('Monarto Zoological Park Questionnaire', Langdon, personal communication. May, 1994). All the guides are volunteers, and their role is to locate the animals in the ecosystem and discuss issues of conservation. Two tour guides suggested that this message ran counter to visitors' initial preferences, which were for entertainment (Graham Goldsmith, tour guide, interviewed on 27 July 1993) or to monitor the development of the site (Jan Tottman, volunteer coordinator of the 28 volunteers, interviewed on 27 July 1993).

In 1994 Monarto was still in a rudimentary stage of development and this was commented on in terms of too few animals (70 per cent of respondents where the total response rate for this item was 13 per cent) and not being close enough to the animals (33 per cent compared with 10 per cent):

> I think that opening the Park before it is completed was disappointing to me and the others with me. We paid $30 (+ petrol to get there) to sit in a bus and view a few animals. Most of the animals we did see were too far away to look at properly. The guide on the bus was constantly telling us about what animals would be at the park in the next few years ... which made me wonder why you had opened the park now and not waited.
>
> (female mothercraft nurse, aged 30–44)

By contrast, in 2002 the vocal members of my small group on Monday 5 August 2002 were impressed to see the animals 'like this in the wild, not like on the telly'. There were gasps when the cheetahs came right up to the bus and comments of 'Oh my God, look at that' when we entered one of the African plains exhibits and ten giraffes and a small herd of zebras trotted in front of our bus.

Respondents to my survey in the mid 1990s were most likely to visit with other family or friends, the site attracting few overseas visitors.[7] The small group on our minibus when I visited again in 2002 consisted of myself and a colleague visiting from Paris, a mature woman with a child, perhaps her granddaughter, a mother and daughter team, loquacious and humorous, and a young Muslim couple, she wearing a headscarf. The passengers in my group had some general knowledge of animal behaviour, apparently gleaned from wildlife films. The Muslim male asked whether there were birds at Monarto that groomed animals like the rhinoceros and whether the cape hunting dog regurgitated meat for its young. There was also some commentary on the sexual behaviour of the animals, the Muslim man saying he 'liked the idea' of the one male Indian black buck stag 'having all the females to himself', as the male guide had put it. The Muslim male also wondered whether the females in one ungulate group didn't 'get bored without a male', to which his female partner said, 'Trust you to ask that'. By contrast, when our female driver told us that the pack of Cape hunting dogs (also called African painted dogs) was headed by a matriarch, the female members of the bus tour voiced approval. The young woman from the team said, 'Yeah, I seen that on a documentary', adding 'the whole pack raises the litter, just like human natives where the whole tribe raises the children'.

We were sternly informed of the endangered status of many of the animals in the park, this information being linked with Monarto's breeding programme. We were told that habitat encroachment was the main reason that the Cape hunting dogs, which 'used to roam in packs of a hundred or more', were now down to 'several thousand'. 'Humans are the worst animals,' echoed a passenger. We were told that the white settlers in the US shot bison for sport and to contain the Indians, reducing bison numbers from 60 million in the 1700s to less than 1000 by the late 1820s. Numbers are now at 200,000 and the Native Americans farm bison. The guide proudly affirmed that Przewalski's horse, described as 'prehistoric' (by a passenger) and a 'walking fossil' over 20,000 years old (by our guide), was being returned to the Gobi desert as a result of a successful breeding programme. One passenger claimed, 'it is not bad when you can breed them here and send them back to their homeland'. Similarly, a passenger lamented the most recent failed breeding attempt with the cheetahs, using artificial insemination: 'it would be terrible if there were no cheetahs left in the world'.

Our guide also spoke of the breeding programme for yellow-footed rock wallabies, in which volunteers release the wallabies in their 'natural habitat'. Killing two birds with one stone, volunteers removed feral goats, which were brought back to Monarto for the carnivores to eat. The Addax and Scimitar Horned Oryx were described as 'extremely endangered', the Addax being plentiful until World War II: a newborn baby was drawn to our attention. The young woman asked 'How many animals go extinct per day?' and the guide answered that he had no idea. She replied, 'It's quite high, isn't it?'

Visitors in the mid-1990s survey also received the conservation message loud and clear, five respondents commenting on the important work of breeding programmes for endangered species:

> Knowing that these animals were in a large, open natural environment and that they were being bred to be returned to the wild.
>
> (female, home duties, aged 30–44)

Warrawong

> Dawn in a rain forest can be an everlasting memory – the creatures of the night and day intermingle as the sun rises through the mist of the Adelaide Hills. Join us for an experience that you will never forget.
>
> (Warrawong Sanctuary, 1991, p1)

> In this increasingly busy and hectic world, many people find themselves removed from nature and the peace and calm that it creates. When it comes to nature and getting back to it, there is nowhere on earth that compares to an Earth Sanctuary. Each of our Earth Sanctuaries ... is the Australia that existed before the arrival of Europeans ... The really pleasing thing about creating a sanctuary for Australia's flora and fauna is that it also becomes a sanctuary for people too.
>
> (Earth Sanctuaries, 2000a, pp30–31)

A stone's throw from Cleland (discussed in Chapter 1), also in the Adelaide Hills, is Warrawong Sanctuary: '25 years ago Cleland was the most visionary thing in Australia'. Now too many cages and mismanagement means that 'There are more animals lost at Cleland than at Gepps Cross [a busy metropolitan traffic intersection]'. 'They don't pay their own wages, their own maintenance or their own development', which the government pays. 'If they had to pay the actual costs it would cost $70 per head to go in' (John Wamsley, interviewed on 19 December 1992).[8] Such criticisms are a constant refrain from Dr John Wamsley, who, until he recently retired, ran his Earth Sanctuaries, not only without any government funding, but also in the face of political opposition.

The survey responses suggest that Warrawong is akin to Monarto in visitors' appreciation of their learning experience and the preservation of endangered animals (see Tables A3.5 and A3.7). John Wamsley encourages Warrawong visitors to turn their 'cute and cuddly' response to the adorable furry marsupials into a conservationist orientation. Previously a lecturer in mathematics at Flinders University, Wamsley was raised in the bush, and was:

> fortunate to live in a part of Australia before foxes and cats got to it.
> When I was seven I used to get up at midnight to watch the animals.
> My parents knew that I'd have to work with animals but they couldn't decide whether I'd be a butcher or a taxidermist.

This, for Wamsley, represents the attitude of many white Australians to the continent's indigenous wildlife: 'One of the sad things about Australians is we pretend we are Europeans and so destroy Australia' (John Wamsley, commentary on dawn walk, 19 December 1992).

John Wamsley's vision to save Australian's small marsupials from extinction commenced in 1969, when he purchased 14 hectares of land, used as a dairy, in the Adelaide Hills. Over time, Wamsley planned to secure sanctuaries in every significant habitat in Australia, the small marsupials protected within by a cat- and fox-proof fence.[9] By 1999, Earth Sanctuaries had set out to achieve 'the impossible', to ensure that not one more of the 100 mammal species expected to become extinct in Australia by the year 2025 actually does become extinct.[10] To achieve this goal, a plan was hatched to acquire 10 million hectares of land that would be covered with appropriate habitat, the total project to cost about $1 billion (about three-quarters of a billion in US$). In February 2000, Earth Sanctuaries became a publicly listed company with a $15 million float (about US$11million), described as 'the world's first publicly listed conservation company (Booth, 2000, p25). This ambitious plan led to overcapitalization and the anticipated investors did not materialize. All the properties, bar Warrawong and Little River Earth Sanctuary (close to Melbourne), were sold. The four sanctuaries of Scotia, Yookamurra, Buckaringa and Dakalanta were sold to Australian Wildlife Conservancy,

Note: Warrawong becomes a listed company (Booth, 2000, p25, photography by Campbell Brodie and courtesy of *The Advertiser*).

Figure 2.2 *'Prospectus that Offers Wild Returns'*

which has similar goals to Earth Sanctuaries (Earth Sanctuaries, 2002, pp1–3; Martin Copley, Director, Australian Wildlife Conservancy, letter to Earth Sanctuaries shareholders, no date but mid-September 2002). John Wamsley retired as director.

A 'natural gem in our midst' (Jory, 1998, p18) or 'Mad John Wamsley', as he is called around Adelaide, often seen in his feral cat hat, John Wamsley became well known for his iconoclastic conservation statements, exchanging insults with opponents across the environmental spectrum. Wamsley has particularly angered cat lovers, for example with his bumper sticker 'the only good cat is a flat cat'. He complained 10 years ago that the Australian Conservation Foundation would not broach the subject of feral cats because too many of their members had pet cats. He was prescient in suggesting that the cat debate would follow the lines of the tobacco debate, it becoming increasingly accepted that cat owners must take responsibility for preventing their pets from becoming feral (interviewed on 19 December 1992). By the time of the 1998 Constitutional Convention on the Australian Constitution, one delegate, Janet Holmes a Court, suggested that 'no feral cats' should be included in a new preamble (Smith, 1999, p292).

Earth Sanctuaries included in its definition of a sanctuary: 'run as an environmental education centre that earns sufficient funds to give a reasonable return to investors and provides for the day-to-day running of the sanctuary' (Wamsley, 1994, pp20–21). Wamsley's refrain was that other sanctuaries, particularly those nearby like Cleland, Monarto and Adelaide Zoo, offered unfair competition because of their government subsidies. Recriminations flowed back and forth.[11] Wamsley's commitment to making sanctuaries economically profitable mechanisms for saving the wild world[12] led to Wamsley's interest in placing a price on nature.

Should the last stand of old mallee in Australia, at Yookamurra Sanctuary, be valued at the price of firewood – $130 a tonne – although protected from being cut down for firewood? Or at the cost of replacement nest boxes for the animals and birds which nest in the trees – $400 a tree? Or at the cost of buying the most advanced trees on sale, at about $2000 for a 100-year-old tree? Or at the replacement value of $100 million per tree? In one calculation, the 400-year-old Yookamurra trees are worth $13,000 trillion (in the Australian government publication, 'Techniques to Value Environmental Resources', and the Australian Institute of Horticulture's 'A System of Assigning a Monetary Value to Amenity Trees': Earth Sanctuaries, 1995, pp7–9). Similarly, an animal might be valued at the price a hunter pays to shoot it (in Zimbabwe, local communities sell the right to shoot an elephant for about US$25,000) or the value of its products (in Australia $50 for a killed red kangaroo). Alternatively, each species of Australian mammal is estimated as worth about $318 million in tourist revenues (Earth Sanctuaries, 1995, pp10, 7, 11).[13] One might value an animal or tree at the net market value, that is the price at which the asset could be sold. On the other hand, it might be claimed the animal is valueless if it is illegal to shoot or (in general) to sell it.[14]

When Wamsley was not attacking the unfair advantage received by 'socialist' government supported sanctuaries, he was extolling the success of his own. 'Six species of mammal have been taken off the endangered list as a direct result of Earth Sanctuaries' work' (Earth Sanctuaries, 2003, p5). People who have a large impact in the world are often single-minded and Wamsley (1994, p22) was convinced that government funded research, which passively recorded the extinction of species, was totally unnecessary. The solution was clear: more sanctuaries like his. Earth Sanctuaries' newsletters were peppered with stories of battles with government zoos to acquire breeding animals or with state governments to acquire land (e.g. John Wamsley, 1999a, p4; see also Wamsley 1994, p22). One prospectus (Earth Sanctuaries, 1996, p9) claimed that Wamsley is 'the only person who has been able to repeat' the 'breeding [of] platypus in captivity'. As David Langdon (interviewed on 7 January 1993),

Note: By the mid 1990s, Warrawong supported more than 200 brush-tailed bettongs (Australia's smallest living kangaroo), over 100 long-nosed potoroos, over 30 of the Sydney subspecies of the red-necked pademelon, and over 200 of the southern brown bandicoot; all breeding from an original two to six individuals (Wamsley, 1994, p20). In 1995, boodies (tiny burrowing kangaroos), were reintroduced to Warrawong from islands off Western Australia, their only remaining habitat (Wamsley, 1995, p1).

Figure 2.3 *Dawn Walk in Warrawong*

who has suffered Wamsley's ire, noted wryly, for the purposes of saving marsupials, Warrawong is a slice of native Australia. For the purposes of platypus breeding, Warrawong becomes a place for 'captive' animals. Indeed one visitor in my survey wondered 'when he [Wamsley] is against so many activities, what he is for – that is what political action he recommends'.

South Australia was chosen as the place for Warrawong simply because it was the only state in which building a sanctuary was not illegal (Wamsley, 1994, p21). About 100,000 trees and shrubs were planted, a kilometre of creeks and pools constructed and the land surrounded by a cat- and fox-proof fence, the first vermin-free area on mainland Australia. Australia's small marsupials, virtually made extinct by humans, foxes and cats, were reintroduced in 1982. Warrawong opened to the public in 1985.

On 19 December 1992, I attended the dawn walk with Dr Wamsley, our group consisting of 8 men and 11 women. Two of our party were Asians, who appeared to be visiting with Adelaide families. This was a low turnout for a Saturday in summer, a result of the uncertain and often cold weather that year. We assembled in the nursery outside the cat-proof fence, where a sign proclaimed: 'Warrawong Sanctuary is a no dog, no cat, no litter, no smoking zone'. As the only animals in cages are the breeding animals, the denizens of Warrawong are lured to the tourists on the dawn walk with gifts of barley. Wamsley defends this inauthentic intrusion by claiming 'this is for you not the animals' (by which he means they have sufficient food in the environment, but the barley draws them close to us). The first stop of the dawn walk is at the crest of a paddock. A medley of kangaroos and wallabies hop up to us, their variety illustrating Wamsley's major theme:

> Anywhere in Australia 200 years ago you would find a full range of kangaroos. The grey kangaroo was the last species living in the wild in the Adelaide Hills. They are coming back at last as people stop shooting them on sight... The fox decimated medium sized mammals and the cat wiped out our small mammals. We lost everything in Australia except our big animals, and that's the tragedy of Australian wildlife... A couple of potoroos are working their way up towards us. These are the most ancient of the kangaroos, real kangaroos. They are the same now as they were ten million years ago, when all kangaroos were as small as potoroos and Australia was all rainforest. This is the largest viable colony in mainland Australia.

Wamsley expands on the conservation theme by repeatedly noting the near extinction of many of the animals that are now breeding successfully at Warrawong:

> That's a brush-tongued bettong, there are only two hundred left in the world; ten years ago half of them were in our sanctuary. We know more about the rare pandas than we do about the bettongs. There's a southern bandicoot, very rare. This subspecies of pademelon: the only place they are known in the world is Warrawong.

Our path lies along a black water lake on the edge of a eucalyptus grove, runs down into a gully where a small rainforest shelters bettongs and bandicoots, and rises past a derelict early settler's cottage and the vermin-proof fence. Wamsley explains his platypus breeding programme, and the cat-proof fence:[15]

> This is the first successful cat and fox proof fence in Australia. It works because it is quite cheap, consisting of a mild current. The fence bends out at the top so animals cannot climb under and over, while it

also goes out underground so animals cannot burrow successfully
under at the base. We get cats thrown over the fence and usually a
phone call with them saying they are from a cat lover!

At our final resting point, a group of 20–30 tamil wallabies emerge and, only
several feet from us, companionably munch on the barley. The sunlight is
stronger. Dazed by waking before light to attend the dawn walk and basking in
the warming sun, we recast the scene before us as a small recaptured utopia.
Clearly Wamsley's message allows very little anthropomorphizing. We gaze at
the rare, invariably furry and large-eyed animals, wanting to sigh 'isn't that
cute' or 'aren't they beautiful'. Wamsley makes them ambassadors of his
politics, proof that time is short and action must be taken: 'My aim is to keep
expanding Warrawong until it's the whole of Australia. I'm another Hussain'.

By 1988, work began on Yookamurra Sanctuary near Swan Reach in the
Murray Mallee of South Australia (Wamsley, 1994, p21). Yookamurra,
meaning yesterday, is described in its brochure as:

> some of the last of our continent's ancient, magical, pristine mallee ...
> being restored to what it was before the arrival of Europeans with
> their sheep, cats, rabbits, foxes and goats.
>
> (Earth Sanctuaries, 1993, p4)

The vermin-proof fence was officially closed by Sir Mark Oliphant in 1990; the
rabbits and foxes were eradicated by 1991 (Earth Sanctuaries, 1996, p24).

When my mother and I visited Yookamurra, in January 1993, the sanctuary
was still very much under development. Two paid workers were assisted by a
number of volunteers, including Margaret and Don, who had become almost a
fixture. The release programme had met with mixed success. The stick nest rats
had found shelter under the accommodation huts, which was felt to be an
inappropriate demonstration of their return to the wild. The mallee fowl were
taken by the remaining fox, whose persistent evasion of the staff's attempts to
trap it was also delaying the numbat programme. Our guide for the night walk
was Jim Grant, for 12 years employed in the Melbourne Zoo but disenchanted
with their strategies for wildlife conservation. The lunchtime walk was
conducted by Justin, a young man in his twenties, a former printer who was
inspired to work at Yookamurra after a visit to Warrawong. Justin took us to
an open clay plan where a sprinkling of flowering native plants were luring
back the native bees, gentle grey insects that have no sting. Justin asked us to
imagine bettongs and other marsupials hopping over the delicate floral carpet
spread before us, combining his image of yesterday with a utopian tomorrow.
Jim was not quite as visionary or as sure that John Wamsley had all the
answers; he outlined a broader ecological picture than the saving of marsupials.

In 2000, it was claimed that 'Warrawong Sanctuary has delighted hundreds
of thousands of visitors, Australian and international, since 1985' (Earth

Sanctuaries, 2000b, p17). In the mid 1990s Warrawong had about 20,000 visitors per annum while in 2003 there were about 50,000 visitors (Earth Sanctuaries, 1996, p30; Table P1.2). Even more so than at Monarto, the 'medium is the message'. When I surveyed them in the mid 1990s, many visitors came to hear John Wamsley tell them how he is saving Australia's small marsupials. Warrawong visitors gave statistically positive responses to enjoying a 'unique experience' and 'learning about the animals' (Table A3.5 in Appendix 3). They 'felt good the animals were being preserved' and eschewed anthropomorphic responses such as feeling affection for the animals or that the animals liked and trusted them (Table A3.7). Visitors commented that Dr Wamsley's message 'enlightened me'; 'I never realized how endangered Australian species are'. 'Long live John Wamsley and his wife and team.' 'Looking over the grass, dams and eucalypts thinking it's good someone's making an effort.' Several commented that the experience was 'fantastic', 'inspirational', 'uplifting'.

Among those in my survey who responded enthusiastically to John Wamsley's message, some identified action they would take as a result (also prompted to action, my mother and I became shareholders). A teacher planned to bring his class of 12-year-olds and to 'give some money'. A woman engaged in home duties hoped to fence her land one day, while another woman wanted more aid to sanctuaries like Warrawong. Wamsley's work does lead to changes in people's behaviour, including Earth Sanctuaries' support for a property owner to build a fence around the nesting site of endangered Bush Stone Curlews on her property (Wamsley 1999c, p4) and Martin Copley's creation of Western Australia's first private sanctuary in jarrah woodland an hour east of Perth. Copley describes his 'Damascene conversion' as a result of visiting Wamsley's sanctuary (Laurie, 1999a, pp38–41). However, even at Warrawong, people arrive by accident or for other reasons. Wamsley (interviewed on 19 December 1992) suggested that maybe 10 per cent are not interested in seeing wildlife in the wild. Meredyth Hope (interviewed on 5 January 1993), a guide at Warrawong, noted that some groups are very 'entertained and enthused' but 'some nights it's a real drag; I don't know what they pick up and how they feel about the place'.

From killing to watching: Whales, penguins and sea lions

> There are some who can live without wild things, and some who cannot. These essays are the delights and dilemmas of one who cannot... For us of the minority, the opportunity to see geese is more important than television and the chance to find a pasque-flower is a right as inalienable as free speech.
>
> (Leopold, 1949, pvii)

Turning to conservation

Sealing and whaling were major industries in colonial Australia. Between 1800 and 1806, well in excess of 100,000 seals were killed. By 1820 the southern seals had been hunted to near extinction. Francois August Peron, on Baudin's voyage of discovery, noted 'the cruelty of nature which seems only to have created such strong, gentle, and such unfortunate beings in order to deliver them' to the 'cruel sailor' (quoted in Lines, 1991, p32). Bands of convict runaways pressed captured Aboriginal women into hunting the few remaining seals (Lines, 1991, p33; Plumwood, 1992, p48), the women lying with the seals, imitating their behaviour to secure their trust. Even today, as many as 3000 fur seals are killed by the Tasmanian fishing industry each year, entangled in plastic fish bait packaging or 'in macho shoot-outs that wipe out whole colonies' (Plumwood, 1992, p51). Crayfishers accuse sea lions of stealing the crayfish out of their pots and salmon farmers accuse them of taking their salmon.[16] The Seal Bay sea lion colony was preserved through all these depredations because of its inaccessibility to sealers (Terry Dennis, District Ranger, National Parks and Wildlife Service, Kangaroo Island District Office, interviewed on 30 December 1992). Seal Bay has become a significant international tourist destination in South Australia.

Australia's international stand on whaling and Antarctica are also examples of a green image, now neatly aligned with the commercial opportunities of tourism. The whale- and dolphin-based tourism industry is estimated to be worth $2 billion worldwide and engage 10 million people each year (Hodge, 2002, p40). Whale watching in Australia is estimated as a $44–50 million-a-year industry, with some estimates of growth rates of 50 per cent per annum (Montgomery, 1997, p3; Richardson, 1993, p10).[17] Each humpback visiting Hervey Bay in Queensland is worth $100,000 in tourism (Brook, 2001, p21). Twelve countries offered whale watching experiences in 1983, climbing to 65 by 1997, including Japan in the Bonin Islands, Okinawa, Shikoku and Hokkaido, which attracts 'a lot of tourists' (Komatsu and Misaki, 2001, p100; see also JijiPress, 2003, p1). However, Komatsu and Misaki (2001, pp107, 106), in their book, *The Truth Behind the Whaling Dispute*, sponsored by the Japan Whaling Association, claim that whale watching 'should never be allowed to replace whaling', the purpose of watching being 'to learn the truth about the wild animals, and to acquire knowledge of proper management'.

Since the mid 1990s, almost every year, at some time between June and October, Australian television audiences are treated to news stories of migrating whales. The story usually contains gruesome black and white footage of the now illegal whaling industry, usually at Cheynes Beach in Albany, the last operational whaling station in Australia, but perhaps at Tangalooma, where dolphins are now a tourist attraction. Project Jonah, in which Friends of the Earth was significantly involved, used graphic images in their arguments against whaling, such as the water boiling with blood as whales thrashed to their death (Jaeckel, 2000, p25).[18] With the cessation of whaling in the late 1970s, numbers have increased (figures are usually offered in the voiceover at this point) and whales can now be spotted at many points around the coast – east, west and south – on their annual migration to the Antarctic waters, sometimes calving on route. This point is illustrated with joyous Australians on cliff tops, enthusing at the clear visibility of whales so close to shore.[19] Indeed lucky ocean-side residents of Sydney view whales from their living room windows. Sometimes, the annual story is precipitated by a whale in Sydney Harbour, sheltering to calve or recovering from an injury.[20]

The message of the annual whale migration story is that Australians are a humane people who protect whales, thus fortuitously creating a much more profitable industry in tourism than whaling ever was. By contrast, we are told, the Japanese have no respect for either international agreements concerning the hunting of whales or the whales themselves, continually pressing for a reopening of the whaling industry which brought so many species to the brink of extinction.[21] The whalers, like other hunters, are 'greedy' and 'savage'; the whales are 'lovely', 'gentle' and 'peace-loving', as are their putative protectors (Kalland, 1994, pp164–165). In fact, in the 1970s and 1980s, protesters sprayed red dye over Japanese delegates to the International Whaling Commission (IWC), while the Korean commissioner was physically assaulted when mistaken for a Japanese person (Komatsu and Misaki, 2001, p163). The racial leverage of this representation is obvious, at least as long as white Westerners are ranged against the shortsighted rapaciousness of the Japanese. But the situation is more complicated, Norway in particular supporting a reintroduction of whaling, and conservationists from around the world, including some in Japan, opposing the industry. According to conservation group sponsored surveys, only 10 per cent of Japanese people support commercial whaling, although Japanese eat 16 kilograms of seafood annually, compared with half a kilogram for people in the US and 1 kilogram for Australians (Fisher, 2001, pp22–23).

A recent book written by two Japanese who have been active in the International Whaling Commission, Masayuki Komatsu, a former official at the Ministry of Agriculture, Forestry and Fisheries, and Shigeko Misaki, an interpreter at the IWC, claims to tell *The Truth Behind the Whaling Dispute*. The 'truth' is opposed to the 'lies' of 'whale huggers', who are 'manipulated' and 'brainwashed' (Komatsu and Misaki, 2001, p91), while the 'anti-whaling majority constantly bullies pro-whaling nations in the IWC' (Komatsu and Misaki, 2001, p95). The anti-whaling nations' 'infantile cynicism' is a 'political ploy' with various aims: to gain electoral support (especially when problems such as 'Agent Orange' in Vietnam threatened faith in the US government: Komatsu and Misaki, 2001, p60), to increase Japanese dependence on imported food, and to exclude Japan from the nations deemed capable of managing ocean resources (Komatsu and Misaki, 2001, pp5, 7).

Continuing in this vein – no doubt sounding slightly hysterical to some Western readers – Japan was 'tricked' into accepting the 1982 moratorium on whaling when the US threatened to deny Japanese access to US fishing grounds if they did not sign, access the US removed two years later anyway (Summers, 2002). According to these authors, 'moratorium' means 'temporary halt', and the IWC promised to reintroduce whaling by 1990 at the latest. In fact, the resolution says that, after a comprehensive assessment, the IWC will 'consider' modifying catch limits (Komatsu and Misaki, 2001, pp4, 64). The Inuit were exempted from the quota on the basis of traditional hunting (Ryder, 1989, pp233–234), while whale-capturing for research was also allowed. At the 52nd annual meeting of the IWC, Australia unsuccessfully proposed a South Pacific Whale Sanctuary to protect the breeding grounds of whales feeding within the Southern Ocean Sanctuary near Antarctica.

Against claims that the Japanese disguise continued whaling for food as scientific research, Komatsu and Misaki claim that '99% of the whale meat in the Japanese market have the legal identifiable source' (Komatsu and Misaki, 2001, p86). Similarly, it is claimed that funding for Caribbean nations, 'great in relation to the GNP', is not to buy pro-whaling votes but is assessed on a 'project by project basis' (Komatsu and Misaki, 2001, p136). In contrast, it is darkly suggested that an Australian anti-whaling group may have attempted to bribe the Makah people not to conduct their traditional whale hunt (Komatsu and Misaki, 2001, p139).

The two major planks of the Japanese pro-whaling lobby are, first, the claim that whales are now so numerous that soon 'there will be no fish left in the sea' (Komatsu and Misaki, 2001, pp7,10). Debates continue as to whether minke whale numbers in the Southern Ocean are as few as 268,000 (IWC) or nearly 1 million, 'cockroaches of the sea', according to a fisheries diplomat in Japan (Brook, 2001, p21). The Japanese are leading attempts to introduce a Revised Management Scheme that will replace the present ban with quotas (Prideaux, 2000, pp8–10).

The second plank of Komatsu and Misaki's (2001, p93) argument is the claim that protecting whales 'because they are lovable and intelligent' is merely 'Anglo-Saxon ethnocentrism': 'Killing any kind of living creature is equally cruel. However, it is inevitable that human life is maintained by eating other biological species.' Australians do not protect lambs, while the Japanese are apparently repulsed at the thought of eating sheep meat (Fisher, 2001, p23) or kangaroos (Komatsu and Misaki, 2001, pp29, 94), and seek to reduce the environmentally damaging methane emissions produced by cattle (Summers, 2002).

Using such arguments, the Japanese government and the Japanese Whaling Association have mounted an increasingly sophisticated campaign for the reintroduction of whaling, reaching even into the homes of South Australians in 2000 when the International Whaling Committee's 52nd annual meeting was held in Adelaide. A pamphlet delivered with the community newspaper asked:

Note: Whale hunting and eating whale meat at Japanese festivals are described as 'endangered' cultural practices (Nakajima, 2000); (top) Minke whale meat, from the Southern Ocean, on sale at Tokyo's Tsukiji fish market; (bottom) the Western press perennially reports stories of savage whale or dolphin killing, for example the 400 years of dolphin hunting by the fishermen of Taiji. Environmentalists describe 'a barbaric anachronism verging on murder'. One fisherman, Kogai san, says: 'In this village, we have only been able to survive by hunting whales and dolphins. We owe so much to them' (Parry, 2004, p12, photograph by AFP/Sea Shepherd Conservation).

Figure 2.4 *Eating Whales*

what if ... Australians were told they couldn't eat their traditional
meat pie or roast dinner because a foreign nation didn't like it? Or
indigenous Australians were banned from hunting crocs or kangaroos
for tucker for no other reason than foreigners thought the animals cute
or – wrongly – endangered?

(signed by Keiichi Nakajima, President of the Japan Whaling Association, 2000)

The authors concede that the IWC must agree to and oversee an international
inspection scheme and implement new humane methods of killing whales
(which now die in 'only a few minutes'), although elsewhere humane killing is
described as an 'irrelevant matter' (Komatsu and Misaki, 2001, p85).[22]

This debate between Japanese and Australian sources reveals a very different
understanding of whales, and, by extension, other animals, indicating the
challenge to finding a compromise. However, if this issue is addressed through
the idea of 'sustainable management' or 'respectful stewardship', the Japanese
attitude to nature can be made meaningful to Western perceptions, this
approach being more common among Japanese people than the total hands-off
approach widely accepted in Australia. One survey suggests that Japanese and
Norwegians approve of the consumption of whale meat and 'know' that whales
are not threatened, compared with Australian ignorance of whale numbers. By
comparison, Australians are more likely to approve of kangaroo meat
consumption and 'know' that kangaroos are not endangered (Freeman and
Kellert, 1994, pp295, 298–299, 312; see also Aslin and Norton, 1995, p79).
Respectful stewardship is based on knowledge as well as emotion. As Catherine
Kemper of the South Australian Museum suggests, 'As a scientist, I have to say
there's no difference in hunting whales or hunting kangaroos so long as we
know how many are being taken and we can regulate' (in Brook, 2001, p21).

Indeed, whale watching is not totally harmless to whales, some of whom
appear to have died from being stressed when chased by tourist boats. In the
Loreto Bay National Park in Mexico, tourists light beach fires, collect shells
and toss cigarette butts and drink cans at the whales when they leap from the
water (Moore, 1999, p20). As a result of such behaviour, governments
increasingly regulate cetacean encounters. As in the US (Orams, 1995, pp99,
180), in Australia such rules are recognized in the breach as well as the
observance. Tour operators strain to offer the almost guaranteed close
encounter, for example using an underwater scooter to move dolphins closer to
the surface and the tourists feed dolphins and swim too close to them (Jarvis,
2000, pp214, 203).

Turning now to the emotional response of 'whale-huggers' (Komatsu and
Misaki, 2001, p91), Iain Greenwood, director of Osprey Wildlife Expeditions,
suggests the effect of the whales is particularly strong on humans because they
are so much larger and more powerful than us (interviewed on 22 July 1993).[23]
And we see cetaceans as our kin, for example in their sociability, intellect, and
their variation on each year's new hit whale song.[24] Indeed, Canberra public

servants and US computer geeks who snorkel with dwarf minke whales 'whoop' with pleasure, go 'gaga like a coven of New Agers', and have tears streaming down their cheeks (Safe, 1998, pp19–21).

A number of Australia's coastal towns have turned their local economies to whale watching, for example Albany on the west coast abounds in whale souvenirs, from pencils to drink coasters. Its best known beach offers a whale lookout and an instructional sign on first aid for stranded whales (Jaeckel, 2000, p82). On Australia's east coast, in 1991 30,000 tourists visited Hervey Bay to see an estimated 2000 whales migrating. At that time, about 25 whale watching boats operated in the bay. Nature Travel promised a 'truly unforgettable experience', where 'you don't just "watch" ... [but] become part of this magical location and event' (Phillips, 1992, p1). Even so, we were told repeatedly by our guide, Dave, from the Pacific Whale Foundation, 'We must show the respect' of 'going into their bedrooms'. 'We're out here so you can have a great day but our ultimate concern is the preservation of whales.' Given the human cruelty of the whaling industry, Dave said we should be surprised and grateful at how careful are the 'gentle giants', who have never been known to harm humans around the boats. Those among us who saw only a whale breach in the distance were disappointed. One woman muttered, 'So much for the stories that they come right up to the boat and you can almost pat them'. On another boat, a young woman recounted how 'fabulous' and 'lovely' it was when two whales passed under their boat. In reply to my query, her mother said, 'It was a wonderful day', before asking what we had for lunch (member of Nature Travel tour, 28–30 August 1992, whale watching on 29 August). If lunch was the major concern, at least according to some of my companions to the Great Australian Bight, one might prefer to stay at home among the culinary delights of Adelaide.

Whale dreaming: Southern Right Whales on the Great Australian Bight

> [both whales and these Aboriginal people] have been battered by
> modern European technology, almost blasted out of existence – the
> Yalata people by nuclear bombs, the whales by harpoons.
>
> (Mike Bossley in Safe, 1999, p.26)

Although far from major population centres such as Sydney, Brisbane and Adelaide, the cliffs above the Great Australian Bight are 'the best whale watching platform in the world', according to Osprey Wildlife Expeditions' publicity literature (see also Reid, 1996, p1). Whales making their way southwards to Antarctica, calves in fin, can be viewed from as close as 20 metres. Seventy Southern Right Whales were counted in 1997 and 104 in 1998 (Safe, 1999, pp22–26). In terms of the resort cycle, the Great Australian Bight experience is for the pioneers. There is no visitor centre, indeed almost no amenities. There are no rangers, and, in 1995, one researcher noted damage to

Notes: (top left) A Southern Right Whale and calf; (top right) viewing from the cliffs; (bottom left) the 'viewing platform'; (bottom right) roadhouses abound with whale maps, posters and even 'big whales' out the front: Clem, the Aboriginal guide, with the author.

Figure 2.5 *Whale Watching in the Great Australian Bight*

vegetation and danger to tourists who did not stay on the white stone marked paths, but clambered to the edge for better views (Reid, 1995, pp22–25). Although declared a sanctuary by the South Australian government, little so far has been done to preserve the site, oil exploration licences for the park even being issued.[25]

I was kindly invited by Iain Greenwood to join the Osprey Tour, 'Wintering with the Whales', 1–7 October 1994, led by Tim Bickmore, a graduate of Aboriginal studies. Clem Lawrie of the Mirning people was our Aboriginal guide, his father and uncle being the last remaining initiated Mirning men. The tour was advertised: 'Apart from meeting with the Mirning people this tour offers a special opportunity to interact with up to 40 massive Southern Right Whales', which traverse the 'great East–West Songline' (Osprey Wildlife Expeditions, 1994, p1). In the Mirning Aboriginal people's dreaming, the whale is a manifestation of the Rainbow Serpent, Djidara. As the Rainbow Serpent crosses the Nullabor to the Bight it makes huge underground limestone caves, also tourist attractions in the area. At the coast, the Rainbow Serpent sheds its skin to become a whale. The Mirning people's land has been marked with stone arrangements in the shape of whales, some of which Clem pointed out to us.

The government relocated the Yalata Aboriginal people in the Bight after their own lands near Maralinga were contaminated by nuclear testing. Thus it is the Yalata and not the Mirning people who control the whale watching cliffs and receive the entrance fee to enter Yalata Aboriginal Trust land (Safe, 1999, pp22–26; see also Johnston, 1991, p416), amounting to US$30–50,000 each year, according to Clem Lawrie. At the time of the tour, Osprey was supporting the Mirning people in developing a Native Title Claim against the Yalata people to regain their coastal lands.

We were a small group and not always a happy one, some members complaining about the quality of food on a trip that cost around US$750 (although 64 per cent of the tourists in my survey did not record any negative aspects of the experience). Our guide, Tim Bickmore, suggested that 80 per cent of tourists to whale sites were women and that in 1994 about 30 per cent were from overseas (in a total of about 100 tourists on the various tours). Indeed, Table A3.1 in Appendix 3 suggests that Osprey does disproportionately attract women, overseas visitors and those on high incomes, while another large survey additionally found that a high proportion were conservation group members.[26]

The Osprey visitor enjoyed the animal encounter because the whales were in their own environment and were wild and free, visitors choosing these responses at a higher rate than any other group (Table A3.3 in Appendix 3). They were more likely to feel close to nature and spiritually uplifted than was the sample as a whole (Table A3.7). They also described a 'unique experience' (Table A3.5). Iain Greenwood (interviewed on 22 July 1993) said to me that by the third day everyone is affected in some way purely by being in the wilderness. According to Iain, one man initially claimed to be there on sufferance with his wife, but after two days was urging everyone to write to Japan protesting whale slaughter. Idiosyncrasies come to the surface as people feel vulnerable to the isolation and the power of the Nullabor: a vast flat land rimmed by sea under a huge sky. As puny as ants caught in our enormous bowl of light, visitors are drenched blue by day and star glittered black by night.

In Reid's (1996, p38) survey, visitors appeared more motivated by whale protection than learning facts about the whales, while respondents expressed a fairly low interest in Aboriginal culture (the highest score was whale protection at 3.7; whale behaviour/life cycle was 3.24 and Aboriginal culture was 2.04). Respondents were pleased or disappointed depending on whether or not whales were numerous, active and close, while calves were an additional interest (Reid, 1996, pp41–42). As with dolphins, discussed in the next chapter, some visitors were lyrical concerning their experience. '"Fascinating" was commonly used to describe the perception of whales', with several giving 'passionate descriptions of their feelings for the animals' (Reid, 1996, p37), often linked with the grandeur of the scenery. Respondents experienced a 'magical place' of 'extreme tranquility'; 'solitude' and the absence of human manipulation of the experience:

> Seeing the whales in their natural environment with no human involvement, e.g. boats, planes, etc.
>
> (Reid, 1996, p43)

Although my tour group was happy to watch the whales, none of us experienced the emotional euphoria reported in these accounts. There was little such euphoria in Seal Bay either, despite the anthropomorphism with which sea lions are often presented in marine shows.

The sea lions of Seal Bay

In Celtic lore seals are 'silkies', mysteriously aligned with humankind and occasionally capable of mating with them.[27] Val Plumwood (1992, p45) describes sea lions as 'creatures of a sociality, sensitivity and sense of fun similar to our own'. One of the appeals, therefore, of the sea lions is our capacity to anthropomorphize them. As at Monarto and Warrawong, the guides at Seal Bay strain against such an interpretation of the 'silkies'.

Kangaroo Island, one hour by SeaLink ferry from Cape Jervis, which is 110 kilometres south of Adelaide, is marketed as a natural and peaceful paradise of spectacular coastal scenery, beaches and fishing. Besides 'walking among the seals in their natural environment' at Seal Bay, Kangaroo Island offers koalas and kangaroos at Flinders Chase Wildlife Sanctuary,[28] and encounters with fairy penguins as they return each night to their burrows built among residents' houses (Tourism South Australia and Kangaroo Island Tourist Association, 1988, pp18–19). Various surveys of Adelaide households reveal that Kangaroo Island is sometimes remembered more for its coastal scenery or its wildlife generally than for Seal Bay or Flinders Chase, with the bad (gravel) roads featuring in some surveys, although many of these roads have since been sealed.[29] Visitor numbers to Kangaroo Island increased dramatically from the mid 1980s when sea transport was supplemented with air transport and the new ferries could accommodate motor vehicles.[30]

There are few accessible sea lion colonies in Australia, although tourists are encouraged to join the 'Endangered Australian Sea Lions' in Baird Bay, Eyre Peninsula (near Streaky Bay)[31] at the only mainland sea lion breeding colony.[32] The sea lion colony at Seal Bay is, apparently, known to the Japanese tourism industry as the best sea lion colony in the world (Terry Dennis, interviewed on 30 December 1992). Indeed, international visitation rates have increased over the years,[33] partly due to Malaysian ownership of the SeaLink ferry connection. On the two days I spent on the beach in December 1993, one bus group consisted entirely of Asian visitors.

Approximately 400 to 500 sea lions live at Seal Bay, declared a sanctuary in

1954 when it was feared the animals were being used for shark bait (Tilbrook, 1989). Despite the name 'sanctuary', visitors could walk unescorted among the sea lions, while locals captured and displayed the sea lions in hotels, forcing them to drink beer (Terry Dennis, interviewed on 30 December 1992). In October 1987, a fee was imposed for access to Seal Bay, accompanied by guiding and an interpretive presentation (Terry Dennis, interviewed on 30 December 1992; Tourism South Australia and Kangaroo Island Tourist Association, 1988, p21). Not everyone approved of the newly mediated encounter: a visitor I interviewed in December 1992 was 'disappointed you can't go and sit with them like you used to, people told us that you could do that'. Another said it was more 'natural' and felt that the sea lions were larger and in greater numbers before the site was regulated by the guides.

In 1987 a Seal Bay Management Plan was developed and boardwalks to the beach were erected (Tourism South Australia and Kangaroo Island Tourist Association, 1988, p21). In January 1992, the major infrastructure was a walkway to the beach with interpretive signs. By January 2004, a visitor centre had been erected, containing a display on pollution, a touch table with sea lion skins and a skeleton of a gastrolith, a service desk and a souvenir sales section. One side was glass plated allowing a view down on to Seal Bay (for those frequent days when the icy winds off Antarctica made the beach uncomfortable for humans and sea lions alike).

Tim, a guide at Seal Bay (interviewed on 30 December 1992) describes the January tourists as 'just here to see the animals put on a show for them' or 'just out for the holidays'. Indeed, Kangaroo Island attracts a disproportionate number of low income tourists (South Australian Department of Tourism, 1984, pp30–31), advertisements luring a sizeable market outside the ecotourism sector. People come for the fishing or general relaxation. A lecturer at Adelaide University came as 'part of Craig's [his son's] education', although his father would rather spend 'two or three days under a gum tree reading a book' in Flinders Chase. One couple thought it was nice to see the sea lions 'in their natural way'. Was it worth it, I asked: 'My word – we're bushies at heart, like to get out on picnics and barbecues'.

I visited Seal Bay in the winter of 1990 and again in the summer of 1992, when I spent two days, 30 and 31 December, talking with the guides – Tim, Steven, Mia and Prue – and the visitors. The 54 staff, mostly casuals, had been trained specifically for interpretive presentations and to prevent visitors creating 'artificial or interruptive behaviour patterns' (Dennis, 1989, p16). Groups of up to 20 visitors are escorted on to the site by each ranger. Before descending to the beach, visitors assemble at a platform that also functions as an interpretive site. The guide introduces the experience with a short talk. Steven says, 'I'm here to protect the seals and secondly to give you as much information as you want'. We must stay at least 4 metres from the animals and make no attempt to interact with them. Although the guides do not mention this, I suspect that the distance is for our protection as well as the welfare of the sea lions, based on my experience with the aggressive SAMs (sub-adult males) on the sub-Antarctic Islands.[34]

During winter, the sea lions seek shelter from the cold winds, sleeping in the sand dunes, including those adjacent to the interpretive signs. In summer, the sea lions stay on the beach, and the first glimpse is caught on the descent from the interpretive platform. Below is a crescent of white sand lacing the blue ocean, bounded at either end by the rookeries in which the mothers give birth (these are banned to tourists). Scattered along the beach are exhausted sea lions on their stomachs, having just spent two or three days at sea. Sometimes a sea lion surfs in on an incoming wave and clambers up the beach to flop on its stomach. In winter there might be only several dozen animals; in summer they crowd along the beach, either at the water's edge or amongst the seaweed. Occasionally a sub-adult male takes on another age mate or a cow. As Stephen says, 'The pleasure is not just the animals, [but also] the smells, the air, the surf'. While the scenery is, as promised, 'spectacular', action is minimal and interaction prohibited.

Tourists' expectations, based on sea lion feeding in zoos or performances at an aquarium, interrupt the guides' message that the (less interesting) behaviour in Seal Bay is natural. The guides are aware of this potential source of disappointment and share information with each other concerning any activity they have spotted, for example a mother suckling a pup or two pups playing in the sand dunes. Almost any movement occasions comment from the tourists. A little girl says, 'Look at that one running'; someone notes, 'Oh look, it's scratching' as a sea lion raises a flipper to ventilate itself. Or, 'Did you see that one run down and he just went splat?' The pups in particular attract visitor responses: 'Oh, the baby one' says a young boy. The 18-month-old sea lions are certainly 'baby releasers', with their pale chests and dark eyes.

The guides work hard to wreathe stories around these apparently lazy ambassadors for conservation. As we look at listless lumps of fur, we are told about the sea lions' life cycle, what they are doing now, what they do in other seasons. The most interested tourists gather around the tour guide and ask questions. Others, disparagingly called 'happy flickers' because they do not listen to their guides, see the beach 'only through the lens of a camera', 'don't want to go beneath the surface, want to accept the glitz' (anthropomorphic fantasies about the life of sea lions) (Mia, a ranger). A meditative mood is deemed the best approach. Tim suggests, 'Rather than try to go along the whole beach and observe the maximum number of sea lions, we will just sit quietly near a few and observe them more closely'. It is pleasant sitting where the sea lions loll among the seaweed in the water pools. Lucky sea lions, the visitors think, in the hot mid-afternoon sun. The pause allows Tim to rest from his trudging up and down the beach all day.

On one occasion, Mia escorted a bus tour of Asian tourists, many of them two or three generation family groups. Probably because of language barriers, their behaviour was much harder to regulate than that of the English-speaking

Notes: (top) Sea lion seeking protection from the wind, winter 1991; (middle) summer visitors to Seal Bay; (bottom) the sea lion colony in summer, 1992.

Figure 2.6 *Seal Bay Sea Lion Colony*

groups. Several times Mia had to call visitors away from excessive proximity to sea lions and she worked hard to keep them together. The guides shared with me a rumour that an Asian tour brochure reputedly tells prospective tourists they can touch the sea lions. Arrival on the beach produced a frenzy of photography: children, lovers, mothers and others being photographed with sea lions behind them. However, I observed one youngish man taking a portrait of the sea lions. Terry Dennis and Mia averred that the Japanese do not know how to conduct themselves around wild animals, with Mia suggesting that Asians have 'no affinity at all with animals' because they know them only in zoos or as a resource.

Frustration with Asian tour groups is all the greater because the Seal Bay guides have their own conservation message to impart. They make no bones about the need to change attitudes. Mia noted:

> At the start it's really new to them and wow it's mind-blowing. If there's action on the beach you've really got them hooked. But if there's no animal behaviour, you have to work hard to convince them that the behaviour of seals in circuses is not their natural behaviour.

Most respondents to my survey 'got' the message, saying they enjoyed seeing the sea lions in their own environment and felt good the animals were being preserved (Table A3.3 and Table A3.7 in Appendix 3). This group of visitors was most likely to feel they had learned about the animals. As one respondent elaborated:

> Having visited this site many times before, it is my experience that many people would get very little out of the visit if it wasn't for the guides. I have often overheard reactions like 'Are they dead??' or 'What lazy animals!' Their attitudes and levels of interest are heightened by the information provided. With the exception of a few visitors, this more than compensates for their inability to touch and feed the Sea Lions.
>
> (female, planning consultant, aged 30–44)

Just as John Wamsley strains against the cuteness of his small marsupials to insist on the environmental message, so too do penguins waddling up the beach in their dinner suits excite an anthropomorphic response from untutored spectators.

Framing penguins

> gross – really for something that's supposed to be quasi-natural, ... all very regimented. It never used to be quite like that, the whole thing should be abandoned, it's been done to death. People should clear out and let the little birdies do what they do.
>
> (Ken, ex-Navy, focus group member 1992, speaking of Phillip Island)

When I came to American River [settlement on Kangaroo Island] four years ago I told my wife I'd like to build an aviary on the front verandah. She said, 'You've got one already'.

(Brian, SeaLink tour bus driver, December 1992)

I was watching Cameron being approached by a penguin; he put his hand out and the penguin leaned towards him before backing away. He turned to me, his eyes glittering with disbelief, and whispered 'It's just magic'. An eighteen-year-old builder, usually of few words, had been captured by the place.

(entry in my diary, Antarctica trip, January 1996)

Just as Wamsley attempts to place a value on threatened marsupials, so too have the Little Penguins (formerly called Fairy Penguins: Jarvis, 2000, p6) at Phillip Island been valued at about US$20,000 for each of the estimated 3,000 that are seen by tourists (in an estimated colony of 30,000) (Jarvis, 2000, pp134,117)[35] The penguins contribute almost US$75 million to the Victorian economy (Jarvis, 2000, p115).

The Penguin Parade advertises itself in two competing registers. The first offers penguins as 'appealing stars of the theatre of nature', indicated by the very name, a 'Parade' (Jarvis, 2000, p119). More commonly, the message is that the penguins are 'a way to "get back to nature"' (Jarvis, 2000, p118). Among the 10 per cent of visitors to Phillip Island who saw it as a theme park, one North American man asked a ranger 'how they trained the penguins to walk up the beach' (Jarvis, 2000, p158). In another survey, 39 per cent of visitors expected to be able to pick up a penguin (Pearce, 1988, p209).

Perhaps its tourist name of 'Penguin Parade' should warn the intending visitor not to expect solitude and a torch on the foreshore, although this is the origin story of Phillip Island (Cherfas, 1984, p215; Jarvis, 2000, p11). Following concern about the decline in penguin numbers in the early 1980s (Jarvis, 2000, p122), an Australian Bicentennial Project grant of about US$2.5 million allowed the construction of infrastructure to support high volume tourist traffic. This includes boardwalks across the dunes, an elaborate Visitor Interpretation Centre (Jarvis, 2000, p123) (incorporating a cafeteria, shop and sophisticated displays such as an interactive computer game) and a viewing structure, not unlike a football ground grandstand, which seats approximately 3000 people. In 1995 there were over 500,000 visitors (Jarvis, 2000, p13). Flash photography is not allowed as cameras 'seriously disorient and disturb the penguins' (Fortescue, 1992, piii).

On the night I visited in 1997, the audience was predominantly Asian with some Europeans and a few Australians. Some people had thermos flasks and blankets, usually those who were staying with Melbourne friends wise to the rigours of concrete seating in Victoria in October. Most, however, had only themselves. Indeed, Jarvis (2000, pp166, 168), conducting her survey in the

Figure 2.7 *The Infrastructure at Phillip Island's 'Penguin Parade'*

summer, found that waiting in the cold was the least enjoyable aspect of her respondents' visit. The announcements were made in Mandarin, Japanese and then English: explaining that this is a natural event and that visitors are observing the penguins' natural habitat. They have been coming here for years before humans came to see them.

As the final light of the sun left the beach, the crowd hushed to a murmuring, before a North American voice called out, 'Here they come off to the right!' People's voices remained low but were coiled with excitement. A ranger announced the first arrivals and repeated the message prohibiting flashlights. Tourists began pointing, as small groups of birds came to shore in various spots. Someone said: 'Here's a bunch, right in front of us'. Another visitor was using a night vision video lens, laughing as the penguins waddled up the beach. After about half an hour, penguins emerged in quite large rafts, closer to the lights. About 70 per cent of the audience had left, including most of the Asians, no doubt herded away by their tour timetables. As the remainder of the visitors returned along the boardwalks, domestic scenes were played out around the burrows. It was possible to imagine tiffs, jealous rivalries, rejections and shifting sexual liaisons as penguins huffed and retreated and squatted near their burrows (Cherfas, 1984, p216; Jarvis, 2000, p161).

Jarvis (2000, pp166, 168) found that the least enjoyable aspects of the visit included crowds pushing and blocking the view (20 per cent). One visitor said the beach area was 'like a concentration camp, all the lights and fences … We're the guards watching the prisoners come up' (Jarvis, 2000, p162). A number of my focus group members also complained about the crowds, specifically the Japanese. Geoff, who had lived in the area as a boy and saved orphaned Fairy penguins, commented that turning on the lights is the scariest experience for penguins:

> The first one goes whack, and 9900 Japanese are running over... It's like coming into their living room while they're eating dinner. [But] It's the biggest money spinner in Victoria so they've got to do it... When I was a kid, it was just beach and bush – and people on the beach. Now the whole thing is totally gross, really.

Kangaroo Island's penguin encounter is still 'beach and bush – and people on the beach'. Twenty years ago, hotels armed their visitors with torches to visit the Fairy penguin colonies around the settlements of Kingscote and Penneshaw. As tourist numbers grew, National Parks and Wildlife developed a tour, described in 1992 when I took it as 'Discovering Penguins: the wildlife experience with a difference'. The tour aimed 'to provide a professional, informative and sensitive insight into the lives of one of Australia's most popular birds' (National Parks and Wildlife SA, 1992, p1). The tour I accompanied commenced with an orientation talk by a ranger, Tony, which included a certain amount of anthropomorphism aimed at children. Young penguins go off to 'see the world' before they start breeding, while parents 'take a holiday' after they raise their young. Because the Penneshaw township was built on a penguin colony, the penguins intermingle with people, crossing roads, digging burrows in front lawns and nesting in garages, 'truly marvellous' according to Tony. Later, about 30 or 40 people saw between five and ten penguins waddle up across the rocks. They were dim shapes in the torchlight. A self-appointed guide told us we were extremely lucky to see the penguins in this natural way; soon it will be like Phillip Island with floodlights and walkways.

For an exceptional penguin encounter, there is little to surpass Macquarie Island, an Australian sub-Antarctic Island (a long way) south of Tasmania. In the summer of 1995/6, my mother and I joined 31 other 'expeditioners' on a tour to the sub-Antarctic Islands and Antarctica, the tour's brochure suggesting this experience was for the more hardy among the ecotourist market. The tour was run by the New Zealand company, Southern Heritage Expeditions Limited (SHEL): 'The objective of SHEL is to create ambassadors for the continued protection of fragile environments'. In this role, SHEL promises to educate clients concerning human impacts on the environments they visit (Southern Heritage Expeditions Limited, 1995, p.4).[36] Our cruise had four guides: Rodney Russ, who owns SHEL (in partnership with his wife), Jeni, Simon and Terry. All our guides had tertiary qualifications, for example in marine biology or botany. Terry was an ex-teacher and previously a ranger on Macquarie Island. Simon became a 'long-haired greenie at school' and has published a book on the plants of Fiordland, New Zealand. Jeni has been involved in research in Antarctica. Our boat was a converted science research vessel, the *Akademic Shokalski*, captained and crewed by Russians.

Ours was a highly educated group (85 per cent having tertiary qualifications compared with 41 per cent for the total sample of animal site visitors), while a majority had professional or managerial jobs (85 per cent compared with 40 per cent for the total sample). The group was also more conservationist in their orientation, with higher scientific society membership and thoughtful approaches to conservation issues. One of the party, Eric, was a geography teacher. Another member, Jim, had an environmental sciences degree and advises companies on environmental investment schemes. These two tourists, in a discussion with Rodney, agreed that feral cats should be eliminated, that it was sensible to farm kangaroos, but were unsure about the impact of exporting live galahs and other native fauna. However, another member of the group was surprised to learn that sea lions had skeletons: not everyone on the trip shared the same high level of scientific knowledge and environmental commitment.

While we were not short of video screenings, lectures or roundtable discussions on those days we did not step on land, learning about the animals did not feature highly as a reason for enjoying the encounter. Some of the results were predictable, for example enjoying seeing animals in their own environment (Tables A3.3 and A3.5 in Appendix 3). However, like the Monkey Mia visitors, a high percentage felt privileged to have the encounter, the highest of any group of site visitors (Table A3.7).

The King penguins at Macquarie Island were the favourite animal encounter, chosen by 14 of the 22 respondents,[37] followed by albatrosses (4 respondents), the Adelie penguins at Commonwealth Bay and seals (3 responses each). Earlier in the trip, Jeni, one of the guides, had promised that, as we approached Macquarie Island, 'The water will boil with penguins'. She was right. A welcoming party of thousands of penguins swarmed around our ship, raising their heads in inspection, before suddenly diving and popping up elsewhere. The Naiad, the ship's inflatable tender, took us into Lusitania Bay. The penguins squatting all over the derelict digesters[38] warmed the cockles of Rodney Russ' heart. It is not an overstatement to say that Macquarie Island teems with penguins, forming a 'mind boggling' 'mass' as respondents said. In particular, adolescent King penguins appear to have little to do in advance of their commitment to reproduction and curiously followed us around.

Behind the beach, the land rises to the Royal penguins' rookery, a noisy area of bare mud cut out of the surrounding vegetation. Alongside the Royals' highway up to their rookery, the sludgy path attracts elephant seals which lie together in snorting mounds, unhappy in their slow moult, large slugs vying for a warm place in the centre of the heap. To the right of the Royals' hill is the King penguins' rookery, where there were a few newly hatched chicks, grey and crinkled in sacks of skin, and more advanced balls of fluff were dotted among the adults. Along the foreshore, elephant seals rose occasionally against each

Notes: (top) The water boils with penguins, the digesters in the background; (bottom) penguin contact

Figure 2.8 *Macquarie Island Penguins*

other in half serious jousting before slumping back into the water. Penguins were coming and going on their fishing trips, some harassed by ropes of kelp as they attempted to gain a foothold onto the rocks.

A number of us were transfixed by physical contact with a King penguin. To achieve this, it was best to sit down and wait. Eventually a small group waddled over; the more adventurous of the gang came ever closer, pecking first at one's boot and then trousers. Even if we were not actually touched by a penguin, either on Macquarie Island or in Commonwealth Bay, Antarctica, we 'could observe them, almost sitting amongst them, as they went on with their animal business' (Netherlands, male, lawyer, humanistic religion, speaking of the Adelie penguins of Commonwealth Bay).

As these three penguin encounter sites reveal, a tourist's encounter with the same animal species can be framed quite variably. Although all these sites are 'authentic' in the sense that the humans go to the animals, go to a location where the animals gather and live their lives, the 'naturalness' of the experience ranges from the more regimented 'penguin parade' at Port Phillip, through the more low key 'discovering penguins' on Kangaroo Island, to the almost indescribable experience of a real inter-species encounter on Macquarie Island. The differences owe something to the balance between humans and penguins, which is reflected in the authenticity of the surroundings. But the site is also 'framed' by guides, with their varying shades of green messages.

Conclusion: Green messages

> Could the tour guide place more accent on encouraging clients to 'like the animals' i.e. 'see the beauty of the giraffe'?
>
> > (female, tap dancer and craft worker, aged 45–60, commenting on her visit to Monarto)

> I love all animals but am inclined to invest them with human qualities.
>
> > (married female, home duties, aged over 60, visitor to Monarto)

> I would have liked to touch.
>
> > (visitor to Seal Bay)

David Langdon envisaged Monarto as a Noak's Ark, where endangered animals could be bred and visitors could learn about the importance of saving the environment. John Wamsley is a passionate advocate of Australia's small marsupials. Terry Dennis (interviewed on 30 December 1992), with some friends, invested in a heritage area in Kangaroo Island, which he describes as 'white land rights'. The land is caveated against certain uses and provides a refuge for animals. Rodney Russ' passion for the sub-Antarctic islands and Antarctica is no less than Wamsley's passion for small Australian marsupials. When I suggested that Rodney was a missionary of sorts, he replied, 'I like to see people learn and if I achieve that it's good'. Russ also puts some of his resources at the disposal of environmental preservation.[39]

At most of the encounter sites described in this chapter, the conservation message is loud and clear. But several visitors expressed their desire for a different and often closer encounter. As a visitor to Monarto said, 'It's hard to interact from a bus' (female, clerical assistant, aged 20–29). The Seal Bay rangers work against this longing to touch or interact with the sea lions, telling people that refusal to interact is what keeps the animals wild. A scientific ecological paradigm generally prevails.[40] Tim says, 'We don't pat the animals, we don't interact with the animals or make any attempt to change their behaviour'. When a young boy told Tim that he was kissed by a sea lion at Sea World, Tim replied, 'How do you know it kissed you? It was just sniffing you, which is how they get their information about something new'. Clearly the naturalness of the encounter is lost on those who ask how many fish the rangers give the seals each day. 'The only help they need is to leave their habitat alone,' Mia noted tartly. She went on to complain: 'People often ask, "What happens if they can't get enough food?" "They'll die." "Can't you do something about that?"' When one innocent tourist asked Tim: 'Do you lose many to sharks?' he retorted 'Not *lose*, sharks are their natural predators'. Mia claims that the guides have succeeded if they change behaviour, for example if people go down to Flinders Chase and think, 'Oh yes, we don't need to feed the kangaroos'.

At Seal Bay, the sea lions are represented as a tableau behind a glass wall. We humans are wrong to think that we can communicate with them and inhumane if we attempt to provoke an interaction. Prue reserved special disparagement for people who claim communication with animals: 'they think they are special but they're no different from anyone else'. As Steven said, the sea lions are 'wild animals which are tolerant of people. You can't actually relate to them'. Mia said: 'Now I grit my teeth and turn away when someone taking a picture asks, "Is it posing for me?" When a sea lion sits up it is disturbed; this is not natural behaviour.'

Our human desire for inter-species communication is more acute in the case of dolphins, although whales also attract the 'New Age crystal-using feminists', as Tim Bickmore, of Osprey Tours, described a certain class of tourist. One such crystal user, according to Tim, had to be prevented from jumping into the sea to 'merge with the whales'. However, such attitudes are not expressed significantly in Table A3.5.

Monkey Mia visitors were the most likely to claim that the animals wanted to interact with them. Thus many people who encounter dolphins are not satisfied merely to know the dolphins are there. Some humans also want the dolphins to know that we are here. Dolphins have captivated the human imagination in a different way from penguins, sea lions or bilbies. As Rodney and Simon (commenting on my lecture on board *Akademic Shokalski*, 21 January 1996) noted, 'we do not see the "shitty" side of dolphins, as we literally do in penguin colonies'. We usually see dolphins intermittently in their lives, little knowing where they go or what they do. We skein our own meanings across the gaps in our knowledge about dolphins. It is to such dreams of dolphins we now turn.

3
So Long and Thanks For All the Fish[1]

Watching for Dolphins

In the summer months on every crossing to Piraeus
One noticed that certain passengers soon rose
From seats in the packed saloon and with serious
Looks and no acknowledgement of a common purpose
Passed forward through the small door into the bows
To watch for dolphins. One saw them lose

Every other wish. ...

... and had they then
On the waves, on the climax of our longing come

Smiling, snub-nosed, domed like satyrs, oh
We should have laughed and lifted the children up
Stranger to stranger, pointing how with a leap
They left their element, three or four times, centred
On grace, and heavy and warm re-entered,
Looping the keel. We should have felt them go

Further and further into the deep parts ...

(David Constantine, 1983, pp26–27)

We humans project onto dolphins our own dreams and desires. However it remains a moot point why dolphins are such splendid bearers of our fantasies. Such is the quest of this chapter, exploring the putative characteristics of dolphins as they are enmeshed in our cultural nets of meaning.

Oceanic anchors: Dolphin dreaming

Dolphins to some extent are kind of an ambiguous subject that people can project all kinds of things on to. For some people, I think they're the essence of freedom and joy, and we all wish we could live that kind of life. For some, they're a symbol of greenness and ecological things. For others, I think just the sheer beauty of them gets them. Surprisingly, it is a bit of a gender issue because I take lots and lots of people out to see the dolphins. I'd say nineteen out of twenty are women. I've often wondered whether it is even almost a Freudian thing, but I don't know – because of the shape and all that sort of thing.

(Mike Bossley, Australian Dolphin Research Foundation, interviewed on
19 December 2000)

So what is it that we see when we look into the eye of a dolphin and are struck immediately and powerfully with a sense that theirs is an intelligence of extraordinary measure? What we see in an eye that is not obsessively hopeful and approving like that of a dog, or absently self-absorbed like that of a cat, or fearfully distracted like that of a bird. Rather, it is an eye that seems somehow familiar even as it defies description... It is an eye that can strategize, empathize, and, perhaps above all, recognize when its gaze is met by another, similarly complicated and sentient being.

(Rachel Smolker, 2001, pp254–255)

Rachel Smolker (2001, p3), who has researched the dolphins of Shark Bay for over 15 years, echoes Galdikas (1995, p390) when she suggests that the 'privilege' of sharing the dolphins' world and her 'deep affection' for the mammals is:

the sort of eager affection I have felt at times when encountering some unusually interesting and exotic foreigners while travelling in their country. Though we can barely communicate and I know little about their world, somehow the juxtaposition of what is common and what differs between us inspires in me both a deep sense of kinship and a keen and inescapable awareness of being merely an observer.

Humanity's relationship with the dolphin appears to date back to Crete, possibly more than 5000 years ago (Montagu, 1963, pp6–7; Charbonneau-Lassay, 1991, p306). Over the centuries, dolphins have come and gone as objects of human desire. Given their contemporary ubiquity, it is perhaps surprising that the most recent North American love affair with dolphins commenced only 40 years ago. 'Since the 1960s, dolphins have occupied the cultural imaginary as bearers of alternative values such as collectivity, compassion, friendliness, creativity, joyful sexuality, androgyny, spiritual wisdom and intuitive intelligence' (Bryld and Lykke, 2000, p2).

The dolphin has possibly supplanted the whale, described as the 'metonym for nature' (Kalland, 1994, p163) in the 1960s and 1970s. Greenpeace began as an antinuclear organization in the mid 1970s but soon turned its attention to whaling. The defence of the 'nation of armless Buddhas', as one journalist described whales, took activists beyond merely saving whales. They wanted to meet them, 'encourage them, encounter them, touch them', according to Robert Hunter, a Greenpeace activist (Bryld and Lykke, 2000, p207). Similarly, dolphins have become the source of psychic healing, ecological answers, spiritual sustenance, and role models for social relations. When dreams of dolphins jumped the Iron Curtain and entered Russia, they carried different meanings with them. The dolphins were appropriated as 'our true sea brothers', peace-loving, with high morals; creatures who 'always rush to help at the first call, even at the risk of their own lives' (in Bryld and Lykke, 2000, p203). In Russia, as in the US, it was suggested that dolphins control their environment with telepathy, ordering sharks away[2] or paralysing their prey, thus reducing the working day to a few hours (Bryld and Lykke, 2000, p206).

Dolphin intelligence is pivotal in this idealization, but its connection with a number of other desired traits is also crucial. Arne Kalland (1994, pp160, 163) suggests that we combine a number of whale and dolphin species into a 'super-whale', which exhibits intelligence, singing, being endangered, caring for its young, friendly, as though all the species share all these characteristics. Jim Nollman (1987, p55) ruminates that 'in this last quarter of the twentieth century, more people love dolphins than just about any other wild animal'. Hugh Edwards (1989, p1) comments on the 'charming' smile and 'peg-toothed enjoyment' of the dolphin. This aspect is brought to the fore in television representations like Flipper and in performances in aquaria. Besides their smile, actually an aerodynamic feature, the ubiquity of dolphins might also be a significant aspect of humans' attraction to them, reflecting numerous encounters with dolphins in the wild (comments from passengers in response to my lecture on board *Akademic Shokalski*, 21 January 1996).

Dolphins like us

Another explanation for human fondness for dolphins is that we are returning the favour: 'dolphins like us' and have characteristics, such as intelligence or sociability, which make human–dolphin interaction pleasurable to both parties. Oppian (AD 183–213) and Plutarch (AD 46–120) noted dolphins' friendship for purely altruistic reasons (Johnson, 1990, p165). Melody Horrill, from the Australian Dolphin Research Foundation (ADRF), suggests an 'unconditional friendship [that] is something we do not find every day' (Portside Messenger, 1996, p4). Mike Bossley (interviewed on 19 December 2000), also of the ADRF, believes this special relationship is one of equality between the species, neither of us (consistently or significantly) being predators of the other. Dolphins 'are interested in us as a species'. 'There's no sense of subservience, and they're not looking at you as a predator. It's just kind of eye to eye.' Bossley suspects that dolphins, with their echolocation abilities, have established that

Notes: Dolphins abound in advertising representing communalism, intelligence and environmental awareness: (top left) Andersen Consulting advertises itself with 'The organization that performs together transforms together'; (top right) a bathroom sink and (bottom left) a biodegradable cleanser promise environmental friendliness, or merely friendliness; (bottom right) the Australian Conservation Foundation's membership form: photograph courtesy of the Australian Conservation Foundation.

Figure 3.1 *Ubiquitous Dolphins*

humans have brains of about the same size as theirs and feel we warrant further investigation. Rachel Smolker, quoted above, agrees with this analysis. As a male visitor to Monkey Mia suggested, humans 'seem to be really isolated' from other species and respond emotionally when that species separation is bridged (interview with Sue Doye, July 1995, courtesy of Sue Doye). Jim Nollman (1987, pp178–179), in *Animal Dreaming*, suggests that dolphins have made a pact of 'interspecies comradeship'. Humans allowed into their idyllic world may long to 'merge' with the dolphins, because human thoughts and consciousness are obstacles to accessing 'natural' wisdom and 'innocence'.[3]

Dolphins' legendary helpfulness towards humans is persistently reported in histories of dolphin–human encounters. Dolphins have saved drowning people in stories told by Aesop, recorded by Herodotus, Pliny the Elder and Younger (nephew of Pliny the Elder), and been mentioned by Shakespeare. Once dolphins gained a Christian meaning, at the end of the second century (Charbonneau-Lassay, 1991, pp306–307), Christian saints joined the ranks of those saved by dolphins (Montagu, 1963, p13). In Maori legends, dolphins, *taniwha*, rescue the sons of chiefs, come when called and attend funerals (Alpers, 1960, pp187–188). Over the last century, dolphins have nudged to shore shipwrecked sailors and women (Johnson, 1990, p70; Hahn, 1990 p314; Montagu, 1963, p17). The pink *boufo* dolphins of the Amazon River push helpless persons ashore when their boats capsize (Montagu, 1963, p20). Scientists, ever sceptical, suggest that dolphins are not deliberately saving people but have an instinct to carry objects on their heads or are interested in floating objects (Johnson, 1990, pp71–72; Montagu, 1963, p18).

Dolphins have also been aided by humans. Fishermen of pre-Christian times were said carefully to disentangle any dolphins caught in their nets (Charbonneau-Lassay, 1991, p306). Dolphins escorted Russian sailors to a dolphin trapped in a fishing net where sailors set it free to whistles of thanks (Johnson, 1990, p71). Ice-trapped beluga were reportedly enticed out to their freedom when played classical music by the Russian icebreaker sent to rescue them (May, 1990, p60).

Such love of dolphins for people questions their intelligence, given the slaughter we impose and imposed (Johnson, 1990, p165; Alpers, 1960, p35). I remember being shown a US cookery book in the early 1970s. A section on dolphins opened with a paragraph praising dolphins who guided ships through tricky passages and saved drowning people. The next paragraph commenced along the lines: 'To prepare your dolphin meat for cooking'. Around the world dolphins die by the thousand in tuna fishers' driftnets.[4]

A second explanation for dolphin desire suggests that dolphins are the Western world's pangolin, ambiguous or liminal creatures at the borderlands of our classification system. Given this location, we ritualize dolphins in order to align the contradictions of good and evil, death and life (Douglas, 1970, p53). Dolphins and whales are 'intelligent mammals of the sea', fish with brains but no hands (Kalland, 1994, p162). Mette Bryld and Nina Lykke (2000, pp18, 183) claim that dolphins are 'playfully erotic' and androgynous. Their ambiguity makes dolphins something of a blank slate. Even so, if we are to weave our own meanings for them, dolphins must be sufficiently like us to allow a sense of connection and sufficiently different to be inscrutable. We are kin in that dolphins are mammals that once lived on land; they are strangers as they now live in the ocean (Bryld and Lykke, 2000, p4).

Communicating with dolphins

Dolphins have also become a favourite icon with New Age followers. In this manifestation, dolphin spirituality is 'sustained by feelings of global oneness and empathic communication across the borders of space and time' (Bryld and Lykke, 2000, p7). Dolphins have the intelligence to destroy the planet as humans have done; but lack the hands and, of course, the desire to do so (Bryld and Lykke, 2000, p202). Dolphins possess wisdom that transcends rational intelligence (Bryld and Lykke, 2000, p66). Dolphins do not labour long and hard for their livelihood, instead enjoying themselves and their family and friends (Bryld and Lykke, 2000, p7).

Unlike parrots who talk, chimpanzees who learn sign language, even our pet dogs and cats who use body language, dolphins and humans have been required to rely on more unmediated forms of communication, described as intuition or telepathy. Gregory Bateson suggests dolphin communication is probably less about things and events and more about relationships (Fichtelius and Sjölander, 1973, pp74–75). In Freudian terms, such wordless communication belongs to the pre-linguistic developmental period when the child feels oceanic oneness with the mother (Torgovnick, 1990, pp204–205). We give up this sense of connection with woman/nature to become civilized, to leave behind childish ways of understanding the world.

A medical doctor and brain specialist, John Lilly is most closely associated with the holy grail of communicating with dolphins. In 1960, Lilly's claims concerning dolphins' high intelligence and the immanence of communication with them hit the front page of the *New York Times* (Bryld and Lykke, 2000, p8). Lilly established the 'Human–Dolphin Foundation', wrote *Man and Dolphin* (1961), *The Mind of the Dolphin: A Nonhuman Intelligence* (1967) and *Lilly on Dolphins: Humans of the Sea* (1975). However, Lilly was also considered 'wacky but calling himself a scientist' so that, for a period a budding scientist interested in dolphins was seen as a 'weird-head dolphin fan' (Richard Connor, in an interview with Sue Doye, July 1994, courtesy of Sue Doye;[5] see also Norris 1991, p298). Not only was Lilly 'whacky'; reading his books is also perplexing and dismaying. He inflicted death and pain on creatures he claimed to love and respect, an oscillation between sacralization and cannibalism, to use Bryld and Lykke's (2000, p4) typology.

Several dolphins died under anaesthetic before Lilly became aware that they breathed voluntarily. The research continued without anaesthetic, the dolphins' brains being probed with electrodes. This meant drilling a sheath 30 mm into their skulls and hammering the probe down into their brains (Bryld and Lykke, 2000, p193). Although it was 'painful' for the dolphins and Lilly was 'haunted by the deaths' of the five dolphins they lost (Lilly, 1962, p55), this did not stop him sacrificing a sixth. This dolphin stimulated itself to death when Lilly found its pleasure centre and allowed the dolphin to operate the electrodes (Lilly, 1962, p75; Bryld and Lykke, 2000, p 193). Lilly's defence was 'Despite disappointment and sadness, we had to go on with the research: our responsibilities lie with finding the truth' (Lilly, 1962, p70). Sponsored by agencies like NASA, the US Navy and Air Force and the National Science Foundation, Lilly continued his work until 1968 when the funding ceased and he realized he was imprisoning his friends, the dolphins, in a 'concentration camp' (Bryld and Lykke, 2000, p 194).

It is now suggested that bottlenose dolphins imitate each other's signature whistles, which appear to be akin to a dolphin's name (Masson and McCarthy, 1996, p48). Baby dolphins are not born with a signature but acquire it at about six months, after experimenting with different sounds (Smolker, 2001, p191). Some male dolphins in an alliance who spend time together seem to develop a common signature (Smolker, 2001, p203). Dolphins also achieve communication through the body language of rubbing, stroking and biting (May, 1990, pp28–29).

Akin to the European's construction of the native, many scientists and trainers suggest that dolphins have a premodern childish intelligence (Bryld and Lykke, 2000, p198). When he discusses how dolphins would bring the props for the Flipper filming and never expected or received a reward, Richard O'Barry (1991, p212) says they were like 'children who want to help, happy children eager to be a part of things'. However, some trainers speak of being trained by the dolphins (May, 1990, p28); many stories of dolphin ingenuity are told by trainers (May, 1990, p28; Lee, 1970, p219; Edwards, 1989, p29; Griffin, 1992, pp211–212; Mitchell, 1993, p240). Research in Hawaii has produced dolphins that perform the 'most complex trained behavior ever achieved for cetaceans, including responding to questions, classifying objects, and remembering absent articles' (Norris, 1991, p302). Dolphins at Sea World in Durban South Africa have proven themselves more intelligent than the average three-year-old human (Mee, 2000, p4).

Dolphin intelligence was further accredited when it was discovered that, like people and apes, they use tools in the wild, carrying sponges on their beaks (Telegraph Group, 2001a, p8). The most likely explanation is that dolphins use the sponges as protection from abrasive rocks and the spines of poisonous fish in their foraging along a deep channel in Shark Bay (Smolker et al, 1997, pp454, 455, 459, 461, 462). Science now flirts with New Age claims that dolphins shape their physical environment with their sonar. Studies suggest that dolphin sounds make 'anchovies swim in circles, stay still or die' or make 'buried eels jump out of the sand, ... giving the dolphins time to catch them'. 'Other researchers were skeptical' of these findings published in the *New Scientist* (Telegraph Group, 2001b, p3).

It is against this background of dolphins being like us and dolphins liking us that many people make sense of their encounters with dolphins.

Human–dolphin encounters

> 'Tuna is a fun food,' said Heinz [Starkist] vice-president Ted Smyth. 'If
> it's associated with the harassment and killing of a noble creature like
> the dolphin, that's not right'.
>
> (Rajecki et al, 1993, p45)

There are five kinds of human–dolphin encounter: in captivity in aquaria, in
regulated tactile encounters as at Monkey Mia, in unregulated locations where
lone 'hermit' dolphins choose to socialize with humans, in communities of
known dolphins living close to human settlement, and in chance encounters
with unknown dolphins in open waters. One might argue that these represent
interactions along a continuum from 'staged' to 'authentic', and our discussion
starts with the dolphin in captivity.

Like modern zoos, aquaria have a long and often imperial lineage, starting
with the ancient Romans (Jarvis, 2000, p79). The first records of marine
aquaria in England can be traced to the mid 1800s (Jarvis, 2000, p80). An
aquarium in Melbourne was opened in 1885 with others set up later at Sydney's
Bondi and Coogee beaches (Jarvis, 2000, p83). The New York Aquarium was
opened in 1914. In the 1920s, parents complained that the animals were
misbehaving sexually (no details are provided) and the dolphins were banned
(Hahn, 1990, pp317–318). The next marineland was formed serendipitously in
1938, when tanks were filled with marine life as background drama for a film
shoot. Somehow dolphins got into the tanks and people started coming to see
them, this becoming Marine Studios (Hahn, 1990, pp318–319).

There is extensive discussion in the literature concerning how stressful life is
for dolphins in captivity, deafened by ricocheting echolocation, prevented from
swimming the hundreds of miles a day they would cover in the oceans, bored
from lack of stimulation and lonely for their kin. Children who kiss dolphins
give them fatal diseases or dolphins die swallowing objects fed to them by
tourists (Hanes, 2001, pA10; Johnson, 1990, pp167–168, 170–172, 180–184,
193, 213). Dolphins live in the wild up to 30 years and in captivity for an
average of 5.3 years (Johnson, 1990, p168). Dolphins have been confined to
small hotel swimming pools, where swimming with the dolphin experiences are
offered (Horne, 1992, p10; Johnson, 1990, p209), or are pressed into primitive
travelling circuses and nightclubs as part of striptease revues (Johnson, 1990,
p17; see Murray, 1991, p73 for Ancol Fantasyland in Jakarta).

As with zoos, promotional literature for aquaria dwells on convenience and
close encounters, occasionally including touch, sometimes lacing entertainment
with a little education, but more often resorting to a 'cute and cuddly' register
(Davis, 1997, p35). Indeed, while dolphinaria are justified as educational, in
one survey less than 1 per cent of visitors to the zoo and dolpinarium in London
went for educational reasons (Johnson, 1990, p194). Oceanworld in Sydney is
the equivalent of 'day trips to the Barrier Reef', 'so close you can touch'. At the

Figure 3.2 *Close Dolphin Encounters*

Notes: (top) An in-flight magazine advertisement in the US in April–May 1992 for Sea World in Orlando, Florida, shows 'Shamu, the central trademark, animal attraction and logo at Sea World' (Davis, 1997, p1), the 'world-renowned killer whale' leaping out of the water. 'To get any closer, you'd need gills.' Here one comes 'nose-to-nose' with the orca, can 'stare down steely-eyed sharks', 'chat with a dolphin', 'touch the sleek skin of a bat ray', 'lunch with a seal' (Sea World, advertisement, *Sky* in-flight magazine March 1992, p31: © 1992 Sea World Inc. Reproduced by kind permission). (bottom) Futami Sea Paradise, Ise Shima Region, Japan invites visitors to 'Come (over/and) touch!' Under a picture of two young girls holding the dolphins' dorsal fins, the caption reads 'Let's make friends with the dolphins. The dolphins swim ree-ally well. So, do you think you'll be able to make friends with these dolphins?' Beneath that, framing the dolphins and sea lions, is 'Play with us. Let's play together!' (My thanks to Romit Dasgupta for translating the text, Alison Main for bringing the pamphlet back from Japan and Futami Sea Paradise, for allowing me to reproduce the photograph.)

New York Aquarium, you can 'see eye-to-eye with 400-pound sand tiger sharks'. At the Vancouver Aquarium in the early 1990s, visitors were told 'Our naturalistic approach means MORE variety for the animals – and you!' In the mid 1980s, Sea World on the Queensland Gold Coast asked visitors to sign a petition that their experience had been educational and encouraged conservation attitudes in people. Managers of Sea World claim that they make a contribution to animal research and rescue through their Sea World Research and Rescue Foundation. They also assert that a visit produces educational outcomes, particularly through Project Neptune, which involves worksheets and guided talks for school classes (Jarvis, 2000, p95). But the site has virtually no interpretive displays or signs; almost all information being passed through commentaries at the animal 'shows' (Jarvis, 2000, p96, 101).[6]

By contrast, the only mammals in captivity at UnderWater World at Mooloolaba in Queensland's Sunshine Coast are the seals. As they swim into the show aquarium, plastic waste is discharged from a storm water drain into their pool, the commentary explaining the impact of plastic waste on marine life. Visitors are also shown how the seals are trained (Jarvis, 2000, p111). At AQWA (the Aquarium of Western Australia) in Perth, 'The animals in our care are fed according to their needs, and there are no shows' (Aquarium of Western Australia, 2001, p5). Instead there are information sessions throughout the day, including at the touch pool, the 'Discovery Pool'. At the information session (1 December 2001), we were told 'We'd rather treat our animals with dignity and respect' than have them do a show, although they are 'perfectly capable of performing tricks'. Instead the keepers demonstrated how they cared for the animals, the seal standing against the wall so its height could be measured; the fur seal swimming with a flipper out of the water to demonstrate its 'thermoregulation' strategy. However, at the end, the fur seal was asked 'Are you going to say goodbye, Mont?' and waved a flipper as he exited. As Susan Davis (1997, p8) suggests, a 'theme park about wild nature' is a massive contradiction, 'so peculiar that it makes no sense, or contemporary culture is so thoroughly rationalized that it makes perfect sense'. Indeed, many aquaria in Canada are choosing not to replace their cetacean displays (Hanes, 2001, pA10). The Morecambe Dolphin Campaign by animal rights activists from 1989 to 1991 'brought about the closure of a dolphinarium through a combination of direct communication with tourists and through lobbying the licensing local authority' (Hughes, 2001, p321).

There are two places in Australia where regulated tourist-oriented feeding of dolphins occurs, the internationally famous Monkey Mia in Western Australia and the less well known Tangalooma in Queensland, where the experience has been developed in the light of difficulties encountered at Monkey Mia.

Monkey Mia

according to a number of reliable organisations who take an interest in such things, this is the only instance ever reported of a whole group of dolphins, who, on their own initiative, come regularly to the same beach, and right into shallow water, seeking to be touched.

(Elizabeth Gawain, 1981, p10)

it doesn't sound good when other people say it was a magical experience but it was for me ... it really was special for me ... it was the only time in my life when I've had that kind of contact with a wild animal at all. ... They have an awareness, they have an intelligence, they know how you're feeling... They responded perfectly to what we needed at the time, which was a lot of cheering up.

(Simon, focus group, 1992)

Monkey Mia is often described in Gawain's terms, as the only place in the world where dolphins have, for some time, chosen to come regularly to the beach to relate to humans (see also Leimbach, 1984, p11; Edwards, 1989, p2; Orams, 1995, p89). The west Gascoyne region or Shark Bay area of Western Australia is steeped in history, indeed prehistory. Stromatolites, made famous by David Attenborough's *Life on Earth* (BBC), waver on the verge of life at Hamelin Pool. Aboriginal people lived in the location on and off for at least 30,000 years, when the region was several hundred kilomotres inland, as well as some 6000 years ago when it became coastal (Bowdler, 1999). More recently, in 1616, Dirk Hartog is considered to be the first European to visit Australia.

Monkey Mia, however, is the jewel in the crown, with visitation rates of close to 100,000 per year, 'one of the most significant tourism attractions in Western Australia' (Orams, 1995, p93).

As with a number of the authentic animal encounter sites discussed in this book, Monkey Mia has an origin story, or stories, in which the serendipity of human–animal interaction leads to the development of the famous site. In one origin story, the dolphins once helped Aborigines fish in the area (A 'Discovery' Program, according to Barb, 'host' of DolphInsight, Dolphin Research Centre, Grassy Key, 17 May 1992).[7] Another story suggests that in the 1950s a dolphin rounded up fish for the fishermen and was given some of the catch in thanks (Gawain, 1981, pp10–13). In the most common story, one night in 1964, Alice 'Nin' Watts took a yellowtail fish, used as fishing bait, out of the icebox and threw it to a dolphin that was splashing and blowing around the boat. The next fish was taken right from her hand. They called the dolphin 'Charlie' and, says Alice, within a few nights he was bringing his 'wife and a tiny baby'. A young girl then succeeded in coaxing Charlie onto the beach and he began taking fish from the hands of people on the beach. Other dolphins became emboldened to follow suit. For his part, Charlie assisted the fishermen, rounding up a school of bony herring every morning for fishermen on the jetty to catch for bait (Edwards, 1989, p3). Charlie was later shot by a 'mean spirited amateur fisherman' who resented Charlie stealing his bait (Edwards, 1989, p4).

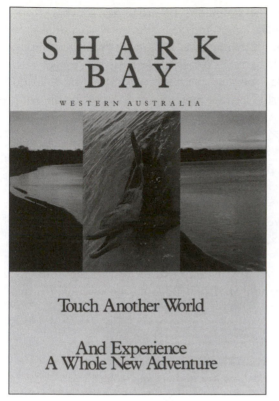

Note: 'The high point of any visit to Shark Bay is sure to be the dolphins of Monkey Mia. The magical thrill of being touched by these beautiful wild mammals has to be experienced to be believed... Rangers are always on hand who'll show you how to approach the dolphins and answer your every question. People come from around the world to meet these magnificent dolphins. When you've been there you'll understand why': 'Touch Another World – And experience a Whole New Adventure'. Images of dolphins adorn the front and back covers of this tourist brochure. An inside page featuring the Monkey Mia dolphins is headed 'One of the world's natural wonders' (Shark Bay Visitor and Travel Centre, c1991, pp1–2).

Source: WA Tourism Commission

Figure 3.3 *Advertising the Monkey Mia Dolphins*

In 1974, Wilf and Hazel Mason arrived to take over the caravan park, which was no more than a primitive bush toilet and a couple of shacks. Although they arrived knowing nothing of the dolphins, Hazel quickly became 'unofficial guardian' of the dolphins, all of whom she named, 'Holey Fin' being the most famous.[8] As the fame of Monkey Mia spread, increasing numbers of people arrived. They did not always know how to treat the dolphins, throwing bread, chicken carcasses and steak bones into the water, and crab spears from the jetty. Little girls persisted in trying to touch the dolphins' blowholes and a man held a cigarette to a dolphin's open mouth (Gawain, 1981, p99; Edwards, 1989, p5). The Masons erected signs on the beach (Edwards, 1989, p5) and formed the 'Dolphin Welfare Foundation', which aimed to raise funds for wardens and to petition the government for protection of the dolphins. Official protection was given in 1985 (Edwards, 1989, p6). In 1986, the first rangers, from Denham Shire, were stationed in the area and an interpretive centre was built (Orams, 1995, p93). In January 1988, when I visited Monkey Mia, the beach sign warned 'Dolphins are wild animals' and 'their behaviour is unpredictable'. The caution, presumably a result of visitor complaints concerning the bites and bumps they suffered from the dolphins, was tacked above a more alluring billboard headed 'How to meet the dolphins'. In order to reduce visitors' negative experiences, more formal rules and regulations were established (Orams, 1995, p93), for example touching was no longer permitted during feeding (Orams, 1995, p95).

In December 1991, Shark Bay became Western Australia's first World Heritage Area, the Shark Bay World Heritage Site, jointly operated by the Shire of Shark Bay and the Western Australian Department of Conservation and Land Management (CALM).

About half those who visit the Shark Bay area also go to Monkey Mia, for example 114,000 of the 201,600 tourists in 1990 (Wilson, 1994, p33), including over 1000 on the beach one particular day (Doye, 1995, p37). In 1990, 70 per cent came from within Western Australia, 22 per cent from interstate and 8 per cent from overseas, generating between them about US$3 million in revenue (Dowling, 1992, p130). When I visited the site in January 1988, the group of a dozen or so people on the beach (later supplemented by more than 30 bus tourists) were all able to buy fish to feed to the dolphins. Chris Sauer, my travelling companion in 1988, updated me with a postcard dated 12 November 1992:

> The dolphins are still regular visitors to Monkey Mia. We saw them yesterday. However, MM now has a sealed road and resort – there is a $3 entry charge, and the rangers allow selected visitors to feed them just a single fish.

Indeed, when I returned in 1999, over 100,000 visitors came each year (Gauntlett, 2002) and they could sip gin and tonic on the verandas of the resort while searching the dazzling waters for a sign of dolphins. With the increase in tourist numbers, the town of Denham became divided into pro-development and preservationist lobbies (Doye, 1995, p53).

In 1992, a resident ecologist was hired, and Monkey Mia claimed to be the first tourist resort in Australia to do this (Doye, 1995, p23). Six full-time rangers were employed in 1994, four men and two women, two indigenous and four white (Doye, 1995, p22). In January 1989, the death of seven of the regularly visiting 15 dolphins provoked international concern and condemnation of the feeding practices (Edwards, 1989, p84).[9] To avert one possible cause of death – contamination of near shore water – probably by overflowing septic systems (Edwards, 1989, pp89–90), the EPA ordered all septic systems to be pumped out and sealed, which was done at great expense (Edwards, 1989, pp89–91).

In a 1994 investigation of the low survival rate of calves born to provisioned dolphins, it was found the calves were malnourished, because of lack of training by their mothers in fishing and socializing with other dolphins (Wilson, 1994, pp8–9).[10] There was a clear contradiction between the 'immense enjoyment' people experienced from feeding the dolphins combined with

Notes: (top) From close encounter in 1988 to gin and tonic resort for (bottom) the many tourists visiting a decade later (David Charles, Monkey Mia ranger).

Source: Copyright © Marc Muller, 'Dolphins' morning greeting, Monkey Mia, Western Australia'

Figure 3.4 *The Resort Cycle at Monkey Mia*

economic livelihoods dependent on the practice as opposed to dolphin welfare (Wilson, 1994, p2). The compromise was a restriction in feeding, including barring male calves and unweaned females from the provisioned group. It was recommended that feeding be done regularly, twice a day, rather than erratically which encouraged the dolphins to stay at the beach (Wilson, 1994, pp10–11, 16). One female student in my survey recommended a much stronger conservation message 'to justify the interruption of these dolphins' natural lives'. She recommended the involvement of Greenpeace, banning recreational boating and fishing and touching the dolphins, expostulating that 'nobody knows what the hell they are doing! Result – dead calves'. By contrast, in 2002, only three regularly provisioned dolphins came in for feeding, and they were middle-aged. The Shark Bay Shire President asked the Marine Parks and Reserves Authority for more dolphins to be fed, to attract more tourists, as there was now sufficient employment arising from the Monkey Mia tourist attraction that a high school was about to be built. Some scientists accepted this proposal, suggesting that provisioned dolphins could be 'sacrifice' dolphins (Hodge, 2002, p42).

While some visitors are impressed with the intelligence of the dolphins, sometimes combined with their great sense of humour,[11] it is more common for visitors, like Simon quoted above, to report their experience in a spiritual register. People – including myself – feel honoured or privileged that dolphins have chosen the encounter. There was 'peace and harmony', 'time and space in which to find ourselves – and with the dolphins as our teachers, most of us found that unaffected childlike state of playfulness and joy' (Leimbach, 1984, p13). Elizabeth Gawain (1981, pp58, 76, 77) met visitors who 'wept when they left', identified 'a personal treasure just to be in their presence', felt the dolphins were 'trying to tell me something' (Gawain, 1981, p92). People felt trapped by the limitation of words, which define, put down and finish (Gawain, 1981, p203). Visitors interviewed by Sue Doye also noted unspoken communication: 'an overwhelming feeling of gratitude', 'it brings tears to your eyes to see wild animals so trusting' (visitors to Monkey Mia interviewed by Sue Doye, July 1994). In response to my article in the *Portside Messenger*, Sheryl Deed wrote me a letter (dated 23 December 2000) in which she described her experience at Monkey Mia, some 14 years previously, as 'the most amazing experience of my life'. Sheryl Deed has cerebral palsy and feels that 'animals relate to me better than people do'. However, even Elizabeth Gawain (1981, p111) is annoyed the day the dolphins do not wish to be stroked, a sort of feeling 'that I am not getting the show that I paid for'.

My survey revealed that Monkey Mia visitors were different from visitors to the other animal encounter sites. They were most likely to be female, to come from overseas, to profess no religion. Among the Australian visitors, they were the least likely to have one or both non-English speaking background parent (see Table A3.1 in Appendix 3). They were more likely to be young (aged 20–29) and visiting alone (25 per cent compared with a total of 7 per cent). They were of higher socioeconomic status than the average site visitor, but also more likely to be on lower incomes than the average visitor. While the nature of the site led me to place Monkey Mia near the 'authentic' end of the animal encounter spectrum, it is not experienced so much as an interaction with animals in the wild, or perhaps wild animals, as a locale for inter-species interaction and communication (Table A3.5). Visitors focused on dolphins being responsive to people and choosing the encounter (Table A3.3, Table A3.12); they were more likely to feel protective towards the animals than visitors to any other site; they also felt privileged, and felt there was mutual affection (Table A3.7).

Monkey Mia respondents provided the most detailed and extensive comments on their experience, generally enthusing about their close encounter with the dolphins, particularly touching them, feeding them or feeling privileged and awed that wild animals chose to interact with humans. A

Japanese woman said, 'In Japan no dolphins. Only in the pool and no touch them. I'd like to touch a dolphin' (visitors to Monkey Mia interviewed by Sue Doye, July 1994). One respondent commented at length:

> The experience that I have had here at Monkey Mia with the dolphins has been really very fascinating and has left me with such a deep respect and excitement for these special dolphins. I have been fascinated with dolphins for so many years and this is the second time I've ever seen dolphins in the wild and I was actually there!! Of course, my biggest thrill and longing was to touch them – and when I had that chance today, I felt very privileged and felt it so extraordinary at how trusting and loving these dolphins are. They are fascinating, possibly enough to become involved with them as a career or volunteer.
>
> (female, secretary, aged 20–29 visiting from Canada)

Of the negative features of the site, Monkey Mia respondents recorded significantly higher levels of dissatisfaction with the numbers of people present and the regulation of the encounter by a ranger (Table A3.9). A particular pressure point was the large number of people who wished to feed dolphins and the small number who could, given the strict regime concerning provisioning as a result of Wilson's report on high mortality rates.[12] However, one visitor declined the offer to feed a dolphin as 'a pointless experience and not a great honour as seems to be the general air'. The rangers relieve this demand for contact by appointing some members of the crowd as assistant rangers, who select people who will hold the bucket of fish or select members of the crowd for feeding. Five respondents described this role as their best experience at Monkey Mia: a 'privilege', a 'buzz', 'a very special opportunity'.

Thus communion with the dolphins can suddenly shift out of focus, bringing into view the crowds of people and a sordid commercial encounter, although some visitors realized they were part of the problem:

> This morning for the first time I felt that the crowd and triggers of cameras were out of place for such a special meeting – but I was also one of that crowd who so much wanted to see them!

Several were critical of the rangers' approach, one complaining that the rangers were 'dictatorial and unpleasant with no humour. The only time they smiled was at the dolphins and they seemed keen to emphasize *their* special relationship with them' (female TV producer, aged 30–44, visiting from England).

Of course not everyone understands *The Dolphins' Gift* (the title of Gawain's book) or cares to communicate with them. Some visitors are there for other reasons, on their travels round northern Australia, on a fishing trip or because they take the children to see animals, any animals (visitors to Monkey Mia, interviewed by Sue Doye, July 1994). Rachel Smolker (2001, p226) suggests that perhaps even a majority of visitors may be happy snappers, seeking only the photograph of the tourist feeding a fish to the dolphin.

While the feeding regime at Monkey Mia appeared to sign the death warrants of a number of dolphin calves, provisioned dolphins can also place tourists at risk. The pushy behaviour of dolphins, hitting and biting humans, was already evident at Monkey Mia in 1988: as indicated by the warning sign. The response at Monkey Mia was to reduce the amount of food available, thus reducing dependence on provisioning, but there are no data to assess the success of this strategy (Orams, 1995, pp178–179). Sharon Gosper, one of the rangers, noted, 'It's true that dolphins can be aggressive at times. They're quite rough with each other in the wild, and that's something people don't generally realize' (Edwards, 1989, p47). Used to animals in dolphinaria, tourists do not recognize the head nod, open-mouthed squeak and so on as stress signs (Doye, 1995, p59). 'This risk is seldom mentioned in tourist promotions or the popular literature which, perhaps understandably, emphasize the positive aspects of interacting with dolphins' (Orams, 1995, p103). The dolphin feeding experience at Tangalooma is quite different from that at Monkey Mia, the result of Mark Orams' (1995) research and recommendations.

Tangalooma

> Please bear in mind that the dolphins are wild creatures that come into
> the resort each evening of their own choosing, they are not trained or
> tamed dolphins as found in various oceanariums. On that basis we
> don't pat, pet, stroke or swim with them. Our reward is to see their
> trust as they swim up to us and gently take small fish from our hand.
>
> (Tangalooma, 1997)

The front cover of the Telstra White Pages telephone directory for Brisbane 2000 featured the feeding of the 'totally wild' dolphins, as one brochure has it, at Tangalooma (Orams, 1995, p147) in Moreton Bay, a couple of hours by launch from Brisbane, capital of Queensland. Tangalooma is coupled with Monkey Mia as the 'only other location where tourists regularly feed wild dolphins' (Orams, 1995, p82). Advertised in Asia, Tangalooma was incorporated into a Japanese tour after its dolphins and sand tobogganing appeared on Japanese television.

Tangalooma shares with Monkey Mia a large shallow enclosed body of water where recreational and commercial fishing occurs. As with Monkey Mia, it appears dolphins were at first fed intermittently by fishers, then started coming more regularly. By 1994, about four to six dolphins regularly accompanied 'Beauty' and her third calf, 'Shadow' (Orams, 1995, p124). As the dolphins became more confident, they began to exhibit pushy behaviour, on occasions biting, particularly characteristic of adult male dolphins (Orams, 1995, p173, 152).

Notes: (top) The Tangalooma bus invites us to 'Feed the wild dolphins'; (bottom) a postcard sold at Tangalooma features two dolphins as 'Good Friends'. Tangalooma 'helps as much as it can but we rely on charity for research funding'. One funding strategy was a shingle drive to clad the Dolphin Research Centre, at the cost of $20 per personally inscribed shingle.

Figure 3.5 *Tangalooma*

Like Wilson in his review of Monkey Mia, Orams (1995, p200), who was charged with researching a better feeding strategy, was constrained by the resort's unwillingness to abandon regular feeding. Between 1989 and 1993, Orams (1995, pp205–208, 111) trialled various strategies and my Tangalooma experience was shaped by his findings. Just as Christina Jarvis (2000, p119) notes that aspects of the 'Penguin Parade' offer the penguins as 'appealing stars of the theatre of nature', the 17 April 1997 dolphin feeding at Tangalooma was billed 'Dolphins as Divas'.

As the dolphins receive no more than one-third of their daily food requirements through provisioning, only guests who have collected one of the limited number of tokens may participate in the feeding (Orams, 1995, p200). Much of the dolphin feeding occurs in the dark, because Orams recommended feeding at a regular time each day but at a time when the water is likely to be shallow and so minimize dolphin manoeuvrability and hence aggression. At about 5.55 pm a dolphin and calf and two other dolphins arrived, causing some excitement among the half dozen people gathered on the jetty. A microphone in the water relayed the dolphins' sounds to us. By 6.15 pm there were more dolphins in the water and the jetty was fairly full of people; attendants roped off the feeding area. Megan commenced her talk by saying, 'You can see the dolphins do their natural behaviours', one doing a tail stand on the sand and drawing some gasps. At about 6.30 pm, those with feeding tokens were called down to the beach and given instructions. The other 'majorly important thing' that Megan almost forgot was, 'Don't touch the dolphins. They are wild and we aren't allowed to touch them and neither are you as we don't know how it affects their behaviour.'

The guests assembled in three or four lines on the beach, were told again not to touch the dolphins, to refrain from loud noises, and instructed how to feed the dolphins. The briefing was heavy with anthropomorphic phrases such as 'Put yourself in the dolphins' shoes' with 50 strangers 'coming up to you every 30 seconds and patting you on the head' (which creates dolphin aggression). We were told to:

> line up in pairs, turn around your rings so the jewels are on the inside, wash your hands in the antiseptic, hold fish firmly in the palm of your hand so it doesn't slip out and you miss out on a dolphin feeding experience, and put the fish down deep into the water.

The fish must be placed well below the surface because dolphins see horizontally and down; if they have to rise for the fish, they may take it more aggressively than they need to. Visitors are usually told to place their second fish in the water quickly to avoid any impatience and nudging from the dolphins.

The rangers fed the dolphins several fish each from the jetty to count them and for a 'photo opportunity' for people on the jetty. The guests then lined up on the beach and the dolphins in the water, assisted by rangers. We went down in pairs in four lines. The attendants stood between the pairs in each line, catching each other's eyes to give a simultaneous signal to feed. We entered the water, fed the dolphin and then walked backwards out of the water. Each dolphin took a fish, swam past and returned to the dolphin queues for further fish, a sight that could be enjoyed from the jetty. One dolphin, Nick, disrupted the dolphin feeding lines, providing some interest for those who could see, but the light was poor.

The party of Japanese tourists, who had been briefed separately in Japanese, were told to link arms with the attendant as they went down to the water to feed. Sandra, my companion, expanding on the theatrical theme, felt this looked highly ritualized, 'like Kabuki Theatre'. As we fed the dolphins, our photographs were taken from the jetty. These images, suitably computer redigitized to bring the dolphin closer to the tourist, could be purchased the next day. The Japanese wore coloured vests to allow their photographs to be identified and posted to them.

Presentations from the rangers during the feeding concentrate on educating people about dolphin behaviour and biology (Orams, 1995, p204). We received quite a long lecture on echolocation, sight, breathing and so on. We were told to be careful with our rubbish as plastic bags look like jellyfish to a loggerhead turtle, while cigarette butts, washed down drains in storms and then into the sea, harm dolphins. The Dolphin Education Centre, a small demountable building, also encourages visitors to learn about dolphins and contribute to environmental conservation through its small collection of videos, books and exhibits, while rangers answer questions and offer specific educational programmes for children. There was a petition against whaling.

When asked by Orams what they enjoyed most about their experience with the dolphins, the major response categories were watching behaviour, experiencing the dolphins in ways that did not change their natural behaviour, the close proximity of the dolphins and feeding the dolphins. As with respondents at Monkey Mia, participants were uplifted, and had a once in a lifetime experience. One family came 6000 kilometres to 'see dolphins in the wild'. Orams found that the educational programme produced a sense of learning while not reducing enjoyment. A number expressed concern about provisioning dependence, danger to the dolphins from humans and tourist greed (Orams, 1995, p224, 227, 229, 232). Others made unsolicited comments stating that they had become more environmentally aware as a result of their experience (Orams, 1995, p254). By contrast, on the nights I participated in the dolphin feed, there appeared to be limited interest in the educational aspects of the encounter. Once the group on the jetty were treated to an educational lecture, they began to dissipate, several older women whingeing, 'Why couldn't they have done this before? Why don't they get on with it?' Such complaints point to the difficulty of harnessing people's emotional response for the conservational lesson.

While Flipper's Florida scenery might 'burst from their television sets like a miracle' (O'Barry, 1991, p140) and Monkey Mia and Tangalooma offer warmth and sunshine almost all year round, seeing dolphins in their most northerly location was a less sparkling affair. At Cromarty, on the Moray Firth, Dolphin Ecosse is run by Bill and Victoria Fraser. Although it was summer in Scotland on a July day in 1997, the thick fog, or har, had lifted from the bay only by noon to reveal a grey cold day. The dolphins neither interacted with the people on the boat nor came very close. The passengers remained subdued, even when a group of dolphins were spotted. Just as the experience of my whale watching group at Hervey Bay was almost in a different universe from tourists who spoke with awe of breaching whales or whales swimming under the boat, closeness can be everything.

Swimming with dolphins

> increasingly tourists are prepared to experience some risk (e.g.
> swimming well away from shore) and discomfort (e.g. cold water) for
> the chance to see an animal in its own place.
>
> (Christina Jarvis, 2000, p180)

Over 15,000 people participate in dolphin swim tours each year in Victoria, which means that dolphin pods are visited every 60 to 90 seconds on busy summer days (Prideaux and Bossley, 2000, p3). In 1995, Mark Orams (1995, pp97, 99) identified dolphin-spotting cruises operating from the Bay of Islands and three other locations in New Zealand, Port Phillip Bay (Victoria) and Nelson's Bay (New South Wales). People could also swim with the dolphins in Rockingham (WA), while applications for a further 20 permits were before the New Zealand government (Orams, 1995, p99).

Orams did not list the Bunbury Dolphin Discovery Centre in south-west Western Australia, now host to 600 visitors daily. This, like Monkey Mia, grew out of the relationship one woman developed with dolphins (Edwards, 1989, p101).[13] A no longer functioning website urges, 'People ... not to touch, chase or feed them. It's up to the Dolphins if they want to interact.' However, 'some' dolphins are fed 'occasionally', while sick or injured dolphins, which 'treat the beach as a haven', are given medical attention if appropriate (www.southwest.com.au/~adreyer). A 'special beachfront interaction zone', initiated in January 1990, allows visitors to swim, paddle or snorkel with the dolphins 'in a strictly controlled environment' (according to Fleur O'Neill, manager of the Discovery Centre, in Amalfi, 2000, p53). For example, people in the water may only float and must not swim; they must stay within the interaction zone. A core group of five to six dolphins regularly visit the beach, on average 260 days each year. The usual interaction time is 20–30 minutes (Webb and Drummond, 2001, p83).

Although having to brave the cold to swim with dolphins, some members of a cruise who did so on the Bay of Islands, New Zealand, in the early 1990s emerged from the choppy waters, their voices quavering with awe and emotion. Similarly, some who swam with dolphins in Port Phillip Bay had 'a life-transforming event... Such visitors equated seeing the dolphins with major personal events, such as the birth of their children or their wedding night.' Children likened the experience to the Melbourne Grand Prix, Christmas presents, to 'other big events in their lives' (Jarvis, 2000, p243). Where 'privilege' was a common term used by my Monkey Mia respondents, Jarvis (2000, p234) noted a number who used the term 'respect'. 'Here, the dolphin was envisaged as other, as a utopian being, inherently peaceful, altruistic and in harmony with their environment and one another' (Jarvis, 2000, p238). Again, like the Monkey Mia visitors, communication was a key theme, achieving closeness with the dolphins, spiritually or physically (Jarvis, 2000, p241), or

Notes: (top) Braving the har at Dolphin Ecosse, Cromarty, Scotland; (bottom) swimming with dolphins in cold and choppy waters, the Bay of Islands, New Zealand/Aotearoa.

Figure 3.6: *Dolphins in the Cold*

describing them as 'friends' (Jarvis, 2000, p242). 'I just wanted to be in their world,' said one; another wished to 'visualise their human nature' (Jarvis, 2000, p244); a third 'wanted to see what they thought of me' (Jarvis, 2000, p243), a reversal of the gaze.

Dolphins in the community

> I can't understand anyone not liking dolphins; they must have something missing in their life.
>
> (female focus group member, 1992)

The city of Malibu has granted citizenship to cetaceans (Rajecki et al, 1993, p48). While Port Adelaide in South Australia has not gone quite as far, the city takes pride in its resident dolphins. Dolphins feature in locally produced plays and pageants, murals and stencils near storm water drains warn against littering. Fundraising events are held for dolphins, housing is advertised as 'the perfect place to watch dolphins at play' (*Portside Messenger*, 5 February 1992, p10; 17 November 1999, pPA1; 12 May 1999, p1; 18 May 1994, p11; 22 March 1995, p7; 3 February 1999, p1; 2 August 2000, p31).[14]

A common way to make a family connection with dolphins is through 'adopt-a-dolphin' schemes, advertised on the Moray Firth and for the Port Adelaide dolphins.[15] In 1995, The Australian Dolphin Research Foundation, a new organization of South Australian marine researchers, offered the public a chance to sponsor a dolphin for $35 (about US$25; corporate sponsorships were $100 to $500, US$75 to US$350). The sponsors received a dossier on their dolphin and a newsletter. Foundation member, Melody Horrill, said 'The money will be used to support non-invasive research into their behavior and ecology' (*Portside Messenger*, 1995, p7; 3 July 1996, p4). Mike Bossley, a key player in the Australian Dolphin Research Foundation, described the research of the Foundation as facilitating 'a relationship between the people of Adelaide and the dolphins' (Digirolamo, 1998, p4). The presumption of 'adopt-a-dolphin' schemes is that dolphins are available for adoption but not capture or killing (Kalland, 1994, pp175, 178). This section explores those occasions when dolphins become part of human communities, either as 'hermit' or 'sociable' dolphins or, less intensely, as pods living close to dense human settlements.

Hermit or sociable dolphins

> I used to spend hours and hours and hours near him, but he wouldn't let anybody get too close. Eventually he kind of got accustomed to me and it got to the stage where I'd give him hugs and we had a very, very close relationship... It's still one of the most significant experiences of my life.
>
> (Mike Bossley, speaking of 'Jock', a 'hermit dolphin' in Port Adelaide, interviewed on 19 December 2000)

Another staple of dolphin histories is stories of dolphins who fall in love with individual people, often children whom they take for rides, sometimes to school. The stories usually end in tragedy, the dolphin stranding itself on the shore, sometimes inconsolable that its child companion has died (Alpers, 1960, pp11–14; Johnson, 1990, p67). Accounts of wild individual dolphins who become accustomed to human presence include 'Pelorus Jack' in the Marlborough Sounds of New Zealand/Aotearoa early in the 19th century, as well as 'Opo' and 'Horace' more recently in New Zealand (Orams, 1995, p86). Sociable dolphins have also been reported for Dingle, Ireland ('Fungi'), the Isle of Man ('Donald'), the south-west coast of England ('Percy'), the Turks and Caicos Islands ('Sandy'), off the coast of South Carolina and Georgia (an albino), Florida ('Nudgy') and in Tin Can Bay Inlet, Queensland ('Scaree') (Orams, 1995, pp96–97), as well as off Spain, Wales, France, Florida, the Red Sea and the Bahamas. Indeed, 'extended and regular social interaction between humans and a single friendly dolphin is not particularly unusual' (Orams, 1995, pp86–88).

However, 'sociable' may not always be the best adjective for these dolphins' behaviour. Donald has carried people out to sea and pinned divers to the seabed for short periods. 'Horace' roughhoused with swimmers at Napier. 'Percy' pushed swimmers out to sea and prevented them from returning, smashed surfboards and injured people, as well as making sexual overtures. 'Simo' became sexually aggressive with swimmers, his penis erect as he attempted belly-to-belly contact and thrusting with female swimmers. Male swimmers were butted until they left the water, 'leaving the dolphin alone with the female' (Orams, 1995, pp101–102).

Two of New Zealand's famous friendly dolphins are 'Pelorus Jack' and 'Oppo'. From 1888 onwards, 'Pelorus Jack', a Risso's dolphin, regularly met and accompanied ships crossing Cook Strait between the North and South Islands, Wellington to Nelson (Alpers, 1960, pp198, 204). An Order in Council was proclaimed in 1904 by the Governor, 'Prohibiting the taking of Risso's Dolphin in Cook Strait, etc' (Alpers, 1960, pp209, 202), making Pelorus Jack 'the first dolphin that ever caused a country to enact a law especially for his protection' (Alpers, 1960, pp196–197). In Opononi, in the far north of New Zealand in 1955, 'A dolphin, friendly and gentle, came to the beach and played with the children there'. 'Opo' was a young *Tursiops* (Alpers, 1960, p225) who 'cast its spell over all New Zealand' (Lee-Johnson and Lee-Johnson, 1994, p20). Crowds of up to 2000 people (Lee-Johnson and Lee-Johnson, 1994, p22) became 'friends with total strangers in an instant, all because of the dolphin' (Alpers, 1960, p233). An 'entirely self-taught juggler of balls and bottle' (Lee-Johnson and Lee-Johnson, 1994, p10), Opo allowed children to be photographed astride her (Lee-Johnson and Lee-Johnson, 1994, p26). Few Maori were among the crowds, it being claimed that Maori believed she was a *taniwha*, messenger, sent by Kupe and that treating her 'as a mere plaything' was demeaning (Lee-Johnson and Lee-Johnson, 1994, p38). An Opononi Gay Dolphin Protection Committee was formed, which placed notices like 'don't try to shoot our gay dolphin' (Lee-Johnson and Lee-Johnson, 1994, p31), gay being a nickname the children had conferred on her (Alpers, 1960, p227). 'Throughout the country', there were claims Opo should be given the same protection as Pelorus Jack. Indeed a proclamation was passed but, a few hours before it came into force, Opo was found dead in a shallow pool (Alpers, 1960, pp233–235). '(T)he people buried her beside the Memorial Hall, and covered her grave with flowers.' At Whangarei a hockey team came onto the field wearing black armbands, while wreaths, telegrams and letters, including one from the Governor-General, poured in (Alpers 1960, p236; Lee-Johnson and Lee-Johnson 1994, p43).

Mike Bossley (interviewed on 19 December 2000) describes dolphins like Opo as 'hermit dolphins'. From the dolphins' perspective, the lone dolphin is a hermit, usually orphaned or losing its pod when young. 'People basically become substitute dolphins for them, I think', says Mike Bossley, whose close relationship with Jock opens this section. Not everyone was as enamoured of Jock as Mike was. Another local resident and sometime tour operator, Patricia Irvine (interviewed on 20 December 2000), described Jock as 'a sex-driven "deviant" with a fetish for rubber and wet fibreglass'. He would hammer away under her kayak for 20 minutes or more (Cooper, 1995a, p3). Another resident, Pat Wundersitz, agreed that Jock had a sexual nature, but stressed: 'My friend took many people to meet Jock, and all were profoundly moved to have the privilege of swimming with a wild sea creature'.

Fans of Jock 'mourned across the State' when his corpse 'was found washed ashore in mysterious circumstances' (Cooper, 1995, p3). The other well known sociable dolphin of Port Adelaide, Billy, also succumbed to pollution. Mike Bossley, in his campaign to 'clean up' these dolphins' environment, claims that the 'Port River is the slum of the dolphin world' (Ferguson, 1995, p5).

Port Adelaide's 'slum' dolphins

> I always get a happy tingle when I see them there ... the dolphins are part of the treasures that our Port Adelaide can be proud of.
>
> (Patricia Candis, letter to *Portside Messenger*, 8 February 1989, p10)

> I don't know of another place anywhere in the world where you have these animals so close to the population of a big city.
>
> (Mike Bossley, Australian Dolphin Research Foundation, in McGarry, 1998, p5)

Mike Bossley (interviewed on 19 December 2000) describes Monkey Mia and Tangalooma as 'predictable, orchestrated, choreographed', 'feeding time at the zoo', where the dolphins are 'lured and they're bribed to be friends with you'. Orams (1995, p142) locates the Tangalooma experience between the semi-captive and wild categories. This is not the case with the Port Adelaide dolphins, of whom Mike Bossley says, 'as far as I know, we are the only city which has dolphins in its midst', a 'unique privilege' (Wesolwoski, 1998, p3).[16] In 1992, visiting children, orphaned by the Chernobyl disaster, delighted to see the dolphins (*Portside Messenger*, 1992, p1). In 1993, a 'rendezvous with a playful dolphin' heartened marathon Port River rower, Max Herriman (Starick, 1993, p8). A Swiss couple who married while sailing on the river were 'overwhelmed when the dolphins arrived to pay their respects', 'the highlight of their world trip' (Susan Brame, letter to the editor, *Portside Messenger*, 12 May 1999, p2). Birkenhead horse trainer, Sandy Sandford, and his horses swam with 'Billy' in the Port River each morning at Cruickshank's corner (15 November 1989, p9; 1 November 1989, p8; 25 October 1989, p11; 11 October 1989, p3;

13 September 1989, p1).[17] So popular are the Port dolphins that they featured in the election campaign of both major political parties in the 2002 State election (Tilbrook, 2002, p12). The Australian Labor Party supported 'a "real" sanctuary for the Port River dolphins', which 'will create vitally important environmental benefits and has the potential to create a rare tourist drawcard' (Labor South Australia, 2001, p7).

Although the response was disappointing (see Appendix 1), the handful of residents who completed my questionnaire echoed these newspaper reports. A male pensioner noted that dolphins play about his boat when he goes fishing: 'I swim with them and they talk to me.' Janet Crease (email dated 6 January 2001, who has since published a book on her dogs) and Patricia Irvine (interviewed on 20 December 2000) described their dogs swimming with dolphins. Patricia Irvine has 'swum with them a lot', including a time shortly after her husband died, in which the dolphins gave her comfort in a 'New Age'-like experience.

In 1995, Mike Bossley drew attention to the high pollution levels in the Port River (Ferguson, 1995, p5).[18] Bossley claims that the highest level of mercury ever recorded in a dolphin was in a Port River dolphin (Mike Bossley, interviewed on 3 November 2000). The *Portside Messenger* has carried numerous stories concerning Port River pollution, including excessive nutrients, industrial effluent, storm water runoff, plastics and discarded fishing tackle, which can choke and kill dolphins and sea birds. The assistance of residents, including school students, in protesting the pollution and its effects include protests to parliamentarians, removal of polluting materials from the river (some items as large as shopping trolleys), donations for dolphin research (for example *Portside Messenger*, 4 October 1989, p3; 19 February 1997, p7; 19 March 1997, p3; 15 November 2000, p10). A major rescue operation for the dolphin 'Float Baby' involved removing floats and sinkers from her dorsal fin, as well as a length of rope around her girth which would have slowly choked or crushed her as she grew. The story was featured on Channel 9 television (Cooper, 1995, p4). From 1993, residents became involved in an action to prevent a power station being built at Pelican Point, it being feared that the increase in water temperatures would threaten marine life.[19] The power station was built in 2000.

The well known dolphin, Jock, appears to have died as a result of pollution. In 1997, there was a controversy between the EPA and Port dolphin researchers concerning whether the high levels of polychlorinated biphenyls (PCBs), discovered during the autopsy of Jock, meant that the Port River is polluted with PCBs (*Portside Messenger*, 1997, p6). Billy's story was linked to the issue of pollution when her calf died, apparently from toxic mother's milk (Gunther, 1994, p1). This provoked a number of articles and several letters to the editors, including dolphin researcher, Melody Horrill, who noted 'the Port River is seen as a bit of a toxic rubbish dump, a ... cesspool' (letter to the editor, *Portside Messenger*, 24 May 1995, p3). Pollution was also 'wiping out' their habitat, killing vital seagrasses and fish, so dolphins could not 'get a decent feed' (Gunther, 1994, p1). A cleanup followed, using the slogan 'Dolphins Don't Ask For Much, Just Clean Water' (Littleton, 1995, p3). Articles noting the pollution levels continued to link the 'grim picture' of Port River pollution to the death and illness of dolphins (*Portside Messenger*, 27 August 1997, p6; 23 July 1997, p1; 22 April 1997, p5; 1 August 1998, p5; 30 August 2000, p9).

Mike Bossley (interviewed on 19 December 2000) 'shamelessly' and deliberately uses the dolphins and people's response to them as vehicles for his message about pollution and the environment: 'I don't feel I'm exploiting them [the dolphins]; I feel I'm taking advantage of an extraordinarily convenient symbol that can be used to benefit the dolphins in the long run.' Bossley, involved in research on dolphins for more than 20 years, believes that people have become more responsive to the environmental issues, understanding that 'if you love dolphins, it's not enough just to protect them; you have to protect their environment as well. It's not just dolphins; any species'.

Port residents are only more outraged when they discover dolphins have been deliberately killed, for example shot in the head (*Portside Messenger*, 1998b, p13; McGarry, 1998, p5) or run over by watercraft operated by 'a hoon convention' (Wesolwoski, 1998, p3). Resident Sheryl Deed wrote me a letter, dated 23 December 2000, saying, 'It makes me very angry and hurt that people kill such trustworthy and lovely creatures of the ocean. It just sickens me to hear these things go on.' Senator Amanda Vanstone, then Federal Justice Minister, the newspaper *The Advertiser* and radio talkback host, Jeremy Cordeaux, offered rewards when the dolphins Monika and HiLo were killed in 1998 (*Advertiser*, 1998, p13; *Portside Messenger*, 1998a, p13). For the first time, Crime Stoppers was used to coordinate a search for people who killed wildlife (Kemp, 1998, p13). In 1999, when a three-month-old dolphin calf was fatally stabbed (Hurrell, 1999b, p6), a group of local traders formed a river patrol (Digirolamo, 1999, p7). According to SA Museum Animal Curator, Catherine Kemper, while a dolphin appears to die annually of gunshot wounds in South Australia, this was the first time a dolphin had been killed in metropolitan waters (*Portside Messenger*, 1998b, p7).

Interestingly, the Port River dolphins have not become a major tourist attraction, although articles periodically note that they are a hidden treasure (for example Hullick, 1998, p9; Weir, 1998, p11). Due to the absence of regular tourist encounters with the Port dolphins, I employed a combination of content analysis of the local newspaper and advertising for residents to complete a modified questionnaire, both through the local newspaper and through Mike Bossley. As Mike Bossley's major purpose is not interaction with dolphins but monitoring the population and their environment, the passengers on his boat were not 'tourists' in the same sense as respondents at the other animal encounter sites. I also interviewed Mike Bossley and Patricia Irvine, two people who are, or have been, involved in showing people the Port dolphins (see Appendix 1 for more details).

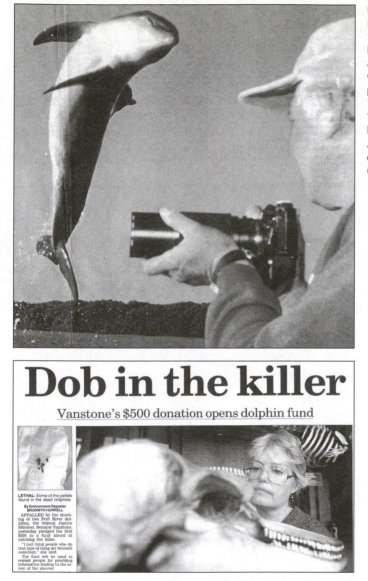

Notes: (top) Dr Mike Bossley warns that 'toxic gulf waters are killing baby dolphins and could eventually wipe out local dolphin populations' (Weir, 1998, p11); (bottom) 'Dob in the killer' to the local newspaper, *The Advertiser*, which offered a reward (Hurrell, 1998a, p3).

Figure 3.7 *Dangers to Dolphins: Pollution and Killers*

Turning first to the content analysis of the local newspaper, I draw on Adrian Franklin's and Robert White's (2001) analysis of *The Mercury*, a Hobart-based newspaper (Hobart is in Tasmania, Australia), from 1949 to 1998. The authors argue that the late 1970s were a watershed, during which the trends shifted from anthropocentric to zoocentric, unsentimental to sentimental, and from animals posing a risk to humans to animals being at risk. My analysis of the local Port Adelaide newspaper suggests a similar shift in almost the same timeframe. There is a move away from anthropomorphic attitudes to pets, which are also increasingly understood to be a nuisance, towards an expression of affection towards wild animals, particularly dolphins. There is also an obvious trend showing increased interest in pollution issues, both generally and specifically in relation to Port River pollution (Table 3.1). The most significant changes occur in the 1970s and 1980s. The trends are particularly clear if the proportion of articles in the three categories of dolphins, pollution and pets is compared (Figure 3.10), a strategy that controls for the changing size of the newspaper and its changing ratio between articles and advertising as it went through three metamorphoses in the half century from 1949 (see Appendix 1 for details). Figure 3.10 reveals a clear shift from pets to dolphins and an increase in interest in pollution issues, with 1979–1980 appearing to be a crucial moment in these trends.

There is also a trend away from environmental issues that focus on suburban amenities such as unauthorized rubbish dumping, littering on beaches, sewerage sludge, towards issues concerned with environmental degradation as a result of chemicals and other pollutants and associated threats to wildlife. The latter are more invisible, comprising the 'riskier' pollution in Beck's (1992) terminology, as discussed in Chapter 5. The first mention of pollution in the

Table 3.1: *Distribution of Articles in* Portside Messenger *1949–2002 as Percentage of All Articles on Animals and the Environment*

Articles, etc	1949–1950	1959–1960	1969–1970	1979–1980	1989–1990	1995–1996	2000–2002
Dolphin/s	0	0	0	4	12	12	12
Pollution	18	26	45	55	72	58	66
Of which: Port River Pollution	1	0	0	0	0	10	18
Dogs and pets	82	74	55	41	16	30	22
feral cats	0	0	0	0	0	1	0
Sub-Total (Number)	11	57	38	56	133	200	95
Other environment issues (Number)	1	2	15	36	0	70	6
Other animals (Number)[1]	8	17	29	46	0	8	14
TOTAL	13	71	67	140	133	287	116

Note: 1 Sporting animal articles, e.g. horse racing, pigeon racing, are most of 'other' animal articles along with occasional discussions of animal nuisances or interesting animals stories (e.g. bees). In 2000–2002, six articles concerned culling pigeons

2000–2002: The first search was undertaken in November 2001. Due to refurbishment of the State Library it then became impossible to access the remainder of 2001's newspapers. Instead, and to include the most recent editions available at the time of the second search, the period January to November 21, 2000 was supplemented with November 21, 2001 to April 2002

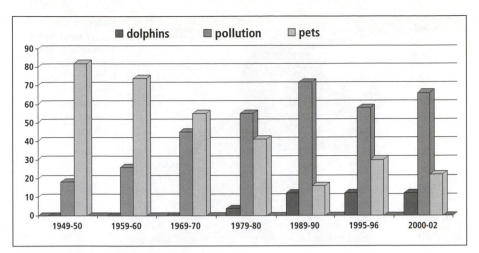

Figure 3.8: *Distribution of Articles Between 'Dolphins', 'Pollution' and 'Pets'*

Port River occurs in an article in 1950 (*The Progressive Times*, January 1950, p15). In the 1990s, pollution levels in the Port River became a significant issue as did the effects of the power station, often linked with the wellbeing of the dolphins.

There were no articles concerning feral cats before 1989, although an article in 1960 claimed that 'stray cats' wandering outside their yard should be shot (*The Messenger*, 2 November 1960, p2). Feral cats were the subject of 13 articles from 1989 to 2002. In 1997 and 1999, articles discuss a plan to release native animals on Torrens Island after removing the feral cats, John Wamsley warning this will not be successful (*Portside Messenger*, 3 February 1999, p7; 27 August 1997, p5).

It is interesting that the local newspaper is silent on the issue of 'wild' dolphins until the 1980s, after which dolphins become a regular feature of newspaper stories. The very first article on dolphins uncovered by the content analysis concerns a 'family fun day' to raise money for the Lions Club and the Marineland dolphins (*The Messenger*, 7 March 1979, p6). Indeed, the Marineland dolphins are the subject of the first articles on dolphins, particularly the controversy concerning their destiny when the West Beach Marineland building was condemned in 1988. The campaign triggered Mike Bossley to start his increasingly systematic study of the Port River dolphins, as he 'intensely' disliked the Marineland (interviewed on 19 December 2000). Despite pleas to release them into the Port River, the dolphins were sent to Queensland, where 'They're still in captivity there, but in a more benign sort of captivity' (Mike Bossley, interviewed on 19 December 2000). Subsequent to the Marineland story, pollution is the main hook for dolphin stories, before a rash of articles in 1998 dealing with the killing of dolphins (seven articles). The theme of senseless killing of dolphins (three articles) and of pollution is continued in 1999.

Notes: (top) Mike Bossley surveying the dolphins in the Port River; (bottom) 'slum' dolphins in the Port River, against the industrial backdrop (Prideaux and Bossley, 2000, p3).

Figure 3.9 *The Port River Dolphins*

Although Mike Bossley does not offer tourist cruises to see the dolphins, he does regularly take passengers out on his research visits to count and monitor the Port River dolphins. As with John Wamsley's personality at Warrawong, the personality of Mike Bossley as guide is a crucial ingredient of the dolphin encounter. When she left the Australian Dolphin Research Foundation, Melody Horrill, in a letter to the editor (*Portside Messenger*, 12 July 1996, p2) said of Mike Bossley: 'Dr Bossley has dedicated many years of his life and a great deal of his own finances to continue his work with the Port's dolphins'. He is 'a man with great patience, wisdom and empathy for all animals, especially dolphins'. Bossley believes science 'shall not exclude beauty or empathy, or a concern for the wellbeing of all the individuals whose ocean I share' (Bossley, 1998, p32). Mike Bossley is unusual in his interdisciplinary training, including biology, anthropology and 'comparative' or 'environmental' psychology, which explores the relationship of people with their physical and biological environment. Bossley worked for Greenpeace for five years in the early 1970s, prompted by his students in environmental studies at Australian National University, who asked in relation to whale killing, 'Why doesn't anyone do anything?' For a time Bossley offered authentic dolphin encounters through Iain Greenwood's Osprey Tours (discussed in Chapter 2). He has been an academic at several of Adelaide's universities, as well as interstate and overseas. He now concentrates his research on the Port dolphins, supporting his work with occasional ecotours of four or five people each year, who stay on his property in the Adelaide hills. Most of these are European, particularly Swiss, who find him through his personal website. I interviewed Mike Bossley on 19 December 2000 and went out on his boat the following day and again in May 2001.

Like John Wamsley, Mike Bossley requires those who will have an authentic animal encounter to rise before dawn. We drove through the empty dark streets of Adelaide to arrive with the sunrise at the marina where Bossley's boat is moored. Nobody was about, not even the caretaker. Water slapped lazily against boat hulls, rigging creaked in the slow breeze, fish slipped through the shallows, a few gulls wheeled overhead. At the start of our journey down the river, it seemed that we were the only humans in this whole horizontal world stretched pale and flat around us, rimmed by the mangroves, domed by the sky. The trip of about three hours took us out of the estuary into the sea and back. Later we met other humans: a couple of fishermen moored in a dinghy, a launch busily ploughing its way to the ocean, a cargo ship towering above us as it left the Port, a tug returning up river with dolphins surfing its bow waves. Once in the ocean, we could see distant trees and houses beyond the beach line. We returned past power stations and half-sunken wrecks of rusting ships. We saw visible pollution, including discarded esky ice boxes and plastic bags.

The first time we saw dolphins was in the river. Mike turned off the motor. In the sudden still silence of the early morning, the world contained only us and them. If the dolphins were not otherwise engaged – fishing or 'bonking' (as Mike calls it) being favourite activities – they swam around the boat while he identified them and recorded his observations. They jumped and played and made eye contact with those on the boat. We did not stroke the dolphins, and this may disappoint some visitors. Those dolphins who were largely 'strangers' to Mike ignored the boat and had to be identified through binoculars. Very, very occasionally Mike does not see any dolphins on his almost daily trip.

As at Monkey Mia, people who accompanied Bossley commonly said they felt 'privileged' to have had the encounter, the dolphins bestowing their presence like a royal favour (four of the seven Port Adelaide respondents). As Mike Bossley (interviewed on 19 December 2000) puts it, encountering wild dolphins may be the closest thing to an equal relationship with an animal: bearing in mind both 'equal' and 'relationship'. Paradoxically, the relationship might be more 'equal' than that with primates because dolphins do not have conversations with (most) humans. Signing chimpanzees have demonstrated disappointingly childish enthusiasms for food and games, making it more difficult to believe that they hold the secrets of the universe. Mike suggests that most people who go out on his boat have 'very intense experiences', including weeping. Men are also affected, although the performance of masculinity in our society means they usually try to hide their feelings. As with Jarvis' respondents, Bossley's passengers compare their dolphins encounter with: 'it's like when they were 14 or 15 and fell in love for the first time'; 'this is far more important than the day I got married'; 'it's more important than having my child'. A little girl said, 'It feels just like the night before Christmas'. Mike finds the intensity of these responses 'almost scary in some ways' (interviewed on 19 December 2000).

Again, as with the Monkey Mia respondents, interaction was important. One respondent was excited to swim with dolphins so close to her, on this, 'the best day of my life'. A British woman working as a secretarial coordinator, who has always felt a 'connection' with dolphins, expressed 'a huge sense of relief and an idea of "returning home"'. She described her religion as 'a more universal spirituality': 'I have spent nights dreaming of dolphins where I swim with them, they teach me things... I firmly believe they have much to teach us about joy'.

Patricia Irvine (interviewed on 20 December 2000), who in the mid 1990s ran canoeing expeditions to see dolphins, describes her customers as a mix of people, from New Age through to ecotourists more interested in mangroves or birds. Tourists often asked whether Patricia could 'guarantee the dolphins' and her reply was similar to other ecotourism operators, but with a twist:

> I can't guarantee the dolphins; the dolphins are wild animals!' I just
> made it quite clear. I said, 'They come – they please themselves'. I said,
> 'I keep tabs on the movement of dolphins; I log it in my diary... So
> there's a good chance, but if you want guarantees go get yourself a
> barbecue lunch or something and ... go out to [nearby] Garden Island
> for half a day and sit and watch.

Not everyone feels the same intensity for dolphins, some people merely mouthing support for them now that certain attitudes to animals have become 'politically correct', 'a bit like gender equality, I suppose' (Mike Bossley, interviewed on 19 December 2000). The articles and letters in the *Portside Messenger* are proof that polluters persist in the community, jet skis and fishing lines endangering sea birds and dolphins (*Portside Messenger*, 31 May 1995, p2; 12 July 1995, p2; 26 August 1998, p2; 12 February 1997, p2; 17 November 2000, p2). On top of this is the deliberate shooting of dolphins. It is also an heroic claim to suggest that the *Portside Messenger* reflects the total community, rather than the inclinations of journalists, editors and even letter writers. The population is diverse, containing, apart from environmentalists, YUMIES (young urban males into extreme sports), working class and unemployed people, Vietnamese and Cambodian first generation migrants, who more often fish for utilitarian than leisure reasons and thus sometimes infringe catch size regulations.

Patricia Irvine (interviewed on 20 December 2000) remembers that every Sunday morning during one summer a group of louts camped on the eastern side of Garden Island:

> hollering and hooting. And just firing over the mud flats and all around that area – firing into the water. I didn't even consider the dolphins. I thought about myself and my customers.

Patricia believes that the kind of people who shoot dolphins are 'the wife beaters and the child abusers': 'It's just, if you're violent, you're violent. If you're cruel, you're cruel, and you don't think about it. It's just reflexive.' Mike Bossley (interviewed on 19 December 2000) drew the same analogy, saying that 'I can't explain why people shoot dolphins, but I can't explain men who beat up their wives, or mothers and fathers that abuse their kids.' 'We humans are mostly very nice, but there are arseholes out there.' However, lest Anglo intellectuals run away with a sense of our own superiority, Mike recounted an anecdote:

> Just last week I was out there [on the Port River observing dolphins] and a big, burly bloke in a blue t-shirt who was unshaven and had an esky full of tinnies [of beer] in front of him was out there fishing. The dolphins started to swim past and he very carefully pulled his fishing line in and waited until they went past. I went over to him and said, 'That's great what you did; thanks very much'. And he said, 'Oh, any fuckin' bastard that doesn't do that needs to have his balls cut off'.

In telling the story, Mike Bossley implies that this man is acting out of the character of blue collar masculinity, is adopting a response to the dolphins that would be coded as 'feminine' in our society. However, in his very action, the 'big, burly bloke' nudges at and shifts the boundaries of working class masculinity.

Despite the shooters and looters, the indifferent and untouched, many humans in late modern Western societies find dolphins the best of all animals to think with. The meanings we project onto them depend not only on who we are – our gender, ethnicity, experience and individual needs – but also where we are when we experience the dolphins, perhaps, in a sense, who the dolphins are.

Conclusion: Wolves of the sea

> all happiness is animal happiness, even the happiness of the philosopher [but non-human animals may] have a greater gift for accepting happiness than we do.
>
> (animal trainer and philosopher, Vicki Hearne, 1994, pxv)

All questionnaire respondents were asked to describe the last time they saw a dolphin and then tick any of the boxes that described their feelings at the time

Note: Images of orcas are prevalent on Vancouver Island, Canada, used by the Kwakiutl on their totem poles, by Greenpeace to represent the infinite cycle of nature in their logo for the Save the Whales campaign, by white Canadians in posters, postcards and even to fashion letter boxes ('Skahna' Image by Clarence Steven Mills, Gah-ghin-skuss, member of the Eagle Clan, Skidegate).

Figure 3.10 *Images of Orcas*

(Table A3.23 in Appendix 3). Reflecting the ubiquity of dolphins, almost half the respondents last saw a dolphin in the wild. In such encounters, dolphins were often usually too far away, although some 'MAGIC!' (boat trip on Port River, Adelaide) or 'beautiful' (swimming close to a beach) experiences were reported. Most of the Port Adelaide respondents ticked all the boxes, several commenting on the sense of 'rightness' in the world when they see dolphins. Not unexpectedly, many respondents were disconcerted by dolphins 'exploited' in captivity, but some were happy to see the 'show'.[20]

A number of 'New Age'-style responses comment, not only on dolphins' great love for humans, but also their affection for each other. 'Dolphins have a reputation for being cooperative and altruistic', even across species and genera (Connor and Peterson, 1994, p132; see also Jarvis, 2000, p199). Dolphins support wounded companions, females surround a mother about to give birth and raise a newborn calf to the surface to breathe (Johnson, 1990, p71). Given the common belief in dolphin altruism, the use of dolphins in military operations, as kamikaze submarine bombers or minesweepers, for example,[21] has caused particularly outraged commentary (Johnson, 1990, p300; O'Barry, 1991, p302).

The peace-loving dolphin image is increasingly contested with evidence that orcas are 'wolves of the sea' (the name of a celebrated documentary by wildlife filmmaker David Attenborough) and that dolphins can be 'quite aggressive' and 'occasionally rape' (Masson and McCarthy, 1996, p54). Orcas have been recorded assisting whalers to catch the Southern Right and Humpback whales at Eden in New South Wales (Orams, 1995, p83–85; and Montagu, 1963, p19, who are drawing on Alpers, 1960, pp162–164). Driven into the bay and harassed by both boat and orcas, a whale could be captured within an hour rather than the 12 hours that might be required without orca assistance. Orcas will attack a baleen whale many times their size, seizing the flippers and tail flukes, tormenting it until the tongue lolls out. They then eat the tongue and lips and 'leave the rest' (Bryld and Lykke, 2000, p207; May, 1990, p139).

The other dent in dolphin publicity is their proclivity for sex, amounting to rape, even gang rape (Masson and McCarthy, 1996, p81) and necrophilia (Caldwell and Caldwell, 1966, p773), both of trainers and of other dolphins. Only humans and bonobos have been observed to indulge in non-reproductive sex with the same frequency as dolphins. Dorsal fins, beaks and penises are inserted into vulva, genital slits or anuses in various combinations of male and female partners, including incestuous copulations between young males and their mothers. Females carry small balls with the muscles of their vagina and rub their genitals against them (Bagemihl, 1999, pp343–346). Mike Bossley (interviewed on 19 December 2000) claims:

> I have seen some female dolphins basically trying to seduce males, and sometimes without success actually. But by and large, it's two or more males trying to persuade a female that she really loves them, so to speak. And the females usually do their damnedest to avoid penetration.

Patricia Irvine (interviewed on 20 December 2000) suggests her clients were 'gobsmacked' to learn that the nicks and cuts in dolphins' tails and dorsal fins did not come from sharks but from fights with other dolphins. Irvine is much more critical of the male dolphins than is Bossley, describing them as 'louts' who rape mothers with calves. As she says of her terminology, 'That's anthropomorphic' but 'if it was up to the female, I don't think she would have come across, but she didn't have a choice'.

Research with the 350 bottlenose dolphins in Shark Bay has found that males form alliances, including rival gangs, to 'attempt to monopolise mating opportunities by forcing oestrus females to swim with them' (Connor et al, 1993, p25; Ron Shepherd in Wilson, 1994, p29). Male dolphins charge, hit, chase, bite and slam into uncooperative females (Connor and Peterson, 1994, pp125–126).

sweet little
monsters

We go potty over cats and dolphins but both animals have a dangerous dark side. In the wake of the controversy over the City of Stirling's cat clampdown last week, **WENDY PAYNE** looks at how cat owners can do more to protect wildlife and **PAM BROWN** talks to the makers of a revealing television documentary about dolphins.

DOLPHINS are not playful and happy, and people have to get away from being so impressed by their perpetual grins, says American marine biologist Paul Atkins.

Atkins and his wife, Grace Niska Atkins, have travelled the world to make a documentary for National Geographic called Dolphins: The Wild Side, and they despair at the new age view of dolphins as being somehow in tune with man.

"Dolphins are wild animals," says Paul Atkins. "They are like tigers and lions. They are hunters and predators and they have the instincts of preda-

in the case of the Shark Bay dolphins, a lot has to do with predation by sharks.

Paul Atkins says the figure for Shark Bay is on the high end of the scale but not abnormal.

"If you look at elephant seals, about 50 per cent won't survive their first year. Humans used to be that way until they developed modern medicine.

"It is the law of the natural

Paul and Grace Atkins, right

Note: Payne and Brown (1999, p12) compare cats and dolphins

Figure 3.11 *Dolphins Lose Their Lustre*

The purpose of male gangs is 'skulduggery'; 'sex and violence'; 'kidnapping'. A kidnapped sexually receptive female can be held prisoner for a month or more, the males mating with her either one at a time or sometimes simultaneously (Douglas, 1999, p3636; see also Connor et al, 1999, p571). Pro-feminist researchers, including Smolker (2001, pp183–184), wonder why female dolphins do not form defensive alliances against the males. Smolker suggests that they may be too busy foraging and raising young, but she is clearly frustrated at the females' failure to combine in their own defence. Females support each other occasionally by 'hiding' a victim from herding males, surrounding two or three herding males who might then give up the chase, or allowing a harassed female to rest a flipper against their side (Connor and Peterson, 1994, p129).

Rachel Smolker (2001, p146) notes that, 'because of our preconceived ideas about dolphins' as 'always gentle and kind and playful', it was some time before researchers identified this bad behaviour. As these findings enter the popular domain, articles often include caveats such as 'if you find yourself taking a dip with Flipper, don't be fooled by his beatific smile' or 'their cuter-than-thou image'; instead beware of 'Flipper's dark side'.[22] A report headed 'sweet little monsters' shows a basket of kittens (incipient feral cats and destroyers of Australia's wildlife) alongside two smiling dolphins (Brown, 1999, pp12–13). A similar correction is offered in the 1999 documentary *The Ultimate Guide to Dolphins*, produced and directed by Nigel Ashcroft (*West Australian*, 2001, p32). Usually seen as peaceful, intelligent and friendly creatures, dolphins have also been known to torture and kill porpoises. The narrator suggests, 'Maybe we see dolphins how we like to see ourselves': 'they kill to eat', 'they fight each other for dominance' and 'so do we'. Similarly, Smolker (2001, p170) claims that her own respect for dolphins has been enhanced in discovering that the dolphins are 'more like us' and have more complex behaviour than suggested by the 'perpetually sweet' stereotype.

Furthermore, complex social relationships might be a sign of intelligence, if Nicholas Humphrey's (1988) claim is correct (Smolker, 2001, p242). Humphrey suggests that the intelligence of higher primates, including humans, has been developed to navigate complex social relationships. Understanding the environment does not require such brain development. This means that 'Like us, their minds are on each other' (Smolker, 2001, p254), perhaps, like humans, scenario building, imagining the outcome of certain encounters before actually engaging in them (Smolker, 2001, p248). As a feminist, I would argue that an even higher level of intelligence and social skill is required to manage social relationships without resorting to aggression.

Two contradictions have been introduced in this conclusion. The first is that between dolphins imagined as spiritual and harmonious as opposed to dolphins imagined as complex and aggressive. The second is the contradiction between scientific knowledge and emotional connection. Indeed, even scientists change the tone of their voice depending on their audience. Richard Connor and Rachel Smolker, part of the team that has been studying the Monkey Mia dolphins for over 20 years, discuss their experiences and research findings in quite different registers in a popular book (Connor and Peterson, 1994, p135) and in scientific journals (see Connor et al, 1999; Smolker et al, 1997). In the former, the Monkey Mia dolphins are given the names by which they are known to the rangers and tourists at the resort, names like 'Puck' and 'Nicky'. In scientific articles discussing the very same issues, the researchers abbreviate the dolphins' names to the more scientific sounding PUC, BOT, VAX and so on.

Table A3.16 reveals that, while the trends are only approximate, visitors to authentic animal encounter sites are more likely to be members of conservation and field naturalist societies; visitors to Monkey Mia are members of animal welfare societies; visitors to the more staged sites are members of hunting societies (although note the high Warrawong response rate). Table A3.18 reveals different orientations to nature-related issues at the different sites. Warrawong visitors tend to be the most conservationist, for example in opposing woodchipping of native forests or accepting the extermination of feral cats. Monkey Mia visitors tend to be more humanistic, for example demonstrating comparatively high disapproval rates for experimenting on animals and either culling or farming indigenous animals. The Cleland sample reveals some utilitarian orientations, for example in relation to hunting, woodchipping native forests, experimentation on animals.

What does it mean that some people are left unaffected by encounters with wild animals in natural destinations? Are those who are affected yearning for a return to premodern certainties? Or are they seeking an authentic encounter that allows reinvigoration of modernist political and moral certainties: that humans can and should act to save the world? Or are they postmodern tourists, playing with the notions of 'authenticity', ironically performing as the tourist/child who wants to cuddle a koala, stroke a dolphin, feed a lorikeet? Would they be just as happy with a pink plastic flamingo or a CD of whale songs? What am I saying about nature, both human and other, when I hierarchize experiences along a gradient of authenticity? And, finally, 'Is it already too late?'

The next part explores these questions by addressing the oppositions in our understanding of culture and nature, of humans and other animals, of tame and wild, of male and female, of rationality and sensuousness. I argue that we need to overcome these dualistic understandings; we need a new philosophy, a 'loving knowing' of animals and a 'respectful stewardship' of the non-human world. In this, it is important not merely to invert the dualisms that mark Western philosophy, in the way that, for example, New Age approaches do, but to combine the opposites into a new understanding and practice. As Gregory Bateson (in Berman, 1981, pp220, 238) suggests, a new mode of thought is required, based on deciphering meta-communication (communication about communication, communication beyond language). The scientific logic of either/or is replaced by a logic of both/and; wholes have properties that are more than the sum of their parts. We must build our new understanding on both scientific knowledge and the commonsense desire of many people for more communion, connection and communication. As these ideas come from often competing domains of social life, this will require us to overcome some of the black and white categories by which we classify the world, both 'ours' – culture – and 'theirs' – nature.

PART 2

The Nature of Modern Society

How are love, power, and science intertwined in the constructions of nature in the late twentieth century?... In what specific places, out of which social and intellectual histories, and with what tools is nature constructed as an object of erotic and intellectual desire?... Who may contest what the body of nature will be?

(Donna Haraway, 1992, p1)

Throughout the Middle Ages men and women continued to see the world primarily as a garment they wore rather than a collection of discrete objects they confronted.

(Morris Berman, 1981, p73)

Introduction – Part 2

One of us, we admit, speaks with snakes. ...She hears what is said, and she also hears what is not said. Oh, she is a marvellous listener!

(Susan Griffin, 1978, p180)

The concepts used in this book – 'nature', 'civilization', 'animals', 'humans' – contain the complex and contradictory detritus of their intellectual history. Culture/nature, along with mind/body, rational/emotional, male/female, self/other, civilized/primitive, is among the dualistic couplets considered to frame Western thought. Jennifer Price (1999, pp160–161) suggests that, for the postwar generation, the opposition between Nature and Artifice became an ur-boundary, used to 'mark and challenge the boundaries of aesthetics, taste, class, reality, sexuality'. In this formulation, nature is all that is authentic; the rest is all that is culture, artifice. As can readily be imagined, there are a number of problems in using these simple oppositions to carve up the known universe. For example in focusing on the human–nature divide, we possibly neglect human–machine relations. Perhaps computers are replacing pets in some households: electronic products are marketed as 'personal companions' including palm-size personal computers, handheld electronic books, the smart card (Millar, 1998, p121; Turkle, 1991, pp230, 232–233).

Raymond Williams suggested 'nature' might be the most complex word in the English language. Indeed 'Any full history of the uses of nature would be a history of a large part of human thought' (in Coates, 1998, p1). Williams defined nature as 'what man has not made, though if he made it long enough ago – a hedgerow or a desert – it will usually be included as *natural*' (in Coates, 1998, p3). Thomas Dunlap (1999, pp4–5), in his history of science and nature in the USA, Canada, Australia and New Zealand, defines nature as 'the culture's understanding of the land and the living creatures on it at the level of "unaided observation"'. It is the land as understood within culture, the picture of the land made significant in national myths and hung in art galleries. Kate Soper (1995, p11) suggests that the nature that preoccupies political movements is a 'surface' or 'lay' concept of nature. Rather than being a set of physical and biological laws, this nature is a set of utilities, a source of aesthetic pleasure, a site of intrinsic value. Social scientists are not so much interested in nature 'out there' as its meaning in human society: 'the nature of being human itself' (Fudge, 2000, p2).

Thus various things may constitute the non-natural, for example the human, the cultural, the artificial. Furthermore, the boundary line is diffuse. As Sarah Franklin et al (2000, p1) open their book: 'This book is about the power of nature, not as a static concept or even as a flexible sign, but rather as a shifting classificatory process'. Thus there is human nature (Soper, 1995, p2) and there are animal societies: 'An anthill is an artifact just as a highway is' (Elliot Sober in Bradford, 1993, p425). Nature is found in the most central business district, such as Central Park: trees, sparrows, mosquitoes, even rain and air. Many national parks have become little more than culture reserves with picnic areas and tagged animals (Bryld and Lykke, 2000, pp19, 24), while the imprint of humanity can be found in almost every corner of seemingly desolate or isolated wilderness. Nature is commodified as a 'culture of nature', expressed in purchasing 'natural' products, employing images of nature in marketing, financially supporting conservationist organizations, engaging in practices to enhance the naturalness of one's body (Macnaghten and Urry, 2000a, p1). To be in nature often requires artifacts of industry and science: boots, boats, cars, motor cycles. We imagine that we live in an increasingly speedy or fast world, comparing it with the slow rhythms of nature, but at least one thing in nature moves at the speed of light (Thrift, 2000, p41). Reproductive technologies have made 'nature and technology ... mutually substitutable'. Technology gives nature 'a helping hand'; biology generates the new technologies; reproduction is no longer a given sequence of events but an 'achievement' (Carsten, 2000, pp11–12).

Additionally, too much variety is contained in each side. It is clear that trees are not the same as dolphins, that chimpanzees are more our kin than slugs, that wilderness means something different from the ocean or a suburban garden. We speak of 'the deer' as though one deer can represent all deer (Shapiro, 1993, p3). The claim that 'Humans exploit, animals suffer' (Stone and Stone, 1986, p6) is simplistic. Perhaps some domesticated animals chose their covenant with humanity (Budiansky, 1992; Noske, 1989, p3; Lorenz, 1954; Tapper, 1988, pp52–53; Hearne, 1987). Sharks and lions are predators and killers of humans; parasites, mosquitoes and bats suck our blood. Humans displace animals, competing with them for resources like water, fresh air and food. Humans then act in a less than equal attempt to protect these very same animals, in wildlife sanctuaries or in outlawing animal cruelty (Stone and Stone, 1986, pp6–7). Attitudes to animals, to the very same animal, are often paradoxical. The pet is both loved and controlled, like a child (Szasz, 1968; Tuan, 1984, p102). The hunter admires his prey, but also destroys it. The ranger kills feral cats and culls indigenous animals (Stone and Stone, 1986, p8).

In this part of the book, I focus on the issues arising from visitors' contradictory experiences of animal destination sites, the ways in which their desires and emotions butt up against the guides' messages derived from knowledge and science; how they wrestle with their longing for the authentic experience as against their knowledge of sites as constructed encounters; how they evaluate environmental manipulation by humans, for ill and for good. While nature–culture is the 'ur-boundary' in this discussion, its realization in the contest between science and a number of non-scientific discourses is a central issue for understanding how we speak about the natural world. These non-scientific discourses include commonsense, emotional responses, spirituality and religion, even the humanities as opposed to the natural sciences. As long as academic analysis refuses to assess the limitations of science, it leaves the field open to the advocates of New Age and other new philosophies to express the search for meaning, which appears to be a quest of many of us who live in contemporary secular capitalist societies.

I will set the stage for disrupting these oppositions by considering how visitors to animal encounter sites express 'nature dispositions', a concept adapted from Bourdieu's (1984) notion of aesthetic dispositions. How did they imagine animals? What environmental attitudes do they have? What do they do in relation to experiencing and preserving the environment?

Nature dispositions

[Jellylorum Cat has again caught the mouse Elaine Stratford saved and put outside yesterday. Stratford retrieves the mouse another time and puts it in an ice cream container with some bread and apple]: So here she is trying to save a declared pest that causes mass devastation throughout Australia, making the 'natural' environment sick. But she has held it and stroked it, and she feels that, as an individual creature with feeling, it deserves to die as peacefully as she will want to. And here she is again wondering if all these anthropomorphic and anthropocentric values are appropriate. She puts Mouse, in its little plastic Vanilla Ice Cream sarcophagus, straight in the big green Council bin. Bugger the recycling.

(Stratford, 1994, pp35–39)

As a result of a nationwide survey in the US, Stephen Kellert (1978a; 1978b) developed and refined a set of orientations to animals. As Table A4.1 in Appendix 4 reveals, Kellert initially identified ten orientations towards animals, of which he selected four as the significant categories. These are:

- *neutralistic*: avoidance of animals, endorsed by 35 per cent of the population;[1]
- *humanistic*: deep emotional attachment or love for nature, but more usually domestic animals, endorsed by 35 per cent of the population;
- *moralistic*: belief in right and wrong way to treat animals, equality of all animals, endorsed by 20 per cent of the population;
- *utilitarian*: assessing animals on the basis of their usefulness for humans, endorsed by 20 per cent of the population.

My research suggests interest in a further category identified by Kellert:

- the *ecologistic*, a systematic conceptual understanding of and concern for the environment as a system, endorsed by 7 per cent of the population.

Kellert (1978a, p65) found that farmers had the highest utilitarian scores while students had the highest moralistic and ecologistic scores. The humanistic and moralistic oriented people tended to be urban-dwelling, reasonably well-educated females living on the Pacific coast; the utilitarian and neutralistic (and those who wished to dominate or had negative attitudes) tended to be older, male, less well-educated farmers living in the South (Kellert, 1989, p18).

It is important to note that one-third of the US population is, in fact, indifferent to animals and has little knowledge of animals (the neutralistic orientation). This finding challenges claims about universal human needs and desires in relation to animals, for example as proposed by the ethologist, Edward O. Wilson, in the 'biophilia' hypothesis.[2] Research reveals little concern among the public for the natural world in both Japan and the US, where survey respondents express interest in only a small range of species and landscapes, those laden with symbolic meaning. The Japanese respondents often emphasized 'control, manipulation, and contrivance' in relation to the small number of species and objects they wanted preserved (Kellert, 1993b, p63). The US respondents expressed little concern for lower life forms (Kellert, 1993b, p64), while there was widespread ignorance concerning animals, particularly among those with a neutralistic orientation, those aged under 25 and those aged over 75. For example only 54 per cent of the US sample knew that veal does not come from lamb (Kellert, 1989, pp19–20).

I adapted Kellert's orientations to suit the range of responses in my own Australian survey.[3] The utilitarian orientation was treated as the lack of any one of the three positive orientations, identified as follows:

- A humanistic orientation is a largely emotional approach, in which animals are treated as 'subjects' and are most often pets and 'cute' wild animals, for example kangaroos and dolphins. Often these animals are also constructed as cute by the media (for example Flipper), while some are morphologically childlike in appearance and so are 'baby-releasers' (Lorenz, 1954, pp104–106). People with this orientation drew on their everyday experience (of pets for example) to frame their responses to wild animals. According to James Jasper and Dorothy Nelkin (1992, p38), animal rights organization supporters are predominantly city dwellers, 60–70 per cent are women, while very many own pets. Animal rights campaigners often see scientists as corrupted by the 'system', insensitive, arrogant, narrow-minded or materialistic (Paul, 1995, p15).
- A moralistic orientation means a moral response, identifying a philosophy concerning the correct treatment of animals. 'There is a world of difference between animal love and animal rights' (Tester, 1991, p177). According to

the moralistic orientation, animals, however cute or loveable they are, should be treated equally if they share the same characteristics, for example equal sentience (Singer, 1977) or the same chance to achieve 'genetically programmed potentialities' (Stephen Clark, discussed in Tester, 1991, pp3–11, who provides a summary). Animal liberationists and animal rightists have tended to focus their concern on the ill-treatment of animals in human 'captivity', for example experimental animals, stock animals, zoo animals, rather than on pets or wild animals at large.

- A conservationist orientation (adapted from Kellert's ecologistic orientation) is a political and/or ecological response that identifies animals within an ecosystem. Mary Midgley (1983, p19) distinguishes the moral claims that might arise on behalf of individual creatures and ecological claims that arise on behalf of whole populations or species. Environmentalists are sometimes condemned for ignoring individual animals because their gaze embraces populations of species, particularly those facing extinction. The green movement has been charged with 'environmental fascism' (Tom Regan in Nash, 1990, p159; Lawrence, 1994, p183), a criticism ecofeminists also make of the wilderness movement, which positions itself as the 'manager' of the ecosystem. There are two major strands in the conservationist orientation: deep ecology and sustainable development (for example see Eder, 1996, pp177–185, who presents a synthesis of various approaches to nature, including frameworks for analysing the conservation movement). Deep ecology expresses a conviction that nature has rights independent of human needs. Sustainable development is more often accused of corruption by science and the capitalism-induced demands of human beings. Sustainable development conservationists 'mastermind' the preservation of the wild under its patronage, reproducing (if for different purposes) man in dominion over nature. Where the humanistic orientation focuses on pets, the environmentalists have been accused of ignoring animals within human settlement because they are not part of 'the environment' (Noske, 1989, p2).

The humanistic orientation is the more everyday one, referring to the treatment of animals that are close to humans. The moralistic and conservationist orientations concern the treatment of animals in more demanding categories: livestock, game and wild animals. Also, following Bourdieu (1984), one would expect various activities to be associated with these attitudes. For example people with neutralistic and utilitarian/doministic attitudes are unlikely to visit animal sites or watch wildlife films. This, of course, indicates some of the ways in which my sample is not representative of Australians as a whole. Those with humanistic attitudes are likely to want to fondle, touch and feed animals. They are more likely to be pet owners who derive pleasure from their pets. They read about animals in anthropomorphic fiction rather than in scientific journals. Those with moralistic attitudes are likely to be vegetarians and members of animal liberation groups. The conservation oriented would be members of wilderness societies, and probably engage in considerable wilderness activities, embedding their concern for animals within concern for preserving ecosystems.

The orientations of the visitors to animal encounter sites in my research are shown in Tables A3.19 and A3.20 in Appendix 3 (for a more detailed discussion of how the 'nature dispositions' were formulated, see Bulbeck, 1999). In my questionnaire, 25 questions asked respondents to express their agreement or disagreement with a range of activities in relation to animals and wilderness. As outlined in Appendix 3, answers to a selection of these questions indicated which of the above three orientations was adopted by the respondent. Three questions were litmus test questions, distinguishing between orientations: the attitude to killing feral cats, 'culling' indigenous animals like kangaroos, and breeding native animals for human consumption. Those with a humanistic orientation would disapprove of exterminating feral cats because they align them with domestic cats, animals with whom they are familiar. Those with a conservationist orientation would put the needs of the environment as an ecosystem ahead of the needs of individual members of species, and culling is sometimes necessary to protect other animals or vegetation. Farming native animals is less destructive of Australia's fragile soils than farming stock animals, and so would be endorsed by those with a conservationist orientation but not those with a humanistic or moralistic orientation. One would expect those with a moralistic orientation to disapprove just as much of farming indigenous animals as they would of farming stock animals, basing their analysis on the 'rights' of animals as sentient beings (Rolls, 1981, p408).[4]

Table A3.19 shows that those with a university education had the strongest conservationist orientation, although the results are not clear-cut for the other two orientations. The summary of nature orientations provided in Table A3.19 thus confirms one of Kellert's findings for the US in terms of educational, gender and regional differences.[5] More highly educated respondents tended to be naturalistic or moralistic while those with low education tended to have negativistic attitudes towards animals (Kellert and Berry, 1978, p75). Income differences tended in the same direction as education but were not as impressive (Kellert and Berry, 1978, p76). Table A3.17 shows the answers for individual items, revealing that those with a tertiary education tend to be more conservationist, particularly in relation to wood-chipping, preserving wilderness for its own sake, culling indigenous animals and imposing a tax to cover environmental destruction. They are also statistically more likely to oppose experimentation on animals to develop life-saving drugs (moralistic orientation). A number of statistically significant items reveal women's greater humanistic orientation, for example animal experimentation, bullfighting and hunting. However, there are some stalwart animal liberationists/moralists among those who have not completed secondary education. This group has the highest disapproval rate for bullfighting, hunting for economic reasons and experimentation on anaesthetized animals. These results support indicative evidence which contests that only highly educated people seek and enjoy naturalistic animal encounters (Urry, 1992, pp16–17); see South Australian Department of Tourism (1984, pp30–31) for high 'working class' visitation rates to Kangaroo Island, akin to Bennett et al's (1991) discovery of unexpectedly high rates of historical activity among a segment of working class visitors to museums.

Kellert (1978b, p135) found that the young and affluent were most often involved in animal-related activities, especially environmental protection and scientific lobbying. In Australia, too, economic and cultural capital combined make those with high education and income, doers, joiners and readers (see Tables A3.13 and A3.14 in Appendix 3). Table A3.14 shows that better educated people are such avid joiners that they are even more likely to be a member of a hunting association, despite their more conservationist orientation. The greatest difference is for scientific association membership and the least is for humane association membership, again suggesting that the humanistic orientation was less appealing to the better educated.

Given the significance of male–female as companion oppositions to culture–nature, one would expect gender differences in responses to animal and environmental issues. In various US surveys, men know more about animals, although 'in a somewhat emotionally detached matter-of-fact manner not found among females' (Kellert and Berry, 1978, p59); are more concerned to maintain viable habitats (Stange, 1997, p86); are more likely to be doministic, for example to be cruel to animals, while women are more likely to report cruelty (Arluke and Carter, 1997).[6] The Australian sample bears out these findings that women tend to be more humanistic or moralistic and men either more conservationist or doministic (see Tables A3.17 and A3.19, compared with Kellert's findings in Table A4.2 in Appendix 4). As one female Australian respondent, quoted above in Chapter 2, ruefully resisted the scientific conservation message: 'I love all animals but am inclined to invest them with *human* qualities'. For example, in each of the categories of experimentation on animals (1) to produce cosmetics, (2) under anaesthetic and (3) to develop life-saving drugs, women were significantly more opposed than men (Table A3.17). The focus groups were quite distressed during their discussion of animal experimentation, commenting they 'should experiment on the bastards who do it'; 'humans can fight back (to torture) whereas animals cannot'; 'what they do to animals is the same thing as what Hitler did to the Jews, they've got no choice'.

Adelma Hills (1993, p117) argues that women are more likely to connect with individual animals, to reframe wild animals – perhaps even stock animals – as pets, as something more akin to children or human kin than other. These results conform with psychoanalytic explanations that masculinity is developed in differentiation from others, whether human or natural others. Femininity, by contrast, is forged in connection with others (for example see Chodorow, 1978). Mike Bossley (interviewed on 19 December 2000) notes that the main sponsors in his 'adopt-a-dolphin scheme' are '90 per cent women, and of those, 90 per cent would be teenage girls from age 15 to 18, almost all ... the lower socioeconomic groups'. Such a gender bias is not so noticeable in relation to animal sponsorship at the Adelaide Zoo, where 59 per cent of new sponsors were female and 41 per cent were male for the period March 1998 to December 1999 (extracted from reports in 1998 and 1999 issues of Royal Zoological Society of South Australia Incorporated, 'Zoo Times'). However, this gender balance may also reflect men's higher disposable income. Furthermore, as reported in the preceding chapters, it is clear that some men have intense emotional reactions to animals and the environment. Perhaps many disguise their responses because of the requirements of masculine performance.

Put simply, these results suggest that men and the better educated are more likely to adopt an environmental approach to the natural world, based on their greater scientific knowledge, while women and the lesser educated are more likely to adopt either a humanistic or moralistic approach, which appears to be related to an emotional empathy with animals. There is a tendency in the literature to assume that the former approach is superior, although feminist writers challenge this.

Interestingly, Kellert subsumes the spiritual or religious dimension in attitudes to animals under the moralistic orientation. The spiritual dimension is sometimes expressed as part of New Age philosophies and with reference to particular animals like dolphins, as discussed in Chapter 3. Heather Aslin (1996, pp170–172), conducting interviews with 51 members of environmental, farming, hunting and scientific organizations and running focus groups in capital cities and rural towns in south-eastern Australia, uncovered this spiritual dimension. Among Aslin's (1996, p189) members of environmental and other organizations, many talked in spiritual terms: of 'wondrous things' in the bush; a 'quasi-religious' experience (a biologist); whale watching 10 years ago 'changed my life'. Indeed, among the wildlife and other organization members and the more representative focus groups, a major constellation of responses to wildlife was fascination/wonder/spiritual. Also a significant category among the organization members was discussion of dependence/balance, responsibility/care and priceless/precious (Aslin 1996, pp182–183). The next chapter explores this gap in scientific understanding of the natural world, a sense of wonder or awe, which must perforce often be expressed in New Age and other philosophies.

4
Recapturing Lost Meanings

To the environmentalist a day can be as full of religious observance as a monk's. He can choose his food to avoid chemicals, factory-farming and blighted origin. He can reject over-elaborate packaging, conscientiously re-use plastic bags and walk or cycle rather than drive.

(Bryan Appleyard, 1993, p134)

Where has all the meaning gone?

what has for long distinguished us from the 'primitive' is the belief that we can establish the meaningfulness of our private existence in the absence of any collective cosmology or teleology. The search for spiritual fulfillment has for some time been left to the individual – who seeks it 'in the logic of childhood, dreams and desires'. Psychoanalysis is the ultimate guide in this quest.

(Kate Soper, 1990, p83)

According to Metta Bryld and Nina Lykke (2000), dolphins can be inserted into the triplet of nature–native–woman, just as Donna Haraway (1992) makes a similar argument for primates.[1] Dolphins have replaced the noble savage of early modernity as the guides to a simple, true and sacred life in harmony with nature (Bryld and Lykke, 2000, pp2–3). Several visitors to Monkey Mia suggested that dolphins communicated with them telepathically: 'It's like they put thoughts into your mind' (visitors to Monkey Mia interviewed by Sue Doye in July 1994). Trainer of the Flipper dolphin actors, Richard O'Barry (1991, pp112, 167), thought the dolphins were reading his mind, or even his soul. In 1967, O'Barry became a liberator and 'untrainer' of captive dolphins when his favourite Flipper actress died in his arms of a 'broken heart' (Bryld and Lykke, 2000, p182; Johnson, 1990, p315). Others who claim telepathic communication with dolphins include Frank Robson (1988, p113) and Timothy Wyllie (1984, pp60–61, 79).

Perhaps because of their telepathic capacities, dolphins are said to have healing effects on neurologically impaired children (Smith, 1983), the chronically depressed (Dobbs, 1992, p49), children with disabilities, 'criminal youth, substance abusers' (Muir, 2000, p14) and even the merely unhappy (Dobbs, 1992, p129) or already happy.[2] As a result, dolphin therapy is a booming business (Bryld and Lykke, 2000, p181). William McDougall, a civil engineer, and Olivia De Bergerac, a psychotherapist, management consultant and neuro-feedback trainer (interviewed in February 1997 at a Sydney-based conservation organization, Planet Ark) target workplaces with their training for 'tomorrow' that 'belongs to the dolphin: inventive, sensitive, responsible, cooperative and highly intelligent'. They offer dolphin therapy at Port Stephens, assessing the dolphin encounter with EEG machines to measure brain wave patterns, questionnaires, videos and so on.

David Nathanson (interviewed on 23 March 1989), working at the Dolphin Research Centre at Grassy Key in Florida, describes his approach as totally medical and humanistic rather than spiritual and dolphin-centred. Nathanson says, 'I love people, I also love dolphins but I do this for people. You've gotta love kids to do this. You get peed on'. Interaction with dolphins extends the children's attention span. This is the key explanatory factor for his success with children with profound learning disabilities, as far as Nathanson is concerned, although he adds that dolphins are intelligent and cooperative, while swimming may release endorphins (Nathanson, 1989, pp233, 235, 239; David Nathanson, interviewed on 23 March 1992).

The New Age cult book, *Into the Deep* (1996) by Ken Grimwood, claims that only 8 per cent of First World people can manage mind-to-mind contact with dolphins compared with 79 per cent of Australian Aborigines and certain other native populations (Bryld and Lykke, 2000, p168; see also Robson, 1988, pp79–83, and Dobbs, 1992, p11). Claims that dolphins communicate telepathically are statements that dolphins are outside civilization in the same way that the 'primitive' is beyond Western rationality. Dolphin telepathy is both inferior to Western science and knowledge and superior to Western disconnection from authenticity.

This chapter explores the ways in which Woman–Native–Nature form a (contradictory) other to Universal Man, 'the civilized, enlightened self' (Bryld and Lykke, 2000, p7; see also Soper, 1995). According to Kate Soper, nature has been represented as a woman in three ways: as virgin, lover and mother. Nature as mother *and* lover means that men who approach nature as a lover commit incest (Soper, 1995, pp103, 105). Perhaps this is why some men feel they violate nature, including Thomas Jefferson, William Wordsworth and John Montague (Soper, 1995, p104). Scientists sought 'nature out in her Concealments, and unfold[ed] her dark Mysteries', as Isaac Newton's teacher, Isaac Barrow, put it. Isaac Newton was described as 'penetrating far into the abstrusest secrets of Nature' (Easlea, 1980, pp246–248). There is a 'genuine tension' between the impulse to dominate and the impulse to be nurtured, or, as Annette Kolodny put it, the 'phallic' and 'foetal' aspects (Soper, 1995, p106). 'Feminized nature is not therefore emblematic simply of mastered nature, but also of regrets and guilts over the mastering itself; of nostalgia felt for what is lost or defiled in the very act of possession; and of the emasculating fears inspired by her awesome resistance to seduction' (Soper, 1995, p107).

Note: At the Dolphin Research Centre, Grassy Key, Florida, Nathanson works with two children at a time, a dolphin working with each child under the guidance of a trainer. Nathanson says to the child, 'say ball and you can shake flippers with the dolphin'. Rewards include feeding, touching, watching the dolphin perform tricks, swimming with the dolphin, or kissing the dolphin (Nathanson, 1989, p237). In two of the three cases on the day of my visit in March 1989, parents were overjoyed, claiming that it was the first time their children had said recognizable words.

Figure 4.1 *Dolphin Therapy*

Similarly, there are two contradictory constellations of meaning for the 'primitive' in Western culture. European culture has inherited both the notion of 'violent, in need of control ... cannibals' and of the 'noble savage', 'gentle, in tune with nature, paradisal, ideal ... what we should emulate' (Torgovnick, 1990, p3). The former image fits with social Darwinism in which European civilization stands at the apex of development. The latter idea belongs to fear or concern that Western culture has lost something authentic in its march of progress. While teleological narratives of colonialism and imperialism constructed the barbaric backward native, the Romantic tradition, repelled by the excesses of industrialization, constructed the authentic, honest, spiritually superior native. This alternative vision is most often associated with Jean-Jacques Rousseau's *locus classicus* on the 'noble savage', written in 1755 (Torgovnick, 1998, p13). Such romanticism was comfortably accommodated as long as Europeans felt their pity described a dying race (Mulvey, 1987, p259).[3]

From a psychoanalytic perspective, the role of the 'primitive' in modern consciousness is to signal the desired but repressed 'other'. Rational heterosexual adult man only achieves his maturity by repressing his desire for the feminine: the mother, oceanic consciousness, primitive unbridled emotions, connection with the supernatural and embodied sensual experiences (Torgovnick, 1998, pp14–15, 122; Price, 1989, pp40, 50). Clearly, this analysis owes a debt to both Jung and Freud who, in different ways, explored the price civilization exacts on the psyche.

Deracinated Westerners seek to recapture their lost sense of direction, their authenticity, through indigenous peoples' spirituality rendered in New Age or fundamentalist religions, Jungian psychology and self-help movements (Lattas, 1992, pp45–46) and a romanticized experience of nature and animals. That the gates all open onto the same utopia is suggested by the connections between these strategies. Jung and indigenous spirituality are grist to the New Age mill. Indigenous people are sometimes imagined as the original ecologists, exemplars for modern environmentalists. Ecofeminism[4] aligns subjugated woman with exploited nature under patriarchy (Ynestra King in Sturgeon, 1997, p67) and celebrates 'native' women as ecologists. Ecofeminists also look to those Third World women thought to embody appropriate care of the earth, an 'othering' expressed in Lohmann's notion of 'Green Orientalism' (Kalland and Asquith, 1997, p25). Pre-Christian European pagan women provide exemplars both for New Age spiritualists and ecofeminists. The national parks movement grew out of romanticism's rejection of industrialization. Nature-worship is, for some, a new religion (Appleyard, 1993, pp130–133). This chapter explores the ways some Westerners seek 'self-health' (Franklin et al, 2000, p13) in nature, to assess the claim that the construction of an 'authentic' untouched nature has become a locus of meaning and cradle of healing for Western humanity.

Woman–native–nature

> a discourse dissolving the 'West' and its highest product – the one who is not animal, barbarian, or woman; man, that is, the author of a cosmos called history.
>
> (Haraway, 1991, p156)

Susan Griffin (1978, p38), in *Woman and Nature: The Roaring Inside Her*, suggests that women, animals and primitive peoples are assumed to have less libido, less ego, and less awareness of the necessities of life. This section explores the overlapping natures of native, nature and woman, using the example of New Age spirituality.

New Age Spirituality

> One image is imprinted indelibly in my mind – an image of almost ten years ago when feminism was a fresh force raging in my spirit.

Travelling up the island, enjoying the voluptuously feminine shapes, the alluring contours and creases of the landscape, I suddenly encountered a scene of abysmal ugliness and grief. The leaking, stark clay scars of a formerly green and forested hillside, red soil exposed like bleeding viscera across a gaping, jagged gash of earth.

(Ngahuia Te Awekotuku, 1991, p69)

It is sometimes claimed that ancient matriarchal religions as well as contemporary pantheisic religions, like Hinduism, Shinto, Buddhism and Taoism, maintain permeable borders between human and natural worlds (Ryder, 1989, pp25–26; Kaplan and Talbot, 1983, p164; Nash, 1973, pp20–21; Cesaresco, 1909, pp19, 266). According to this story, matriarchal antecedents were repressed by the rise of patriarchal monotheistic religions (see Spretnak, 1990; Eisler, 1988; Goodison, 1990; Gimbutas, 1989 and the critiques of one prop for ancient matriarchies, the Venus figurines: Nelson, 1993; Russell, 1993, pp95–96). The turn to goddess worship is a return to these ancient matriarchies.

Despite its title, the 'New Age', the Age of Aquarius, which embraces yoga, holistic healing, veganism, contact with UFOs or angels, wilderness trips, self-help and Jungian psychology, goddess revivals and the mythopoetic men's movement, has precedents as far back as theosophy in the 1890s (Roe, 1998, pp170, 185).[5] Even so, there has been a recent explosion in the publication of books with 'soul' or 'goddess' in the title (Cimino and Lattin, 1998, p28). In one US survey, 15 per cent of respondents described themselves as holding some New Age beliefs and another 12 per cent expressed interest in learning more (Wuthnow, 1998, p123). It is estimated that there are now more than 200,000 adherents to Wicca and other related 'neopagan' faiths in the US, making Goddess spirituality the fastest growing religion in the country (Allen, 2001, p18). 'New Age spirituality' or the 'Goddess movement' has attracted largely white, heterosexual, tertiary educated women, although advocates are disproportionately lesbian or bisexual, often marginally employed and come from unconventional religious backgrounds (Eller, 1993, pp58, 7–8, 20–21, 30, 70–79, 231–232 for North America; Puttick, 1997, p206 for Britain). Capturing both its ubiquity and its amorphousness, Marianna Torgovnick (1998, p172) suggests that 'The New Age seems to be everywhere but continues to elude specific definition'. However, perhaps all the practices share a commitment to discovering how to integrate body, mind and spirit with the powers of the universe (Torgovnick, 1998, p173).

Some Australian 'New Agers' seek the 'soul' in Aboriginal spirituality. The President of the New South Wales Aboriginal Education Consultative Group and member of the Wiradjuri nation, Linda Burney (1994, p23), suggests that New Age interest in indigenous spirituality may be a form of denial concerning the reality of colonial relations (see also Morton, 1993, p39; Lattas, 1992, p45 for Australia; Highwater, 1981, p203 for the US). 'The "primitivist" yearns for an arrangement in which Aboriginal people have spiritual beliefs (sacredness) but no property rights' (Gelder and Jacobs, 1998, p64; see also Donaldson, 1999, p677). The appropriation of rituals by New Age practitioners alongside their refusal to engage in any political actions has angered many indigenous people (see Torgovnick, 1998, p187 for the US; Helena Gulash in Cuthbert and Grossman, 1997, pp50–51, 56–57 for Australia). This is not to say that all spiritualists lack political interest, which ranges from Starhawk's nature religion to the young ferals in Australia.[6]

Many indigenous writers are also critical of the bowdlerized mish-mash of native spiritual beliefs and practices that are used by New Age practitioners (for example Donaldson, 1999; see also Torgovnick, 1998, pp209–210). This 'nostalgia for the Native That Never Was' desires an innately spiritual being living in perfect egalitarian harmony who 'redresses all the wrongs of patriarchal capitalism' (Donaldson, 1999, p683). It has been argued that white women cannot understand the symbols of another culture 'grown on different soil, under a different sky within the nexus of different spirits', whether Native American spirits or Anglo-Saxon goddesses (Paula Gunn Allen in Gaard, 1993, p307). Indeed, the belief that traditions from other cultures can be appropriated is a peculiarly Western notion, based on our reverence for property relations rather than for things spiritual. Indian traditions and ideas are 'put in the service of a thoroughly modern worldview that takes the self as a thing to be owned, cultivated, and coddled' (Torgovnick, 1998, p176). One purchases spirituality, in art and artifacts or in pilgrimages to sacred places. New Age pilgrimages listed in the *Pilgrim's Guide to Planet Earth* include Uluru, Mt Fuji, Stonehenge, the Pyramids and the Easter Island statues, producing potential conflicts over usage and homage, for example between the Aboriginal custodians of Uluru and New Age pilgrims (Marcus, 1997, p41). Such consumption of grace assumes that knowledge is not embedded in relationships, tied to place nor does it involve responsibilities to others (Smith, 1999, p101). The Western conception of the self is quite different from the construction of identity embedded in community and cosmos (Allen, 1986, pp62–63; see also Willis, 1990, p7; Highwater, 1981, p67). Furthermore, New Age spirituality often amounts only to reassurance: one goes on doing what one is already doing but feels better about it (Wuthnow, 1998, p101).

Karl Marx (1965, p72) long ago attacked the alienation produced by commodity fetishism in capitalism, the valuing of things as persons and persons only as things. Today, commodity fetishism has become so entrenched that even critiques of capitalism are recycled in a commodified form. This includes the marketing of environmentally friendly goods, nostalgia in the tourist industry, and an enormous range of New Age products (Tacey, 1995, p132; Eastwood, 2000, pp135–136; Coates, 1998, p9). Nature itself is commodified when 'mountains, deserts, birds' are used to 'hawk soda, jeans, makeup, beer' and a host of other commodities that have very little obvious connection with nature (Price, 1999, p236). Nature Company stores personnel in the US describe their

For those who appreciate speed.

Notes: (top) Cheetahs suggest speed in printing by Brother International (Aust) Pty Ltd: 'For those who appreciate speed: Brother'; photography by Andrew Gardner; (bottom) Aboriginal art has become popular in Australia, fetching high prices and adorning public buildings such as Parliament House in Canberra and a Qantas jumbo jet painted with the Aboriginal design, Wunala Dreaming (Qantas, 1994, p8, image courtesy of Qantas; see also Nicoll, 1993, pp705, 710).

Figure 4.2 *Advertising Nature and Indigenous Themes*

products terms like 'simplicity', 'leisure', 'adventure', 'authenticity'. These products provide relief from 'the urbanism, anonymity, commercialism, technological control, complexity, white-collar work, artifice and alienation of the postwar era' (Price, 1999, p175). The aim of the products is that customers '*feel good* about themselves and the world in which they live [emphasis added by Price]' (Price, 1999, p178). The few human images and voices that are included are confined to indigenous people, revealing the alignment of nature and native (Price, 1999, pp172–175).

Fourth World Peoples: The 'Original' Ecologists?

We Ngarinyin are developing up a Bush University to take people into our country, to teach them the meaning of Relationship in land. We are doing this because we are sorry for people who are looking for meaning

in their lives, and are lost to their identity. We want to share our
knowledge and our lives with them... When they are grounded in the
real world which is the Earth, they become happy... This is our gift.

(Kamilia Council and its Chair, Paddy Neowarra, 1997, p16)

[Osprey] is actually welding western and Aboriginal men of high
degree of knowledge – wisdom of the elders is exactly what we are
doing.

(Mike Bossley, interviewed by telephone on 2 January 1993)

How did hunter-gatherers understand and respond to the natural world? Did
they cower close to the brief protection of their campfires, fearing the animals,
whose speed, sight and strength defeated human intelligence (Nash, 1973, px)?
Or did they express respect, reverence, love, for the wild world from which they
were hardly a species apart? Did hunters exchange a relatively easy life full of
play and ritual for the hard labour of the farmer and herder (see Clutton-Brock,
1999, pp63–64)? There are two contradictory tales here: an ascent of humanity
towards civilization or a descent of humanity away from the meaning-filled life
of people in tune with their environment.

Wilderness was poetically defined (if also in sexist terms) in the 1964 US
Wilderness Act as a place where 'man himself is a visitor and does not remain',
a place offering 'outstanding opportunities for solitude' (Vest, 1987, p303). The
Australian Conservation Foundation (ACF) describes wilderness as 'a large
tract of pristine country ... substantially unmodified by humans and their
works' (in Davis, 1989, p11). In the eyes of Aboriginal people, an
understanding of wilderness as pristine appears little different to the notion of
terra nullius or a land empty of people, by which the British crown justified its
accession of Australia, US national park officials sought to remove Indians
from the parks (Spence, 1999), as did the South African government the local
Africans (Kirschenblatt-Gimblett, 1998, p163). More recently, the World
Conservation Society has been attacked for supporting the expulsion and
enslavement of the Karen people in Burma to create the Myinmoletkat Nature
Reserve (Levy et al, 1997, p5). An attempt to repopulate the wilderness in Perth
Zoo's African savannah actually suggests the inappropriateness of humans on
the African plains: 'To add to the verisimilitude, there is a recreation of an
African village nearby. Visitors, particularly young ones, won't be duped into
thinking the savannah is devoid of human *encroachment*' (Williams, 1993, p94,
italics mine; see also Laurie, 1994, p66).

The celebrated statement by Chief Seattle in 1854 concerning the
connectedness of all things and lamenting the demise of humanity for refusing
to recognize this truth is famous both for its sudden popularity among
conservation groups and its lack of authenticity (Knudtson and Suzuki, 1992,
pxvi). In his contemporary garb, Rousseau's 'noble savage' has become 'Eco-
Indians' or Indians as 'ecological gurus' (Howard Harrod in Stange, 1997,

p100). Indigenous people possess the 'wisdom of the elders', living in a natural balance with the land (for example see Accoom, 1992, pp29–30; Highwater, 1981, p203; Sackett, 1991, p241; Martin, 1978, p15). Indigenous peoples have become high priests of meaning and wisdom in a fractured amoral world. 'Perhaps the earliest [Australian] writer to promulgate the idea of the Aborigine as an ecological angel was Mary Gilmore, in *Old Days, Old Ways* (1933)' (Poppenbeek, 1994, p35). More recently, a spate of widely publicized works sought to confer the status of scientific truths on indigenous knowledge. These books include *The Wisdom of the Elders*, by Peter Knudtson and David Suzuki (1992), *Millenium: Tribal Wisdom and the Modern World* by David Maybury-Lewis (1992), also made into a television series (funded by Boston Television, the Body Shop and Cultural Revival), *Voices of the First Day* by Robert Lawlor (1991) and *Messengers of the Gods* by James Cowan (1993). It is interesting that these authors find it necessary to 'prove' the value of indigenous knowledge by reference to scientific discoveries.

Once passing this test, indigenous knowledge is actually superior to Western science. Indigenous people have 'wisdom' rather than the mere factual knowledge of 'science'. Cowan (1993, p3) says we must turn to 'this earth-wisdom possessed by traditional people throughout the world' (see also Maybury-Lewis, 1992, p234). Wisdom indicates 'awe' and 'wonder' (Cowan, 1993, p204; Knudtson and Suzuki, 1992, p13), the sense of the 'interconnectedness' of all life (known to science as 'ecology') (Knudtson and Suzuki, 1992, p3; see also Maybury-Lewis, 1992, p180; Lines, 1991, p3). By contrast, science is attacked for its false separation of intellect from emotion (Knudtson and Suzuki, 1992, p183).

Given that hunter-gatherers, by definition, are meat eaters, their spiritual connections with the land are presumably also expressed in relation to the animals they kill. To many New Agers, with their love of dolphins, this might seem contradictory. Some commentators argue that the tension is and has been resolved by hunter-gatherers with a respectful, even sacred, relationship with their game. 'The relationship was full of responsibilities – to the animals, to himself, and to his family' (Lopez, 1986, p199). Eskimos do not grasp that animals are objects to Westerners and 'have difficulty in imagining themselves entirely removed from the world of animals' (Lopez, 1986, p200). The Waswanipi say a successful kill is partly due to the moose or beaver or whitefish willingly laying down its life so the Waswanipi can live (Knudtson and Suzuki, 1992, p87; see also Lawlor, 1991, p303). Rituals before the hunt and at the kill 'excused' and explained hunting and eating the animals, overcoming the 'cognitive dissonance' of cannibalism (Oelschlaeger, 1991, p17; see also McNeely and Wachtel, 1988, pp161–162; Highwater, 1981, p83; Regan, 1982, pp216, 219, 222).

This respectful attitude to hunted game contradicts Europeans' eyewitness accounts of cruelty and wastage (Martin, 1978, pp164–165). While some commentators suggest that Europeans observed indigenous hunters already corrupted by European attitudes to environmental destruction, or adrift in the wake of decimation by disease and invaders (Martin, 1978), archaeological evidence indicates that exploitative relations with nature preceded white contact in most locations, although not Australia (Flannery, 1994, pp206–207; Lourandos, 1997, pp109–110). The truth of this archaeological debate is less significant than its contemporary meaning, the investment by some in the white environmental movement in their version of the 'noble savage' (Christopher Anderson, 1994, p44; Torgovnick, 1998, pp154–155; Barsh, 1990, p729).

Indeed, some indigenous people draw on the trope of the original ecologist, and not without justification, given the impact of white settlement. Furthermore, to some extent, indigenous people are forced into the straitjacket of the 'noble savage' because the only alternative is barbaric primitive. This is forcefully demonstrated in Roger Sandall's (2001, pp106, 176, 152–155) critique of 'culture cultists' and 'designer tribalism'. He claims that 'the difference between London today and the world inhabited by the Ice Man 5000 years ago in Europe can be studied on a hundred different scales'. 'The curative claims of shamanism are idealized, not because people take them seriously or intend to consult shamans rather than the nearest doctor', but because 'culture cultists' are intent on demeaning Western 'civilization' and arguing it is a 'culture' no better than any of the myriad cultures around the globe. Indigenous people appear to have little choice but either to accept that they are the barbaric cannibals that Sandall and his ilk claim them to be or to don the mantle of 'noble savage' conferred by designer tribalism. Success in pursuing their own agenda, for example land rights, will be more likely if indigenous people can conform to preconceptions found in dominant society and which, at least partially, support their aims. Furthermore, it is likely that indigenous people's understanding of their ecological past is influenced by both indigenous and settler conceptions and knowledge, including anthropological and historical records (During, 1991, p34).

Australian environmentalists have, on the whole, accepted that notions of wilderness as empty land are abusive to Aboriginal people. Now they are grappling with the logical outcome of that understanding, their need to accept Aboriginal people's 'inalienable full title to terrestrial and marine resources' and proper consultation with Aboriginal communities 'in the identification, declaration and management of land for nature conservation' (Green Groups, 1993, no page numbers). This statement is premised on the belief that 'For thousands of years, Australian Aboriginal people have been living in harmony with their natural environment' as 'an old and infinitely wise culture'. Environmentalists have moved beyond this utopian vision to be more aware that there will be conflicts, sometimes generated by the conditions of poverty and inadequate health care for Aboriginal people with few economic opportunities (Evans, 1997, pp12, 13). In contemporary Aboriginal settlements, these limitations often cause overuse of resources, although this might not be desired by Aboriginal groups themselves (Hill, 1992, p271; see also Sackett, 1991, p243).

Notes: (left) The Wilderness Society works with the local Aboriginal people in the campaign for Cape York Wilderness: cover photograph, Wilderness News, number 134, 1993, © The Wilderness Society; (right) 'Wilderness: we call it home', repudiating the application of the *terra nullius* concept to understandings of wilderness in Australia; photograph courtesy of photographer, David Tatnall.

Figure 4.3 *Repopulating the Wilderness*

Despite the joint agreement in 1993, there remain those in the movement who disapprove of Aboriginal hunting in national parks (Hutton and Connors, 1999, p252; Langton, 1995, pp16, 17; see Tables A3.17 and A318 in Appendix 3 for the survey results on this issue), indicating both European Australians' preference for the 'noble savage' and their lack of trust in Aboriginal people armed with guns and assisted by speed boats (Anderson, 1994, p45). Barry Lopez (1986, p148–149) notes that indigenous autonomy means that the voices of Eskimo hunters must be included in the decision-making bodies that set kill quotas, while Eskimos also need assistance in devising hunting behaviour more consistent with the power and reach of modern weapons (see for Australia, Omeenyo, 1992, p31, and Baird, 1992, p34).

Aboriginal tourist guides

While Indigenous people are written into wilderness stories as the original ecologists who hunt game and love the land even more reverentially than do white hunters, only about 10 per cent of the Australian ecotours and nature-based holidays surveyed by Janet Richardson (1993) explored Aboriginal culture, while only 5 per cent had Aboriginal guides. Two well known national parks, Uluru and Kakadu, are under joint management regimes with traditional Aboriginal owners (Langton, 1995, p16), while a dozen parks are either Aboriginal-owned or jointly managed with the National Parks and Wildlife Service (for example four in South Australia) (Young, 1995, pp200–201). Uluru, 'Australia's geographic and spiritual or emotional centre' (McGrath, 1991, p115), is an icon for white Australians and tourists, as Ayers Rock, the biggest rock in the world. There are problems of managing differing expectations between Aboriginal custodians and non-indigenous visitors, the

Notes: Irian Jaya was described in an Australian newspaper as 'My own cannibal paradise' (Mullins, 1992, p8, text courtesy of News Limited); the Northern Territory government has long promoted Aboriginal cultural tourism. The first and, for many years, only Aboriginal cultural tour brochure was the Northern Territory's 'Come Share Our Culture: A Guide to Australia's Northern Territory Aboriginal Tours, Arts and Crafts'. The brochure conveys the message of personal contact with Aboriginal people and participation in Aboriginal traditions (Zeppel, 2000, p31). A subsequent brochure, 'Experience Aboriginal Culture in Australia's Northern Territory' (1997) replaces 'come share our culture' with 'come share our country' and features direct quotations from landowners on the meanings attached to their Dreaming sites and country (Zeppel, 1998, p29). (top and middle) In the photographs, Aboriginal tour guides display 'bush tucker' and Tiwi culture (photographs courtesy of the Northern Territory Tourist Commission); (bottom) Aboriginal tour guide, Clem, on the Great Australian Bight.

Figure 4.4 *From 'Noble Savage' to Indigenous Tour Guide*

best known being that traditional owners do not want visitors to climb the rock (the top of the rock is for Aboriginal men only) (Central Land Council et al, 1987, p11).

Aboriginal tourist guides are often employed as the translators between culture (white tourists) and nature (the land). Primitives 'represent a real and timeless present – the impossible compound tense of colonizing discourse' which denies both the history which destroyed their particular past, and hurries forward to the future which recreates them as tourist spectacle (Haraway, 1992, pp194–195). A Northern Territory tourist pamphlet notes 'these tours are very special, for your guide will have had up to 40,000 years of training in Aboriginal culture, lore and the land' (Northern Territory Tourist Commission, 1993, p3). As Maria Mies (1993, p133) puts it, Westerners do not yearn for the nature that surrounds them, but for 'backward, exotic, distant and dangerous, the nature of Asia, Africa, South America'. In aligning them with nature, tourists expect their indigenous guides and translators to be ecologically sound nature-lovers, just as David Suzuki and others have described them. They are not impressed by guides in Africa more interested in describing game as edible food than in being a prop to the 'vision quest' for the 'outstanding' inward experience (Almagor, 1985, pp39–40). They are not amused when they think Aborigines have substituted road-killed kangaroo for traditionally hunted game (Zeppel, 1998, p33). The local Canadian Indian communities on Prince Edward Island distressed the local tour operators when they claimed that billboards and abandoned cars were 'part of their culture' (Wilson, 1992, p48).

The only animal encounter site in my survey that included an Indigenous element was the trip to the Great Australian Bight, organized by Osprey. South Australia's first Indigenous tourism brochure, *The South Australian Aboriginal Tourism Experience* (1996), features a 'Mirning elder calling whales' on the Nullabor cliffs (quoted in Zeppel, 1998, p32). Tours combine Aboriginal and whitefella teaching techniques at Aboriginal request: 'they appreciate we have things to offer, but they have a lot more' (interview with Iain Greenwood, director of Osprey Wildlife Expeditions, on 22 July 1993). The whale calling is done either by a Mirning elder or Iain Greenwood, Osprey's director, who has been taught by a Mirning elder (Osprey Wildlife Expeditions, 1992, p2). Iain uses a didgeridoo to call the whales, 'and, occasionally, the whales will respond'. He twirls and twists the didgeridoo as the whales circle clockwise and then anticlockwise in response, something they will not do if someone else manipulates the didgeridoo (Armstrong, 1992, p45). Iain Greenwood (interviewed on 22 July 1993) says the communication is achieved through telepathy, and only enhanced by visual and sound cues. The communication can be 'healing'. It is 'magic', with the 'realization from the human that the whale knows you're there and acknowledges it' (interview with Iain Greenwood on 22 July 1993). Fern Hames, expedition coordinator for scientific research assistance expeditions, which monitor the behaviour of Southern Right whales, says 'It's very, very powerful. Many people do describe it as a life-changing experience'

(Illing, 1994, p16). Such tales put pressure on Clem, the Aboriginal guide on the tour I accompanied, to call the whales, Iain not being with us at the head of the Bight. On one day, a calf came barrelling straight over to Clem as he stood at the cliff edge and swam along the shoreline as Clem moved along the cliff. However, on another day, no whales came when Clem went over to the cliff edge, and Clem stopped going to look over the cliffs.

On an earlier day in the tour, we spent some time with Iain Greenwood, who told us things of a mystical bent. Iain has a medicine stick, made for him by an Aboriginal elder, which represents a serpent climbing a tree. The stick is a magical length, which Iain demonstrated by placing it over rock arrangements or in bends of trees at sacred sites. Iain believes that Mirning spirituality may be connected with Egyptian, Druid and American Indian beliefs, while Aboriginal women can fly on their sticks. An elder has an altered state of consciousness, akin to the use of hallucinogenic drugs. White people so repress our capacities in this direction that we rarely feel these parts of ourselves (Iain Greenwood, lecture, 3 October 1993). Iain also claimed that Mirning people carried their whale dreaming on their bodies, in the form of beauty spots shaped like whales or a serpent's tooth. Indeed, Clem had a birthmark on his torso, a largish and pale whale-shaped spot. Iain has been documenting these birthmarks as potential evidence of Mirning people's knowledge of genetic engineering or the structure of DNA (interviewed on 22 July 1993). The birthmark is echoed by the Mirning people across their country, which has been marked with stone arrangements in the shape of whales. For those who strain towards rationality, such stories are discomforting and likely to be rejected; someone in my group unkindly suggested that Iain smoked a lot of hash.

'Repressive authenticity' means that urban Aborigines are somehow deemed as inauthentic, not real Aborigines (Bayet, 1994, p31; Langton, 1995, p16). 'True' Aborigines do not desire capitalist commodities, monetary income or political power. It is not acceptable for indigenous people to receive mining royalties (Johnston, 1991, p403). Even more horrifyingly, some Indians want to collect fees by allowing nuclear waste to be stored on their land (such an outcome allowing waste depositors to avoid state environmental laws) (Coates, 1998, p91). Indigenous people are thought to be more suited to projects that grow or harvest bush tucker, for example crocodile or emu farming (Wilson et al, 1992), or bush medicines like melaleuca or tea tree oil. It could be argued that Aborigines will only have found their rightful place in tourism when they can be imagined as tourists themselves,[7] as bilingual tour guides for a Japanese group, and as the minister of tourism, as easily as the interpreter of rock art or the bush tucker guide.

Given the native–nature couplet, New Age dolphins are often assumed to have particular affinity with indigenous people.[8] Indeed, there are many documented cases of cooperative fishing between cetaceans and humans, not only Australasian indigenous people but also reported for Europe, Africa, India, China and Brazil (Alpers, 1960, p154). The stories from around the globe and across the ages generally consist of the fishermen 'calling' the dolphins by beating the water or side of the boat and the dolphins and the humans encircling the fish between them (Alpers, 1960, p150). In an article published in 1926, Heber Longman collected all eight published references to the Moreton Bay Aborigines' cooperation with dolphins in hunting mullet (Orams, 1995, pp83–85 and Montagu, 1963, p19 who are drawing on Alpers' study). The Aborigines were witnessed in 1856 calling the dolphins by splashing the water with their spears. The dolphins drove the mullet before them into hand nets, later taking fish from the end of a spear held out to them (Alpers, 1960, p152). Shane, a member of the Quandamooka people of Moreton Bay, told me (on 25 April 1997 at the dig on Peel Island organized by Annie Ross) that he had seen his father and others use dolphins to herd mullet into the shore. After the herding was finished, each pod of dolphins came up to their associated Quandamooka family group and Aborigines and dolphins shared the catch half and half. Let me turn now, therefore, to the connections forged with animals through hunting.

The masculinity of hunting

> Hunting was a total experience... The outdoors... And the killing, ... the killing was the best part. It was the dying I couldn't take.
>
> (Fleishman, in *Northern Exposure*, screened on Channel 10, 22 April 1993, after wounding a bird which he later attempted to save by putting its wing in a sling)

> Skin out the neck until the ears are reached then proceed with utmost care and detach the ears... Take care not to cut into the eyelids as it may spoil some of the features of your trophy. The best way is to push your index finger on the eye itself from the outside and place your thumb on the flesh side and use it to pull the skin away from the bone while skinning.
>
> ('Preparing a Trophy Head in the Bush', *Archery Action*, 1986, pp8–9 at 9)

Where the Western woman's path to the other lies through New Age spirituality or ecofeminism, men are more likely to find their wild selves through wilderness experiences, whether hunting or saving national parks. These activities also have their resonances with the imagined native, the 'original ecologist' who hunts his game with awe and reverence.

Jean-Jacques Rousseau believed that wild animals were stronger and more admirable than their domesticated descendants. 'It is the same with man himself: as he becomes a creature of society and a slave, he becomes weak, fearful and servile' (in Thacker, 1983, p97). The masculinity of hunting belongs to a tradition that poses the city and its comforts as dangerously feminizing. As the frontier almost disappeared, it was preserved in the safe microcosm of hunting: the Boy Scouts, the Woodcraft Indians, the Sons of Daniel Boone and other outdoors movements (Nash, 1973, pp147–148; Huhndorf, 2001, pp70–73), championed by President Theodore Roosevelt (Nash, 1973, p149; Wilson, 1992, p251). With its purpose of overcoming the 'degeneracy of the city', the Boy Scout movement rapidly became the largest youth organization in the US (Huhndorf, 2001, p73).

The *sine qua non* of masculine outdoor activities is hunting big, dangerous and wily game worthy of a man's opposition. The noblest quarry is male, and fights tenaciously to the end (Ritvo, 1987, p266; Haraway, 1992, p33). By contrast, most animals bred for eating are female (Adams, 1990, p73). Many feminists oppose hunting as killing (as do many women: see Table A3.17 in Appendix 3). Some hunters equate the rape of women with the killing of animals (Adams, 1994, p151; see also Masson and McCarthy, 1996, p50; King, 1991, p75). Paul Shepard (1973, p173) talks about the 'woman-prey' and his love for her: 'The ecstatic consummation of this love is the killing itself'. Furthermore, some hunters engage in 'commodified bear-hunting' or hunting at ranches stocked with animals one has ordered (Franklin, 1999, p110). Such unskilled men are decried by romantic hunters, just as would be a mountaineer who used aluminium ladders and pneumatic drills to scale cliffs: 'he violated the mountain and betrayed the love of nature that should be at the heart of mountaineering' (Gaita, 2002, p150).

But other hunters claim respect for their game and desire to preserve a land they come to love and know intimately. Andy Russell, well known conservationist in Alberta and 'top rifle big bore shot in Alberta 1953' (Andy Russell, interviewed on 17 June 1992), spent his adult life as a trapper, broncobuster, hunter, rancher, professional guide, and, in the early 1990s, when I interviewed him, was a fulltime author and photographer (Russell, 1984, p246). Russell suggests

> it's a sense of respect for the game which you're hunting... You honour
> an animal which you hunt. The Indians in the old days, you know,
> when they killed something, they actually said a prayer asking
> forgiveness for taking their life... We come along, and we shoot any
> old damn thing and call the Indians uncivilized savages.
>
> (Andy Russell, interviewed on 17 June 1992)

Hunting is not a rational experience; rather it is intensely sensual, involving identification with the hunted prey as well as immersion in the land. Barry Lopez says, 'To hunt means to have the land around you like clothing' (Lopez, 1986, pp199–200). In Japan, the famous bear hunter, Fujiwara Chōtarō, calls hunting 'ascetic training for the heart' and 'the only path to enlightenment' (Knight, 2000a, p154). Unlike the tourist, whose gaze merely slides across the landscape (Shepard, 1973, p147), the attentiveness of the hunter is a 'premodern' involvement, usually with a specific natural location, an embodied experience involving sound, taste, smell, touch, rather than just the sight on which the tourist largely relies, surrounded by the chatter and noise of other tourists (Franklin, 2001, pp65–66, 58). Like meditation, this attention tries to be at all points without attending to any one thing (Turner, 1996, pp26–27). Hunting is a return to 'that bitter impulse that we have inherited from primitive man', 'rehabilitating that part of himself which is still an animal' (Ortega y Gasset, 1972, p139).

Paul Shephard (1973, pp100–101, 30) goes further, claiming that 'The mystery of life does not reveal its secrets to bean-eaters' (Shepard, 1973, p152). Hunters deplore the hypocrisy of meat-eating animal lovers. There is more honour and honesty to be had from only eating that which one has killed, be it in the hunt, on the farm (Budiansky, 1992, ppvi–vii), or even in the humble backyard chook run (Gaynor, 1999, p30). Indeed, most of those who disapprove of hunting also eat meat, if Table A3.17 in Appendix 3 is a guide to more general attitudes.

Hunters also make much of their contribution to conservation, for example in culling and restoring the ecological balance, in the information they provide for environmental programmes, in their use of barbless hooks or fish friendly nets (Franklin, 1999, pp110, 115–116, 119–120). Given this love of land and prey, perhaps it is not surprising that some hunters, like Andy Russell and Aldo Leopold, find sympathy replaces empathy (Serpell, 1986, p142) and hunters become conservationists. Andy Russell says:

> I'd like to see the wilderness preserved, instead of just wasted like it's been ... I mean we don't know it yet, but we are thoroughly dependent on it and if we ever lose our wilderness completely we're going with it... It's like racial discrimination – environmental discrimination.
>
> (Andy Russell, 17 June 1992)

Dualistic constructions of self and other also deform understandings of Western culture, emptying it of spirituality and emotion,[9] denying the West's 'mystical traditions' (Torgovnick, 1998, p5), expressed not only in hunting, but also in artistic imaginaries, including cyborgs, mermaids and satyrs (Torgovnick, 1998, p18). Western practices that amplify the passions include dance, theatre, mime, art, massage therapy, body–mind centring (Thrift, 2000, p45). Indeed the longevity of the romantic tradition suggests a centuries-old desire among Westerners for tactile and emotional experiences.

Tourism and the Romantic movement

The Romantics sought solace and spiritual recuperation in the countryside, which they reconfigured from farmed land to landscape. The landscape is painted by an observer, perhaps with remote figures of humans working in the distance (Fuller, 1988, p19, 26).[10] The romantic orientation was no mean feat, given that the countryside 'was at the time rich with odours of farm animals, sewage, rotting vegetables, smoke and especially foul-smelling stagnant water' (Macnaghten and Urry, 2000a, p5).

Almost no history of tourism fails to locate its origins in the romantic movement's search for the sublime in nature. Indeed Patricia Jasen (1995, p11) wonders if it is too 'farfetched' to argue that 'romanticism's association between images, commodities, feelings, and personal fulfillment was a vital contributing factor to the development of consumer capitalism, including the growth of the tourist industry'. The Romantic movement extended or transferred 'feelings formerly associated with religious experience to the secular realm, to imbue "wild nature" with new meaning and value' (Jasen, 1995, p7). Contra Dean MacCannell's notion that the angst-ridden tourist has been with us for only a few decades, Jasen (1995, p6), in her analysis of nature-oriented tourism in Ontario from 1790 to 1914, argues that, for at least 200 years, the tourism industry has stirred romantic sensibility with 'oldness': ruins, graveyards and quaintly dressed people apparently doomed to extinction, whether Scottish crofters or indigenous villagers (Jasen, 1995, p10).

Nature's cathedrals

Think of our life in nature, – daily to be shown matter, to come in contact with it, – rocks, trees, wind on our cheeks! the solid earth! the actual world! the common sense! Contact! Contact! Who are we? Where are we?

(Henry David Thoreau in Oelschlaeger, 1991, p141)

The romantic tradition 'was characteristically one of intense personal involvement with and aesthetic response to nature' (Oelschlaeger, 1991, p111). Solitude, the capacity of the *individual*, was also essential (Thomas, 1983, p268). The third Earl of Shaftsbury said in 1709, 'The Wildness pleases, we seem to live alone with Nature. We view her in her inmost recesses' (in Julia Horne, 1991, p87). Scenery had become the 'cathedrals of the modern world', to the American Charles Eliot in 1896 (in Thomas, 1983, pp260, 269). The authenticity of nature was often represented in visual, visceral or tactile experiences (Nash, 1973, p126). Henry David Thoreau described 'a delicious evening, when the whole body is one sense, and imbibes delight through every pore' (in Oelschlaeger, 1991, p158).

Wilderness thus offers a sacred, redemptive experience, these terms finding expression in the environmental movement (Langton, 1995, p17)[11], media commentaries and popular culture. Australia's once dead centre is now a 'redemptive wilderness heartland' (Fergie, 1994, p5). In its Romantic register, wilderness represents the alternative to over-industrialized humanity. For the conformist, wilderness provides a chance to be delinquent; for the delinquent a chance to conserve and protect. In contrast to an aggressive culture, wilderness is a dream of gentleness and peace; against materialism it is a spiritual transcendence. In a life-negating society, a river tells the phases of human life; in a sexually repressed society, wilderness recharges the senses, and 'where emotion is denied, it speaks what is unfelt' (Salleh, 1996, pp26–27).

Antarctica as white wilderness

> Plan a wild Christmas or New Year. Shock your family and friends …
> it is difficult to imagine a wilder place to celebrate or take time out
> from your busy schedules.
>
> (Southern Heritage Expeditions Limited, 'Plan a wild Christmas or New Year',
> 'Heritage News', newsletter of Southern Heritage Expeditions, June 2000, p3)

> To dine with a glacier on a sunny day is a glorious thing and makes
> feasts of meat and wine ridiculous. The glacier eats hills and drinks
> sunbeams.
>
> (John Muir's comment is repeated in tour brochures for cruises to Alaska and other
> ice-bound destinations, for example see Pearson's Pond Luxury Inn & Adventure
> Spa, Juneau, Alaska (www.lanierbb.com/inns.bb5338.html) and Travelocity.com
> (leisure.travelocity.com/Vacations/Cruise/Ship/0,2416,TRAVELOCITY_166,00.html),
> accessed March 2004)

Antarctica has all the cachet of the ultimate ecotourist experience. Due to cost
and the days of seasickness that stand between the visitor and any hope of
landfall, which may then be impossible due to inclement weather and the short
tourist season, very few humans in the world can claim to have set foot on
Antarctica. Annual visitor numbers to Antarctica, including the Antarctic
Peninsula, are about 10,000 to 17,500, rising from less than 2000 in the late
1980s and 6500 in 1992–1993. Only about 500 people each season visit the
Ross Sea area (Herr, 1989, p61; Wexham, 1995, p10; New Zealand Antarctic
Institute, 2000; Gateway Antarctica, c2000; Rodney Russ, communication 20
January 1996; Crossley, 1995, p96). By contrast, the great majority visit the
Antarctic Peninsula off Argentina, which even has a hotel (Wiltsie, 1990, p25),
and is visited so frequently by large cruise ships that Lemaire Channel has been
nicknamed Kodak Gap (Innes, 1992,'Travel', p1). Those who have set foot on
Antarctica are usually passionate about something, whether it is ice, penguins,
getting to a point like the south magnetic pole, or Antarctic exploration history
(Rodney Russ in discussion on the bridge, 6 January 1996). Among my fellow
passengers to Antarctica, Floriss, from the Netherlands, said he had wanted to
come since he was four years old and his father read him the diaries of the
Antarctic explorers, Scott and Amundsen. Dorothy, from Britain, was piqued
by David Attenborough's series *Life in the Freezer*. Rocky, from Hong Kong,
was an assiduous photographer, with masses of equipment, always on the last
boat to return from each landing (conversations, 3 January 1996 and
discussion on the bridge, 6 January 1996).

Unlike the visitors to Monkey Mia, whose sense of privilege is located in an
anthropomorphic register, my fellow expeditioners to Antarctica were awed by
their experience rather than connected with other creatures; we were in
communion ('fellowship') rather than in communication ('conversation') with

nature. One of our guides, Simon (18 January, debriefing on ship), said of Macquarie Island: 'After a while I felt immersed in another culture'. This response is indicated by low scores, especially compared with Monkey Mia, for feeling an affection for the animals (5 per cent compared with 33 per cent of the total and 50 per cent of Monkey Mia) or feeling the animals trusted and liked us (5 per cent compared with 25 per cent for Monkey Mia). Of course, there were some passengers, particularly those who chose seals as their favourite encounter, who adopted a 'cute and cuddly' approach, noting, for example, the 'innocent big-eyed sweet faced young elephant seals' (debriefing, 12 January 1996).

Antarctica is often described as a white wilderness and it certainly had such an impact on many of us. After three weeks in the time capsule of our ship, a number of my co-expeditioners experienced a sense of shock when we visited the Australian research base at Buckles Bay on Macquarie Island, being 'irritated', 'ashamed', or 'depressed'. I wrote in my diary that 'even a few days amongst the animals can make you harshly critical of ockers and even ordinary humans and their self-centred ways'. A male researcher took us for a tour of the area around the base. I recorded this in my diary:

> at last we had all learned Jeni's lesson of quiet patience and sat upon
> the sands for our Gentoo penguin experience. On the whole they kept
> their distance, a little line of inquisitive eyes locking with ours. We
> watched the wild grey sea at Hasselborough Bay, the giant petrel
> swoop and land, before we were told to move on, to visit the brewery
> at the base for crying out loud![12]

Not usually one to sit still and do nothing, I had gradually learned this watchful meditation from one of our guides, Jeni. She attempted to orient us to a 'solitary wilderness experience' as one of our group, Luke, a wildlife technician, described it. Jeni (discussion, 3 January 1996) realized such an orientation worked against the gregarious nature of humans as well as the desire of many of us to be told scientific facts rather than to be content with emotional narratives. Even so, a considerable number of respondents in their questionnaires described a moment of connection, a point at which human, landscape and animal clicked into a seamless union of only two sentient beings in the whole world, observer and observed. I remember the remains of a bitter afternoon on Campbell Island where our patience was rewarded with the delicately magical gamming (courting) of two Royal Albatross. Albatross mate for life, so courting is a serious business: 'They are tentative and speculative with each other, clicking and rubbing beaks together, putting beaks hesitantly into the other's feathers; one pulls at another by the wing'.

The balance is in favour of the wildlife in Antarctica, particularly if one also weighs in the scales the landscape of towering icebergs and mile-long glaciers. It was our conceit that the pleasure – and perhaps pain – of Antarctica goes on and on without us. We were spectators of penguin societies, breeding, feeding, swimming, fishing. There were so few of us and so many of them that humans felt peripheral. Phil, a Technical and Further Education sector course manager (debriefing, 12 January 1996), described the 'privilege to be here' for this fraction of time, while the albatross will survive for centuries when we have gone. For months after I returned, I could pause in my urban routine and imagine Antarctica pursuing its self-sufficient course: the Adelies plodding across the ice, the elephant seals vying for a spot in the warm centre of their massive huddle, the albatross on their extended flight around the Antarctic circle. We human interlopers felt totally incidental to the great intractability of this last place on earth. The length of time that separated us from 'civilization' and our puny numbers in the landscape meant we saw ourselves briefly as the environment saw us. In a sense, the environment did not see us. The animals paid us no mind and we humans had been 'rendered absolutely marginal', to use Berger's (1980, p22) phrase.

Mike Bossley (interviewed on 19 December 2000) suggests that the 'Attenborough effect' means people are sometimes disappointed with their dolphin experience. Because of wildlife films, because of the hyper-reality[13] of dolphins, people expect a spectacle of dolphins leaping about and taking an intense interest in humans. In Antarctica and the Galapagos Islands, the animal encounter is not only as close as the best of a wildlife film, but it is better. We were THERE, smelling, hearing, sometimes touching it – certainly being touched by it. If you can prise your eyes away from the animal dramas in front of you, your field of vision does not take in lounge room furniture and your ears become attuned to the motor vehicles on the street outside. Instead you see seals playing in the surf as it rolls into the beach or icebergs glistening serenely in the sun.

At various debriefings, we peppered our descriptions with 'stunning', 'incredible', 'magical', 'indescribable', 'spellbound'. Floriss, a Netherlands lawyer, said it is 'like being reborn, everything I see here is new, my first albatross, my first penguin' (debriefing, 12 January 1996). Jill described a 'magic scene' watching a young male albatross which 'really was stunning. I find it very hard to describe in words …'. She wound down, as many of us did, knowing our descriptions were dust in our mouths by comparison with what had vibrated through our bodies (debriefing, 4 January 1996). At our final debriefing on 20 January, everyone was very moved, a number to tears. Several confessed that, while on shore somewhere, we had wept or kissed a rock, so transformed were we by the stillness, the solitude, the mystery of life, our unbelievable luck to be there.

As Lenore Layman (personal communication, 2001) suggested to me, our Antarctica experiences were 'romantic' encounters, a secular pilgrimage. Indeed, as with the Romantics, the landscape impressed on many of us more than the animals did. We may have been too coy to use the words 'sublime', 'natural cathedrals' or 'spirit-beams', but we contemplated a vast empty nature in near-solitude. We were thrilled by the danger of the white wilderness even as we were not really afraid for ourselves:

Note: Icebergs and snowdrifts dwarf all living creatures, and slowly demolish Douglas Mawson's Hut in Commonwealth Bay

Figure 4.5 *Romantic Antarctica*

The paradox of sublime landscapes is that they ought to be beyond human description. Likewise, the wilderness cannot be fully compassed by even the most lyrical and poetic language. Sublime landscapes and wilderness alike derive their power from their inhumanity. Not necessarily hostile, not necessarily brutal, but always indifferent to human presence, the sublime wilderness drives human beings from solipsism to humility. *Yet for people to care about wilderness there must be some relationship between the human observer and the wild place, some sense that the human experience does, in the end, matter,* if only as witness to the wonders of nature. Antarctica promises to be the most sublime of all wilderness, yet the most indifferent.

(Hains, 2002, pp31–32, italics mine)

'There must be some relationship between the human observer and the wild place': of course Antarctica cannot go on without us. The Australian government and conservation groups have acted on the international stage to preserve Antarctica as a 'last wilderness', a status intermittently threatened with mining, scientific research and even ecotourism itself (Bowden, 1997, p408). Against those trying to protect Antarctica from 'human impact', Rodney Russ advocates 'experience impact'. Both Jeni and Russ believe that ecotourists can have a Damascene experience, taking their conservation commitment back home. Jeni instanced people from Florida who had never previously picked up a pair of binoculars, but who returned to become involved in bird preservation in the Florida Keys. Russ distinguishes himself from deep ecologists who sometimes define humans as everyone but themselves. 'Unique' and 'rare' are human terms that have no meaning without humans to experience the 'unique' and 'rare' (Rodney Russ and Jeni, interviewed on 3 January 1996). Ultimately, Russ believes the fate of the Antarctic region will be determined in the courts, where economic interests will seek access. Thus the islands need their advocates in the general populace to influence the judges. We were often reminded of the conservation aspects of our experience, although, as Table A3.7 (Appendix 3) suggests, other aspects overwhelmed our joy that the animals were being preserved.

Conclusion

Westerners escape their rational work routines for embodied hedonistic pleasures or for authentic ecotourist destinations. Along with personal self-help and New Age spirituality, we also find that encounters with animals and environmental politics assist us in the search for meaning and authenticity. Such involvements are seen as the antidote to our secular, commodified, scientistic, complex and contradictory lives. However, ecofeminists and environmentalists celebrate 'untouched nature' when there can be no such thing. Nature 'is made', 'a co-construction among humans and non-humans' (Scott, 2001, p368).

The advocates of Romanticism did not recognize this hybridization of nature and culture. They did not question the mind–body dualism; they merely inverted its values. Nature was superior to culture, *because* it was natural, connected with bodily or emotional sensations. Val Plumwood (1993, p62) calls this approach the cavern of reversal. It merely reverses the dominant evaluations (man = good; woman = bad) without reconceiving and reordering the relations between the elements. Concepts of healing and reweaving focus on women's 'naturalised roles, not rights', which may create the expectation that women will 'mother earth' without necessarily sharing in the products of that labour (Agarwal, 1998, p83). Gaia[14] becomes a housewife who uncomplainingly cleans up humanity's mess (Plumwood, 1990, p625; see also Heller, 1993, pp222–224; Seager, 1993, p219). The 'angel in the ecosystem' (Plumwood, 1992, p9) is a simplistic way to connect women with nature. In this essentialist and ahistorical merging, insufficient attention is paid to how the link between women and the natural world emerged historically and under what material conditions it changes (Agarwal, 1992, p120; Agarwal, 1998, pp64–67).

Unlike our more innocent Romantic forbears, some of us at least are afraid for the environment. We are inhabitants of a world and time forever darkened by the shadow of Rachel Carson's (1962) *Silent Spring* and Paul Erlich's ([1968] 1971) *The Population Time Bomb*. Encounters with wild animals feed nostalgia and give pleasure, but they also remind us that the natural world is at risk, and that moral or scientific certainties have dissolved. Neither the scientific paradigm nor New Age romanticism on its own allows us to move into a successful relationship with the wild world (Bryld and Lykke, 2000, p25). We might hunger to be modern subjects secure in our possession of Antarctica or Romantics satisfied with its independence from us, but we cannot reconcile our desires and our knowledge. How will this ambivalence influence environmental politics? This is the question of the next chapter.

5
Loving Knowing

Changing scientific paradigms

In the olden days the voice of man, raised in reason, was confronted by the roar of the lion, the bellow of the bull. Man went to war with the lion and the bull, and after many generations won that war definitively. Today these creatures have no more power. Animals have only their silence left with which to confront us. Generation after generation, heroically, our captives refuse to speak to us. All save Red Peter, all save the great apes.

(Elizabeth Costello, protagonist author and vegetarian, in J. M. Coetzee's novel, *The Lives of Animals*, 1999, p30. Red Peter is the ape in a story by Franz Kafka (1952.)

It is so clean: animals live without moral searching, so, without a sense of corruption. For animals, pain is physical only. Or is that all a projection, a delusion?

(Anastasia, in French, 1987, p853)

According to one view, science and industrialization mark humanity's progress, our ever-increasing freedom from reliance on the chancy beneficence of the soil or climate. In this story, reason and observation give men dominion over the natural world. 'The clear voice of Aristotle, writing more than 300 years BC' (Mabey, 1997, pviii), is contrasted with 'The Dark Ages' during which religion displaces science. Humans no longer attempted to observe animals, and the bestiary, 'probably the most popular tome after the Bible itself' (Ryder, 1989, p45) in 12th century England (Rowland, 1971, p4), was didactic and moralistic (Clark and McMunn, 1989, pp2–3). As St Augustine summarized the theological attitude of the times, it was not important whether an animal existed or not, but rather its meaning (Rowland, 1971, p4).

After the Dark Ages, came the light of the Enlightenment. In the mid-18th century, natural history emerged as a distinct field of inquiry (Foucault, 1973, p133). During the first half of the 19th century, a craze for collecting, whether bugs, ferns, flowers or birds, touched almost every section of English society (Thomas, 1983, p283). Nature studies were added to the school curriculum in Britain in 1870 and 'Wattle Days', school bird days and so on featured in

Australian schools (Dunlap, 1999, p116). By the 1890s every Australian colony sustained a royal society or natural history society or both (Hutton and Connors, 1999, p31). The shift from the classification of the natural world, associated with Carolus Linnaeus, to the modern episteme or scientific approach is usually marked by the publication of Darwin's *On the Origin of Species* in 1859 (Barber, 1980, p57). While the publication of *On the Origin of Species* did not immediately stop amateurs in their tracks, when natural history became part of university training (Barber, 1980, p28), finding new species was no longer considered a significant contribution to knowledge (Barber, 1980, p66). The word 'scientist' was coined by William Whewell in 1833; over the 19th century science developed as a profession with a social role. This chapter explores how science first constructed the natural world as utterly inferior to the human world, drawing a deep gulf between humans and the rest of nature, but has, in more recently emerging disciplines, begun to close the gap and produce an emotional connection with a more holistically conceived natural world. We then move on to claims that physical connection might be a better way to know the natural world than through scientific facts, at least if we want people to change the world. Finally, and presaging Chapter 6, we explore the role of feral animals in challenging the dualism of nature and culture, wild and tame.

Dualism: Are humans different animals?

Barbara Noske (1989, p44) describes Aristotle as a dualist, identifying a clear distinction between the anima of animals and 'anima rationalis' which only humans had: 'of all animals man alone is capable of deliberation' (Aristotle in Klingender, 1971, p89). The dualists have a stronger tradition in Western science, one of the most radical versions being found in Descartes' claim in the 1630s that animals are automata, no more sentient than plants (Soper, 1995, p53; Brumbaugh, 1978, pp6–8; Thomas, 1983, p33),[1] and which could not feel pain and had no reason (Walker, 1983, p9). Descartes 'nailed his wife's pet dog to a board by its four paws and dissected it alive. His wife, by the way, then left him' (Rothschild, 1986, p11).

By contrast, Darwin argued that, although differences between people and animals in intellectual powers are 'immense', there was no fundamental distinction between humans and higher mammals in mental faculties (Ritvo, 1987, p39), in moral sensibilities (Jasper and Nelkin, 1992, p16), or indeed in having a 'coherent language' (Beer, 1986, p219). Even so, as with religious writers before Darwin (Salisbury, 1994, pp4–5, 84–85), scientists since have continued their search for a clear boundary between humans and animals. Animals have been considered inferior, and therefore not deserving any special treatment, due to a lack of reason, speech, soul, morality, a higher nature, culture, humour, or knowledge of death (Masson and McCarthy, 1996, pp38–39). Thus Mary Midgley (1978, p207) half-jokingly suggests that 'man [is] perhaps centrally a test-passing animal'.

Many of us outside the world of science accept a continuum with animals, expressed in the popularity of books which not only assert that 'elephants weep', that animals have emotions, but ask if animals wrongly project their emotions onto us, commit zoomorphism (Masson and McCarthy, 1996, p54). Despite the exposure of Clever Hans, the counting horse who actually read its master's body language, animals can 'count' whatever this might mean in their minds.[2] Animals are capable of joking, for example when they learn sign language (Noske, 1989, pp142–143). Sheep can recall the features of familiar people and other sheep for up to two years (Connor, 2001, p13), while fish have a memory span of up to three months, 'can be manipulative and socially aware … and are able to recognize their shoal-mates' (Henderson, 2003, p29).[3] Elephants have learned to paint to save themselves. Once elephants moved logs, but with the deforestation of Thailand, two Russian artists, Vitaly Komar and Alex Melamid, hatched a scheme to sell elephants' paintings to hotel chains to decorate their hundreds of rooms (Komar and Melamid, 2000, pp2–3: extract from their book *When Elephants Paint* by Perennial/HarperCollins; see also Masson and McCarthy, 1996, p198). Picasso hung a painting by a chimpanzee on his wall (de Waal, 1999, pp40–41); Jarvis (2000, p100) reproduces a photograph of a dolphin 'artist' at Sea World.

Those that deny animals a language imply that, until they spoke English or some human language, animals were mute. But animals are clearly capable of verbal as well as nonverbal communication, as are humans when engaged in dance, music, sculpting and athletics (Wise, 2000, p162; see also Noske, 1989, p130). Alex, the African grey parrot, learned to talk by watching two experimenters ask and answer questions of each other (Barber, 1993, pp4–5; Griffin, 1992, pp172–173). In the 'first report of an ape making sounds that seem to hold their meaning across different situations', Kanzi, an adult bonobo, 'adept at communicating with symbols' and understanding some broken English, has invented four distinct sounds: for 'banana', 'juice', 'grapes' and 'yes' (Ananthaswamy, 2003, p12). Perhaps the most famous signing chimpanzee is Washoe, her tale told by Roger Fouts (1997), Professor of Psychology at Central Washington University. When Washoe first met other chimpanzees, she referred to them disdainfully as BLACK BUGS although she later overcame her cultural arrogance (Fouts, 1997, pp384–385).

J. M. Coetzee's (1999, pp34–38)[4] protagonist in *The Lives of Animals*, Elizabeth Costello, criticizes scientific experiments to assess animal intelligence because they circumscribe the animal's capacity to display its talents. The ape is oriented 'toward acceptance of himself as primarily an organism with an appetite that needs to be satisfied … a carefully plotted psychological regimen conducts him *away* from ethics and metaphysics toward the humbler reaches of practical reason' (Coetzee, 1999, p37). This is a poetic construction of animals: the primates who are capable of communication do seem preoccupied with simple pleasures such as food and drink. Chimpanzees' use of American Sign Language is akin to a toddler's (Fouts, 1997, pp88–89). The orangutans who learned sign language were interested largely in signing for food and contact. As Galdikas (1995, p400) disappointedly concluded, 'I realized why orangutans don't have spoken language'.

Wittgenstein claims that language is a form of life; we could not understand a lion even if it spoke. Nagel, akin to Wittgenstein, claims that humans cannot think like a bat because we lack sonar (Wolch, 1998, p122). Sanders and Arluke (1993, pp378–383) add that sociological investigators have been unsuccessful in their attempts to capture the 'emotive discourse' of companion animals, the 'perspectives of animals themselves' despite the excellent strategies suggested by animal trainers like Vicki Hearne, or a researcher on feral cats who learned to speak 'pidgin cat'. In response to claims concerning the impossibility of inter-species recognition, J. M. Coetzee's (1999, p49) protagonist, Elizabeth Costello, notes that we can 'think our way into the existence of a being who never existed', a fictional character (Coetzee, 1999, p45). Of course, it may be that the overlap in primate and human forms of life is indeed circumscribed to common interests in 'eating, sleeping, sex, avoiding encroachments on our environments'. We may not share the lion's interest in how to anticipate a gazelle's next turn or questions concerning gazelles' rights. However, 'that sort of thing often happens when I'm talking to fundamentalist ministers or accountants, whose forms of life and language games are also incomprehensible to me' (Rollin, 1990, p143).

The last bastion of humanity is the claim that animals do not share with humans the capacity 'to be conscious that they are conscious' (Wise, 2000, p129). Chimpanzees, orangutans, dolphins and humans have proven that they recognize themselves in mirrors, which is said to indicate that 'the creatures are capable of self-awareness' (Telegraph Group, 2001a, p8).

Given the evidence, it is hard to believe any scientists still accept the Cartesian construction of animal automata. It seems more likely that they repress the evidence of their senses to avoid an 'empathy crisis' (Randall Lockwood in Ryder, 1989, p315; Birke, 1994, pp2–4) or disparagement from their scientific peers (Rollin, 1990, p31; Birke, 1994, pp52–54).[5] Mike Bossley (interviewed on 19 December 2000), who combines psychology and environmental science in his research and teaching, thinks 'it's legitimate and appropriate to accept some kind of an emotional bond or connection between me and what I'm studying'. He believes that most biology students also have this connection when they commence their studies but it is 'stomped' out of them as they learn the 'almost antiseptic approach' of the lab-coated professional. Andy Russell (interviewed on 17 June 1992), a hunter and well-known conservationist from Alberta, says of scientists:

> They come here to talk to me, spend some time with me, and
> inevitably they do not understand the holistic approach. It's called
> science, there's got to be a reason for everything which is utter bullshit,
> if you don't mind my saying so.

Indeed some scientists also know that it's 'bullshit'.

Connection: Ethology, ecology and environmentalism

The sense of interconnection, the need both for observation of the particular and the development of fervent commitment to the preservation of ecosystems and 'their' species within them (Dunlap, 1999, pp156–157, 159; Barber, 1980, p287), marks ethology and ecology out from other natural sciences. Ethology asks the researcher to 'think like an animal' (Konrad Lorenz, 1954), usually based on close observation of animals. Konrad Lorenz, an animal lover, is the pioneering ethologist.

Exceptional in the annals of science, as Donna Haraway (1992) argues, is the role of three female primatologists: Jane Goodall, Dian Fossey and Biruté Galdikas, all fostered by the Anglo-Kenyan paleontologist-anthropologist, Louis Leakey (for example see Galdikas, 1995, p385). The gap between humans and other animals was already imagined as narrower for women, configured as closer to nature and less needful of asserting their masculinity with mastery and rifle. These primatologists reached across the gap to touch and love another species (Haraway, 1992, p149).[6] In her history of primate relations, Donna Haraway (1992, p135) suggests that communication, 'the immediate sharing of meanings', with apes became the holy grail of the 1980s. The female primatologists went into the wilds to connect, with touch instead of sight, through understanding and not mastery, accepting the 'honour' of being 'chosen' (Montgomery, 1991, pp15, 55). Indeed, a former student of Fossey's said of gorillas, 'they don't like us as much as we like them' (quoted in Montgomery, 1991, p273).

Michael Hutchins, a conservation biologist with the New York Zoological Society, says 'good conservationists can't afford to be that emotionally involved with the populations they're trying to save. Individuals can't mean that much when you have to do large-scale manipulations of populations' (Montgomery, 1991, p229). As the farmer knows and the old military adage goes, 'Don't name the chickens' (Montgomery, 1991, p228), which of course Goodall, Galdikas and Fossey contravened: they named their apes and focused on individuals (Montgomery, 1991, p104). In the middle of the 20th century, scientists studied animals from behind blinds, secretly, like hunters. 'The idea that animals might have thoughts, emotions, and personalities was considered a projection of human traits' (Galdikas, 1995, p386). Goodall wrote of the chimpanzees as 'she' and 'he', the editors substituting 'it' in the first paper she submitted to the *Annals of the New York Academy of Science*. In her first six months in the field, Goodall made two of her most important discoveries, that chimpanzees use tools and hunt omnivores, working in teams to hunt their prey. All three primatologists became involved in seeking to save 'their' apes (Torgovnick, 1998, p101; Montgomery, 1991, pp194–195; see also Peterson and Goodall, 1993).

The story of the evolution of the ecological approach to understanding the natural world is told in gripping terms and careful detail by Donald Worster

(1977),[7] albeit with a US and British focus. The story is extended to settler societies like Australia by Thomas Dunlap (1999), who claims that 'The transition from natural history to ecology [is] the single most important change affecting the settlers' understanding of the land and their relationship to it in the nineteenth century' (Dunlap, 1999, p138).

Ecology works in the opposite direction of the reductionist ethos of other natural sciences, which start from the smallest element. Thus, atomic particles, studied by physicists, explain the chemical reactions studied by chemists, which in turn, explain the behaviour of organisms, studied by biologists. Instead, a holistic approach is advocated to explain organisms in the context of their environment. The term 'oecologie' was coined in 1866, by Ernst Haeckel, a German disciple of Darwin's (Worster, 1977, p192). However, Worster (1977, p7) traces ecology back to Gilbert White's *The Natural History of Selborne*, first published in 1789, and appearing in over 100 editions by the middle of the 20th century (Worster, 1977, p5). White's project was to see how many species the Selborne parish contained and how they formed an interrelated system (Worster, 1977, p81). The book was largely ignored for 50 years, until the Romantic tradition took up White from 1830 (Worster, 1977, p14). In the latter half of the 19th century, nature essayists noted an alienation from god/spirituality produced by science and industrialization, but which they felt could be recovered in nature (Worster, 1977, p16). They expressed this 'longing to reestablish an inner sense of harmony between man and nature through an outer physical reconciliation' (Worster, 1977, p10). In this tradition are Henry David Thoreau (1817–1862), Waldo Emerson (1803–1882), John Muir (1838–1914) and landscape painters (see discussion in Oelschlaeger, 1991).

One of the most dramatic changes in outlook is attributed to Aldo Leopold and his shift from utilitarianism to preservation, expressed in the idea of the 'land ethic' and the ecosystem (Worster, 1977, p256). As a forest assistant, between the 1880s and 1930, Leopold participated in programmes to exterminate wolves (Emel, 1998, pp98–100). Indeed, without a notion of the ecosystem, it was hard to grasp what was wrong with exterminating predators like the wolf and coyote (Worster, 1977, p262; Dunlap, 1999, p273). With the concept of ecosystem, ecologists could recognize and then argue for the balance of species. Indeed coyotes were necessary to save grain crops, as they limited the number of deer who stripped the forests and then went in search of food among the farmer's crops (Dunlap, 1999, pp211, 214, 224). In 1934, predator hunting in national parks was banned (Worster, 1977, p277). Leopold went on to become a wildlife researcher and professor at the University of Wisconsin, and was instrumental in founding the Wilderness Society. In Australia, Ratcliffe, in 1929, was an early pioneer who recommended against killing flying foxes who attacked the orchards, instead suggesting frightening them off to their preferred eucalyptus blooms (Dunlap, 1999, pp184–185).

Ecology became a scientific discipline in the 1930s (Collard, 1989, p137; Dann, 1991, p348), displacing natural history at the same time as universities displaced museums 'as the locus of research, and professionals replaced amateurs' (Dunlap, 1999, p16). Ecologists' explanation of the Dust Bowl of the 1930s was accorded public attention, revealing them as public figures and trusted advisors (Worster, 1977, p190). Worster (1977, pp22–23) claims that Rachel Carson has done more than anyone else to launch the 'recent ecology movement'. Indeed, Carson disputed the idea that the 'ecosystem' is like the economy, a great *productive* organism, with each species paying its own way (Worster, 1977, p291). Carson pointed out that the notion of 'economy' allowed farmers to use pesticides, but if they had a notion of an ecological sustainability they would not intervene in this manner (Worster, 1977, p340). From 1970, an image of the fragile blue planet from outer space (Worster, 1977, p341) became an icon of holism and humanity's obligation to preserve the world with economic self-restraint (Worster, 1977, p342). The term 'biodiversity' was coined in the mid 1980s (Mazur, 2001, p82).

Richard Grove (1995, p6) suggests that preoccupation with the national parks movement may tell the story of environmentalism in the US, but it represses an alternative that 'has long eluded scholarly attention'. Instead of ecology arising with the publication in 1864 of *Man and Nature* by G. P. Marsh (Grove, 1995, p470) or with Aldo Leopold's discernment of the 'land ethic', in the colonies of British and other empires, the mid-17th century saw the emergence of 'a coherent and relatively organised awareness of the ecological impact of the demands of emergent capitalism and colonial rule' (Grove, 1995, p6). Alexander von Humboldt, at the turn into the 19th century, systematized these ideas, drawing on Indian and Chinese forestry and horticultural techniques (Grove, 1995, pp367, 11).

Given these shifts in scientific outlook, it is perhaps unsurprising that in Australia there is debate concerning the degree of continuity in more than 100 years of Australia's conservation politics. Was there a sharp break between a world-transforming anthropocentric preservationism and a new breed of environmentalists in the 1960s, who sought to stop oil exploration on the Great Barrier Reef and to save Lake Pedder in Tasmania from flooding to produce hydro-electricity (Hutton and Connors, 1999, p91 of Lines, 1991; Christoff, 1999, p21 the latter adopting the disjunction approach)? In 1966, the Australian Conservation Foundation (ACF) was founded, mostly by Canberra-based scientists (Hutton and Connors, 1999, p107). By 1969, the ACF was condemned for its conciliatory approach to oil drilling on the Great Barrier Reef (Hutton and Connors, 1999, p1) and more radical environmental groups and responses quickly developed. The damming of Lake Pedder was opposed with a petition of 10,000 signatures, the largest in Tasmania's history (Kiernan, 1990, p21). In 1978, Greenpeace Australia began operations in Sydney, their first national campaign against whaling conducted in Western Australia (Stacker, 1985, p6; see also Ryder, 1989, p231). This was followed by efforts to reduce drift net fishing because of its impact on dolphins (Jarvis,

2000, p104). The first Commonwealth environmental legislation in Australia was the Environment Protection Act 1974 (Carroll, 1991b, p40). In 1983, the damming of the last 'wild' river, the Franklin, became an election issue, the damming successfully resisted by a movement spearheaded by Bob Brown and the Wilderness Society (for example see *Wild Rivers* (1983) by Peter Dombrovskis and Bob Brown).

In the late 1980s, environmental movement organizations in Australia claimed 300,000 members Australia-wide, more than all the members of political parties combined (Hutton and Connors, 1999, p1). Young people in Britain are disaffected from nation and neighbourhood, although concerned about the environment, AIDS 'and above all animals' (Wilkinson and Mulgan, 1995, pp16, 96, 106). An Australian survey commissioned by the Australian Heritage Commission in 1997 revealed there was 'overwhelming community support for protecting our remaining wilderness areas' (Young 1997, p2; see also Table A3.17 in Appendix 3).

However, while membership of environmental groups in the US increased between 1969 and 1995, it has since declined, while few environmental organizations have local chapters (Putnam, 2000, pp156, 160).[9] This decline has been attributed to the sexism, scientific managerialism and economic rationalism of a new breed of male leaders, scientists and management-oriented careerists who seek alliances with corporations. Some male environmentalists blame women for overpopulation (Seager, 1993, p214) or wearing fur coats (Adams, 1994, p135; Seager, 1993, pp202–207), and express other forms of sexism and racism (Elder et al, 1998, p78; Sanderson, 1994, p197). These managers focus on fish and wildlife management, neglecting issues closer to home, such as zoological and botanical gardens, nuclear power and weapons dangers. Similarly, Hutton and Connors (1999, pp127, 169, 251) note that, in Australia, the high profile struggles have involved resource exploitation, whether sand mining on Fraser Island or wood-chipping old growth forests.

Joni Seager (1993, pp176–9, 188, 193–194) suggests that in accepting economic arguments, often smuggled in through claims to environmental sustainability, environmentalists deny themselves the right to make moral or aesthetic claims. Similarly, Heather Aslin (1996, pp27–28) suggests that, in Australia, a consumptive approach to Australian wildlife, indeed putting an economic value on individual species of wildlife, may only reinforce the doministic attitude to animals, and extend it to 'wild' animals, rather than promoting the protection of nature. Scientifically trained men displace the potential contributions of women in animal welfare, arts and entertainment activities. This means that affective, tactile or aesthetic understandings of animals are deemed irrelevant to conservation (Aslin, 1996, p 329). Experience of the 'concrete wild' has no purchase.

Experiencing the wild

Adrian Franklin (2002, pp18, 49) suggests that the sudden turn to nature in the 1970s was due to disaffection with capitalism's 'rationalized individualism', with the failure of collectivism and welfarism. People began to seek comfort in the 'principles of sustainability' and nature still seems to offer the panacea for our seriously disharmonious world (Franklin, 2002, p18). Franklin (1999, pp3–4; 2002, p53) contrasts the consumptive modernist approach to nature with his definition of a postmodernist approach. This registers 'the absence of paradigm assumptions about the true or proper relationships between society and the natural world' (Franklin, 2002, p53). Ironically, perhaps, people retreat from the impossibilities of postmodern life to value animals and nature (Franklin, 1999, p194). Franklin links the angst of uprooted postmodern individuals, denied connection with place, kin and meaning in their political and community engagements, to a renewed sense of kinship with and caring for animals. Pets substitute for distant kin and children; wild animals substitute for political and social causes embracing other humans; game animals provide access to wilderness intimacy. Similarly, Jennifer Price (1999, p252) suggests that nature is 'a refuge from modern life, it is a *reprieve* from irony and self-awareness'.

The growing intimacy with animals is a response to three ills produced by the collapse of the modernist project, ills that characterize the postmodern condition: misanthropy, risk and ontological insecurity (Franklin, 1999, pp194–195). Misanthropy suggests humans are destructive, pestilent, mad and out of control. Animals are essentially innocent victims of a greedy global economy (Franklin, 1999, p3). Where trees are cut down or animal species destroyed, 'people feel victimized *themselves* in a certain sense'; they also feel they bear responsibility for the animals and nature so destroyed (Beck, 1992, p75).

In relation to risk, Franklin draws on Ulrich Beck's (1992) classic text, *Risk Society: Towards a New Modernity*. Beck explores the explosion of insidious and invisible risks in modern societies, risks uncovered by science but also refuted by science. Where oil spills are at least visible, the impact of radioactive leakage or of greenhouse gases is intangible and long in incubation, requiring scientific validation to prove its existence and effects (Beck, 1992, pp156, 162–163, 72). But scientists may also refuse the risks, obfuscating with denials of causation or alternative data (Beck, 1992, pp58–64). In reply, activists engage in moral crusades proffering their sick children as the proof of environmental degradation (Beck, 1992, pp76–77). Franklin (2002, p13) incorporates Phil Macnaghten and John Urry's (1998, pp219ff) contribution, based on their focus group findings. The focus groups felt disenfranchised from the public discourses concerning 'quality of life' and 'sustainable development' (Macnaghten and Urry, 1998, pp223, 225–226). They were suspicious of 'rational' discourses offered by scientists, preferring to rely on the evidence of their own senses and bodies (smells and illnesses for example) (Macnaghten and Urry, 1998, p228). Even so, they did not totally trust their own experiences: 'people were also concerned with dangers that were distant, unseen, unknown or delayed' (Macnaghten and Urry, 1998, p235). They expressed extreme distrust of both corporations and governments over environmental issues (Macnaghten and Urry, 1998, p224).

The third aspect of the postmodern turn to nature, ontological insecurity, refers to the 'churning nature of postmodernity', its directionlessness, its social isolation as fragmented mobile families lose contact with kin, community and neighbourhoods (Franklin, 1999, p56). People respond with individual self-cultivation to 'work out insecurity by oneself' (Beck, 1992, p76) through education, self-help, psychoanalysis, diet, exercise and modern taboos against smoking and over-eating (Appleyard, 1993, p213). People without secure livelihoods do not experience ontological insecurity, they experience poverty (Beck, 1992, pp53, 75; Soper 1995, pp267–268). The previous chapter explored the search for meaning in response to ontological insecurity.

Franklin claims that, on the whole, humans do not like these conditions of postmodernity, and so turn to animals. There are two reasons for this. First, animals provide moral certainty in times when it is hard to know how to treat human others and also avoid charges of ethnocentrism, paternalism and so on (from Appleyard, 1993, pp238, 240). Animals are 'available, reliable, stable and predictable in their relations with humans at a time when human social relations are the opposite' (Franklin, 1999, pp194–195). Indeed, some animal liberationists are willing to endanger human lives to reduce the suffering of animals (Jasper and Nelkin, 1992, p 44; Baker, 1993, pp219, 222).[10] Another way to read the sexism and racism of some environmentalists might be through Franklin's (1999, p3) suggestion that (some) humans are found to be 'destructive' and 'pestilent' (by other humans).

Macnaghten and Urry's findings are pessimistic concerning the potential for environmental activism. Their focus group respondents felt unable to solve what were clearly global problems within the ambit of their own capacities and interests, which were local (Macnaghten and Urry, 1998, p227). 'Think globally, act locally' only works in the second element of its admonition, although even here people had done little to change their lifestyles, some expressing ambivalence in relation to using motor vehicles, and none being engaged in 'collective forms of protest or lobbying' (Macnaghten and Urry, 1998, p237). The most commonly proffered political interventions were educating children (for example in not being wasteful) and expressing consumer choice (for example dolphin-friendly tuna or aerosols that do not contain CFCs). A rare few believed voting and democratic accountability would have some impact (Macnaghten and Urry, 1998, p244).

By contrast, Franklin (1999, p198) suggests that, while we cannot solve the human condition that now overwhelms us, humans can express small actions of care. We assist frogs to cross the road, feed birds in our garden (Franklin, 1999, p194),[11] or save turtles from the soup kettle in our Manhattan apartments.[12] We love our pets as our equals. Aslin's conclusion is similarly optimistic. 'Most interviewees and group members did not question either the human right or ability to manage wildlife' (Aslin, 1996, pp304–305). Organization members were all aware of the effects of their daily activities on wildlife, expressing concern about the environmental consequences of agriculture, pollution in waterways and so on. Some identified the personal action they took or could take (Aslin, 1996, p289). Aslin (1996, p48) suggests that, while men know more about environmental issues, women are more likely to change their behaviour as a result of environmental concerns. One example of 'integration' of wildlife in some people's daily lives is work with wild animals.

The concrete wild

> Our ability to perceive quality in nature begins, as in art, with the pretty. It expands through successive stages of the beautiful to values as yet uncaptured by language.
>
> (Aldo Leopold, 1969, in Domm, 1988, p7)

> We recycle. We spend a hundred dollars to attend a star-studded fund-raiser or a rock concert to Save the Earth. We make a donation to help save the whales or the elephants. And then we go about our daily business more or less as before.
>
> (Biruté Galdikas, 1995, p255)

> Abstraction ... leaves us without an explanation of our emotional relations to animals.
>
> (Jack Turner, 1996, p34)

One of my focus group participants, Geoff, who grew up on the Victorian coast at Hastings, compared his animal encounter experiences with the highly artificial Penguin Parade on Phillip Island. As a child, Geoff nursed sick penguins back to health, saying it is 'so different to have penguins in your hand or in a box in the kitchen near the stove'. Alison, one of a half dozen focus group members who go fishing, said of her Penguin Parade experience: 'I don't think it was any great experience for me; if you go fishing, [there are] dolphins and turtles around the boat, and sharks trying to nibble at your toes'.

Geoff realized he was 'getting close to those animals people don't get to experience these days'. As the Australian population expands and the economy shifts, each generation moves farther away from country lifestyles to a city or suburban existence, losing connection as they lose relatives on the land or the geographical proximity of the bush. In a British study, the English focus group participants remembered walking in the woods as children and wanted their own children to have the same experience. By contrast, inner city Asian youth identified woods and forests as important for global ecological reasons but their own experiences suggested the city was more civilized, trees were messy or woods were a resource for firewood (Macnaghten and Urry, 2000b, p174).

Rural dwellers are often condemned for their ignorance of and utilitarian attitudes towards nature.[13] In fact, surveys suggest that those living in the country often have more knowledge of the natural world, expressed in higher naturalistic or ecologistic scores, even if they do not necessarily express a greater commitment to conservation (Kellert and Berry, 1978, pp83, 89 for the US; Aslin, 1996, p46 for a New South Wales survey that also found higher ecological scores among the young (aged 25–34) and the tertiary educated). Table A3.19 in Appendix 3 reveals that people who grew up in the country tend to have a lower environmental orientation and, contrary to other findings, a more humanistic orientation. Explanations for these contradictory results include the fact that people who grew up in a rural area do not necessarily still live there, that those who are drawn to animal encounter sites (my sample) are not representative of all those who live in rural areas, and that different kinds of people live in the country, for example farmers, hunters and environmentalists. In terms of responses to the animal encounter, in my survey those who grew up in capital cities were more likely to identify a 'unique experience'. Those who grew up in rural areas were less likely to say they felt close to nature and more likely to feel that the animals were unhappy. It was more important that the site be peaceful and relaxing to those who grew up in a capital city (these data are not shown in Appendix 3). Putting these findings together suggests that people who grew up in cities are more likely to experience the animal encounter as a special moment of proximity and peace contrasted with their everyday lives. Those who grew up in rural areas express concern for the animals based on a humanistic identification with them: are these animals happy? They may be in a better position to answer the question, given their concrete experiences of owning stock animals, rescuing wild animals, even hunting animals or birds (see Table A3.13 in Appendix 3). Similarly Heather Aslin's (1996, pp329–330) research suggests the importance of 'contact with living animals' and 'personal knowledge' in forming attitudes to wildlife, for example killing wildlife when young or working for a veterinarian. However, the significance of physical contact is missed in most of the wildlife management literature.

Aslin (1996, pp330, 303) found that wildlife attitudes were not usually formed by limited experiences such as viewing an isolated video or participating in a single field trip. In like vein, Jack Turner (1996, pxv), one time university lecturer, who resigned to be a guide in Wyoming, suggests that the greatest threat to the environment is what he calls 'abstract nature'. 'We only value what we know and love, and we no longer know and love the wild.' We accept substitutes, 'a diminished wild', caricatures and reproductions (Turner, 1996, pp25, 27). These cannot produce a desire for the wild; all they invoke is a desire to experience more fakes (Turner, 1996, p35).

The experience most urbanites have of the bush is so short-lived and so sanitized that our minds remain saturated with human concerns. A 'clear majority' of children who lived within 25 miles of two national parks in the US 'had never spent more than half an hour alone in a wild landscape' (Hancocks, 2001, p245). Wilderness becomes a place of vacation: vacant and empty (Turner, 1996, p86). Mike Bossley (interviewed on 19 December 2000) once conducted wilderness expeditions for students as part of their university studies. The students came with mixed motivations. Nevertheless most (but not all) had intense emotional responses to the wilderness environment. 'They feel very much in touch with both themselves and with the world'. Many re-evaluate their lives as 'trivial and inconsequential' and want to do 'something' with their lives. Bossley offers various reasons for this response. Instead of following their watches, students responded to the 'natural rhythm' telling them when to eat or sleep. As opposed to city life, social interactions were more intense, involving a smaller group of people. 'There's something about being in that environment that makes people laugh a lot ... often at the most trivial things'. This releases endorphins that make people feel good and more inclined to laugh; the face muscles relax and 'change the whole way you look'. Urban environments have lots of vertical lines while some wilderness environments, like the Coorong, are horizontal, which 'seems to be incredibly restful for the eyes'.[14]

My focus group respondents echoed Mike Bossley's argument, saying that bushwalking was 'peaceful', 'relaxing' and 'serene': 'you're more relaxed and you accept it'. One also noted the greater intensity of experiences, remembering a spider's web that was 'really clear'. By contrast, in the house, a spider is a nuisance that has to be removed. While many readers who have spent time in the bush might well remember the relaxation, laughter, even intensity of visual and physical experiences that emerge from simple (non)routines, they might be more surprised by Mike Bossley's claim that some, but not all, of these wilderness expeditioners go on to change their lives; this is not a passing fancy.

Rescuing wild animals

Many researchers have suggested that pets are surrogates for human companions in our 'atomistic society' (Thomas, 1983, p119; see also studies by Weisman, 1991, p246; Salmon and Salmon, 1983, p254; Peretti, 1990, pp153, 155). Kathleen Szasz (1968, p214–215) claims that excessive reliance on society, a fear of being abandoned and a focus on the acquisition of things has thrown neurotic modern people back onto their pets as proof of their worth. Lacanian-informed psychoanalysis tells us that human encounters are always frustrating, failing to meet the desire invested in them; pets fill the psychic gap (Soper, 1995, p85). However, some commentators note that the idea of 'companion animal' represses the unequal aspect of human–pet relations (for example see Tuan, 1984, p102; Soulsby, 1988, pp3–8; Ryder, 1989, p319). The literal meaning of pet is small (Tuan, 1984, p100) and domesticated breeds retain juvenile characteristics and a lifelong dependence on their master

Notes: (top left) 'Rescue success for dolphins in distress': 'It's like if you see a family in trouble you try to help them' (Linda Thompson, one of the 100 volunteers who helped rescue a pod of dolphins stranded on Kangaroo Island (in Hurrell, 1999c, p3, picture by Chris Mangan and photograph courtesy of *The Advertiser*); (top right) 'John King, 8, cries over whales beached at Seal Rocks' (Nationwide News, 1992, p23, picture by Gary Graham and photograph courtesy of Newspix); (bottom left) volunteers knitted jumpers for Phillip Island penguins to prevent them from ingesting oil by preening after they were caught in an oil spill (Gough, 2000, p3, picture by Colin Murty and photograph courtesy of Newspix); (bottom right) 'Young lifesaver visits a sick mate': an Australian sea lion, mauled by a shark, was 'saved' by a boy who alerted the RSPCA via his father. Warren Gray, the 11-year-old boy, opined, 'It makes me very, very happy that he's now safe. And all the kids at school think I'm pretty cool' (O'Brien, 2000b, p9, picture by Michael Milner and photograph courtesy of *The Advertiser*).

Figure 5.1 *Rescuing Wild Animals*

Note: Schoolchildren in Minnesota discovered frog deformities in 1995, bringing the amphibian crisis into the media spotlight. In Australia and the Americas the chytrid fungus is thought to have caused massive die-outs (Crane, 2000). So well known is the frog in its role as an environmental barometer that, when the South Australian bakery Balfours went into receivership, a picture of one of its cakes featuring a green iced frog was captioned: 'endangered: a frog cake' (*The Advertiser*, 'Crisis puts Balfours in receivership', 17 October 2000, p4, picture by Greg Adams, photograph courtesy of *The Advertiser*).

Figure 5.2 *Frogs as Environmental Barometers*

(Lorenz, 1954, p23; Tuan, 1984, p101–102). Other favoured characteristics are care-soliciting and dependence behaviour (Budiansky, 1992, pp65–66). Thus '(t)he pet *completes* him [sic – the owner], offering responses to aspects of his character that would otherwise remain unconfirmed' (Berger, 1980, p12). By contrast, Franklin (1999, p86) claims that pet owners are 'engaged in an exercise of decentring: attempting to understand the needs of others', realizing that these will be different from but overlapping with human needs.

Stories of firemen saving an elderly woman's kitten caught up a tree once denoted intimacy and connection between humans and animals (as well as humans and humans). Today, newspapers are more likely to applaud the saviours of beached whales or sea lions caught in fishing nets, as Figure 5.1 suggests. Volunteers knit jumpers for penguins to stop them preening when they are caught in oil spills or convert their backyards into habitat for frogs, which have displaced canaries down coal mines as environmental barometers. Echoing Franklin's claim, the author of a newspaper magazine cover story on Frogwatch concludes that her daughter's involvement is 'an act of faith in the future, a declaration that we, the world and our frogs are not entirely going to hell in a handcart' (Laurie, 1999b, p8). Volunteering SA executive director, Rosemary Sage, believes that volunteering work has shifted away from door-knocking for the homeless or raising funds for art foundations to environmental care (Messenger Press, 2000, p15).

Almost half the respondents at animal encounter sites, 44 per cent, had at some time rescued or helped a wild animal. Women were significantly more likely than men to have helped a wild animal in the last six months (Table

A3.13 in Appendix 3). Birds were by far the largest recipients of rescue or help, magpies being the most often nominated bird. Eight respondents rescued lizards, while a diamond python, turtles, tortoises and frogs were also rescued, particularly 'off the road'. A dolphin, 4 echidnas, 11 kangaroos, 9 possums, a sea otter, a sea lion pup and 'a wombat (but it died)' were amongst the larger animals rescued or helped. Mike Bossley (interviewed on 19 December 2000) notes that people involved in rescuing stranded whales and dolphins 'get so emotionally connected with these animals lying on the beach that they're trying to save. That's a very potent kind of experience'.

While 44 per cent of my sample had rescued an animal, one-quarter said they had been rescued or helped by an animal, women receiving this succour more often than men.[15] The responses fall into four categories. In the first, and largest group, are 'Lassie' type stories of useful intervention by animals, almost always a dog who warns of snakes or strangers, although one 'dog b[r]ought me a beer' (a comment probably offered in jest). The second category referred to the companionship offered by pets, dogs and cats. In the third, and related, category, four respondents noted the pleasure they received from wild animals and birds. Patricia Irvine records that she was 'helped when pod of dolphins I see most often turned up and swam with me a few days after my husband's death'. Balanced against these three categories, two respondents jokingly noted 'veal for dinner last night'; 'beef for dinner'. All these respondents, even the meat eating utilitarians, recognized their dependence on animals.

As Adrian Franklin (1999, p4) suggests, these new sensibilities are spreading beyond Western societies. Chinese people are applauded for 'helping' animals in the same way that Victorians are commended for knitting zoot suits for Phillip Island penguins. The Chinese care for baby elephants rescued from accidents in the forest,[16] feed birds,[17] celebrate the births and mourn the deaths of pandas in captivity.[18] In a booklet produced in conjunction with local teachers by Kinmen National Park in Taiwan, children are advised always to carry a pair of scissors so that they can cut free birds caught in farmers' nets. There is sometimes an edge to these articles, hinting at an excessive concern for animals. 'Some people ask "What else on earth is better treated than the giant panda, except man himself?" Indeed.' (Yang and Li, 1993, p5).[19]

Aslin (1996, p329) suggests that the response of wildlife rescuers to animals struck by motor vehicles is far removed from the mechanistic worldviews of highway engineers and bulldozer drivers. Like the animal orphanage at Currumbin that so enthralled a number of visitors, the Animal Reception Centre at Healesville Sanctuary in Victoria rehabilitates injured native animals. Nick Ordinans suggests:

> I find it very satisfying trying to save these little guys. Almost all of
> these orphans have been produced because of something mankind has
> done. We've done the damage so I think it's nice if, in a very small
> way, we can try to compensate for it.

Notes: (top) In Australia, 'millions' of animals are killed on New South Wales roads every year (Young, 2003, p21, photograph by Eric and David Hosking/Corbis); (bottom) in August 1990, in Canada's Yoho National Park, a Wildlife Memorial week consisted of placing orange flags at the side of the road to commemorate road-killed animals. Between 1979 and 1989, over 3000 elk, moose, bears and other large animals were killed by vehicles in Banff, Jasper, Yoho, Kootenay, Mount Revelstoke and Glacier National Parks (Minister of the Environment and Minister of Supply and Services, 1990, p6).

Figure 5.3 *Road Kill and Cure*

A dozen highly skilled vets, keepers and assistants work to save a four-inch-long sugar glider, shown in the television series 'Zoo's Company' (produced by Jill Lomas, screened on ABC television in 1998: Pitt, 1998, pp15–17). The assistant producer of the television programme, Steve Westh, believes this 'rekindles your faith in humanity and possibilities for the planet'. Similarly, Suzanne Michel (1998, p174) argues that 'wildlife rehabilitation is a form of community activism', expressing an ethics of care.[20]

Golden eagle rescuers are less accepting than is Nick Ordinans of the negligent people or mere human presence behind the constant stream of wounded eagles. Because they must make triage decisions concerning which animals are to be put down and which might be saved (Michel, 1998, p176), carers express anger at the eagles' deaths and have strong views concerning wildlife protection (Michel, 1998, pp176, 178). Their opinions grow out of their experiences. Heather Aslin's (1996, p321) research with members of wildlife associations and focus groups in cities and country towns found that farmers, who have extensive contact with animals, favoured an experience-based learning style compared with the more abstract scientistic approach of city dwellers. The value of experience, of physical connection with the wild, as opposed to the mere knowledge offered by science, is one strand of my argument for respectful stewardship. The other strand, explored in the previous chapter, is the need to transcend dualist understandings of the world, of nature as opposed to culture, of the authentic as opposed to the managed. Both these problems are exposed in a discussion of feral animals.

Feral and wild animals

On the subject of feral children, a commentator in 1977 wrote, 'the raising of a human child by a wolf is not in itself of much scientific interest' (quoted in Noske, 1989, p162). In these more anthropomorphic times, we are as interested in why an animal might adopt a child as in how the child might turn out.[21] However, following Edmund Leach's (1964) notion that the continuum of life must be divided into categories to acquire human meaning, despite the closing of the gap between animals and humans, many people may prefer the distinction to remain clear (Baker, 1993, p224; Nash, 1982, pp137–139; Midgley, 1993, p11; Davidson, 1991, pp51–53). Indeed some of the anxiety concerning genetic engineering may be due to a perceived blurring of human–other animal boundaries.

Acknowledging the work of Mary Douglas (then largely unpublished) and Radcliffe-Browne, Edmund Leach (1964) argues that, while the natural world is a continuum, human societies feel impelled to break it up into discontinuous categories. Leach suggests that animals are strung out along the gradient represented in Table 5.1. Mary Douglas (1970, p53) suggests that species at the boundary between categories are either repressed or ritualized (Douglas, 1970, p53): 'the search for purity is ... an attempt to force experience into logical categories of non-contradiction' (Douglas, 1970, p192). In Leach's schema, animals close to home are friendly. They are our kin, our pets. Those far away are hostile; they are wild animals.

Table 5.1 *Leach's Classification of Animals*

Relationship	Sister	Cousin	Neighbour	Stranger
Location	house	farm	field	remote
Type of animal	pet	livestock	game	wild animals

Source: Leach, 1964, pp23–63

Adrian Franklin (1999, p10) points out that Leach's analysis is static and one might ask what happens when Europeans bring their classification system to new countries, as in the settlement of the US, Australia and South America. We might also ask what happens when wild animals become less remote through the agency of zoos, wildlife films and so on. Instead of Leach's continuum, Klaus Eder (1996, pp87–88) suggests a u-shaped curve, at least for some animals, in which 'Pets and predators are the most similar to humans in the sense of being either interaction partners or hunters and carnivores'. Farm animals and non-predators living in the wild are most dissimilar. 'People do not

Note: ANDi, 'a rhesus monkey genetically modified with a fluorescent "marker gene" found in jellyfish', is represented with this illustration by Kenton Miller (Phelps, 2001, p26).

Figure 5.4 *Disturbing Genetic Engineering*

eat that which they admire, conquer or spin yarns about.'[22] While I disagree with Eder that we feel closer to animal predators than animal prey, as this does not really explain our contemporary obsession with whales and dolphins, I agree that the u-shaped curve indicates that both 'tame' (pets) and (some, like us) 'wild' animals are now considered near.

One of the boundary maintenance categories troubling conservationists is that between indigenous and exotic animals, between feral and wild. Cats have become a monstrous 'feral peril', the feature article by this name illustrated with a cat holding a rosella in its jaws. Supercats are 'capable of pulling down full-grown wallabies' (Porter, 1988, pp12, 15). The feral peril is destroying 'beautiful' native trees and 'rare' species. '(G)orgeously coloured native parrots' are ousted by 'unscrupulous and competitive' starlings (Cribb, 1988, p4). As this terminology suggests, an emotive discourse describes feral cats as 'cold-blooded, inhumane killers', 'murderers' of 104 million indigenous animals each

Notes: (top) As a sign of changing sensibilities, the Anti-Rabbit League of Australia has increasing success in replacing the chocolate rabbit with the bilby at Easter (Dunlap, 1999, p313). John Wamsley claims that the first chocolate Easter bilbies were made nearby but sold at Warrawong Sanctuary (Earth Sanctuaries, *Earth News*, number 19, April 1997, p3); Haigh's, the Adelaide chocolate company, now sells chocolate Easter bilbies, donating some of the proceeds to assist in the eradication of rabbits in Australia. (top) Cadbury's also sold Easter bilbies in 2004, although it made no promises concerning its commitment to rabbit eradication; (bottom) 'In touch': Senator Natasha Stott Despoja pats a bilby held by zookeeper James Morrison at Adelaide Zoo yesterday' (Innes, 2000, p24; picture by Tricia Johnson and courtesy of *The Advertiser*).

Figure 5.5 *Eating the Easter Bilby*

year (Smith, 1999, pp295, 297, 299). The feral cat is made particularly culpable in the public mind, by comparison with the fox, domestic dog or dingo (Smith, 1999, p299). Nicholas Smith (1999, p301) claims that this is a form of species sexism, an attack on the feminine aspects of the cat as opposed to the masculine traits of the dog, 'man's best friend'.

As discussed in Chapter 2, John Wamsley, the founder of Earth Sanctuaries, is famous for his cat skin hat and his conviction that domestic cats and introduced foxes are culprits in the extinction of many of Australia's small marsupials (see also discussion by Rolls, 1981, pp365–407).[23] My respondents showed strong support for exterminating feral cats (77 per cent of respondents approving and only 8 per cent disapproving), some support for culling indigenous animals (36 per cent approving and 24 per cent disapproving) and for farming native animals (44 per cent approving and 22 per cent disapproving), although support for these interventions was correlated with education (Table A3.17 in Appendix 3).

The acclimatization societies of the 1860s and 1870s deliberately sought to reproduce Europe's gardens and parkscapes in the new worlds (Dunlap, 1999, p54). While rabbits, foxes and English plants were imported, indigenous animals were hunted, often with bounties on their heads. The fur trade in Australia reduced koalas and platypuses to remnant populations (Dunlap, 1999, p51). In 1903 absolute protection was conferred by the New South Wales parliament on echidnas, platypuses and koalas (Walker, 1991, p22). From 1922, penalties were imposed, rangers appointed and protection became more effective. These protective measures were famously too late to save the Tasmanian tiger, or thylacine, whose story of persecution is movingly told by Robert Paddle (2000). Scapegoated for managerial failure and the impact of the climate on sheep, thylacines had a bounty on their heads (Paddle, 2000, pp109–110, 114, 128, 136–137). The last Tasmanian tiger died of exposure in 1936, during the Depression (Alice Reid in an interview with Paddle, 2000, pp193–195). The Protection of Animals Act in 1966 emphasized protection irrespective of hunters' needs and eradication programmes. The Flora and Fauna Guarantee Act of 1988 took an ecological approach and reserved native ecosystems to ensure protection of native animals and birds (Seebeck, 1995, pp55–56).

Note: The North American bullfrog, imported as a pet in the 1980s and 1990s, is now threatening its 'diminutive cousin', the common English frog (*Guardian Weekly*, 2000, p10; photograph courtesy of Martin Godwin).

Figure 5.6 *Ecological Nationalism*

In her interviews, Aslin found that most people seemed to be aware of the native/exotic distinction when discussing wildlife (Aslin, 1996, pp176, 178–179, 210, 215, 304, 306).[24] Apart from a fish farmer who saw crocodiles as 'pests', because they ate the fish, and some who refused to use the term 'pest' for 'innocent' animals, most were happy to name introduced animals as 'pests' (Aslin, 1996, pp178–179); 'ecological nationalism' as Dunlap calls it (Aslin, 1996, p 215). Smith (1999, p289) provides examples of writers whose deployment of ecological nationalism suggests that both feral animals and human Australians are 'spoiling' (Geoffrey Bolton in 1981), 'taming' (William Lines in 1992), 'wasting' (A. J. Marshall in 1966) and 'future-eating' (Tim Flannery in 1995) the 'authentic' 'native' land. As a result of the importation of exotic species, deliberate and otherwise,[25] Australia's feral monsters include brumbies (wild horses), water buffalo, camels and feral pigs. Attempts to solve a feral animal problem can produce another feral species. In the late 19th century, to control the rabbit plague, a problem also created by human intervention, thousands of domestic cats were released into farming land (Smith, 1999, pp295, 297, 299).

However, the apparent chasm between 'good wild' and 'bad feral' animals is not entirely clear. The dingo came to Australia with one of the Aboriginal migrations about 4000 years ago, and so might be described as feral. Its advocates claim that the dingo 'has been in Australia long enough to be regarded as a native animal' and are more concerned about threats to 'genetic integrity' from feral dogs (Breckwoldt, 1989, pp19, 18; see also discussion in Dunlap, 1993, p313). It is possible that the red-backed spider is introduced, given that it was first described as late as 1870 and first collected at the port of Rockhampton (Low, 1988, p22). Marie Bishop, publicity officer for Coffin Bay Pony Preservation Society, argues that Australia was built on the backs of horses and they are part of Australia's heritage. Conservationists, by contrast, note that, in national parks, horses muddy river courses and kill the invertebrate life on which platypuses feed (Carruthers, 2000, pp20–21).

Aboriginal people do not draw dualist distinctions between native and feral, between that which can be hunted and that which is protected. Some Aboriginal people see feral animals as an important source of food and income; the abundance of feral animals is 'a sign that their country is in good heart' (Sackett, 1991, p243) and they express concern at attempts to eliminate feral rabbits (Young, 1995, p204). Other Aborigines are surprised that they cannot hunt protected native species, such as echidnas, which are also 'good tucker' (Nationwide News Pty Ltd, 1993, p2). Indeed, Low (1999, pp254–255) notes that it is often difficult, in the absence of a fossil record, to establish whether a species is 'exotic' or 'native', many being 'cryptogenic', a term coined by James Carlton in 1996, and already applied to 95 species in Australian waters.

When plants or animals leave their former 'natural' range, do they become 'exotic' (Low, 1999, p257)? Koalas, the platypus and Gang-gang Cockatoos are 'all introduced species' to Kangaroo Island (Kent, 1990, p337). Certainly the

'White thugs' killing their cocky cousins

By SCOTT MONK

THE short-beaked corella is not only an environmental vandal. It's killing one of its rare cousins.

Corellas are evicting glossy black cockatoo chicks and other birds from their tree-hollow nests on Kangaroo Island so they can move in themselves.

The cockatoo chicks cannot fend for themselves on the ground, so they are doomed.

"It's tantamount to murder because it exposes them to predators and the elements," Kangaroo Island ornithologist Mr Terry Dennis said yesterday.

The latest observation follows attempts by metropolitan and rural councils to introduce corella culling prog-

HOME INVASION: The corella, left, and a pair of glossy black cockatoos.

rams. The birds are under siege for their constant squawking, fouling of council property, stripping tree boughs bare and eating newly-planted seeds.

On Kangaroo Island, as well as pulling chicks out, corellas engage in

their brand of "psychological warfare".

Mr Dennis said they spent hours screeching at any chicks living in hollows or the island's nest boxes in an attempt to "demoralise" and intimidate them.

"They really are white

thugs," he said. Other hollow-nesting birds such as crimson rosellas, yellow-tailed black cockatoos and boobook owls were also in danger.

Compounding the problem are corellas taking over the island's nest box project, which is federally funded and sponsored by *Australian Geographic*.

With a shortage of suitable habitat on the island, the boxes are designed to provide artificial nesting for some of the island's 200 glossy-black cockatoos as part of a breeding program.

The corella is not indigenous to Kangaroo Island. The first sighting was about 30 years ago but the first recorded breeding was only in 1990.

ENVIRONMENTAL EXPERT'S VIEW ON SAVING KANGAROO ISLAND TREES

Shooting koalas the best answer

By JAMES WAKELIN

KANGAROO Island's koala controls had failed and shooting remained the best option to stop them wrecking trees and the environment, a South Australian environmental expert said yesterday.

Adelaide University chairman of environmental science Hugh Possingham said koalas were eating their way through more than 4000ha of prime natural habitat, consisting mainly of manna gums.

"I still believe that shooting is the best option," Professor Possingham said.

But he conceded that this would not happen because of the local and international outcry.

Instead, he believed the koalas should be feared out of parks and other areas most at risk.

Professor Possingham said the...

BARE: A koala on a manna tree almost stripped bare of leaves. The program of sterilisation and relocation, which began in 1997, has not successfully reduced the

"They are not

Figure 5.7 *'Good' and 'Bad' Indigenous Creatures*

Notes: (top) Corellas are described as 'white thugs' killing their black cousins, the glossy black cockatoo (Monk, 1998, p5). The photograph is captioned: 'Home invasion: the corella, left, and a pair of glossy black cockatoos'. Low (2002, pp205–206) notes that possums, galahs and honey bees also threaten the glossy black cockatoo; (middle) the Australian white ibis has spread through much of Victoria, New South Wales and southern Queensland: 'Now there are ibises patrolling parks and slinking down back alleys in Kings Cross. They raid bins and scare children' (Low, 2002, p119). At Currumbin sanctuary, as the photograph suggests, 'Ibises were soon jabbing tourists, upturning bins, frightening children, milling about cafes (in flocks of up to seventy)' (Low, 2002, p 119); (bottom) Adelaide University's then professor of environmental science, Hugh Possingham, opines that 'shooting remained the best option' for culling the koalas stripping the rare manna gums on Kangaroo Island (Wakelin, 2000b, p12).

now over-abundant population of koalas strip trees, endangering prime natural habitat, mainly manna gums, and then face starvation, although the recommendation to cull the koalas causes community outrage (Canfield, 1987a, p27; Baxter and Halstead, 1989, p7; Hurrell, 1997, p3; Plane, 1997, p4). Is the dingo exotic because it was brought here by human agency but the cattle egret is not because it flew in from Asia of its own accord in the 1940s, although it survives because of cattle in Australia? What of the wanderer butterfly that island hopped west across the Pacific, perhaps aided by ships, its caterpillars now feeding on cotton bushes in Australia? (Low, 1999, p257).

An 'imbalance' between 'wild' animals and other elements of the ecosystem can occur due to the impact of human settlement. In March 2000, seagulls 'decimated' a colony of the rare banded stilt, breeding after the flooding of Lake Eyre in central Australia (Pengelley, 2000, p13). Fortunately, although the flooding of Lake Eyre is a rare occurrence, in June 2000 the lake filled again and National Parks officers were prepared. They laid thousands of poison baits; 3500 gulls died while 36,000 stilts produced 40,000 chicks under the watchful gaze of rangers flying over the island almost every day (Low, 2002, p68). In a growing war with humans, populations of gulls in many British towns explode, doubling every eight years, even while they are forced out of cliff-top nesting sites by coastal developments. Gulls retaliate by stealing food from tourists, striking bystanders and deliberately defecating on people (Vidal, 2003, p21). However, proposals to cull overabundant indigenous species often cause public outcry. As one 'weary' environmental scientist noted, in response to 'conservationists complaining to his vice-chancellor and head of department', 'Few other professionals have to slog it out with amateurs on the ground', where scientific debate is displaced by emotional issues (Powell, 1999, p8).

Some introduced elements of the ecosystem become part of the survival strategies of indigenous species. Wedge-tailed eagles rely on road-killed animals, exposing themselves to the same fate, or on dead sheep in paddocks, bringing down on their heads the rifles and poison of graziers (Rolls, 1981, p385). In Belair National Park in Adelaide, the southern brown bandicoot avoids feral cats by surviving in exotic blackberry (Wanke, 1989, p6). The despised lantana 'furnish[es] much-needed cover for wallabies, bandicoots, fairy wrens, reptiles, and almost everything else ... its nectar sates honeyeaters and butterflies, including rare birdwings. Its tiny fruits feed possums, silvereyes, bowerbirds and rosellas, and reed bees nest in the stems' (Low, 2002, p92).

What should be done about dangerous animals in the contact zone, such as mountain lions, dingoes, crocodiles and sharks? Periodically, shark attacks provoke public debate, for example following the death of Ken Crew, taken on suburban North Cottesloe beach in Perth in November 2000. A number of letters to the editor noted the shark was in its own habitat: 'Sharks are not just out for summertime kicks'. Others said that it was a case of 'mistaken identity', the shark believing the human to be a seal: 'they didn't want to kill us at all' (Drewe, 2001, p18–19).[26] The shark nets deployed to protect bathers in eastern waters are a 'wall of death' to sharks, rays, dugong, dolphins and sea turtles (Freeman, 1994, p152). One victim's father attributes the increased numbers of sharks to the ban on killing white pointer sharks, depleted fish stocks and environmental changes (warmer currents coming closer to shore) (Robson, 2001, p1).

Similarly, following the death of a boy, taken by a dingo on Fraser Island, environmentalists and the Aboriginal people of Fraser Island claimed it was unfair to punish dingoes, because people exercise their assumed 'right' to see and feed these animals. However, the Queensland Premier insisted on a dingo cull (Ian McVale, Director of Queensland's Environment Protection Authority, interviewed on 'The World Today', Australian Broadcasting Corporation, Radio National, 5 November 2001). The formerly 'purebred' dingo was reclassified as a 'wild dog' attacking 'innocent people' (Pearce, 2001, pp183–184). '[N]atural behaviours' (including fear of humans) have been 'polluted by their contact with culture', with people (Pearce, 2001, p 189).

While still accounting for few deaths in comparison with dogs, bees and snakes, mountain lions have killed more people in the last 10 years than in the preceding 50 (Baron, 2004, p234). The first adult to be killed by a mountain lion in a century was a jogger in Boulder, Colorado in 1991 (Baron, 2004, p7). '[I]n the Northeast, black bears have encroached on Boston's inner suburbs for the first time in almost two centuries.' The gray wolf, once endangered, now frequently crosses highways in Wisconsin and Minnesota. Coyotes have spread out of the western plains and desert southwest to be seen in major cities such as New York – where one was captured in Central Park – and running into a waiting elevator in Seattle, after triggering the automatic door to a building (Baron, 2004, pp10–11). Just as the dingo's 'natural' behaviour of running from people was altered by habituation, so too have mountain lions been lured to Boulder by the irrigated lawns that attracted the deer on which cougars feed, and the lack of wolves, made extinct by humans, which hunt cougars (Baron, 2004, pp47–51, 134). The mountain lions shifted their habits from nighttime hunting activity to daytime hunting of pets and later humans in Boulder (Baron, 2004, p228). However, even when an 18-year-old young man was killed by a cougar while jogging in 1991, there was no backlash (Baron, 2004, pp211, 226): 'We need to learn to live with them. They were here first' (Baron, 2004, p158).

Kay Milton (2000) explores the dilemma of managing 'wildlife' in relation to the ruddy duck (*Oxyura Jamaicensis*) campaign in the UK. Introduced in the 1940s from North America into wildfowl collections, the ruddy duck now dominates other wildfowl, especially indigenous white-headed ducks (Milton, 2000, p231). Conservationists wish to exterminate the ruddy duck. In their campaign, they apply three culturally defined, but wavering and contestable boundaries: between one species and another, between natives and aliens and between human and non-human processes.

Each of these distinctions collapses under interrogation, as already discussed for the exotic–native distinction. In relation to species boundaries, Tim Low (2002, p262) notes that some Australian bird and other species would disappear if the hybrids in their midst were culled out. The third boundary between human and non-human processes, or 'culture' and 'nature', is contradicted by conservationists at the very moment of their intervention:

> acting like nature's housekeepers, obsessively restoring order by putting things where they belong – eliminating species that are in the wrong place, returning them to where they used to be – tidying up the mess that others (sometimes, ironically, other conservationists) have created.
>
> (Milton, 2000, pp242–243)

Nature conservationists' very self-definition, as conserving the natural, is challenged by the examples of indigenous animals becoming 'dirt' or 'matter out of place' (Milton, 2000, p238), or of endangered indigenous animals finding their survival strategies in sewerage ponds or cattle-grazed paddocks, as Low (2002) so amply documents. But conservationists are loathe to abandon the distinction between nature and human intervention, as 'natural nature' is the very purpose of their work and object of their concern (Milton, 2000, p243). However, in our present world, so utterly trampled by human footprints, this is what we must now confront: 'Doing nothing destroys wilderness. "Wilderness management" is a necessary contradiction' (Low, 2002, p 44).

Conclusion

When Aldo Leopold (1949, p203) grasped the meaning of ecology, he identified the land ethic. We belong to the land as part of a community whose other members we must use with love and respect, rather than identifying the land as being something we own, as men once owned women and slave masters owned slaves. Leopold (1949, p109) argued that, through Darwin, we learned that 'men are only fellow-voyagers with other creatures in the odyssey of evolution'. Later in the century, 'in the broad sweep of Western thought, the conferring of rights to the natural world was a revolutionary, modern concept, in the words of a prominent environmental scholar, 'one of the most extraordinary developments in recent intellectual history' (Nash, cited in Baron, 2004, p156).[27] It is one thing to pass this in our laws and to know this in our minds, as a lesson from ecology, and even science more generally, with its increasingly insistent warnings concerning species decimation and massive climate change. But it is another thing to change our hearts, which is probably also required before most of us will change our actions. Short-term self-interest collides with long-term prognoses. Slavers found it hard to give up their slaves; men find it hard to give up their 'patriarchal dividend' (Connell, 1995, pp82–83); whites find it difficult to relinquish our 'unearned privilege' (McIntosh, 1992, p78). *Homo sapiens* is presented with a huge challenge, being asked to exercise a stewardship of nature that requires, for many of us, material sacrifice. How we might imagine this task is the subject of the final chapter.

6
Respectful Stewardship of a Hybrid Nature

Contesting dualisms in late capitalism

> There are more human babies born daily than there are individuals in all the great ape species combined.
>
> (Richard Cincotta, ecologist and researcher for Population Action International, in Scourfield, 2001, p1)

> The prospect of us making elephants extinct saps the moral authority with which I want to argue that it is preferable to shoot an elephant than to shoot a human baby. I believe that Homo sapiens sapiens does have claims to priority but our behaviour is making it harder and harder to put that case.
>
> (Humphrey McQueen, 1991, p231)

Chapters 4 and 5 touched on the tension in contemporary industrialized societies between the Enlightenment, or turn to reason, and its disenchantment of the world, or loss of spirituality, meaning, a higher realm. As Charles Taylor (1989, p413) suggests, Enlightenment and Romanticism are still in battle today as the 'struggle between the technologically and the ecologically oriented'. It would appear that a rather base form of Enlightenment is winning this battle, in the form of instrumentalism. Marx (1965, p72) presciently foresaw the fetishism of commodities, the way in which capitalism encourages us to treat people as things and value ourselves by the goods and services we can acquire (see also Taylor, 1989, p500). The 'end of history' (Fukuyama, 1992) is one label given to the global spread of capitalist production and neo-liberal ideologies, trumpeted in the transformation of formerly communist economies and the success story of the 'Asian dragons' and their expanding middle classes. A mass of information and cultural production saturates our daily lives and seeps into our psyches, commodifying our subjectivities and social relations, as Naomi Klein (2000) argues in *No Logo*. She links the spread of multinational capitalist production throughout the world with its colonization of public spaces (schools, streetscapes, cultural performances), so that we identify ourselves through our consumption of particular brand names. We become *Branded,* as Quart (2003) discusses for teenagers in the US. '(B)y adulthood the average American can identify 1000 corporate logos, which they began to recognize at the age of six months, but only ten plants' (Kilbourne, 2003, p7). Commodification is expressed in the increased requirements of a good life: a second colour television set was felt necessary by 10 per cent of respondents in a Roper poll in 1975 and 28 per cent in 1991; the importance of a lot of money increased from 38 per cent to 55 per cent, while that of a happy marriage declined from 84 per cent to 77 per cent (Hochschild, 2003, p144).

In commodity fetishism, we express our identities as 'knowing consumers' through self-adornment, home decoration and so on (Andrews and Whorlow, 2000, p253). Self-definition as consumers has displaced the identity of citizenship so that 'self-interested citizens increasingly view government policies like other market transactions, judging them by how well served they feel personally' (Cohen, 2003, p9). Our subjectivities have become individualized, privatized, commodified. We understand ourselves through therapy and self-help, in which the objective is to find our 'authentic self', and to 'love, honour, and cherish yourself' (Hazleden, 2003, pp416–417). Other humans are judged in terms of the pleasure they are likely to deliver, in 'value for money' terms, as 'an investment like all the others', as 'eminently disposable' (Bauman, 2003, pp75, 12–13).

If we have learned to treat other humans as instruments of our satisfaction, it is little wonder that many of us treat animals the same way. Even apparently pro-animal philosophies such as Singer's utilitarianism and Regan's (1982; 1991; see also Stephen Clark, 1977) approach are described by Val Plumwood (2002 p148)[1] as a minimalist position in which very few animals, only those most like humans, are reclassified out of the category of potential 'property' into the category of 'persons': 'Minimalism does not really dispel speciesism, it just extends and disguises it'.

Against instrumentalism and capitalism is pitted Romanticism and nature, including a turn to New Age philosophies and other spiritualities. Based on the last census, Bouma argues that 'New Age' is the fastest growing religious grouping in Australia, with over 30,000 Australians identifying themselves as affiliates (Possamaï, 2000, p374). In one UK Demos Survey, about half the women had an interest in New Age phenomena, spirituality, alternative therapies or using emotions to make decisions (Wilkinson and Howard, 1997, p10). A growing number of 'seekers' pursue their 'keen personal interest in spirituality' outside institutional religious settings, so that 70 per cent of people in the US believe one can be religious without going to church (Cimino and Lattin, 1998, p11). 'Shopping for faith' responds to the intersection of individualization and commodification, as well as the displacement of the rhetoric of sin and judgement by spirituality and mysticism (Wuthnow, 1998, p66; Cimino and Lattin, 1998, p19). At the World Bank, a 'Spiritual Unfoldment Society' meets every week (Cimino and Lattin, 1998, p36). The men's movement retreats to the forest and drumming to recapture industrialized men's lost links with their wild natures (Torgovnick, 1998, p169).

Much of this 'search for meaning' is personalized, commodified, depoliticized, at least in the traditional understandings of politics. New Age and the other (re)turns to nature are often barely disruptive of our ordinary lives, being expressed in the purchase of commodities and practised in the comfort of one's suburban home. Most seekers continue to lead material lives. New Age requires no jettisoning of family, property, bodily health, good company, social acceptance, comfort (Torgovnick, 1998, p186). It has no political goals. American Indian rituals are imitated but there is no call to return US land to its original owners (Torgovnick, 1998, p187). Teen desire for utopianism and spirituality is expressed in the popularity of figures like *Buffy, the Vampire Slayer* (Quart, 2003, p192). Business consultants have enlisted men's movement experts to increase productivity and profitability (Torgovnick, 1998, p169). Self-help has become a management tool for the 'corporate motivators' (Brockes, 1999, p25). These examples contrast with Rousseau's philosophy, whose sympathy for other animals suggested greater material austerity (Taylor, 1989, p359). Indeed, some environmentalists resist the commodification of their culture, for example the 'ferals' dress in recycled garb and folk-jewellery such as feathers, skulls and umbilical cord necklaces. They live in semi-nomadism, relying on welfare benefits to support their political work (St John, 2000, pp213–214).

Where our turn to nature is not framed within capitalist logics, it is sometimes too utopian. Hyperseparation from our non-Western 'others' is expressed variously in environmental ethics and politics. In the nature–native–woman construction, the first world is cause of all environmental degradation while the 'natives' (variously south Asian women, hunter-gatherers, believers in animist or pantheist religions) are the source of all environmental wisdom and are incapable of harming the wild world. Plumwood (1993, p180) claims that deep ecology stresses such continuity and kinship so that difference disappears altogether, producing psychological identification and extreme holism. Indeed, deep ecologists argue that the fate of the sea turtle is their own fate. Pantheism and goddess movements are liable to an oceanic account that anthropomorphizes nature (Plumwood, 1993, pp126–127). Plumwood (2002, pp143–166) avoids the dualism of both deep ecology (our utter and almost helpless submission to awe-inspiring nature) and of science-in-the-service-of-capitalism's domination (the natural world is improved through assimilation into the cultural world of human goods) by claiming that humans must practise dialogic communication with others.

Following Plumwood, this chapter twists and challenges such dualisms. The classic dichotomies constructing woman–native–nature range knowledge against desire, the mind against the body, civilization against nature, the scientific against the romantic. The concept of 'respectful stewardship' of a 'hybrid nature' suggests that we need to overcome these dualisms for a patchwork way of imagining the natural cultural world. We need to combine our desires with our convictions, 'the sensible as well as the intelligible' (Ahmed et al, 2000, p16), seeking a productive dialogue between head and heart. Humans need to see ourselves neither as totally separate from and superior to nature, the perspective of modernism, nor as totally immersed in and undifferentiated from it, the perspective of premodernism. Instead we need to forge a postmodern relationship with the non-human world, one which accepts the vast imbalance in power and destructive potential between humans and the wild world and also notes the epistemological difficulty of seeing the world from the perspective of wild others.

In true postmodern vein, we will need to relinquish our desire for 'authenticity' and learn to love and nourish a hybrid nature, which will encompass our backyards as well as the ozone layer, walking tracks as well as icebergs in Antarctica. How do we treat respectfully with pets, zoo animals, stock animals, experimental animals, as well as the wild animals that spin our dreams? As this list of animal others suggests, one of the greatest barriers to this reconceptualization is self-interest, the difficulty of giving up our 'homo sapiens dividend', to adapt Connell's (1995, pp82–83) notion of the patriarchal dividend.

The guilty pleasures of self-actualizing tourists[2]

> When you're in nature don't try to be someone else, don't try to be
> someone that you can't be, just be yourself and try to be free and put
> all your worries off and have fun. If you're not a very fun person, go
> out in nature and maybe you will be more fun.
>
> (11 year old boy from Dallas, in Lannis Temple, 1992, p63)

> Admiral Bird, when asked what there was to do in Antarctica, replied,
> 'Resist temptation'.
>
> (Simon, Antarctica guide, as we watched an aurora, a mysterious green glimmering
> arc against the soft black heavens, January 1995)

The humane movement, which arose among the urbanized middle class produced by the Industrial Revolution, is said to be the first significant body of champions of cruelly treated animals. However, where the humane movement opposed the vivisection of experimental animals, the beating of horses on London's streets and the cruel treatment of pets, particularly of dogs and cats, they raised hardly a murmur against fox-hunting and ignored the killing of animals for human consumption (Ryder, 1989, pp152–154, 165; Jasper and Nelkin, 1992, p4; Tuan, 1984, p112; Walker, 1991, p27).[3] When the cat lover Jeremy Bentham, founder of utilitarianism and the humane movement (Ryder, 1989, p75), cried, 'The question is not, Can they *reason*? nor, Can they *talk*?

but, Can they *suffer?*' (in Turner, 1980, p13 and Singer, 1977, p219), he referred not so much to cows and sheep but to dogs and cats. Even so, new sensibilities meant that slaughterhouses had to be hidden from the public eye (Thomas, 1983, pp300–301). In France the term, *abattoir*, to fell trees (Franklin, 1999, p156), replaced the term, *tuerie*, meaning to kill an animal, except among rural people and those who work in abattoirs (Vialles, 1994, pp50–51).

Similarly, although my respondents challenged the status quo in relation to a number of environmental issues, they were much readier to endorse a version of the 'status quo', or urban self-interest, as Adelma Hills (1993) calls it, in relation to stock animals. Hills (1993, pp115, 118, 124) discovered that people's empathy for the suffering of animals was mediated by their self-interest, farmers, for example, showing the highest empathy for an image of a shot rhinoceros, suggesting that instrumentality (or necessity) represses feelings of empathy in relation to farm animals. For the urban public, their attitudes varied with the particular issue, depending on 'how much they are directly affected, the emotional appeal of the animal concerned, the degree of cruelty involved, the prevailing social norms, or the persuasiveness of different arguments'.

Meat-eating animal lovers often appear to acknowledge no inconsistency; in 1992 pet owners ate more meat and take-away food than people who did not own pets (Gaynor, 1999, p35). Despite campaigns against battery hens and other intensive animal raising (Knight, 2000b, pp300–31), very few of my respondents at the animal encounter sites were troubled by meat-eating, killing pests around the house, or farming stock animals for human consumption (between 4 and 5 per cent), although women were more opposed to these activities than men. This can be compared with much greater outrage at using animals for experimentation (for example to develop cosmetics: 90 per cent disapproval) (see Table A3.17 in Appendix 3). Among my focus groups, only two had ever been vegetarian, one a sometime member of Animal Liberation and one a member of Greenpeace. Most drew the meat-eating line at dolphins or kangaroos ('eating Skippy'). One focus group member also drew the line at battery hens: 'there's no need for that' and 'the humane way will always sell in the nineties'. Again reflecting self-interest, my survey respondents were not, on the whole, opposed to breeding and keeping animals in zoos (17 per cent), although there was greater opposition to keeping dolphins in aquaria (60 per cent) (Table A3.17 in Appendix 3).

Ecotourism presents something of a similar contradiction and dilemma, not only for site managers but also for ecotourists ourselves. Some visitors to Phillip Island have 'a sense of unease and even guilt about visiting the penguins, a feeling that their presence is not good for the birds' (Jarvis, 2000, p171). Such a sense of guilty pleasure, a tension between our enjoyment of the animal encounter and a suspicion that the animal is not enjoying the encounter, is a thread running through my research findings:

> In theory I am against their [dolphins'] captivity, but am grateful for
> the experience as I have never had a chance to see them in the wild.
>
> (male, company director, speaking of his visit to Sea World in San Diego)

One of the focus group members said of his Hamilton Island dolphin experience, 'I don't approve but I was lucky enough to get in with dolphins'. An Antarctica respondent 'took advantage of the situation'. A handful of visitors to Auckland Zoological Park and Currumbin commented on the apparent unhappiness of the animals (discussed in Chapter 1). Several visitors to Monkey Mia knew something of the management dilemmas, one contrasting pleasure and anxiety:

> They are possibly becoming too tame and dependent on humans…
> I enjoy seeing the dolphins because they are so gentle and friendly –
> I hope the humans visiting the dolphins can be worthy of the trust and
> never abuse this or hurt the dolphins.
>
> (female, administrative assistant, aged 20–29)

Given their socioeconomic background, many ecotourists desire the David Attenborough experience without forgoing the creature comforts of home: the lodge, hot shower, warm bed, gin and tonic. A flood of research documents the cost to host communities, particularly in developing countries, of the tourism industry. One white middle class person in the US consumes 100 times the food and energy mass of a Third World person.[4] First world corporations are the biggest polluters and resource consumers (Heller, 1993, p225), and they dominate tourism (McLaren, 1998, p14),[5] offering experiences to suit the tastes of wealthy Westerners. Criticisms of tourism include low multiplier effects due to foreign ownership of hotels and resorts (Pattullo, 1996, p39; Brockelman and Dearden, 1990, p142) combined with high cultural and environmental degradation. Some tourist resorts use obscene amounts of water and fuel compared with local usage rates.[6] Despite claims that ecotourism sometimes encourages restoration of the environment, McLaren (1998, pp12–13) retorts: 'Developers are notorious for filling in swamps, mangroves, and coral reefs' and ultimately recreating 'the environment and culture on top of the real thing'. As a result, tourism might narrow, rather than expand, the mind (Crick, 1989, p331).[7]

In hunter-gatherer communities, national parks present a bursting larder to the land hungry people forced to live outside them (Ritvo, 1987, pp284, 279; Marsh, 1987, p35; Daltabuit and Pi-Sunyer, 1990, p10). One solution is to share the profits of ecotourism with the locals, for example locals earn money as guides (Brockelman and Dearden, 1990, p142 in Thailand), receive the meat as well as some proceeds from the sale of limited elephant hunting licences (Peterson, 1994, pp99, 103–104) in Zimbabwe's Communal Areas Program for Indigenous Resources (CAMPFIRE), or share in the revenues from wildlife viewing. While such arrangements support poaching patrols and land reclamation for wildlife in some locations, elsewhere it appears there are too many claimants on the national park's resources to readily buy them off (e.g. in the Galapagos: Bellos, 2001, p5).

In response to these dilemmas, ecotourists are encouraged to become ethical tourists, to seek experiences that are less 'abstract' and more 'concrete'. They should use local produce and accommodation; allow local guides and people to determine the content of the tour; and learn about social issues from local intellectuals, labour leaders, religious community workers, radicalized students or peasant groups (Ryel and Grasse, 1991, p167; O'Grady, 1982, p10).These recommendations formed the basis of Community Aid Abroad's 'One World Travel', until the name was sold to Qantas – clearly indicating its cachet (Martin Wurt, Visual Media Coordinator, Oxfam Community Aid Abroad, email communication, 16 March 2004). Ecotourists might work with scientific research projects 'monitoring crocodile populations, protecting the Eastern Barred Bandicoot and conducting koala surveys', or building boardwalks in national parks (Fincke, 1992, pp12–14 describing the Australian Trust for Conservation Volunteers).

Even better, according to some writers, ecotourists should 'stay at home from time to time' (Krippendorf in Miller and Kaae, 1993, p40). In this vein, the greenest zoo might be the virtual zoo with satellite links to the Amazon, Great Barrier Reef and Antarctica and a virtual reality sensorium in downtown New York or Sydney (Healey, 1992, p33).[8] Of course staying at home puts us back in front of our television sets where we experience only the 'abstract wild', and perhaps fail to change our views and ways.

The research reported in this book suggests several factors that encourage a possibly life-shifting response from visitors to animal encounter sites. As long as humans outnumber animals, their messages and impact are muted. On the Port River, there was just Mike, me and 30 or so dolphins over the course of the morning: the human–dolphin ratio favours the dolphins. It is the other way round at Monkey Mia. A telling finding from my survey is that too many people and too few animals are the most frequently cited reasons for not enjoying the animal encounter (Table A3.8 in Appendix 3). But something more is at stake here than merely the mass versus elite tourist market (Craik, 1991, p111), the cachet of being among the very few tourists to the site. Another factor is the degree of separation between the encounter experience and daily life, separation by both time and distance. Mike Bossley (interviewed on 19 December 2000) can understand people being changed by a week in the bush, but finds it 'pretty amazing' that they would report such a dramatic impact 'after only three or four hours of being with dolphins'.

Some encounters, in their timing, accentuate this separation from dailiness. Both Warrawong and the Port River are about half an hour's drive from the centre of Adelaide, but these encounters start just after dawn. The visitor has been absent from 'civilization', and certainly from great crowds of people, for at least 12 hours – first in sleep and then in navigating the almost deserted streets of a darkened city. In a sense, one wakes up in the Australian bush surrounded by bettongs (rat-kangaroos) or on a river with dolphins huffing and splashing around the boat. Another factor influencing the intensity of the encounter is the frequency of animal encounters between the 'dulling' time in cities. I felt the pain of separation from Antarctica for months, but not years. It is only with difficulty that I can now summon a remnant of those heart-tearing emotions. The environment is also important, not only that it is 'natural' but also that it is 'magical', full of 'solitude', 'romantic' with no apparent human manipulation, as in places like the Great Australian Bight (Reid, 1996, p43)[9] or Antarctica.

The next section explores how these animal encounters can be turned to new forms of awareness and political action. It is actually quite difficult to deny the benefits of living in an industrialized but polluting society (for example our use of motor vehicles or aeroplanes, of commodities that are produced by destroying the environment). It is less difficult, but still an achievement, to refuse to use any animal products in one's daily round.[10] Given this, it is hardly surprising that more than knowledge is required to shift our environmental attitudes.

Hybrid nature

[I want to] translate the words of animals to my friends and teachers.

We should consider the feelings of trees and grass to make man become more friendly with nature.

Eating animal meat is cruel to animals but if we don't eat them, we can't survive.

I want to become rich without destroying nature in the future.

[instead of playing video games indoors] I would like to be able to play freely in nature for just one single day.

(Japanese children's letters on the environment contributed to Temple, 1992, pp78, 79, 15, 12)

Rey Chow (1991) criticizes approaches to Chinese studies that either involve incorporation, assimilation of the other into the self, or submission to the totally different and uncontaminated other. Paradoxically, the submission approach also recasts the other as an extension of the self, so that in neither incorporation nor submission does the other retain a separate identity. Stories concerning how others – non-Westerners – treat animals veer between a noble savage approach and an orientalist approach, between submission and incorporation.

Sometimes 'they' are more reverential, connected, vegetarian than 'we' are. At other times, 'they' are cruel, hunt animals to extinction, do not value nature

Notes: That many Westerners may be more diffident than many Asians to honestly confronting the animal sources of their steaks, leather and furs is suggested by the happy cow yielding slices of her buttocks as steaks to advertise a Beijing restaurant in 2001; (bottom) and 'Models [who] stun a New Year's Eve fashion parade in Beijing with costumes designed to look like cuts of meat' (MATP, 'Tender is the night in fashion steaks' *The Australian*, 3–4 January 2004, p10, photograph courtesy of AFP).

Figure 6.1 *Eating Meat and Saving the Environment*

or wilderness, and so need to be improved to our level. Asian countries, like Bali and the Philippines (and even some southern European countries like Spain) are berated for their cockfights, cricket fights and bull races (Baker, 1993, p7; McNeely and Wachtel, 1988, p153; Rolls, 1992, pp370–371). Australian newspapers decry the 'cruel death' of dogs killed for food in Hanoi or Seoul (Bolt, 1998, p23; King, 1999, p26).[11] Colin Thubron (1987, pp184–185) finds it incongruous that the menu in the Wild Game restaurant in southern China includes 'Steamed Cat and Shredded Cat Thick Soup' while a pet cat lives in the restaurant and the windows are glazed 'with pretty pictures of the animals concerned: deer and cats wearing necklaces'. But how is this different from enthusiastic chickens and cows in advertisements on Western television screens encouraging us to cannibalize them? Asians' use of animal extracts for naturopathic medicines is decried, for example the use of Asiatic or Moon bears to produce traditional Chinese medicines (e.g. O'Donnell, 2000b, p14; O'Donnell, 2001, pp23–24), while Western women take hormone replacement therapy derived from pregnant mares' urine.

Any dualist opposition that homogenizes one side against the other, and which almost always makes one side 'good' and the other 'bad', excuses adherents from difficult analysis. My notion of 'respectful stewardship' of a 'hybrid nature' seeks to avoid the domination advocated by the Bible and science, while also eschewing the abrogation of responsibility that merging with the 'native' appears to offer New Age spiritualists, even some deep ecologists and ecofeminists.

Postmodern ironies

> we are not tourists here.
>
> (Mary Midgley, 1978, p195)

Aspects more peculiar to Western culture than perhaps to other cultures are hurdles to this quest. For many in predictable urban environments, nature is no longer 'dangerous and powerful' (Kalland and Asquith, 1997, p21), perhaps no longer an element in the world that requires our respect, instead being reduced to Flipper, Skippy, or the nightly weather forecast (Turner, 1996, p28). Few citysiders ever experience that attention, perception and emotion of confronting a grizzly bear, when 'you feel yourself as part of the biological order known as the food chain'. For mountaineers, the 'beauty of the mountains' is a 'gift granted to them only because they have risked their life for it' (Gaita, 2002, p145). So too are the Inuit more afraid than Westerners, 'because they accept fully what is violent and tragic in nature', that sudden cataclysms are as much a part of life as the pause to look at something beautiful (Lopez, 1986, p201). Lack of awe and fear may make it hard to develop *respectful* stewardship.

Second, Western scientific approaches to the world are reductionist and mechanistic, whereas, for example, 'nature in Japan is understood holistically and spiritually', as 'situational or contextual' (Kalland and Asquith, 1997, pp19, 9, 11; see also Ackermann, 1997, p51). While it is an expression of orientalism to oppose the Japanese view of nature to the Western view, the blending of science with Shintoism makes the Japanese approach less dualistic, less calculative, more emotional. Even so, the ultimate superiority of humans and the quest for modernist development explain the extreme forms of environmental degradation happily carried out by the construction industry in alliance with politicians (McCormack, 1996).

Third, not only is Western philosophy shot through with dualist ways to carve up our understanding of the world, but the search for 'authenticity', and the spiritual yearning associated with this, may be a peculiar quest for contemporary industrialized Westerners. This desire makes it harder for us to give up the idea of untouched wilderness, of wild free animals.[12] Yet stewardship requires us to learn to love a manipulated nature, to value it as much as the imagined wilderness of our romantic dreams. Some commentators suggest that this willingness to accept hybridization is a mark of the postmodern approach.

Evidence of playful postmodern ironies include genre-knowing nature documentaries, 'dark' tourism and parodies in animal shows at animal encounter sites. At the end of the seal show at UnderWater World at Mooloolaba on Queensland's Sunshine Coast, if the seals choose to swim back out, there is a photo opportunity for visitors. When Christina Jarvis (2000, p114) was there, the seals declined to swim back, the audience applauding this expression of agency rather than being annoyed they could not take a photograph. At San Diego's Sea World, the audience also enjoyed built-in misbehaviour by the orcas (Davis, 1997, p191).

As Franklin (1999, p48) suggests, wildlife shows now include punk presenters, audience questions and do-it-yourself pet care. *Big Cat Diary* is billed as 'Simon King and crew are back in Kenya to give the very latest on the Big Cat "soap opera"' (no author, television programme, *The Weekend Australian*, 20–21 June 1998, p33). In parodying the documentary genre, the commentator asks the viewer both to understand that animals are closer kin than nature documentaries once accepted, but not quite as close as the voiceover implies. These documentaries address television-literate viewers who can laugh at themselves believing in the truth of nature. An example of the self-parody mode is *In the Wild: Lemurs with John Cleese* (Kershaw, 1998), made by the BBC in 1998. John Cleese sets out to discover how a captive lemur breeding and release programme is faring in Madagascar: 'Here I am, a British comedian bred in captivity, ... about to be released in the wild, thousands of miles from the nearest cappuccino'. While we are offered the obligatory environmental message – their main predator is 'us, I'm afraid', '*Homo sapiens*? *Homo hooliganus* more like' – the gushiness of wildlife documentaries is also parodied. At the end of a gruelling journey into the jungle, Cleese catches a glimpse of one of the lemurs. He asks, 'Was it worth it, just a glimpse, for a second and a half, 150 yards away? Of course it wasn't worth it! You little bastards!' he shouts at the lemurs.

Where the search for authenticity is the preoccupation of modern humans, postmodern people are far too sophisticated to believe in the 'real': 'we would argue, in contrast to MacCannell, that many tourists are in search of inauthenticity' (Ritzer and Liska, 1997, p107). Such tourists are happy to visit historic sites or animal encounters remade as theme parks or installations. An amusement park in Lithuania is known as Stalin World (created by Viliumas Malinauskas: Associated Press, 2001, p41). In East German theme park shops, clerks are surly and unhelpful and the only goods are those that were available in communist times. At Williamsburg, slave auctions are re-enacted (Kirschenblatt-Gimblatt, 1998, p173).

According to some academics, postmodernist post-tourists play the tourist game, recognizing that there is no authentic tourist experience (Urry, 1990, p11; Ritzer and Liska, 1997, p102). So popular is a sub-genre, 'dark tourism', that a book has been dedicated to it. 'It is clear from a number of sources that tourist interest in recent death, disaster and atrocity is a growing phenomenon in the late twentieth and early twenty-first centuries' (Lennon and Foley, 2000, p3), including tours of 'death sites' such as the Graceland home of Elvis Presley; victims of serial killers such as Sharon Tate (Lennon and Foley, 2000, pp5,10). The *Schindler's List* film sets now function as a Schindler's Tour which is nearer and more concentrated than Auschwitz I and Birkenau (Lennon and Foley, 2000, p64; see also Rojek, 1997, p70). But whether these tourists are playfully ironic about their tourism is another matter. Donald Horne (1992, p375) suggests that tourists rarely act as semioticians. Most tourists do not even look properly, let alone 'give up sight-*seeing* for sight-*experiencing*'.[13]

A postmodern approach reveals that understandings of the natural world are not immutable but change with the lessons of history and the impact of technologies; are refracted through different landscapes and different cultures. Brigid Hains (2002) argues that two Australian frontiers, Antarctica and the Inland, did not function as escape from the femininity of the city, a point argued in Chapter 4. They were hybridized as both frontier and a place improved by civilization. The Inland was like the desert of the Old Testament, a wilderness, yes (Hains, 2002, p101), but one that could be transformed into a 'civilized, modern, scientific Australia' (Hains, 2002, p106). Exploring their frontiers at a later date, Mawson and Flynn combine the earlier edge of empire frontier notions with a more scientific, rational, capitalist, masculinity (as defined by Connell, 1997, p9). For example an Antarctic team member ironically poses as the great white hunter over a Weddell seal (they being easy prey), thus self-deprecatingly aping the earlier masculinist frontiersmen. The image also refers to the naturalist's calculative rationality, his accumulation of knowledge, which is the actual purpose of killing the seal (Hains, 2002, pp60–61).

Mawson and Flynn 'celebrated the frontier and its individualism', as 'an essential complement to civilization, as an opportunity for liberation from confining domesticity and settled life', and as something that would be 'moderated and restrained by a sense of wider community and responsibility'. Their hybrid utopia was of a 'wilderness civilisation', 'a paradigm shift' in understanding 'what bound a nation as an imagined community together'. Technology enabled this remote civilization, Mawson leading the first Antarctic mainland expedition to use a wireless (Hains, 2002, p55) and Flynn introducing nursing care, the wireless, and, of course, the flying doctor aeroplane to the outback (Hains, 2002, p149). Technology also incorporated this imagined frontier into the imagined community that was Australian nationalism, via the photograph, the wireless, the motor vehicle, the aeroplane (Hains 2002, pp74–75).

The ironies and hybridities with which Flynn and Mawson played have multiplied to such an extent that some commentators suggest that our present time, our postmodern time, is a time without a 'grand narrative' (Burawoy, 2000b, p348). We have lost 'the master narrative of progress that informed the social movements of the 1960s and 70s' (Scott, 1997, piii). Nancy Fraser (1997, p3) agrees that there is no credible, progressive alternative to 'marketizing social relations, eroding social protections, and worsening the life-chances of billions'. Not everyone is as pessimistic. For some who take their philosophical sustenance from nature, we can forge new narratives in a dialogue with nature, but only by eschewing the modernist dualisms of nature–culture and human–other species. Val Plumwood (2002) suggests a hybridized approach which acknowledges human instrumentalism but limits it through a meaningful dialogue with earth others.

Putting 'respect' into stewardship

> Our intelligence gives us immense responsibility as stewards of the planet. I just hope we have time.
>
> (Jane Goodall in Goldberg, 2000)

> At this turning point in our relationship with Earth,
> We work for an evolution from dominance to partnership,
> From fragmentation to connection, from insecurity to interdependence.
>
> (David Suzuki Foundation, 1992, 'Declaration of Interdependence', distributed at 'Wisdom of the Elders', public lecture, Adelaide 16 May 1992)

The notion of wilderness as 'the cathedral of spiritual uplift' or 'the salvation of the world' (Plumwood, 1993, p163) proposes a hyperseparation between wilderness and culture, the idea of a terrain untouched by humans. Until the Pleistocene, humans owned no more than a few thousandths of 1 per cent of the earth's surface. Today, by contrast, there is no wilderness anywhere on the planet, 'no footprint-free world' (Janzen, 1998, pp1312–1313). Thus intervention in the natural world is a fact, but it is often far from stewardship.

Indeed, deep ecologists are horrified by the hubris suggested by the notion of stewardship, seeing it as little different from the dominion advocated by the Bible. They feel that nature should be left alone to get on with its own healing.

By contrast, Heather Aslin's (1996, pp304–305) respondents 'tacitly accepted that humans have a stewardship responsibility' towards wildlife. And they believed that humans were perfectly competent to acquit this. My focus group members were similarly confident (if not always knowledgeable!). Someone suggested that elephants had to be culled to preserve the environment and a woman replied, 'I don't like it'. 'But you can understand why it has to be done,' chorused some others. 'Yes,' she said, 'I can understand it, but I don't like it.' She was expressing a reluctant admission to human stewardship.[14]

Humanity needs to find a connection with the natural world that does not pretend humans are incapable of mass destruction, a connection in which humans accept the responsibility of our power. Daniel Janzen (1998, pp1312–1313) suggests that we understand so-called wilderness as 'wildland gardens', gardens that grow 'wilds'. As gardens, we use them for sustenance but we also expend on them 'care, planning, investment, zoning, insurance, fine-tuning, research, and premeditated harvest'. Applying Janzen's idea to reefs, Jeremy Jackson (1998) defines sustainability as 'putting your money in the bank and living on the interest'. He believes no wild system is sustainable; nothing now can survive if left alone. Almost all coral reefs in the world are dying, showing signs of stress, or becoming unbalanced because of human impacts, for example too many turtles or seals cause faeces that encourage plankton blooms or close beaches. Jackson (1998) also calls for 'reef gardens': to meet the needs of tourists, for food, as a source of pets and so on. Biruté Galdikas (1995, p252) was lured by the 'naturalistic fallacy' of 'going back to nature', to a 'Garden of Eden', but now knows it must be weeded, pruned, sprayed. As David Baron concludes from his study of mountain lions in Boulder, 'We can bring the lions and wolves and bears back to America, and there are many good reasons to do so – ecological reasons, spiritual ones – but these great animals will not restore a mythic past, cannot erase the need for human intervention' (Baron, 2004, p239).

Unfortunately, we do not yet know how to garden reefs and will have to learn through debates and experiments, the wet equivalents of culling and controlled fires in national parks.[15] Indeed, wildlife 'management' in the US still means managing fish and game stocks for hunters and fishers.[16] However, a few organizations are providing remedial training for problem bears habituated to humans, chased with dogs or shot with non-lethal shot; wolves which are scared from sheep flocks with strobe lighting and sounds of highway traffic; does which are given contraceptives (Baron, 2004, pp238–239). But the real need is to change human behaviour, with people planting gardens, disposing of rubbish and so on in the acceptance that 'we are participants in the natural world, not mere observers' (Baron, 2004, p239).

If we are to *manage* nature instead of merely to love it or destroy it, perhaps our knowledge, and our willingness to forgo some creature comforts and material rewards, will derive from working in nature, rather than merely reading about it or even viewing it. John Berger (1980, pp4–5) suggests that in hunting and farming times, animals were 'mortal and immortal' in perhaps the 'first existential dualism'. 'They were subjected *and* worshipped, bred *and* sacrificed.' People who no longer live intimately with animals on which they depend cannot understand this. To us, 'but' should separate the terms of treatment rather than 'and'. To pastoralists and farmers, there is no contradiction in the 'and'. Those who live with nature as loggers, Inuit whale hunters, fishermen, 'often oppose the preserving of nature' (Turner, 1996, p83), as did a greater percentage of my respondents who grew up in the bush (see Table A3.17 in Appendix 3, for example in relation to expanding national parks or wood-chipping native forests).

I am not advocating we copy the 'hoons' who kill dolphins, discussed at the end of Chapter 3. Neither am I claiming that farmers are the only true ecologists. I am arguing that we listen to the claims made by some apologists for hunting. There are forms of connection with the wild that involve killing, sacrificing it, even dominating it in some ways. One of my Port Adelaide respondents, a male pensioner, who said of swimming with dolphins, 'I swim with them and they talk to me', also noted:

> I shoot vermin [feral animals] to try to protect the environment and
> give the natural fauna a chance to survive... I'm a bushy. I live alone in
> the scrub. I fish and shoot to live. I usually eat what I shoot, also I tan
> the hides.

Hunting for food might be a perspective that situates people in the environment, having rights of harvest but not destruction, as much for traditional people who live off the land as for modern citizens. In Chapter 4, as a retort to hunters who accuse other meat eaters of hypocrisy, I mentioned Andrea Gaynor's (1999, p34) proffered solution of the suburban chook run. Gaynor suggests that many suburban backyards have become a microcosm of our loss of connection with nature and an assertion of abstract control. Patios have replaced duck ponds; barbecues and flowerbeds have displaced vegetable gardens. The killing, plucking and eating of chooks (a memorable practice in my own childhood):

> served as a humble and immediate reminder that death is necessary for
> life, that human control of nature is limited, and that we are all part of
> larger cycles of nutrient recycling, growth and decay.
>
> (Gaynor, 1999, p37)

Gaynor (1999, pp26–27) criticizes environmentalists' lack of interest in the relations between people and domestic animals, just as Aslin criticizes a focus on knowing about animals and nature from television and books rather than from our hands and hearts.[17] We need to combine science/rationality/ abstraction and emotion/empathy/intimacy, seeming opposites. Thus Mike Bossley (interviewed on 19 December 2000) insisted I go out with him to see the dolphins and have the experience that he couldn't describe and I could only feel.

Bent Flyvbjerg (2001, p99) suggests that dualistic thinking 'makes it easy to think but hard to understand'. Plumwood (1993, p66), among a number of environmental philosophers (e.g. Sagan and Druyan, 1992, p413; Oelschlaeger, 1991, p297; and Lynn, 1998 for an overview), claims we need to break out of dualism altogether with 'liberatory analogues' that produce new values. This will not be easy as humans are used to thinking of ourselves as powerful, all-knowing actors who are not dependent on the rest of the natural world (Plumwood, 2002, p194). Instead, we must recognize our continuity with others as 'ecological collaborators in our lives' (Plumwood, 2002, p195), and as independent beings who have knowledge that humanity lacks (Plumwood, 2002, p194). Furthermore, we must then act on this knowledge with 'generosity', resource distribution, to save both other lives and our own futures (Plumwood, 2002, pp132, 194). Working towards such a balance between a 'them' on which we are intimately dependent, and from whom we learn with respect, and an 'us', who perhaps will remain central in our ethics,[18] is much more intellectually and emotionally demanding than any absolutist position. It will be an endlessly renegotiated trapeze act.

We must 'take some distance from our own immediate impulses, desires and interests in order to consider their relation to the demands of others, their consequences if acted upon, and so on'. But this does not mean taking up some cosmic 'view from nowhere' 'emptied of its particularity and all trace of our own location'. Rather, we should practise empathy: 'putting ourselves in the other's place, seeing the world to some degree from the perspective of an other with needs and experiences both similar to and different from our own' (Plumwood, 2002, p132). Plumwood (2002, p189) suggests that '(p)erhaps the most important task for human beings', and the most difficult, will be this dialogic communication.

In an earlier book, Plumwood (1993, p160) offers two examples of a communication with others whose needs we neither completely understand nor see as our own. 'The mother does not have to give herself over to the oral pleasures of the child. We can be delighted that our local bandicoot colony is thriving without ourselves acquiring a taste for beetles.' But how does the mother know the child's oral pleasures? How do we know that beetles are in bandicoots' 'interests', part of their 'flourishing'? Philosophical debate concerning human obligations to animals often turns on how we can possibly know animals' rights, needs or interests. This assumes that animals are so different from humans that it is ridiculous to extend rights to them (e.g. see Frey, 1980 and Midgley, 1983 in reply). Plumwood and Midgley, among others, argue for sufficient continuity between humans and other animals that humans can understand their needs, at least to some extent, but should also value animals for their difference from humans: 'loneliness and play, and maternal affection, ambition and rivalry and fear, turn out to be shared with other social creatures' (Midgley, 1983, p14). Furthermore, following Kant (although he limited this claim to humans only), 'we value other people *because* they are other ... as ends in themselves, not as means to any end of ours' (Midgley 1978, p354). 'Our dignity arises *within* nature, not against it' (Midgley 1978, p203).

Like Aslin, Plumwood (2002, p186) suggests that 'abstract affirmation' will not take us very far, and that emotional, and sometimes physical, connection is required. Carers of golden eagles never expect thanks or even intimacy from the eagles they rehabilitate. However, they must become aware of the bird's subjectivity if they are successfully to heal it (Michel, 1998, pp176, 178). Michel (1998, p182) describes this as an example of 'borderland politics', based on 'an ethic of respect and care for local native wildlife communities'.

Vicki Hearne (1987, pp48–49), an animal trainer who has studied philosophy, retorts to critics who consider it cruel to 'work' a dog or horse: 'We are in charge already, like it or not'. Good training enables a domestic animal to find its most noble self, indeed a trained tracking dog can do something the trainer cannot. The training is based on 'love' as well as knowledge, and its objective is 'shared commitments and collaboration, ... a mutual autonomy'. This occurs when the dog has taken the idea of 'fetch' to be something she wishes to do to the best of her ability (Hearne, 1987, p53). In tracking, then, the handler cannot merge with the dog, because 'it is only in the dog's answering illuminations that you know whether you have said anything at all, or what you have said' (Hearne 1987, p106). Hearne (1987, p76) asks

> What gives us the right to say 'Fetch!'? Something very like reverence, humility and obedience, of course. We can follow, understand, only things and people we can command, and we can command only whom and what we can follow.

As Raimond Gaita (2002, p41) puts it, an animal's 'freedom' 'exists only when a concern for its welfare is transformed by respect for its dignity' (Gaita, 2002, p41).

These examples suggest that respectful stewardship requires responsiveness to the particularities of relationships rather than monochrome worldviews. It requires knowledge as well as love. It requires patience as well as conviction. It requires submission as well as mastery.

We need narratives built on long-standing connection with particular places and particular others, to 'yield relationships that are two-way and two-place, in which you belong to the land as much as the land belongs to you'; 'telling its story in ways that show a deep and loving acquaintance with it and a history of dialogical interaction' (Plumwood, 2002, p230):

A spirituality of place is challenging because it is at odds with the western system of dualisms that has made the particular and immediate, the bodily, the sensory, the experiential and the emotional, the inferior 'others' to the abstract, the mental and the rational-dispassionate. A spirituality of place is not then something that will just fall into the laps of people with these kinds of traditions behind them. …the development of a non-superficial spirituality of place that locates the sacred as immanent in particular places … requires major rethinking and re-imagining.

(Plumwood 2002, p231)

Militating against this deep acquaintance with place is the mobility of modernity and the time poverty of our capitalist-dominated lives (Plumwood, 2002, p233; see also Franklin 1999, p194). We tend to conceive relationships with place as a property relationship, reflecting the commodification of the universe by capitalism (Plumwood, 2002, p234). The return to place may sound like a desire to go back to the premodern locale, both impossible and counterproductive. Plumwood (2002, pp233–234) is aware of the impact of globalization and calls for an ethical 'journeying' between places rather than a fixation with one locale. Authentic animal encounter destinations are candidates for such journeying towards spiritual inspiration. They are also open to commodification, to visitation as expressions of our consumer identities. Which messages will they deliver? What chance do we really have of decentring ourselves and our needs to attend carefully to the desires of others?

'Keepers of the game' at animal encounter sites

conservation is not something you think about every day; it's not something you learn at school.

(Jovan, focus group member 1992)

If we have inherited a world that is so disjointed by human action that it now requires our intervention to heal and repair it, then we will have to learn how to accept that we must try to manage it on the basis of Nature's systems and not our standards. But we have much to learn to become better managers.

(David Hancocks, 2001, p175, former director of Werribee Zoo, Melbourne)

Some of the minds we encounter are able to tell us basic ecological things long forgotten or grown oddly unfamiliar, … canny animals who gaze back, size you up and tell you who you are – a dangerous predator! – and where you get off.

(Plumwood, 2002, p177)

Fancifully we might imagine animal encounter sites as Noah's arks dotted across the Australian and New Zealand landscape, providing safe harbour for small marsupials or temporary refuge for Przewalski's horse. Critics claim that these tiny vessels are too fragile to ride the tidal wave of environmental destruction and that their messages contradict the conditions of their existence. They propose nature as commodity, not as an indecipherable other. Their conservation messages are blunted by the requirements of earning an income. BHP and Esso are sponsors of the Phillip Island Penguin Parade: the Visitor Centre does not discuss the major threat to penguins posed by oil spills, focusing instead on feral animals (Jarvis, 2000, p134–135).[19] 'At Sea World [San Diego] pollution and extinction and endangerment are only obliquely mentioned; when they are, they come up as more problems that research will solve. They have no discernible social locations or causes' (Davis, 1997, p231). At Adelaide Zoo, McDonald's trumpets its sponsored rainforest, inviting visitors to 'see the first rainforest bred in captivity'. McDonald's claims it shares with Auckland Zoo the top priorities of 'children, families, fun, education and the environment'. The message is 'that saving the environment does not require substantial changes to individual, commercial and industrial activities; it merely calls for reconstructing a "habitat" for rainforest species' (Mazur, 2001, p203). Such representations make it seem that 'Wildness itself is really obedient – to human beings, especially those that run corporations' (Davis, 1997, p231).

Nicole Mazur (2001) suggests further limitations in zoos' self-description as arks against species extinction. Given accelerating habitat destruction, there is decreasing likelihood of sanctuary for animals after the 'flood' (Mazur, 2001, p73). Since 1950, about one-third of the world's forests and one-third of the world's topsoil have been lost and not replaced. Biological diversity is 'diminishing hundreds of times more rapidly than at any time during the past 65 million years' (Hancocks, 2001, p244).[20] To some critics, claims that zoos aid in species preservation are akin to art galleries putting their Rembrandts out in the rain with a sign next to them: 'rare pictures, only 200 left in the world' (Jim Grant, interviewed on 3 January 1993; see also Mazur, 1994, pp4, 6). Mike Bossley (interviewed on 19 December 2000) suggests that zoos are 'counter-educational, in the sense that they don't really make it clear to people what is important and what isn't'. Their behaviour contradicts their message, which must ultimately be about habitat preservation:

> you can't save animals by locking them up in cages, really. It's pretty
> much the equivalent of a stuffed animal in a museum. The only way
> you can save animals is preserve their habitat.

Indeed, given the way animals are displayed, visitors have sometimes left a zoo with more negativistic or doministic attitudes than they had when they entered (Hancocks, 2001, pxviii, citing Kellert and Dunlap's research).

Furthermore, zoo research often adopts the values of science, including objectification – 'non-human nature is seen largely as an object for human use and benefit' – and reductionism, breaking nature down into 'sets of knowable or observable elements and events', thus ignoring complex interactions (Mazur, 2001, p75). From the 1970s and 1980s, zoos attempted to 'move away from the narrow notion of wildlife management to the broader concept of conserving biodiversity' (Mazur, 2001, p82). But most zoo research still neglects *in situ* conservation or endangered animals in the habitat beyond the zoo (Mazur, 2001, pp96–99; see also Hancocks, 2001, pxvii). In many cases, the 'need for intensive and technological intervention in conservation is presented as absolute', leaving little space to discuss other kinds of intervention or the outcomes a scientific approach might fail to address (Mazur, 2001, p102).[21] Little attention is given to the fact that the scientific and wildlife management community is made up of humans with particular 'political, social and cultural commitments' which orient their research and interventions in particular directions (Mazur, 2001, p103).

But change is in the air. Bronx Zoo's worldwide conservation programme now involves biologists, lawyers, economists, sociologists, and anthropologists. The New York Wildlife Conservation Society has weighed long-term benefits to conservation against short-term detriment to individual animals, and supported hunting in Zambia, helped Patagonians farm inside a wilderness area and refrained from condemning a hydroelectric project in Laos (Hancocks, 2001, pp174–175). In these ways, scientists attached to zoos are addressing the complexities of a hybrid nature, neither a pure untouched wilderness nor a smug conviction of science's ability to save the planet.

Many of the new 'keepers of the game' (Martin, 1978) – rangers and guides – resist visitors' anthropomorphic responses with scientific facts or environmental messages. Indeed, visitors were pleased to discover conservation initiatives, even professing their own desire to become engaged. At Monarto and Warrawong, visitors are 'uplifted' by the vision of a better future for Australia's endangered marsupials and the world's rare animals. Among the ecotourists operating dolphin tours on Port Phillip Bay, one 'proudly' states 'we do not swim with the dolphins': this crew 'see true ecotourism as belonging to the visual not the visceral' (Jarvis, 2000, p218).

However, many visitors at my research sites enjoyed being close to animals: cuddling koalas, feeding lorikeets or swimming with dolphins. For some this tactile experience may have been more meaningful than the ecological messages. Some people must hold a sugar glider before they want to save it, an emotional and tactile connection John Wamsley offers as justification for allowing Australians to own native marsupials as pets.[22] By contrast, as a warning that emotional connection by itself is not enough, corporations who build nature theme parks focus on emotional connection: 'the only wildlife we'll be able to save is the one we care about' (Davis, 1997, p237). While Nick Ordinans and his team attempt to save the tiny sugar glider at

Healesville (Pitt, 1998, pp15–17), the voiceover does not suggest to the television audience that many more sugar gliders might be saved by dealing with the real culprits of species extinction: habitat loss, feral animals, road kills. Thus pulling at emotional heartstrings is insufficient if it includes a smokescreen against the economic causes of, and our own investments in, environmental destruction.

By the same token, it is too easy to blame environmental degradation on 'greedy corporations' and fail to take responsibility for our own actions, for example exotic plants in our gardens: 'gardening is harming Australia's environment more than mining' (Low, 1999, p296). Those versions of green activism that implicitly assume an 'us', the helpless citizen-consumers, against 'them', the 'modern industrial juggernaut', disguise our pleasures and our options in consumption (Soper, 1995, p266). We might usefully practise urban rituals, for example pausing as we turn on a light to think of where electricity comes and what it costs environmentally (David Suzuki, 'Wisdom of the Elders', public lecture, Adelaide, 16 May 1992), and so change our use of this precious resource.

Respectful stewardship of hybrid nature allows both small intimate gestures as well as large political causes. At the larger level is the paradox of 'increasingly local politics in a world structured by increasingly global processes' (in Bauman, 2003, p101).[23] Macnaghten and Urry (1998, p273) suggest that many environmental problems cannot be solved at the local level; many cannot even be solved at the national level, which is why international bodies such as the United Nations, the World Bank, Greenpeace, the Commission for Sustainable Development, Friends of the Earth, the European Union and so on are needed (Macnaghten and Urry, 1998, p274).

Respectful stewardship at a community level requires working with people who have very different interests and resources, working to produce 'reflexive modernisation' or 'deliberate self-reflection about the future we are designing' (Ulrich Beck in Jiggins and Röling, 2000, p29). People do not benefit equally from various nature policies or politics. As noted in Chapter 4, the idea of untouched wilderness, precious to environmentalists in settler societies, has been challenged and reconfigured to allow alliances with previously excluded indigenous people. The effluent from cane farms and retirement condominiums along the north Queensland coast threatens the fishing and tourism industries of the Great Barrier Reef. 'Social learning' or collective learning (Jiggins and Röling, 2000, p33) requires time, patience and goodwill. Social learning is almost impossible if the problems are big, like global warming (Jiggins and Röling, 2000, p35) or there is a crisis situation with a high degree of conflict (Jiggins and Röling, 2000, p33), suggesting that concepts like respectful stewardship may be somewhat utopian.

However, Landcare is an Australian example of social learning. To stop soil degradation, the Australian Conservation Foundation understood it had to work with farmers, not just to change them but also to draw on their knowledge and respect their needs, thus securing $326.7 million over 10 years for the National Landcare Program, which 'builds on a program originally championed by the Australian Conservation Foundation and the National Farmers' Federation'. This programme is part of the Howard government's $1.5 billion Natural Heritage Trust (NHT), funded from 1996 to 2002. There have been high levels of local volunteer commitment, but the Australian Conservation Foundation (2000) is critical of the outcomes, due to a 'lack of national leadership and strategic focus', revealing the need for interactive engagement at many levels.[24]

While 'the Commonwealth [government] has not tackled the major underlying factors degrading the environment' (Australian Conservation Foundation, 2000), citing the continued deterioration of Australia's major river system, the Murray-Darling, social learning has since been expressed in some halting steps to protect the future of this river system (featured in a campaign in *The Australian* during 2001). A quantity of 500 gigalitres of water (less than 1 per cent of the volume of water taken out of the river each year) is to be released upstream from the middle of 2004 to improve the environmental health of six key sites along the river (Crosweller, 2003, p5). The community who produced this small, but hopeful, gesture consisted of the governments of Victoria, New South Wales, Queensland and South Australia as well as the farmers, orchardists, environmentalists, indigenous people and others who live along or are nurtured by the length of the river system.

Respectful stewardship is forged from a combination of the affective and intellectual domains. On the one hand, scientists respond to the experiences of people who rescue wild animals or visit zoos. On the other hand, sentimental pet owners or dolphin lovers show their willingness to learn about aspects of the natural world that are not extensions of Lassie or Flipper. As Richard Jakob-Hoff, then Senior Curator, Auckland Zoological Park, suggests:

> I don't believe that conservation happens *in* zoos any more than I
> believe conservation happens on Little Barrier Island [where kakapo,
> an endangered bird, live]. Conservation can only really be achieved by
> changes in the human mind which result in changes in our behaviour.
>
> (Jakob-Hoff, 1993, no page)

Rather than seeing the affective response to animals as a barrier to new cognitive frameworks (Duffus and Dearden, 1990, p221), or the visual excitement of the sea lions dashing after fish as a distraction from the keeper's talk,[25] the 'empathy' that people feel for animals might deflect the false dichotomy of the entertainment–education opposition. Jakob-Hoff (1993, no page) suggests that 'people are powerfully attracted to animals' and zoos and other animal encounter sites can use this to change attitudes,[26] to promote environmental efforts beyond their bars, locally and internationally.

David Hancocks (2001, pxviii), in arguing that education is the only justification for zoos, suggests that legislation should be passed so that only zoos 'that aim to create respect for wildlife and a desire to save wildlife habitat', that 'make animal welfare their first priority', that adopt 'conservation strategies' as their central tenet, and that inject 'passion and daring into their interaction with visitors' should be allowed to survive (Hancocks, 2001, pxviii). Within this remit, because not everyone experiences animal encounter sites in the same way, a pluralistic presence of sites and activities and approaches is advocated, at least until we learn how to farm reefs and whether zoos do create conservationists.

Not even in Antarctica, filtered as we were by the cost and discomfort of the trip, did we all speak in a romantic or environmental register, one woman wanting to 'foster a penguin' (debriefing, 12 January 1996). This humanistic connection must not be degraded as less correct, less valuable, than the ecological apprehension. The humanistic orientation may act just as powerfully for the planet as the politically correct. Out at the animal encounter sites, mute ambassadors from utopia may catch the I/eye of the visitor and provoke the stirrings of respectful stewardship of a hybrid nature:

Of course we can splice genes. But can we not splice genes?

(Bill McKibben in 1990 in Mabey, 1997, p241)

This task is urgent.

(Plumwood, 2002, p238)

Appendices

Appendix 1: Research Methods

Although observation is labour-intensive and expensive (Gale and Jacobs, 1987, p27), in order to identify aspects of visitor behaviour[1] the researcher visited each site on at least one occasion. I conducted informal conversations with visitors and more formal interviews with staff and managers at most of the sites. I made notes of visitors' reactions and the geography of the site, photographed visitor behaviour and interpretive signs. I collected promotional and publicity material at each site, particularly that given to site visitors, for example maps and pamphlets. In some instances, I acquired additional material about the site that was on sale or examined archives, as at Currumbin and Adelaide Zoo (for Monarto). I had access to newsletters and annual reports from Warrawong, as a shareholder, and for Monarto through my mother's life membership of the Royal Zoological Society of South Australia (RZSSA).

However, the main research tool was a questionnaire administered to visitors to the animal encounter sites. The questionnaire was based on an extensive literature review and feedback from three focus groups consisting of 25 people in total, conducted in September 1992.[2] The focus group members were chosen on the basis that they had visited either Monkey Mia, Phillip Island or Kangaroo Island (first group), an aquarium where dolphins were displayed (usually Sea World; second group), Currumbin or Lone Pine (zoo-like sanctuaries) (third group).[3] As most had visited more than one site and each focus group discussed several sites, 17 focus group respondents commented on Sea World, 12 on Lone Pine, 10 on Currumbin, 7 each on Phillip Island and Monkey Mia, while one individual had visited Seal Bay and another had seen the whales at Hervey Bay.[4]

The questionnaire (see Appendix 2) was trialled at Warrawong and Cleland in April 1995. It was found to be too long and was shortened so that it could be completed in about 15 minutes. The plan was that site workers would distribute 80 questionnaires to people at a relaxation point in the site, ask them to complete the questionnaire and deposit it in a box provided. From this procedure 50 completed survey forms were expected. Variations on this strategy were adopted to deal with site exigencies, in three cases requesting that the questionnaires be posted back to either the researcher or the site (up to 100 blank questionnaires were provided in these cases). Surveys were conducted between July 1994 and January 1996.

The following is a short description of procedures at each site:

- At Cleland, 100 questionnaires were distributed by the Friends of Cleland, a group of volunteers, to be placed on completion in a box in the bistro. This process yielded 45 useable questionnaires.
- Although 110 surveys were sent to Currumbin, the completed number, 17, was disappointingly low. The logistical problem of securing respondents who had experienced the major bird feeding, which occurs at day's end (the breakfast feeding being less well attended), was not satisfactorily solved by attaching self-addressed envelopes to the questionnaires.
- Due to the lack of onsite eating facilities at Monarto, the director agreed to distribute the questionnaires with self-addressed envelopes (to Monarto), offering a day pass to Adelaide zoo as a prize to a selected respondent. Eighty questionnaires were distributed, and 27 useable responses were obtained.
- Following a training session run by a researcher and evaluator, Maggie Jakob-Hoff, a set of instructions was developed for the Auckland Zoo Volunteers who distributed the questionnaires and offered a zoo sticker to thank respondents for their time. These instructions suggested that respondents miss out questions that were not zoo- or New Zealand-oriented (although this did not seem to reduce the response rate in the nature dispositions section) or were too personal (which did reduce comments made in the demographic section, along the lines of 'none of your business'). Following a low response rate, the researcher visited the site and a further 30 questionnaires were distributed, producing a total of 56 questionnaires.
- Warrawong achieved the highest completion rate, possibly enhanced by handing questionnaires to people who stayed overnight in the recently built tent accommodation. A total of 93 questionnaires were returned from the 100 handed out.
- At Seal Bay, the rangers distributed 120 questionnaires with a self-addressed envelope attached. Sixty-five useable surveys were returned to the researcher, of which five identified Flinders Chase (a wildlife reserve where kangaroos and koalas can be seen) as their most enjoyable experience.
- Due to logistical difficulties in forwarding the 80 questionnaires sent to Osprey's office in Adelaide on to the Great Australian Bight, only 11 questionnaires were completed, four of them by the members of the group I joined. The remaining seven were handed out and collected by Tim Bickmore, the tour guide of the expeditions.
- Sue Doye, who was completing field research for her masters thesis on Monkey Mia, kindly handed out 50 surveys in mid-1994. These were later supplemented by surveys handed out by the rangers and returned to the interpretation area from late 1994 to March 1995. A total of 48 useable surveys were collected from 110 questionnaires distributed.

After visiting Macquarie Island, with the three-day run home to Hobart ahead of us, I handed out questionnaires to my companions on the Antarctica expedition. The group of 31 was made up largely of Australians, most of whom had joined through an adult education group, but also included four passengers from Britain, three from the US, one from Hong Kong and one from the Netherlands. I received 22 completed questionnaires. My estimation is that almost all those with tertiary qualifications or studying at university completed the questionnaire, whereas almost all those without university degrees did not do so. Related to the variable response rate by education, 36 per cent of the passengers were male, whereas 50 per cent of the respondents were male. Such a bias towards more educated respondents is quite likely a feature of responses at other animal encounter sites in this research.

Much later in the research I added a further 'site', one which does not fit the criteria identified above: the dolphins of Port Adelaide. The animal encounter is not regulated by a tour operator, although Mike Bossley occasionally takes people out in his small boat. As I could not, therefore, distribute questionnaires to 'visitors' to the animal encounter site, a small article, a much truncated version of the article I submitted, was published in the local newspaper (text below) on 13 December 2000. I sought Port Adelaide residents who were willing to complete a slightly adapted version of the questionnaire distributed to visitors to the other animal encounter sites. The small article elicited four telephone responses requesting questionnaires, three completed questionnaires, a letter and an email response. Between December 2000 and April 2001, Mike Bossley handed out about 30 questionnaires with self-addressed envelopes to people who accompanied him on his dolphin observations. This secured a further four completed questionnaires. This was a surprisingly low response rate, given the enthusiasm for dolphins in the Port Adelaide area. The disappointing response was probably due to a combination of the small size of the article and the lack of an accompanying photograph and the fact that Mike Bossley asked people to complete the questionnaire and post it to me at the end of the boat trip rather than while still on the boat.

Newspaper article seeking responses from Port Adelaide residents

'Research into dolphin encounters' (*Portside Messenger* 13 December 2000)

A University of Adelaide professor wants to hear about Port Adelaide residents' encounters with dolphins. Chilla Bulbeck, from the University's Social Inquiry Department, is researching attitudes to wild animals, particularly dolphins. Professor Bulbeck wants to learn why people find dolphins attractive. She believes citizens of industrialised societies have developed different understandings of animals. People are less interested in animals for utilitarian purposes and instead feel closer to their pets or wild animals, she says. To participate in Professor Bulbeck's research, phone 8303 4864 and leave your postal address. She can also be contacted by email at chilla.bulbeck@adelaide.edu.au or by post at Social Inquiry, University of Adelaide, SA, 5005.

In addition to the survey, I completed a content analysis of the local newspaper, the *Portside Messenger*, from 1949 to 2000. The *Portside Messenger* (1984–) replaces the *Progressive Times* (1949–1951) and the *Messenger* (1951–1984). The *Progressive Times* was distributed monthly and mainly covered 'what's on' community type issues. The *Messenger* devoted a large proportion of the paper to advertisements for clothing and household goods, motoring outlets and contained few articles of any length. The paper increased from 8 pages in length to 12 by the end of 1959; it was 16 pages in 1960, and 18 pages in 1969–1970, by which time article length had increased and sports no longer dominated the front page. By 1979–1980, the length of the paper was 25 pages and sections such as 'sports', 'social scene' and 'housing' had appeared. By the second half of 1980, the newspaper reached 30–36 pages in length, although it was an average of 21 pages in the first half of the year. Most of the advertisements were now supermarket advertisements.

The content analysis discussion is based on the results of a manual search of microfilm and printed copies (1951–1997) supplemented by an electronic search of a database, commencing in 1989, which recorded all articles, short items and letters to the editor but not photographs. An electronic search of the Newstext database was accessed through Adelaide University Barr Smith Library (www.library.Adelaide.edu.au/news/trials) but is normally located through www.newstext.com.au. Because the database search located all mentions of 'dolphin', it returned results for the theft of a dolphin torch (20 March 1991, p6; 1 May 1991, p7) and a theft on Dolphin street (notes on recent burglaries) and any action by the Australian Dolphin Research Foundation, whether or not it involved dolphins, for example a training course in saving beached whales (19 February 1997, p7; 12 February 1997, p4). The results revealed the significance of dolphins beyond the bounds of the Port River and their representation in the street names, poetry, art work, murals and so on of the residents.

Appendix 2: Questionnaire

Outline of questionnaire

The questionnaire was divided into four sections. The first section asked about the animal encounter itself, consisting of an open-ended question about the 'most enjoyable part of' the respondent's experience and several closed-choice questions on why the experience was enjoyable or was not enjoyable. The second section asked about the site, covering its negative and positive aspects as well as its major purpose. The third section related to 'nature dispositions', a term adapted from Bourdieu's (1984) aesthetic dispositions and Bennett et al's (1991, pp4, 21–23) historical dispositions. Nature dispositions cover:

- nature related *activities* like bushwalking, hunting, watching wildlife films, pet and other animal ownership, membership of naturalist, animal welfare and conservation clubs;
- *attitudes* to animals and nature. In consultation with Professor Kellert, I adapted and applied Kellert's (1978a) US survey instrument which covers (i) an animal-orientations scale (for example doministic, humanistic, moralistic, ecologistic, utlitarian), and (ii) a wildlife issues scale (personal communication, 1992). This thoroughly tested scale has proven applicability in a range of settings including one of the most comprehensive studies of zoo visitors (Kellert and Dunlap, 1989);
- *evaluation* of animals. Due to the length of the questionnaire this was reduced to a question concerning whether animals experience pleasure, pain, guilt and so on (see discussion in Chapter 5 and, for example, Rollin (1990, pp30, 114–115).

To explore the hypothesis that dolphins have replaced primates, and more recently whales, as a particularly important species onto which we map our human attributes, desires and problems, the questionnaire included two questions specifically about dolphins.

Animal Encounter Survey

Conducted by Professor Chilla Bulbeck, Head of Department, Social Inquiry, Pulteney Towers, University of Adelaide, SA 5005, Australia; Phone: +61-8-83034864; Fax: +61-8-83033345; Email: chilla.bulbeck@adelaide.edu.au (these contact details changed over the course of the project)

Thank you very much for agreeing to participate in this survey of [visitors to site X]. I am researching the reactions of people to animals and other aspects of the natural environment, with particular emphasis on your response to the [animal interactions you had at site X today]. For the purposes of this survey animals include insects, fish, birds, mammals; everything which would not be described as 'vegetable' or 'mineral'. After you have completed the questionnaire, please [instructions varied from site to site]. Many thanks!

THE ANIMAL ENCOUNTER

1. Please describe briefly the most enjoyable part of the experience you had at [animal encounter site] today.

....

....

....

....

....

....

2. Please indicate with a tick up to THREE statements which best describe why you enjoyed this animal encounter experience

   I ENJOYED the [animal encounter] because the animals were:

   1. beautiful to look at
   2. cute or cuddly
   3. babies or young
   4. mature or full-grown
   5. large
   6. small
   7. close
   8. wild or free
   9. in enclosures
   10. in their own environment
   11. responsive to people
   12. active
   13. resting
   14. unafraid of people
   15. happy
   16. chose the encounter

3. Please indicate with a tick up to THREE statements below which best describe why you enjoyed this animal encounter experience.

1. The animals wanted to interact with me ....☐
2. This was a unique experience ....☐
3. I was able to interact with the animals without the presence of a guide ....☐
4. I learned something about the animal's habits and characteristics ......☐
5. I was able to interact with the animals in their natural environment ....☐
6. There were few other people present...☐
7. I photographed the animals..☐
8. I smelled the animals ....☐
9. I touched the animals ....☐
10. I fed the animals..☐

4. Please choose up to FIVE statements which describe your FEELINGS about this animal encounter experience.

1. I felt privileged to have this animal encounter....................................☐
2. I felt I had communicated with the animal/s ....☐
3. I felt the animal/s trusted and liked me ....☐
4. I felt I had control of the situation ....☐
5. I felt that I had a deeper understanding of the meaning of life ....☐
6. I felt close to nature..☐
7. I felt good that these animals were being preserved...........................☐
8. I felt protective towards the animals ....☐
9. I felt an affection for the animal/s ....☐
10. I felt spiritually uplifted..☐
11. Other, please specify...☐

5. Below are some reasons people sometimes give for NOT enjoying animal encounters as much as they might do. Please choose up to THREE statements which indicate any aspects of this animal encounter experience which you did NOT enjoy:

1. There were too few animals ....☐
2. The experience was controlled by a keeper, guide or ranger................☐
3. The animals did not want to interact with me......................................☐
4. I was not close enough to the animals..☐
5. The animals were in enclosures ....☐
6. The animals were not doing anything ....☐
7. The animals seemed unhappy..☐
8. There were too many other people present..☐
9. Other, please specify...☐

6. Were you able to feed any animals today? If not, go to the next question. If yes, please indicate which ONE of the following statements best describes how you felt about feeding the animals.

   1. The animals showed they trusted me...☐
   2. It allowed me to enter the world of the animal/s.............................☐
   3. I was able to change the behaviour of the animal/s.........................☐
   4. I was able to get the animal/s to come closer to me ....☐
   5. I was able to touch and feel the animal/s..☐
   6. Other, please specify..☐

THE ANIMAL ENCOUNTER SITE

This section asks you about the nature site.

1. In relation to this nature site in general please tick any of the following which describe either good or bad aspects of this site which you feel are IMPORTANT:

	Important	Unimportant
1. The site is peaceful and relaxing	☐	☐
2. The site is clean and well-kept	☐	☐
3. The site has good transportation to it	☐	☐
4. There are many other leisure activities close to the site	☐	☐
5. The site has good eating and rest facilities	☐	☐
6. The site provides an authentic and unspoilt environment	☐	☐
7. It is possible to explore the site unaccompanied by a guide	☐	☐

2. In relation to this nature site in general, please indicate with a tick for each of the following statements whether they are an IMPORTANT BAD aspect of the site or NOT IMPORTANT to you.

	Important	Unimportant
1. The site is crowded	☐	☐
2. The site does not change much from one visit to another	☐	☐
3. The site does not provide many activities	☐	☐
4. The weather was bad	☐	☐
5. The site was expensive (please indicate how much your party paid to enter ($.....)	☐	☐

3. Please tick which ONE of the following you think should be the major purpose of this animal site:

1. Education for visitors ....☐
2. Entertainment for visitors...☐
3. Conservation and breeding of endangered animals ....☐
4. Providing a natural environment for the animals ....☐
5. Research on animal life and behaviour...☐
6. Allowing visitors to interact with the animals ....☐

4. How did you first learn about this animal site?

1. I have visited it before ....☐
2. Word of mouth: from a friend, work colleague, relative or acquaintance ....☐
3. From a television program ....☐
4. From a magazine or newspaper...☐
5. From a travel agent ....☐
6. Other, please specify..☐
7. Can't recall ....☐

OTHER ANIMAL AND NATURE RELATED ACTIVITIES

1. Please indicate whether you have done any of the following activities, and the most recent such experience:

	never	at some time	last six months
1. Watched a wildlife film	☐	☐	☐
2. Had a subscription to a nature-based magazine like *National Geographic, Geo* ...	☐	☐	☐
3. Purchased a nature or wildlife book	☐	☐	☐
4. Enrolled for a course on animals or some aspect of nature...	☐	☐	☐
5. Gone on a tour which has an environmental component	☐	☐	☐
6. Camped out in the bush	☐	☐	☐
7. Gone on a bushwalk	☐	☐	☐
8. Hunted animals or birds............................	☐	☐	☐
9. Gone fishing...	☐	☐	☐
10. Other than this animal encounter site, visited a zoo or wildlife sanctuary (please name the most recently visited.........)	☐	☐	☐
11. Visited a museum	☐	☐	☐

12. Visited an aquarium (please name the
    most recently visited ....).. □ □ □
13. Visited a national park (please name the
    most recently visited ....).... □ □ □
14. Owned a pet (please specify most recent
    ....) .... □ □ □
15. Owned stock animal/s (please specify
    most recent ....)...................... □ □ □
16. Rescued or helped a wild animal (please
    indicate most recently rescued animal
    ....) .... □ □ □
17. Been rescued or helped by an animal (please
    describe most recent experience briefly
    ....)...................... □ □ □

2. Please tick any of the following of which you are a member:

    1. An environmental group like Greenpeace, Trees for Life, Wilderness
        Society, Australian Conservation Foundation, World Wildlife Fund....□
    2. A zoological association (e.g. 'friends of a zoo' group) ....□
    3. A museum society or group..□
    5. An ornithological or other field naturalist society or group ....□
    5. A hunting group or association (like Sporting Shooters Assn)............□
    6. An animal breeding society (livestock or domestic animals)...............□
    7. A scientific society (like Australian Geographic Society) ....□
    8. An animal welfare society like the RSPCA, Animal Liberation ....□

3. Please indicate whether you □ enjoy □ do not enjoy watching wildlife films.
   If you DO ENJOY watching wildlife films, please tick up to THREE of the
   following as your major reasons. If you do not enjoy wildlife films, please
   go to question 4.

    1. Wildlife films teach you about animal behaviours and lives................□
    2. Close-up and other camera techniques mean you see things you
        would never see in the wild ....□
    3. Stories are told about animals' lives, their victories, defeats,
        and struggles ....□
    4. The wildlife films show beautiful scenery and animals ....□
    5. The films show that animal societies are similar to human societies ..□
    6. The films show natural animal behaviours ....□
    7. The films are set in exotic places with animals I could never hope
        to see myself...□

4. Not all animal encounter experiences feel good. Please tick ANY of the following which were BAD or NEGATIVE experiences for you.

   1. Physically attacked by a domestic animal (e.g. dog, bull) (please indicate the animal/s..) ....☐

   2. Suffered bite, sting or attack by wild animal which required medical attention? (please indicate the animal..............................) ....☐

   3. Suffered property damage from an animal (e.g. to your garden or crops) (please indicate animal/s..) ....☐

   4. Suffered noise disturbance from an animal/s................................) ....☐

5. What are your attitudes to the following?

	Disapprove	neutral	approve
1. Experimentation on animals to develop life-saving drugs	☐	☐	☐
2. Experimentation on animals to develop cosmetics	☐	☐	☐
3. Experimentation on animals which are anaesthetized	☐	☐	☐
4. Hunting for pleasure	☐	☐	☐
5. Hunting for food	☐	☐	☐
6. Hunting for economic reasons, e.g. skins or meat to sell	☐	☐	☐
7. Aboriginal hunting in national parks using 'traditional' methods	☐	☐	☐
9. Aboriginal hunting in national parks using modern technology	☐	☐	☐
10. Culling indigenous animals like kangaroos	☐	☐	☐
11. Eating animal meat	☐	☐	☐
12. Eating animal products, e.g. eggs, milk	☐	☐	☐
13. Bullfighting	☐	☐	☐
14. Rodeos	☐	☐	☐
15. Drift net fishing	☐	☐	☐
16. Farming stock animals such as cattle for human consumption	☐	☐	☐
17. Farming native animals like kangaroos for human consumption	☐	☐	☐
18. Breeding and keeping dolphins and whales in captivity	☐	☐	☐
19. Breeding and keeping animals in zoos	☐	☐	☐
20. Imposing a tax on goods to cover the environmental damage entailed in their production	☐	☐	☐

21. Expanding the area of Australia's national parks .... ☐ ☐ ☐

22. Woodchipping native forests .... ☐ ☐ ☐

23. Using the natural environment to achieve sustainable development .... ☐ ☐ ☐

24. Preserving wilderness for its own sake, even if access for people is denied ...... ☐ ☐ ☐

25. Killing pests around the house, e.g. rodents or cockroaches........................ ☐ ☐ ☐

6. Which of the following statements do you believe to be true (at least in relation to some animals):

	true	false	don't know
1. Animals experience pleasure and happiness ...	☐	☐	☐
2. Animals experience guilt	☐	☐	☐
3. Animals can remember	☐	☐	☐
4. Animals can love or like each other	☐	☐	☐
5. Animals can love or like people	☐	☐	☐

7. Please choose the THREE most important factors below when planning a trip interstate or overseas of more than one week's duration:

1. The chance to relax .... ☐
2. The opportunity to visit friends and relatives .... ☐
3. The range of physical activities that are offered, e.g. tennis, swimming .... ☐
4. The chance to talk to local people.. ☐
5. The chance to see something of an exotic culture, e.g. dance, crafts or art .... ☐
6. The chance to be alone in the natural environment .... ☐
7. The chance to see animals .... ☐
8. The learning experiences which are offered .... ☐
9. The chance to buy things not available at home or to purchase bargains .... ☐
10. Feeling secure that the travel and accommodation arrangements will run smoothly .... ☐

DOLPHINS: I am particularly interested in your reactions to dolphins.

1. Please describe briefly the last time you saw a dolphin:

....

....

Please tick any of the following which describes your feelings at the time:

1. A feeling of fun/pleasure .... ☐
2. A sense of comradeship or oneness with the dolphin/s .... ☐
3. Fondness or affection for the dolphins .... ☐
4. A feeling of peace and tranquility.. ☐
5. A feeling I had communicated with the dolphins .... ☐
6. Other, please specify.. ☐

DEMOGRAPHIC DETAILS

1. Today you came to this site with (tick ALL which apply)

   1. Alone .... ☐   2. A partner or friend................. ☐
   3. Your family .... ☐   4. Other family or friends .... ☐
   5. An interstate visitor.............. ☐   6. An overseas visitor .... ☐

2. Your postcode is ....

3. If you are visiting from overseas please name the country ....

4. Please indicate whether you grew up largely in:
   a capital city ☐   a provincial city ☐   a country town ☐   a rural area ☐

5. Your sex is: Male ☐   Female ☐

6. Your marital status is: Married/de facto ☐   Single/separated ☐

7. Number of children: none ☐   1 ☐   2 ☐   3 or more ☐

8. Your age is: less than 19 ☐   20–29 ☐   30–44 ☐   45–60 ☐   over 60 ☐

9. You are: Aboriginal or Torres Strait Islander .... ☐
             Other Australian resident or citizen .... ☐
             From overseas.. ☐

10. Your birthplace is:
    Australia .... ☐   United Kingdom/Eire ..... ☐   New Zealand .... ☐
    United States/Canada... ☐   Greece .... ☐   Italy .... ☐

    Other, please specify..

11. The birthplace of your parents is:
    Both Australian ☐   One Australian and one (please specify)..................
    Other, please specify...............................and ....

12. Your highest level of education is (please tick box):
    Bachelor's degree or higher degree...☐
    Trade, TAFE or other post-secondary certificate ....☐
    Completed high school ....☐
    Other..☐

13. Your occupation is...
    Please tick the following box which best describes your occupational category:
    Managerial ....☐   Service.......................................☐
    Professional ....☐   Craft worker ....☐
    Administrative ....☐   Labouring ....☐
    Clerical ....☐   Home duties ....☐

14. Please check your income range (use latest census bands)
    less than $6,000 ☐ $6,001–$18,000 ☐ $18,001–$26,000 ☐
    $26,001–$40,000 ☐   over $40,000 ☐

15. Your religious affiliation is:
    none ☐   Protestant denomination ☐   Catholic denomination ☐
    Islamic ☐
    Other, please specify...

Any other comments:

....

....

....

....

....

....

....

....

....

....

Thank you again for your time in completing the questionnaire. It is much appreciated. Please [instructions for return of questionnaires varied by site].

Appendix 3: Survey Results

There were 382 respondents in total, 268 born in Australia, 56 respondents for Auckland Zoo and 58 overseas visitors to an Australian site. Only two respondents were Aboriginal or Torres Strait Islanders, under-represented in relation to the percentage in the population;[5] 7 per cent were Maori or Pacific Islanders (all visitors to Auckland Zoo). Australians from non-English speaking backgrounds were under-represented among the respondents, although there are no significant variations from site to site. Of the overseas visitors, 14 per cent came from the UK with most of the remainder equally from Europe, North America and New Zealand. For some years, the Japanese have been the largest category of overseas visitor to Australia, followed by New Zealand (see Table A5.2 below). However, no Japanese and very few other Asian visitors answered the questionnaire, presumably because of language issues and tight tourist schedules. Table A3.1 provides some socioeconomic data for site visitors.

The only sites for which there were sufficient responses to establish levels of significance were Monkey Mia, Seal Bay, Warrawong, Cleland and Auckland Zoo. There are some potentially confounding correlations in the responses. For example respondents with tertiary qualifications were significantly more likely to be male and have managerial or professional jobs, while 96 per cent of those whose occupation was home duties were female. Females were significantly more likely to have grown up in rural areas and males in a capital city. Those with tertiary qualifications tended to have no children. Women were more likely to be aged 20–29 and men over 60. There was a positive correlation between being of a Protestant denomination and either engaged in home duties or with having parents born in an English-speaking country. Catholic respondents were more likely to have Australian-born parents. Those with tertiary qualifications were statistically less likely to profess a religion. While results for no religion and greater socioeconomic status sometimes move together, results for gender generally displayed different patterns, showing that gender was a variable of influence in its own right.

Those with higher socioeconomic status, no religion and males were more likely to visit animal encounter sites at the 'authentic' end of the spectrum. Warrawong recorded a statistically higher proportion of professional people. Auckland is an exception, recording a statistically significant higher visitation rate for those with managerial jobs; but also those with home duties (21 per cent, compared with 13 per cent for the total population). Monkey Mia recorded a significantly higher proportion of visitors with administrative jobs (13 per cent, compared with 6 per cent for the total). The pattern is not as clear for income, with Monkey Mia and Seal Bay recording statistically higher proportions of respondents on low incomes (17 per cent earned $2000–6000 at Monkey Mia compared with 6 per cent for the total; 14 per cent earned $6000–12,000 at Seal Bay compared with 7 per cent of the total). Auckland Zoo has statistically fewer respondents in the middling income range of $12,000–30,000.

Table A3.1 *Socioeconomic Characteristics of Visitors to Animal Encounter Sites*

	Antarctica	Osprey	Seal Bay	Monkey Mia	Warrawong	Monarto	Cleland	Currumbin	Auckland Zoo	TOTAL %	TOTAL N*
Per cent female	50	73	60	77	55	67	49	71	61	60	226
Per cent visiting with family	0	18	55	35	38	44	33	65	64	45	162
Per cent from overseas	25	27	11	31	18	0	29	6	14	16	59
Per cent tertiary qualification	85	82	49	48	43	33	34	24	32	41	164
Per cent professional and managerial	85	73	53	46	53	34	35	36	48	46	163
Per cent income >$30,000	–	54	31	40	47	26	36	30	45	32	118
Per cent no religion	–	45	37	46	42	30	36	24	29	37	134
Per cent one or both parents born NESB country	–	38	13	3	10	12	8	6	n.a.	10	24
Per cent aged 30–44	25	36	46	40	30	41	42	71	46	41	149
Per cent grew up in capital city	–	64	51	48	49	56	51	29	34	47	171
Number of respondents	20	11	65	48	93	27	45	17	56	100	382*

*N for each question varies according to number of respondents for that question so that numbers in column divided by total will not always produce the percentage indicated.

There were few significant variations in terms of age. Visitors to Warrawong were slightly less likely to be aged 30–44 (and more than the average were aged over 45). Seal Bay visitors were more likely to be aged over 60 (18 per cent compared with 10 per cent for the total sample) and less likely to be aged 20–29 (8 per cent compared with 20 per cent for the whole sample). There were no significant variations in terms of where respondents grew up, except that more grew up in provincial cities in New Zealand, no doubt a reflection of the different geographic distribution of the population there.

One-third of the total respondents had visited the site before, although 80 per cent of Auckland Zoo visitors were previous visitors. One-third learned about the site from someone they knew. Those who had only high school education were likely to learn about the site from television while those with tertiary qualifications were more likely to find out from a magazine or newspaper. Television was twice as likely to be the source of information about the site for Monkey Mia visitors (13 per cent compared with 7 per cent for the total). Monkey Mia was significantly more likely to attract the overseas visitor while Seal Bay respondents were significantly less likely to be from overseas. There is perhaps some gradient tendency for more overseas visitors at the authentic end but it is very weak.

Table A3.2 *Reasons for Enjoying the Animals According to Sex and Educational Achievement (percentage of respondents)* *

	TOTAL	Female	Male	Tertiary education
In their own environment	61	59	63	68 (+)
Wild, free	40	43	39	42
Beautiful	36	42 (++)	24 (---)	29 (-)
Close	34	28 (--)	45 (++)	37
Unafraid of people	30	28	33	25
Happy	21	25 (+)	15 (-)	14 (--)
Babies or young	17	20	11 (-)	18
Responsive to people	16	19	11	12
Active	14	15	15	18
Cute or cuddly	8	6 (-)	9	5 (-)
Chose the encounter	6	6	6	6
Resting	6	3 (-)	10 (++)	8
Large	4	5	3	5
Mature or full grown	3	3	3	4
In enclosures	1	1	1	1
Small	1	1	1	1

*Percentages add up to more than 100 per cent as respondents could nominate more than one response.
+++, --- : positively and negatively significant at .01 level; ++, -- : significant at .05 level; +, - significant at .1 level

Table A3.3 *Reasons for Enjoying the Animals: Percentage of Respondents at that Animal Encounter Site**

	TOTAL	Antarctica	Great Aust Bight	Seal Bay	Monkey Mia	Warrawong	Monarto	Cleland	Currumbin	Auckland Zoo
In their own environment	61	75	91 (+++)	80 (+++)	71	76	63 (---)	33	35 (---)	27
Wild, free	40	46	64	49	48	49 (+)	63	20 (--)	24	14 (---)
Beautiful	36	59	18	23 (-)	48	24 (--)	59	56 (++)	41	38
Close	34	9	27	40	25	39	11	33	47	36
Unafraid of people	30	41	9	35	23	32	15	27	41	34
Happy	21	0	27	23	15	24	19	7 (-)	18	32 (+)
Babies or young	17	–	18	25	4 (-)	22	11	11	12	20
Responsive to people	16	23	9	3 (--)	27 (+)	4 (---)	11	40 (+++)	18	27 (+)
Active	14	–	36	5 (-)	8	15	0	11	18	32 (+++)
Cute or cuddly	8	9	0	3	2	4	0	29 (+++)	24	11
Chose the encounter	6	9	9	2	23 (+++)	4	0	2	12	4
Resting	6	–	0	9	0	1 (-)	7	18 (+++)	0	7
Large	4	–	18	2	0	1	7	2	0	16 (+++)
Mature or full grown	3	–	9	2	2	1	0	2	0	11 (+++)
In enclosures	1	–	0	0	0	1	0	2	0	5 (++)
Small	1	–	0	0	2	0	0	0	0	4 (+)

*Percentages add up to more than 100 per cent as respondents could nominate more than one response.
+++, --- : positively and negatively significant at .01 level; ++, -- : significant at .05 level; +, – significant at .1 level

Table A3.4 *Reasons for Enjoying the Animal Encounter Experience According to Sex and Educational Achievement: Percentage of Respondents by Socioeconomic Variables**

	TOTAL	Female	Male	Tertiary education
Learned about animals	63	65	60	61
Unique experience	56	57	56	58
Able to interact with animals in own environment	48	49	45	45
Photographed animals	29	29	29	33
Touched animals	16	14	17	13
Interact with animals without guide	16	11 (--)	23 (++)	13
Animals wanted to interact with me	13	13	15	12
Fed animals	9	8	6	4 (--)
Smelled animals	3	3	2	1

*Percentages add up to more than 100 per cent as respondents could nominate more than one response.
+++, --- : positively and negatively significant at .01 level; ++, -- : significant at .05 level; +, – significant at .1 level

Table A3.5 *Reasons for Enjoying the Animal Encounter Experience: Percentage of Respondents at Each Animal Encounter Site**

	TOTAL	Antarctica	Great Aust Bight	Seal Bay	Monkey Mia	Warrawong	Monarto	Cleland	Currumbin	Auckland Zoo
Learned about animals	63	50	64	91 (+++)	23 (---)	82 (+++)	81	29	41	57
Unique experience	56	64	82	80 (+++)	56	73 (+++)	56	31 (---)	24	27 (---)
Able to interact with animals in own environment	48	59	27	32 (--)	73 (+++)	70 (+++)	44 (--)	27	35 (-)	32
Photographed animals	29	50	45	58 (+++)	23	16 (--)	19	29	41	18
Touched animals	16	0	0	0 (---)	23	10	0	49 (+++)	35	20
Interact with animals without guide	16	23	18	2 (---)	21	3 (---)	4	42 (+++)	29	29 (++)
Animals wanted to interact with me	13	23	9	0 (---)	31 (+++)	5 (-)	4	22 (+)	18	21 (+)
Fed animals	9	0	0	1 (-)	15	0 (---)	0	31 (+++)	29	9
Smelled animals	3	5	0	0	2 (-)	0	0	4	0	16 (+++)

*Percentages add up to more than 100 per cent as respondents could nominate more than one response.
+++, --- : positively and negatively significant at .01 level; ++, -- : significant at .05 level; +, – significant at .1 level

Table A3.6 *Feelings about the Animal Encounter Experience According to Sex and Educational Achievement (percentage of respondents)* *

	TOTAL	Female	Male	Tertiary education
Felt good animals being preserved	60	58	66	59
Felt privileged to have encounter	51	56 (+)	40 (--)	52
Felt close to nature	44	43	45	42
Felt affection for animals	33	36	29	30
Felt protective towards animals	20	20	19	16
Felt animals trusted/liked me	14	13	15	12
Felt spiritually uplifted	12	12	10	14
Had deeper understanding of meaning of life	9	9	9	6
Felt had communicated with animals	5	5	3	1 (--)
Felt had control of situation	3	2	4	2

*Percentages add up to more than 100 per cent as respondents could nominate more than one response.
+++, --- : positively and negatively significant at .01 level; ++, -- : significant at .05 level; +, – significant at .1 level

Table A3.7 *Feelings about the Animal Encounter Experience: Percentage of Respondents at each Animal Encounter Site**

	TOTAL	Antarctica	Great Aust Bight	Seal Bay	Monkey Mia	Warrawong	Monarto	Cleland	Currumbin	Auckland Zoo
Felt good animals being preserved	60	37	45	75 (++)	33 (--)	76 (+++)	93	47 (-)	41	43 (--)
Felt privileged to have encounter	51	86	55	66 (++)	69 (++)	57	37	31 (--)	35	36 (-)
Felt close to nature	44	45	82	42	31	51	22	44	53	45
Felt affection for animals	33	5	27	22 (-)	50 (++)	23 (-)	22	38	41	52 (++)
Felt protective towards animals	20	9	0	17	40 (+++)	15	11	22	35	14
Felt animals trusted/liked me	14	5	9	9	25 (+)	8 (-)	0	29 (++)	29	13
Felt spiritually uplifted	12	23	36	3 (-)	13	16	7	9	6	14
Had deeper understanding of meaning of life	9	14	9	9	4	13	4	9	6	11
Felt had communicated with animals	5	5	0	2	2	2	0	13 (++)	6	13 (++)
Felt had control of situation	3	–	0	5	0	1	4	2	0	9 (++)

*Percentages add up to more than 100 per cent as respondents could nominate more than one response.
+++, --- : positively and negatively significant at .01 level; ++, -- : significant at .05 level; +, – significant at .1 level

Table A3.8 *Reasons for not Enjoying Animal Encounter Experience According to Sex and Educational Achievement (percentage of respondents)**

	TOTAL	Female	Male	Tertiary education
Too many other people	25	28	23	29
Too few animals	13	13	15	12
Not close enough to animals	10	11	10	9
Animals in enclosures	10	9	12	9
Experience controlled by keeper, guide, ranger	9	7	13 (+)	9
Animals inactive	9	7	10	5
Animals did not want to interact with me	6	7	5	3
Animals seemed unhappy	5	6	2	5
Other	13	16	6	11
None	8	5 (-)	9	5

*Percentages add up to more than 100 per cent as respondents could nominate more than one response.
+++, --- : positively and negatively significant at .01 level; ++, -- : significant at .05 level; +, − significant at .1 level

Table A3.9 *Reasons for not Enjoying Animal Encounter Experience: Percentage of Respondents at Selected Animal Encounter Sites**

	TOTAL	Seal Bay	Monkey Mia	Warrawong	Cleland	Auckland Zoo
Too many other people	25	31	63 (++)	19	18	20
Too few animals	13	8	13	2 (---)	13	9
Not close enough to animals	10	11	15	2 (--)	4	16
Animals in enclosures	10	–	–	5	18	38 (+++)
Experience controlled by keeper, guide, ranger	9	8	19 (++)	10	11	2 (-)
Animals inactive	9	8	2	0 (---)	16	29 (+++)
Animals did not want to interact with me	6	3	4	3	9	16 (++)
Animals seemed unhappy	5	0 (-)	0 (-)	1 (-)	2	23 (+++)
Other	13	15	6	19 (+)	7	2 (--)
None	8	0 (--)	2	5	16 (+)	23 (+++)

*Sites with sufficient respondents to indicate statistical significance
Percentages add up to more than 100 per cent as respondents could nominate more than one response.
+++, --- : positively and negatively significant at .01 level; ++, -- : significant at .05 level; +, − significant at .1 level

Table A3.10 *Feelings about Feeding the Animals at Selected Sites According to Sex, Educational Achievement, Religion and Site*: Percentage of Respondents who Fed the Animals*

	TOTAL	Female	Male	Tertiary education	Secondary, primary education	No religion	Religion	Monkey Mia	Cleland	Currumbin	Auckland Zoo
Touch and feel the animals	34	30	38	34 (43)#	33	38	28	13	47	40	31
Get the animals to come closer	20	24	21	17 (21)	24	20	21	22	21	20	23
Sub-total	*54*	*47*	*59*	*51 (64)*	*57*	*58*	*49*	*35*	*68*	*60*	*54*
Animals showed they trusted and liked me	29	33	24	23 (-) (29)	30	25	30	39	26	40	31
Entered the world of animals	10	9	12	6 (7)	13	8	14	9	6	0	15
Sub-total	*39*	*42*	*36*	*29 (36)*	*43*	*33*	*44*	*48*	*32*	*40*	*46*
Other	7	11	5	20(+)	0	10	7	17	0	0	0
Total number who fed the animals	108	64	42	35 (28)	46	40	43	23	53	10	13

*Sites where feeding was possible
#Percentages in brackets show percentages excluding 'other' category, as this is high (20 per cent) for tertiary educated

Table A3.11 *Important Aspects of the Site According to Sex, Educational Achievement and Occupation of Respondent*

	TOTAL	Female	Male	Tertiary education	Post-secondary	Secondary or primary	Managerial, professional	Administrative, clerical	Blue collar	Home duties
Number of respondents	362	216	124	147	73	117	166	43	52	46
Site is peaceful and relaxing	94	93	98	97	93	94	96	100	96	85(--)
Site provides an authentic and unspoilt environment	90	91	89	90	88	92	90	100 (+)	92	87
Site is clean and well kept	90	90	92	90	92	91	90	91	92	87
Possible to explore site without a guide	47	49	46	46	52	46	50	30 (-)	48	43
Site has good transportation to it	42	43	40	37#	49	44	43	42	35	46~
Many leisure activities close to site	14	14	15	13	16	14	14	7	10	15
Site has good eating and rest facilities	50	53	45	40(--)	60 (+)	57 (+)	49	37#	50	59~
Site does not provide many activities	15	14	17	16	19	12	17	23	4 (-)	7
The weather was bad	14	15	14!	12	21	15	13	16	13	17~
Site was expensive	22	25	19	22	25	23	21	16#	31	20

Note: significant levels indicated: +++, --- : positively and negatively significant at .01 level; ++, -- : significant at .05 level; +, – significant at .1 level
unimportant is significant at .1 level
! unimportant is significant at .05 level
~ unimportant is negatively significant at .01 level

Table A3.12 *Responses to 'What Do You Think Should Be the Major Purpose of this Animal Site? (percentage of respondents)* *

	TOTAL	Female	Male	Tertiary ed	Antarctica	Great Aust Bight	Seal Bay	Monkey Mia	Warrawong	Monarto	Cleland	Currumbin	Auckland Zoo
Conservation & breeding endangered animals	46	48	48	47	23	64	52	17 (---)	65 (+++)	78 (-)	29	35 (-)	34
Natural environment for animals	24	22	24	21	59	36	32	21	20	22	13	24	32
Education for visitors	19	16	22	22	5	0	12	23	13	0	31 (+)	29	32 (++)
Allowing visitors to interact with animals	11	12	10	11	5**	18	3 (-)	27 (+++)	2 (--)	0	29 (+++)	18	9
Research animal life and behaviour	5	3	7	5	5	0	5	10 (-)	1	7	9	0	5
Entertainment for visitors	3	3	2	2	0	0	0	2	1	0	9 (+)	0	9 (++)

*Percentages add up to more than 100 per cent as respondents could nominate more than one response.
** one respondent added 'minimally'
+++, --- : positively and negatively significant at .01 level; ++, -- : significant at .05 level; +, – significant at .1 level

Table A3.13 *Nature-related Activities in Last Six Months According to Sex, Educational Achievement, Where Grew Up, No Religious Affiliation* (Percentage of Respondents)

	TOTAL	Female	Male	Tertiary educated	Secondary, primary education	Capital city	Country, rural	No religion*
Watched wildlife film	69	71	74	74	66	73	72	69
Owned a pet	59	65 (++)	51 (-)	57!	63	58	62	64 #
Went on a bushwalk	56	56	57	63 (+)	55	58	54	61
Visited a national park	54	57	53	62 (+)	47	56	59	64
Visited other zoo or wildlife sanctuary	42	45	38	46	38	44	37	52 (+)
Visited a museum	41	44	39	50 (++)	27 (--)	36	44	50 (++)
Camped out in the bush	29	30	32	31	32	30	34	35
Purchased a nature or wildlife book	28	31 (+)	23	33	26~	27	30	34~
Went on a tour which had environmental component	27	29	27	36 (++)	22	28	31	31
Went fishing	26	24	31	20 (-)	36 (++)	27	28	22
Had subscription to nature-based magazine, e.g. *National Geographic*	22	22	25	25	19~	23	21	21
Visited an aquarium	21	24!	18	22	16	19	21	19
Rescued or helped a wild animal	16	19 (+)	14	16	17	15~	20~	16
Owned stock animals	12	10	14	10~	16	8 (-)	16	10
Enrolled in course on animals or some aspect nature	7	9	5	10	6! ~	8	7	6
Hunted animals or birds	4	2 (-)@	7(+) @	1 (-)	3	2~	5	2
Been rescued or helped by an animal	4	6~	2	5	4	3	7	5

The results were statistically significant at the .01 (+++ or ---), .05 (++ or --) or .1 (+ or -) levels of significance.

*Australian respondents only (excluding New Zealand and overseas visitors)

! significant at .05 level for at some time; # significant at .05 level for has religion and at some time.;

~ significant for never; @ significant for all incidences of activity

Table A3.14 *Present Membership of Nature-based Societies According to Sex, Educational Achievement, Where Grew Up, No Religious Affiliation (Percentage of Respondents)*

	TOTAL	Female	Male	Tertiary educated	Secondary, primary education	Capital city	Country, rural	No religion*
Conservation	25	24	29	34 (+++)	19	25	30	30
Scientific	14	13	19	22 (+++)	7 (--)	16	16	11
Animal welfare	13	14	10	14	13	13	11	7
Zoological association	10	11	19	15 (+)	6	13	7	6
Animal breeding	9	11	9	12	5	12	9	4
Field naturalist	7	8	7	10~	4	9	6	5
Hunting	7	8	6	10 (+)	3	9 (+)	6	4
Museum society or group	6	6	7	9	3	10 (++)	5	3

The results were statistically significant at the .01 (+++ or ---), .05 (++ or --) or .1 (+ or -) levels of significance.
~ significant for have been at some time
*Australian respondents only (excluding New Zealand and overseas visitors). In every category except conservation, those with a religion were more likely to be members of the nominated associations.

Table A3.15 *Selected Nature-related Activities* by Site (Percentage of Respondents)*

	Antarctica	Great Australian Bight	Seal Bay	Monkey Mia	Warrawong	Monarto	Cleland	Currumbin	Auckland Zoo	TOTAL
Never hunted birds or animals	77	73	75	71	69	63	58	82	61	68
Ever joined environmental tour	68	54	32	33	35 (+)	22	18	18	14 (-)	14
Enrolled for course on animals or nature at some time	–	27	18	27	24	22	7 (-)	18	18	20
Visited other sanctuary or zoo in the last 6 months	41	36	55 (+)	65 (+++)	40	44	29	29	23 (--)	42
Bushwalked in the last 6 months	23	45 (+)	68	58	69 (++)	52	36 (--)	41	43 (-)	56
Visited a national park in the last 6 months	64	82	69 (++)	69	62	56	36 (--)	53	21 (---)	54

*Activities showing statistically significant results
The results were statistically significant at the .01 (+++ or ---), .05 (++ or --) or .1 (+ or -) levels of significance.

Table A3.16 *Respondents who Have Ever Been Nature-related Society Members by Site Visited (Percentage of Respondents)*

Type of society	Antarctica	Great Aust Bight	Seal Bay	Monkey Mia	Warrawong	Monarto	Cleland	Currumbin	Auckland Zoo	TOTAL
N	22	11	65	48	93	27	45	17	56	384
Conservation	59	64	42	44 (+)	51 (+)	26	18	33	41	52
Field naturalist	32	36	17 (+)	4	19 (+)	11	15	6	18	15
Scientific	55	26	26	16	26	18	9	18	18	20
Animal welfare	18	9	25	32	26	14	18	18	37 (+)	25
Zoological	27	27	13	15 (+)	15	15	24	0	25 (+++)	17
Animal breeding	14	18	11	14	16	14	6	6	18	13
Hunting	0	0	8	2	12 (+)	0	4	0	16 (+++)	8

The results were statistically significant at the .01 (+++ or ---), .05 (++ or --) or .1 (+ or -) levels of significance.

Table A3.17 *Attitudes to Animal and Nature Issues According to Educational Achievement, Sex, Where Grew Up, No Religious Affiliation: Percentages Disapproving unless Otherwise Specified**

	TOTAL	Tertiary	Post-secondary	Completed secondary or less	Female	Male	Grew up rural area	No religion
Expanding area of Australia's national parks (% approving)	96	81	81	72	76	80	67 (-)	83 (+)
Experimentation on animals to develop cosmetics	90	90	84	73	93 (+)	86	94 (+)	92
Hunting for pleasure	85	89	79	84	89 (+)	81	79	91 (+)
Bullfighting	85	83	84	89	89 (+)	83	93 (++)	84
Drift net fishing	81	83	84	80	82	82	84	83
Wood-chipping native forests	80	90 (+++)	76	74	80	84	53 (---)	86 (+)
Extermination of feral cats and foxes (% approving)	77	84 (+)	45	58	75	82	73	79
Preserving wilderness for its own sake (% approving)	71	79 (++)	69	61 (-)	69	75	66	74
Sustainable environmental use (% approving)	64	70	71	60	58 (-)	76 (++)	64	60
Aboriginal hunting in national parks using modern techniques	63	59	66	71	67	61	80	65
Breeding and keeping dolphins and whales in captivity	60	58	69	60	60	61	63	70 (++)
Rodeos	52	56	53	45	62 (+++)	38 (---)	61	66
Imposing tax on goods to cover environmental damage (% approving)	45	59 (++)	45	39 (-)	46	56	49	54
Experimentation on anaesthetized animals	42	37	41	50	49 (++)	32 (--)	53 (+)	50 (+)

Table A3.17 *continued*

	TOTAL	Tertiary	Post-secondary	Completed secondary or less	Female	Male	Grew up rural area	No religion
Hunting for economic reasons	40	32 (-)	43	46	45 (+)	32 (-)	35	48 (+)
Experimentation on animals to develop life-saving drugs	29	20 (--)	36	34	35 (++)	20 (-)	34	32
Culling indigenous animals like kangaroos	24	23	21	29	29 (+)	18	22	25
Farming native animals, e.g. kangaroos, for human consumption	22	17	22	26	30 (+++)	9 (---)	20	23
Breeding and keeping animals in zoos	17	22	10	13	19	13	12	19
Aboriginal hunting in national parks using traditional methods	15	9 (--)	19	21	30	12	25	15
Hunting for food	13	10	14	16	16 (+)	8	12	18
Farming stock animals, such as cattle, for human consumption	5	5	7	5	7	3	3	9
Killing pests around the house	4	5	2	4	5	3	4	4
Eating animal meat	4	5	3	2	7	4	3	6
Eating animal products, like eggs, milk	1	2	2	0	2	0	1	3 (+)

The results were statistically significant at the .05 (++ or --) or .1 (+ or -) levels of significance.
*Australian sample only, i.e. excludes international visitors to Australia, and New Zealand sample (except for grew up in a rural area where smaller sample not available)

Table A3.18 *Selected Attitudes to Nature for Visitors at Selected Sites*: Percentage Disapproving Unless Otherwise Specified)*

	Monkey Mia	Seal Bay	Warrawong	Cleland	Auckland Zoo	TOTAL
Extermination of feral cats and foxes (% approving)	65	78	81 (+)	67	50 (---)	72
Hunting for food	8	17	11	18	11	13
Hunting for pleasure	90	88	83	64 (--)	68 (--)	81
Hunting for economic reasons	44	29	42	40	34	39
Aboriginal hunting in national parks using traditional methods	19	18	11 (--)	13	59 (+++)	22
Aboriginal hunting in national parks using modern techniques	79 (+)	62	66	36 (---)	73	64
Culling indigenous animals	42 (++)	18	26	16	32	25
Farming native animals for human consumption	35 (+)	14 (-)	17	20	32	23
Drift net fishing	85	85	80	71	88	81
Preserving wilderness for its own sake (% approving)	75	66	75 (+)	58	48 (--)	65
Sustainable environmental use (% approving)	65	66	74 (++)	40 (--)	46 (-)	60
Wood-chipping native forests	81	77	88 (++)	53 (---)	75	77
Imposing tax on goods to cover environmental damage (% approving)	50	51	54 (+)	40	29 (--)	45
Experimentation on animals to develop cosmetics	92	91	86	80 (-)	91	89
Experimentation on anaesthetized animals	56	40	37	38	59 (+)	44
Experimentation on animals to develop life-saving drugs	31	28	27	29	36	31
Breeding and keeping animals in zoos	23	14	19	4 (-)	7	15
Rodeos	48	49	51	49	46	50
Eating animal meat	4	0	5	7	2	3

* Sites with large enough samples to identify levels of significance
The results were statistically significant at the .05 (++ or --) or .1 (+ or -) levels of significance.

Explanation for Tables 3.19 and 3.20

Four questions assessed conservationist orientations: wood-chipping native forests, imposing a tax on goods to cover their environmental damage, preserving wilderness for its own sake and expanding the area of national parks (a question on sustainable environmental use was omitted as the wording 'using the natural environment to achieve sustainable development' focused on development rather than the environment). These form the conservationist score in Tables A3.19 and A3.20. The moralistic score was constituted by: opposition to farming stock animals, eating meat, eating other animal products and killing pests around the house. The low score shows a very low disapproval rate for these activities. The humanistic orientation was made up of opposition to experimentation on animals, rodeos and bullfighting. A further question, concerning the extermination of feral cats and foxes, relates to pet-like animals and this item was also included in the humanistic score.

Table A3.19 *Orientation to Animals According to Educational Achievement, Sex, Where Grew Up, Religious Affiliation: Average of Responses to Items Constituting Orientation**

	TOTAL	Tertiary education	Post-secondary	Completed secondary or less	Female	Male	Grew up rural area	Grew up metro	No religion	Religion
Conservationist orientation	73	77	68	62	68	74	58	65	74	68
Moralistic orientation	3.5	3.5	3.5	2.75	5.25	2.5	2.75	3	5.5	2.25
Humanistic orientation	51	49	51	50	58	44	57	50	56	49
Responses to some individual items:										
Farming native animals for human consumption (disapprove)	22	17	22	26	30 (+++)	9 (---)	20	24	33	21
Farming stock animals for human consumption (disapprove)	5	5	7	5	7	3	3	5	9	3
Extermination of feral cats and foxes (approve)	77	84	45 (+)	58	75	82	73	75	79	76
Culling indigenous animals (disapprove)	24	23	21	29	29 (+)	18	22	27	25	26

* the higher the score the stronger that orientation

Table A3.20 *Orientation to Animals by Site: Percentage of Respondents at Each Site: Average of Responses to Items Constituting Orientation**

	Antarctica	Seal Bay	Monkey Mia	Warrawong	Monarto	Cleland	Currumbin	Auckland Zoo	TOTAL
Conservationist orientation	73	54	66	75	61	52	59	48	63
Moralistic orientation	2.5	2	4.5	3.5	1.5	3.8	0	.75	2.75
Humanistic orientation	58	64	63	61	64	56	63	62	62
Responses to some individual items:									
Farming native animals for human consumption (disapprove)	10	14 (-)	35 (+)	17	15	20	35	32	23
Farming stock animals for human consumption (disapprove)	0	0	10 (+)	5	4	7	0	0	4
Extermination of feral cats and foxes (approve)	85	78	65	81	85	67	50 (---)	50 (---)	72
Culling indigenous animals (disapprove)	10	18	42 (++)	26	15	16	32	32	25

* the higher the score the stronger that orientation
Tests of significance were only applicable at those sites where sufficient returns were collected: Seal Bay, Monkey Mia, Warrawong, Cleland, Auckland Zoo. The results were statistically significant at the .01 (+++ or ---), .05 (++ or --) or .1 (+ or -) levels of significance.

Table A3.21 *Reasons for Liking Nature Films According to Educational Achievement and Sex (Percentage of Respondents)*

	TOTAL	Tertiary	Post-secondary	Secondary or primary	Female	Male
Enjoy watching wildlife films	95	96	96	96	96	95
Learning about animal behaviour and lives	73	72	70	77	76	68
Close-up and other camera techniques	66	70	69	65	67	69
Natural animal behaviours	52	51	46	58	54	49
Show exotic places and animals	33	30	36	36	31	36
Show beautiful scenery and animals	21	17	24	25	20	24
Stories are told about animals' lives, victories, defeats	14	8	17	19	14	14
Show that animal societies are similar to human societies	10	9	20	5	11	8
Total N	343	141	70	112	207	118

Table A3.22 *The Most Important Factors When Planning an Interstate or Overseas Trip According to Sex, Educational Achievement and Occupation (Percentage of Respondents)*

	TOTAL	Female	Male	Tertiary education	Post-secondary education	Secondary or primary education	Managerial, professional	Administrative, clerical	Blue collar	Home duties
Learning experiences	48	50	48	56	55	40	52	47	52	43
Chance to see something of exotic culture	40	48	30	46	40	37	45	42	27	37
Chance to be alone in environment	34	34	38	39	32	34	37	35	42	28
Chance to see animals	26	27	24	19	21	38	22	30	42	28
Chance to talk to local people	24	24	24	25	26	19	25	26	21	17
Chance to relax	52	52	52	52	59	51	53	60	48	59
Opportunity to visit friends and relatives	22	20	27	21	16	28	19	21	29	28
Secure that travel and accommodation arrangements run smoothly	17	17	19	14	19	21	16	12	15	30
Range of physical activities offered	9	8	10	9	12	8	8	14	12	11
Chance to buy things not available at home, purchase bargains	8	9	6	7	10	8	8	5	4	11

Table A3.23 *Feelings When Last Saw Dolphins (Percentages)*

Where saw	In wild	Monkey Mia	Aquarium	Television	TOTAL
Percentage who saw at this location	48	10*	15	6	100
Feelings at time:					
Fondness or affection	68	84	67	45	59
Fun or pleasure	69	58	55	18	55
Peace or tranquillity	43	47	27	27	33
Comradeship or oneness	15	32	7	9	14
Feeling of communication	7	24	2	5	7
Total (numbers)	175	38	55	22	290

*Excluding Monkey Mia sample

Appendix 4: Data from Kellert's Study

Table A4.1 *Animal Attitudes in the US*

Attitude	% popn strongly oriented	Description of attitude	Characteristics of population with attitude
Neutralistic	35	Avoidance of animals by reasons of indifference; believe basic lack in affective or other capacities distinguishes animals from humans	No characteristics given as could not scale Low knowledge of animals (as scored)
Humanistic	35	Strong affection for and attachment to individual animals, typically pets, as sources companionship. Preference for animals phylogenetically closer to humans, anthropomorphism likely; deep emotional attachment or love for nature, but more usually domestic animals (Kellert, 1993b, p52)	Tend to be 18–25 years old, white, female, better educated, higher incomes ($20–35,000), little religious attendance, live on Pacific coast Tend to be members of humane and environmental protection organizations, zoo visitors, anti-hunting, scientific study groups. Tend not to be Alaskans, rural, males, African Americans, elderly, farmers. Tend not to be livestock producers, nature buffs, birdwatchers
Moralistic	20	Ethically appropriate, right and wrong treatment, of animals; oppose infliction of pain or harm, exploitation of animals; fundamental equality of all animals: state of mind rather than necessary involvement, often reflecting the conviction of a fundamental spiritual meaning, order and harmony in nature, often associated with the views of indigenous people (Kellert, 1993b, pp53–54)	Tend to be under 35 years old, women, clerical workers, graduate educated, live on Pacific coast, not religious, live in cities of over 1 million population, zoo enthusiasts Tend not to be Alaskans or from the South, African Americans, rural residents, farmers, males; least moralistic were farmers and rural residents Humane and environmental protection organization members, scientific-study hobbyists scored high; recreation and meat hunters, sportsmen's organizations, trappers, fishermen, livestock producers scored very low

Table A4.1 *continued*

Attitude	% popn strongly oriented	Description of attitude	Characteristics of population with attitude
Utilitarian	20	Assess animals on basis of their practical and material value; assumes animals should serve some human purpose and contribute to personal gain Tend to be aged 65+, farmers, less than 8-grade education, African-Americans, skilled workers, rural residents, residents of South; hunters in this category	Tend not to be Alaskans, single, highly educated, living in towns of >1 million population, under 35 years old, female, students; high scores for livestock producers, meat hunters, fishermen and low scores humane, wildlife protection and environmental protection organizations, and to lesser extent scientific study hobbyists, backpackers, birdwatchers
Aesthetic	15	Attractiveness or symbolic significance of animals, artistic appeal or allegorical bearers of a message aesthetic or symbolic: to facilitate human communication and thought – animals are good to think with – (Kellert, 1993b, p51)	No characteristics given as could not scale
Naturalistic	10	Interest in and affection for active participation in outdoors and wildlife	Tend to be under 35 years old, male, graduates or college educated, professional or businesspeople, white, not religious, live in Alaska or Pacific Coast; Nature hunters and members of environmental protection organizations had the highest scores with meat and recreational hunters, antihunters, livestock raisers and fishermen having comparatively lower scores Tend not to be African-Americans, 65+, highly educated

Table A4.1 *continued*

Attitude	% popn strongly oriented	Description of attitude	Characteristics of population with attitude
Ecologistic	7	Systematic conceptual understanding of and concern for environment as a system, wildife as barometers of natural system: state of mind rather than necessary involvement	Tend to be like naturalistic: 18–29 years old, graduate school and college educated, white, professional and managerial, men, residents of towns <2000 population, Alaska residents. Tend not to be unskilled blue collar workers, less than high school educated, aged 56+. Tend to be members of wildlife organizations, sporting organizations and scientific study hobby groups with particularly high scores for members wildlife, sportsmen related and scientific study/hobby groups. Zoo enthusiasts had comparatively low scores
Doministic	3	Mastery and control of animals, typically in a sporting context like rodeos, trophy hunting, bullfighting; contest with animal provides demonstration of strength, masculinity. Doministic and negativistic: a predisposition to avoid creatures and harmful elements of nature where such avoidance has conferred advantage in the course of evolution (Kellert, 1993b, p56)	Tend to be male, farmers, high income, less than 8th grade education, live in small towns, Alaska and Rocky Mountains; Tend not to be women, clerical workers, professional and businesspeople, earning over $20,000 annual income, graduate educated, non-religious and living on Pacific coast. Most doministic were trappers and hunters with humane organization members, environmental protection group members having lowest scores, zoo visitors

Table A4.1 *continued*

Attitude	% popn strongly oriented	Description of attitude	Characteristics of population with attitude
Negativistic	2	Avoid animals due to active fear or dislike; believe basic lack in affective or other capacities distinguishes animals from humans	Tend to be aged 65+, female, less than 8th grade education, farmer, foreign born, African-Americans;[6] Tend not to be 18–29 years old, college educated, skilled workers, students, professional and business people, single, earning $15,000–20,000 annual income, from Alaska Livestock producers slightly above average and antihunters also comparatively high suggesting concern for ethical treatment is more salient than general interest in animals. Environmental and wildlife protection organizations, scientific study hobbyists, birdwatchers least negativistic
Scientistic/ knowledge of animals	1	Curiosity about biological and physical characteristics of animals. Values animals as objects of study, curiosity and observation; may foster emotional detachment	Tend to be 18–25 years old, college educated, single, live in cities of over 1 million population, professional and businesspeople, from Alaska Tend not to be elderly, blue collar workers, poorly educated, African-American, less than 8th grade education, foreign born Highest scores for scientific study hobby groups with relatively high scores for wildlife protection organization members, bird watchers. Low scores for livestock raisers, fishermen, antihunters, meat hunters

Note: percentages add up to more than 100 per cent because people can be strongly oriented to more than one attitude.

Two orientations, the aesthetic, because of validity problems, and the neutralistic, because it could not be distinguished from the negativistic (Kellert, 1989, p10), could not be scaled.

Source: Kellert, 1978a, pp11, 53, 58, 59, 63, 73, 111, 124; Kellert and Berry, 1978, pp44, 53, 59, 63, 111; Kellert, 1989, pp6–9, 11, 14, 16–18.

Table A4.2 *Animal Orientations According to Sex and Nature-based Activities in the US*

Orientation	% total sample high score	% total sample low score	% males high score	% females high score	Average score: Total sample	Av. Score: Nature hunters	Av. score: Humane orgn member	Av. score: Environment protection orgn member
Naturalistic	20	20	22	18	3.1	8.5	5.6	6.5
Ecologistic	24	24	24	23	3.1	5.7	5.1	7.7
Humanistic	22	24	15	29	4.0	3.9	6.1	4.8
Moralistic	22	22	15	29	5.5	4.8	9.5	9.6
Scientistic*	20	24	20	24	0.9	1.5	1.8	1.9
Utilitarian	22	24	28	16	5.3	3.8	3.0	1.6
Doministic	19	16	22	16	2.0	3.8	.9	1.5
Negativistic	16	24	16	24	4.4	2.9	2.7	1.5

Note: low orientation on the scale is zero; higher scores mean a higher orientation towards that view of animals and nature.
*Instead of 'scientistic', 'knowledge of animals' is used.

Source: Kellert, 1978a, pp73, 77–84, 114–121; Kellert, 1978b, pp146, 147, 149, 150, 151, 152, 153, 155.

Appendix 5: Statistics on International Visitors to Australia

Table A5.1 *International Visitors to Australian Nature Destinations in 1990 Cross-classified by Sex, Nationality and Occupation: Percentage of Visitors in Each Category Who Said They had Visited that Site*

Destination	Male						Female					
	USA		Japan		Rest of Asia		USA		Japan		Rest of Asia	
	Manag and Prof	Blue-collar	Manag and prof	Blue-collar	Manag and Prof	Blue-collar	Manag and Prof	Blue-collar	Manag and Prof	Blue-collar	Manag and Prof	Blue-collar
Taronga	65	8	63	13	57	5	39	4	27	0	31	1
Lone Pine	80	1	52	7	85	4	50	0	20	6	44	0
Currumbin	83	8	75	6	96	4	27	5	23	2	57	5
Cleland	76	18	5	1	87	9	23	0	3	0	25	16
Monkey Mia	7	0	0	0	72	0	0	100	0	22	32	0
Kangaroo Island	42	35	10	9	67	33	30	0	64	0	5	0
Fraser Island/												
Hervey Bay	76	0	0	0	72	0	58	0	100	0	9	84
Kakadu	33	10	6	0	65	0	54	0	9	5	52	0

Source: Bureau of Tourism Research, 1990, data kindly supplied to author

Table A5.2 *International Visitors to Australia by Selected Nationality in 1990 and 1999 (percentages)*

Country	1990	1999
Japan	22.3	16.0
Singapore	3.2	5.7
Malaysia	2.0	3.1
New Zealand	18.5	15.9
UK	13.2	12.3
US	11.6	9.5
Total (000s)	2065.4	4143.1

Source: Bureau of Tourism Research (2004) 'International visitors by country of residence 1990–1999', www.btr.gov.au/service/datacard, Bureau of Tourism Research, Canberra

Table A5.3 *Selected Regions Visited by International Tourists to Australia in 1999 (percentages of international tourists)*

Sydney	55.5
Melbourne	24.4
Gold Coast, Qld	21.4
Brisbane, Qld	17.2
Perth, WA	12.7
Adelaide, SA	7.2
Hervey Bay/Maryborough, Qld	4.3
Kakadu, NT	2.4
Total visitors (000s)	4096.7

Source: Bureau of Tourism Research (2004) 'Top 20 regions visited by international visitors in Australia in 1999', www.btr.gov.au/service/datacard, Bureau of Tourism Research, Canberra

Notes

Introduction

1   As opposed to being valued for their economic utility: 'good(s) to eat'. Leach does not here provide a reference to Lévi-Strauss, although his more general discussion of animals and totemism (Leach, 1970, pp41–44) mentions, but without citation, Lévi-Strauss' *Totemism* (1964), the translation of *Le Totemisme Aujourd'hui* (1962). Many other authors commenting on Lévi-Strauss' notion do not provide specific page references, for example see Keith Tester's (1991, p130) rendition of Lévi-Strauss as 'humans use animals to think their humanity' and Ted Benton's (1993, p65) as 'means of thought, as symbols'. Franklin's (1999, p9ff) chapter heading 'good to think with' discusses Edmund Leach, Mary Douglas and Lévi-Strauss. Anne Scott (2001, p371), in her discussion of the work of Noske, Birke and Haraway, describes non-human animals as 'objects-to-think-with'.

2   Not everyone agrees with Berger's proposition that pet animals cannot present themselves to humans as radically 'other'. The Australian philosopher, Raimond Gaita (2002, p38), commenting on his dog, Gypsy, suggests 'we are struck every so often by the mystery of animals, their otherness to us and to our lives'.

3   For quotations of this phrase see Baker (1993, pp11–12), Benson (1983, p80), Noske (1989, p62) and comment in Franklin (1999, p62).

4   Indeed, Indrani Ganguly's (1992, p3) survey of Australian women of Anglo, Argentinian, Tongan, Vietnamese and Indian background reveals that, despite many other cultural differences concerning what constituted beauty, 'Big eyes were preferred by women from all cultures'.

5   Berman (1981, p69) cites Weber's 'disenchantment of the world' and notes Schiller, a century earlier, speaking of the 'disgodding of nature': the history of the West is 'the progressive removal of mind, or spirit, from phenomenal appearances'. Bateson (1972, p146) makes a similar point: 'mere purposive rationality unaided by such phenomena as art, religion, dream and the like, is necessarily pathogenic and destructive of life'. He advocates a metacommunication that soars beyond the limitations of reason (in Drengson, 1980, p72 and Berman 1981, p223).

6   Aslin (1996, p321) describes her approach in terms of Berman's (1981, p71) notion of 'participating consciousness', which has also been described as 'rational re-enchantment' (King, 1990, p121). Wolff (1991, p209) suggests combining catch and surrender: we surrender to the experience at the same time as we catch or harvest it.

Introduction – Part 1: Back to Nature Tourism

1   US millionaire Dennis Tito was described as 'the world's first paying space tourist' when he paid US$20 million for a window seat in a Russian rocket which circled

the earth and later docked with the International Space Station (Baker, 2001, p32). Space Adventures ™ is taking bookings for flights in space in 2005, the ticket costing US$98,000 (Love, 2000, p213).

2 Although recent predictions are more circumspect, Jim Davidson and Peter Spearritt (2000, pxvii) suggest that tourism 'may be the world's biggest industry'.

3 In 1960, worldwide international arrivals were 60 million (Urry, 1992, p1). There are estimates of 1.6 billion in 2020 (Addley, 2001, p22).

4 Australia received 10,000 international visitors in 1946, 85,000 in 1960, 416,000 in 1970 (Craik, 1991, p17), 2.4 million in 1991 (Bureau of Tourism Research, 1991a, p5) and 4.7 million in 2002–2003 (Australian Bureau of Statistics, 2003).

5 Although Davidson and Spearritt (2000, pxvii) trace tourism to the ancient Romans' use of the Bay of Naples as a resort, a leisure pastime that 'remained unmatched' until the 19th century development of the Riviera.

6 One impediment to holiday-making was the Protestant ethic and its command that work was preferable to 'idle' leisure. Gradually, however, church ministers advocated muscular Christianity, medical doctors commended the value of fresh air and rest (Aron, 1999, p43; Jasen, 1995, p112), magazines celebrated the Canadian wilderness (Jasen, 1995, p110) and organizations, such as the Playground and Recreation Association of America, promoted recreation (Aron, 1999, p202). By the Depression of the 1930s, there was too little work and much unwanted leisure, increasing access to holidays for some people. Following the Depression, the demands of consumption started to outstrip the requirements of production as the basis of the US economy and culture (Aron, 1999, p250).

7 In 1996, there were 600 ecotourist operators in Australia, responsible for 1 per cent of expenditure and employment in tourism and 3 per cent of export earnings (Davidson and Spearritt, 2000, p245).

8 One prediction claimed that wildlife tourism would account for up to 40 per cent of all tourism in 2002 (Hodge, 2002, p40). Australia's ecotourism industry is estimated to be worth $15,000 million annually (about US$11 billion), comprising one-third of total tourists (Ralph Buckley in Chryssides, 2001, p42).

9 The usual suspects against ecotourism, for example, timber and chemical companies, rename themselves or their activities. The Canadian timber company, Fletcher Challenge, offers TimberTours of a forest 'in its pure state' (Fletcher Challenge Canada, 1991). The Agricultural Chemicals Association changed its name to the Crop Protection Institute (Wilson, 1992, p77).

10 Fox's cage diving was used to film *Jaws* scenes, using a midget stunt diver to make the shark look bigger (Robson, 2001, p1).

11 For about $350 a day, one is dropped in a cage in the Great Australian Bight. Amid some concern that this 'shark viewing' has become a 'circus', the dive cage operators are drafting a voluntary code of ethics, to 'make sure the great white sharks are looked after' (Huppatz, 1999, p14). Some Port Lincoln residents suggest that cage diving entices sharks to link food with humans: after following a trail of offal and fish oil they find a person in a wet suit (Robson, 2001, p 2).

12 For example, on Galapagos Islands, boobies might be frightened away from their nests, exposing them to predation from gulls (Edington and Edington, 1986, pp38–39; Burger and Gochfield, 1993, pp256, 258). The Tyro Head Albatross colony near Dunedin in New Zealand has been reduced in size by the several thousand people who visit it each week (Rodney Russ, communication 20 January 1996).

Chapter 1: Zoos and Circuses

1   'A domestic animal can be defined as one that has been bred in captivity for purposes of economic profit to a human community that maintains total control over its breeding, organization of territory, and food supply' (Clutton-Brock, 1999, p32, italics deleted). Some animals, like Indian elephants and reindeer, cannot be bred in captivity and so are 'exploited captives'. The cat is the only domesticated animal that is solitary rather than social in its behaviour (Clutton-Brock, 1981, pp25, 130–131). Over time, domesticated species are bred for a reduction in body and brain size and a shortening of the jaws and facial region (Clutton-Brock, 1999, pp36–37), an infantilization of sorts.

2   Salisbury (1994, p39) claims the first documented animal trial on the European continent was in 1266. She suggests that, prior to the Middle Ages, animals were not generally held liable for their actions, and restitution was made (Salisbury, 1994, p37). Other historians claim reliable evidence of animal trials in classical Athens, where inanimate objects like stones and beams were also tried, although such trials might have been largely symbolic and ceremonial (Beirnes, 1994, p37).

3   Of course, bestial relations with animals persist, a little discussed aspect of animal–human encounters, but explored by Alfred Kinsey (Salisbury, 1994, p84) and Midas Dekkers (1994). As Dekkers (1994, p142) notes, one man walks on the moon and the whole of mankind has been to the moon; 11 Dutchman win a soccer match and the whole of the Netherlands played, but if 1 per cent of Dutch people have sex with animals, that is not considered something Dutch people 'do'.

4   Douglas J in dissent (with two other judges agreeing) in the *Sierra Club* case in the Supreme Court of the US extended rights to trees, arguing that 'trees should have standing' and that environmental issues could be litigated in the name of inanimate objects (in Hardin, 1974, pxv).

5   A survey of 1115 residents of New South Wales in 1994 found that 70 per cent disagreed or strongly disagreed that 'humans were meant to rule over the rest of nature', while 93 per cent agreed or strongly agreed that 'plants and animals have as much right as humans to exist' (Aslin and Norton, 1995, pp77, 79).

6   The Koran is also contradictory or ambivalent concerning whether animals are purely for the use of humanity as Allah's 'viceregent on earth' or whether 'There is no beast on earth ... but the same is a people like unto you' (Johnson, 1990, p35; see also Masri, 1989, pp10–11). The basic Islamic teaching concerning meat-eating (except pig flesh because of the large number of diseases carried) and experimenting on animals and using them more generally is that they are available for the essential needs of life. However, animals should be used in the most humane ways possible (Masri, 1987, p24; Masri, 1989, p18). For another discussion, see J. L. J. Wescoat (1998).

7   The purposive collecting of animals dates to 1490 BC, when Queen Hatshepsut sent the first recorded expedition down the Red Sea, to bring back birds and monkeys for her animal park. In the 12th century BC, Emperor Wen of the Chou Dynasty exhibited specimens (Tuan, 1994, p76).

8   Some sources claim that Regent's Park was established in London in 1826 (e.g. Huxley, 1981, p16) but le Jardin des Plantes was founded earlier, 'started with animals rescued from the mobs of the French Revolution' in 1789 (Allin, 1998, p2; Hahn, 1990, pp54–55). Another contender is the private menagerie of Empress Maria Teresa opened to the public in Vienna in 1765 (Jarvis, 2000, p77). Departing from imperial or scientific purposes, Bristol Zoo was 'founded by commoners for commoners' in 1836 (Hahn, 1990, pp86, 91).

9   Whipsnade's conservationist orientation was prefigured by Charles Waterton, who,

in about 1849, and perhaps being the first Englishman to do so, turned his park into a nature preserve, forbidding the discharge of firearms and seeking to protect animals from the 'depraved and demoralised part of Yorkshire' (Barber, 1980, p106).

10 So famous that Red Peter, the ape, in Franz Kafka's short story 'A report to an academy', speaks of being transported from the African Gold Coast to Europe 'in the Hagenbeck steamer' (Kafka, 1952, p171), going on to note: 'as far as Hagenbeck was concerned, the place for apes was [inside a cage] in front of a locker – well, then, I had to stop being an ape. A fine, clear train of thought, which I must have constructed somehow with my belly, since apes think with their bellies' (Kafka, 1952, p172). Red Peter sets about copying humans so that he can escape caged display.

11 The simulated rainforest in Melbourne Zoo cost $2.4 million (Bell, 1990, p44, about US$2 million). Jungle World at the Bronx Zoo cost US$9.5 million (Mullan and Marvin, 1987, pp53, 56). By the mid-1990s, the most expensive ape or jungle exhibits were estimated at between $15 and $30 million (Sama, 1992, p5D). Hancocks (2001, p126) notes that the high cost of these exhibits is often due to the cost of building suitable accommodation for animals kept outside their natural environment.

12 In May 2000, 'Adelaide Zoo's first purpose-built exhibit for bilbies was opened', sponsored by Haigh's chocolate company as part of the company's 85th anniversary celebrations. Haigh's replaced chocolate Easter bunnies with bilbies in 1997 (Innes, 2000, p24).

13 Research suggests that elephants in zoos survive an average of 15 years, compared with 30 years for working elephants in timber camps and up to 60 years in the wild: 'Zoo elephants are fat and stressed,' said Georgia Mason, one of the authors of the findings, based on zoo records at over 100 European zoos and scientific reports (Radford, 2002, p11).

14 Hearne (1987, p169) says 'even many animal lovers conventionally use the pronoun "it" rather than "he" or "she" to refer to an animal. I find this to be extraordinarily weird, evidence of the superstitions that control the institutionalization of thought.' Thus, some writers use the pronoun 'who' when describing animals, or certainly those animals with names or considerable intelligence (perhaps not slugs and flies). I have generally kept to standard English usage, which may be speciesist. I use 'who' on those occasions when an individual animal with a personality is being discussed or the context suggests that the nominated animals are deemed akin to humans.

15 Animal rights campaigners argue that animals in captivity are bored, degraded, listless – even if they are not exposed to actual cruelty by visitors or neglect by keepers (Mullan and Marvin, 1987, p38; McKenna, 1987, pp29–30; Schoenfeld, 1989; Johnson, 1990, p15; Adams, 1987, p84).

16 The night dens at Melbourne Zoo might look like prison cells but they are warm in winter, cool in summer and safe all year round, viewers are told in 'Zoo's Company' produced by Jill Lomas and screened on ABC in 1998 (Pitt, 1998, pp15–17).

17 There are about 1000 pandas in the wild and about 120 in zoos in China and 20 in other zoos around the world (O'Donnell, 2000a, p12), many rented out by the Chinese government (Wilson, 1992, p250). It would appear that the greatest threat to the pandas is not their notoriously low libido, which has led to recommendations of Viagra, 'sex education and physical exercise', as well showing pandas videos of giant pandas mating (Agence France Presse, 2002, p7), but destruction of habitat (O'Donnell, 2000a, p12).

18 By the late 1970s, there was dispute as to Taronga's objectives, now more often phrased as 'a cultural institution' contributing to education, research and

knowledge (McGrath, 1978, p11). Robert Baker, Director of the Adelaide Zoo, said 'Culture is not just fine paintings in art galleries; it is what is worth having and intrinsic to human survival. ...The beauty and diversity of the natural world and of wild animals ... are of cultural value to mankind' (Bell, 1990, p52).

19 The exhibit of beagles was entitled 'English hunting dogs'. The Chinese visitors were wary of the dogs, pulling their hands away from the beagle pups which came over to beg and whine. Llamas are zoo animals in Adelaide but not in Quito or La Paz where they are work animals and pets (Mullan and Marvin, 1978, p2). At the Chiang Mai Zoo in Thailand, in 2001, there was an exhibit of doves and a large billed crow, which cawed, to my ear, like any other crow. At Higashiyama Park Zoo, Nagoya, there is a 'common rat' exhibit.

20 Another writer suggests that the interpretation or visitor centre functions as a 'time tunnel' or liminal point between highway and park. It should shift the head-space of the visitor as well as offer all the information and equipment needed to experience the park (McDonough, 1982, pp81, 83).

21 Stimulated in part by the suffering caused by the animal trade. Whipsnade pioneered captive breeding in zoos (Huxley, 1981, ppxi–xii). The Captive Breeding Specialist Groups, a subgroup of ISIS (the International Species Information System), identifies all endangered animals in zoos around the world, allowing exchanges to maintain a healthy gene pool. The Australasian Species Management Program, in which zoos participate, has a set of priorities which include 'ethical acquisition', 'charismatic species [as they] may draw support for the protection of their habitat and its biotic community', 'broad representation and the value of thematic displays', 'special significance to Aboriginal or other cultures' and 'of use for medical, veterinary pharmacological or other research' (Jakob-Hoff, 1992, p17).

22 The programme for primary school students is linked with the World Society for Protection of Animals and Animals Asia to whom the Chinese government have granted the release and care of 500 bears. At the zoo, children learn how young bears are taught circus tricks, and when old enough are put into cages for bile farming. When no longer useful for bile farming, the bears might be killed for their paws, a delicacy in restaurants in some parts of South East Asia (Education Officer, Melissa Wyatt, 2000, p5).

23 In late 2001, Richard Jakob-Hoff was seeking a sponsor for a $3.5 million dollar Wildlife Health and Research Centre: 'It's a very exciting project that I think will make a big contribution to threatened species conservation here and abroad. As well as providing support for several species recovery programs in New Zealand we are currently also supporting one for an endangered Silver-eye in the Seychelles' (Richard Jakob-Hoff, email message, 22 October 2001).

24 So evasive is zoo publicity about culling that 'a startled public learned that zoos, Melbourne Zoo in this case, kill healthy animals on a regular basis', sometimes because of space. A bandicoot was killed because of his reluctance to breed, lion cubs because their mother was not inclined to feed them. The article notes that the birth of a gorilla averted the potential PR disaster (Crosweller, 1999, p6). The previous year the documentary 'Zoo's Company' took the viewer behind the scenes at the three Victorian zoos, Melbourne Zoo, Healesville Sanctuary and Werribee, an open plains type zoo. Of the three situations barred to the film crew, two involved animal culling: when zoo staff feared that the old silverback gorilla, Bulaman, would die (he did not) and when they decided to cull possums (Pitt, 1998, pp15–17).

25 The positive correlation for this factor in Table A3.3 is an artefact of which sites had animals in enclosures; it may also reflect a feeling of greater safety for some respondents.

26 The Council spent $60 million (about US$40 million) buying significant habitat and proposed a Brisbane Koala Park as a 'conservation and ecotourism draw-card for the city' which the Council felt would inject 'an extra $4 million a year into the city's economy' (Brisbane City Council, 1993).

27 In the early 1990s, 57 per cent of Japanese tourists went to a zoo or wildlife sanctuary. Among Japanese visitors to Queensland, 25 per cent went to Lone Pine Sanctuary, 51 per cent went to Sea World, 25 per cent visited Currumbin Bird Sanctuary (Bureau of Tourism Research and David H. Jacobs Consultants, 1992, pp61, 77). Of Japanese visitors to Adelaide, 21 per cent went to Cleland Wildlife Park (although only 4 per cent of all Japanese visitors went to Adelaide (Bureau of Tourism Research, 1991b, p16). In 1999, 2 per cent of Japanese visitor nights were spent in South Australia, compared with 37 per cent in New South Wales, 33 per cent in Queensland and 14 per cent in Victoria (Bureau of Tourism Research, 2004).

28 The Tasmanian Devil is justified on the grounds that fossil records of the Devil have been found in South Australia (Martinsen, 1985, p49).

29 In Mitchell's (1992, p12) survey, 47 per cent identified as the highlight either the koalas or the kangaroos or both.

30 Lorikeet feeding on a smaller scale is available elsewhere. I was able to do this at Brampton Island in the 1970s. At Bundaberg Paradise Bird Park (MS 264 Paradise Lane), 'Wild rainbow lorikeets are fed at 9.30 and 3.30 daily' (McNaught, 1991, p12).

31 In 1989, 16 per cent of the visitors came from overseas, 'breakfast with the birds' attracting many Asian and other tourists to the morning bird feed (McNair, 1990, pp3, 16).

32 I learned the term 'deer bums' from Raymond Soneff (interviews between 10 April 1992 and 18 April 1992). In 1992, a video in the Banff Natural Springs foyer warned of the dangers to deer caused by feeding them.

33 The wildlife officer in Renmark South Australia shot two pelicans because parents complained one had bitten their small son's arm. Other residents were 'incensed' and 'astounded', but a spokesman for Parks and Wildlife SA said the birds had become habituated to the public, relying on them for food (Cook, 1998, p5).

34 John Wamsley (dawn walk at Warrawong, 19 December 1992) says, 'They build koala sanctuaries and put them all in together; they know they are cuddly because they have long arms. But then they die, koalas are very solitary and they get chlamidia.' A Gold Coast retired resident, Pat McLaren, has spent over a million dollars to establish a koala breeding programme in his backyard, females selling for $5000 and males for $3500 (about US$3500 and $2600). The secret of his success, he claims, was 'that he kept sightseers out'. Because koalas are shy, they get stressed when touched and so diseased: 'Ironically, most of the places where Mr McLaren sells his koalas will use them as tourist attractions – and that means his stress-free koalas will be subjected to lots of patting, hugs and flash photography' (Macpherson, 1993, p31).

35 A study of three zoos in the US – a city zoo in Philadelphia, a plains type zoo and a country zoo in Arizona – found that scientific and ecological knowledge did not increase at all, even though many visitors appeared to read the signs and even more claimed they did so (Kellert and Dunlap, 1989; see also Jarvis, 2000, pp49, 51, 172, 174, 253, 256).

Chapter 2: Animals as Ambassadors for Conservation

1   New Zealand's Tongariro National Park, gazetted in 1894, has been described as

the 'second true national park of the world, after Yellowstone National Park' (Field, 1995, p48), although the word 'true' qualifies this claim in ambiguous ways.

2   It is sometimes claimed that the Royal National Park is the first national park in the world, although it postdates the land grant forming Yellowstone. However, it does appear to be second to Yellowstone and was the first area in the world with 'national park' designation (Davidson and Spearritt, 2000, p226).

3   Hokusi's 36 views of Mount Fuji from the mid-19th century reveal an interest in both the human figure and surrounding nature (Bosselman, 1978, p229). Indeed, even in relation to the famously romantic Lake District, when visitors were asked to select their favourite photograph, the majority chose images with people in them rather than photographs of lonely lakes and mountains. Visitors placed themselves in the scene and in their holiday via the images of other people enjoying the Lake District (Crawshaw and Urry, 1997, pp188–189, 193), little different from Asian tourists who are stereotyped for wishing to be photographed within their holiday.

4   Among them, the Great Barrier Reef, Kakadu National Park, the Tasmanian Wilderness, Uluru-Kata Tjuta National Park, Shark Bay in Western Australia and Fraser Island (World Heritage Unit, 1996, p3). In November 2000, the Greater Blue Mountains became Australia's 14th World Heritage property (Muir, 2001, p14). It is interesting that the term 'property' is used for World Heritage areas, suggesting a possession that many environmentalists find distasteful. Jack Turner (1996, p81) notes that a quotation from Henry David Thoreau – 'In wildness is the preservation of the world' – is often mistranslated as 'In wilderness is the preservation of the world'. Turner suggests that this is a Freudian slip, a repression, because we do not understand wildness as a quality but only wilderness as property.

5   So named, not because it is white, which it is not, but because the original Afrikaans word 'weit' meant 'wide' and refers to the animal's mouth.

6   This reduces the costs of management. In 1993, there were 350 animals at Monarto managed by two keepers and 1500 at Adelaide Zoo managed by 32 keepers.

7   In January 1994 a survey found that two-thirds came from the Adelaide metropolitan area, 13 per cent from country South Australia and only 3 per cent from overseas ('Monarto Zoological Park Questionnaire', Langdon, pers. comm. May, 1994).

8   By contrast, Martinsen (1985, p64) claimed that Cleland had been required to pay its own way from about 1980.

9   By 2000, sanctuaries opened to the public or under development included the original Warrawong, Yookamurra in the South Australian mallee district, Scotia in outback NSW, Hanson Bay on Kangaroo Island, Buckaringa Earth Sanctuary in the Flinders Ranges, Tiparra Earth Sanctuary on Yorke Peninsula, Dakalanta Earth Sanctuary on Eyre Peninsula, Little River Earth Sanctuary in Victoria, Murrawoollan Earth Sanctuary in the Southern Highlands of NSW, and Blue Mountains Earth Sanctuary (Earth Sanctuaries, 2000b, pp17–26).

10 In 2000, ESLs (Earth Sanctuaries Limited) wildlife conservation success list included the Platypus, Bilby, Quoll, Brush-tailed Bettong, Woylie, Southern Brown Bandicoot, Red-necked Wallaby, Red-necked Pademelon, Rufous Bettong (Earth Sanctuaries, 2003, pp7–9).

11 For example, see Hurrell, 1998, p11.

12 Warrawong has won a number of tourism and business awards (Earth Sanctuaries, 2000b, p16) while Wamsley won the *Australian Geographic* Conservation Award for Excellence in 1992 (Wamsley, 1994, p21). Furthermore, shareholders of Earth Sanctuaries supported the conservation message. A survey of shareholders in 1997 revealed that conservation was their primary reason for shareholding (97 per cent),

with educational services also rated as important (52 per cent); only 34 per cent ranked financial stability as an important factor. The typical ESL shareholder was male (although more females were ESL shareholders than the Stock Exchange's general listing), more likely to be middle aged and older, educated to a tertiary level or above, with either a very low or very high household income, all significantly different from the typical Australian Stock Exchange shareholder (Beal, 1998, pp1–2).

13 It has been estimated that an adult male Amboseli lion will net $515,000 in foreign exchange over its life from 'wildlife viewing' (Hvenegaard, 1994, p26).

14 A 'threatened' species animal is valued at $1250 per animal, a 'rare' species animal at $2500 per animal and an 'endangered' species animal at $5000 per animal (about US$1000, $2000 and $3750: Earth Sanctuaries, 2000b, p41). Australia now has accountancy standards which suggest valuing 'self generating and regenerating assets', those over which a company has exclusive rights, at their 'net market value' (Wamsley, 1999b, pp2–3).

15 The vermin-proof fence has been adopted elsewhere. In April 1999, stick-nest rats were reintroduced into Roxby Downs, outback South Australia, after being extinct for over 60 years on the Australian mainland. This project was a joint initiative of the town community, Western Mining Corporation, Adelaide University and the Environment Department. They are in a fenced enclosure from which all rabbits, foxes and feral cats have been removed (Hurrell, 1999a, p27).

16 Newspaper stories make claims such as $250,000 worth of salmon being taken when 'Big Dada and his harem' attacked a salmon farm (Darby, 1991, p15). Crayfishers neglect to note that seals also prey on the octopus which eat crayfish (Dennis, 1989, p16). Seals in the Shetlands were shot to scarcity until they were protected in 1973 with a total ban on hunting. Even so, in the mid 1990s about 60 'disappeared' and eight carcasses were found. Some members of the fishing industry claim culling or sterilization is necessary to contain the now excessive numbers (Hadley, 1997, pp4–5).

17 US$37.5 million, the growth rate explaining the dramatic increase since 1994, when Environment Australia estimated that cetacean-based tourism was worth $8.9 million (US$6.7m) (Prideaux and Bossley, 2000, p3).

18 Established in 1952 (Jaeckel, 2000, p11) and closed in the late 1970s, Cheynes Beach whaling station was converted into a whaling museum, Whale World. Tourists are told that economics, rather than the environmental movement's opposition to whaling, defeated the industry (tour guide, February 2001). Certainly, as numbers declined between 1972 and 1976, the International Whaling Commission's sperm whale quotas became more specific as to length and gender, making it difficult for Cheynes Beach to maintain profitability (Jaeckel, 2000, pp76–77). But public pressure against whaling was also mounting, including opposition from a majority of Albanians. In 1977, the company had secretly decided to wind up its operations, announcing this in 1978 when the federal government inaugurated an inquiry that was likely to recommend a moratorium on whaling (Jaeckel, 2000, p84). Australia closed down its industry following the Frost Commission Report, and became an active pro-whale lobbyist.

19 See also newspaper coverage such as Montgomery (1997, p3) and – in a somewhat macabre register – 'crowds flocking south of Adelaide to a pack of sharks eating a Southern Right carcass' (Brook, 2001, p21).

20 Whales in Sydney Harbour are protected by rules requiring boats to keep their distance (Healy, 1999, p4). It was also suggested that 10,000 balloons should not be released at a rugby football match final because of a whale in the Harbour (Crawford, 1999, p3).

21 There is some dispute as to whether or not General Macarthur 'ordered' the Japanese to reintroduce whaling following the war or was 'persuaded' to do so by Japanese politicians (Summers, 2002; Komatsu and Misaki, 2001, p3). 'Up until the 1950s, 50 per cent of all protein consumed by the Japanese was from the whale', whereas the British and American whalers threw away the meat (Summers, 2002).

22 In an international survey, all samples identified humane killing as one of their highest priorities, except the Japanese respondents who identified the sustainability of the industry (Freeman and Kellert, 1994, pp298–299).

23 Like the charismatic megafauna so attractive to zoo visitors, a point made also by Michael Bryden, Professor of Veterinary Anatomy at Sydney University (Brook, 2001, p21).

24 Described in a video on Humpbacks shown on the 1992 Hervey Bay whale watching trip I joined. The video, *The Gentle Giants*, was edited by Leslie Parry and written and produced by Colin Gillock.

25 In May 1995, 175 square kilometres of the Bight was proclaimed a whale sanctuary, only 10 per cent of the multiple-use Marine Park Area originally proposed by government agencies, the fishing industry and Aboriginal people (Foster, 1999, p23). In May 1996 the South Australian government declared a permanent sanctuary zone at the Head of the Bight, the primary calving and mating ground for the Southern Right Whales in South Australia (Weir, 1996, p12). Oil exploration licences have been released for 200,000 square kilometres of Bight waters, provoking fears of future oil spills (Safe, 1999, pp22–26).

26 The survey, of 224 visitors between July and October in 1995 (returns from 1500 distributed questionnaires), found that 41 per cent had a tertiary education, almost a third were members of a conservation group, Greenpeace being the most popular; 57 per cent were over 50 years old; 46 per cent were on their way to either South Australia or Western Australia and only 24 per cent came solely for the experience of whale watching (Reid, 1996, pp32–36). Almost a quarter identified a general interest in seeing whales as a significant reason for visiting the site and 13 per cent wanted to see whales in the wild or their 'natural environment' (Reid, 1996, pp36–37).

27 The changeling exchange between seals and humans is explored in Beverley Farmer's (1992) novel *The Seal Woman*, Tom Gilling's (1999) novel, *The Sooterkin*, set in colonial Hobart, and the films, *The Secret of Roan Inish* (1994) and *Selki* (a South Australian film).

28 In my survey, although the questionnaires were handed out at Seal Bay, five of the 65 respondents chose Flinders Chase as their most enjoyable experience.

29 For example see Tourism South Australia and Kangaroo Island Tourist Association (1988, pp9, 18–19) and PPK Consultants in association with KPMG (1991, pp33–38, 65).

30 From about 25,000 visitors per annum before 1985, there were 154,000 in 1986/1987 and 200,000 in 1989/1990 (PPK Consultants in association with KPMG, 1991, p13).

31 'On a hot summer's day, you've probably envied the sea lions ... playing in the pool' at the zoo, reminisces the advertisement. Now, you can enjoy an 'unforgettable experience and the sea lions are lured by nothing more than curiosity and even, you'd swear, a sense of fun' (Tourism South Australia, 2001, p27).

32 There are a number of sea lion colonies on islands that are also conservation parks, for example Olive Island (Robinson and Heard, 1985, p214). There are also some potential tourist destinations to presently inaccessible colonies in Western Australia (Terry Dennis, District Ranger, National Parks and Wildlife Service, Kangaroo Island District Office, interviewed on 30 December 1992).

33 In 1982–1983, 3 per cent of visitors came from overseas; in 1987, it was 14 per cent (Tourism South Australia and Kangaroo Island Tourist Association, 1988, p1; South Australian Department of Tourism, 1984, p27). A quarter of the Japanese tourists who went to Adelaide visited Kangaroo Island (although only 4 per cent of all Japanese visitors to Australia went to Adelaide (Bureau of Tourism Research, 1991b, p16). In 1999, 2 per cent of Japanese visitor nights in Australia were spent in South Australia (Bureau of Tourism Research, 2004, 'Nights in states and territories, 1999').

34 The New Zealand Department of Conservation's 'Sub-Antarctic Islands Minimum Impact Code' says: 'give all animals the right of way' and forbids approaching wildlife closer than 5 metres. We found these rules difficult to obey as sub-adult seals chased us or barred our way by standing on the paths. One group almost appeared to be cognizant of the 5-metre rule, stringing itself out on either side of the path at slightly less than 10-metre intervals, thus barring our passage.

35 So valuable have the penguins become that the government is buying back houses on a holiday housing estate that threatened the colony (Jarvis, 2000, p118), spending over US$7.5 million by 2000 (Jarvis, 2000, p133). Due to the housing estate, many birds were hit by cars or killed by the increased number of foxes, cats and dogs, while spreading Kikuyu grass choked the penguins' burrows (Jarvis, 2000, p130).

36 SHEL has won an Air New Zealand Ecotourism Award for 'high achievement in conservation and public education of the natural environment of New Zealand', and a NZ Tourism award for best natural history operation. SHEL is a member of IAATO, the International Association of Antarctic Tour Operators, established in 1991 (Southern Heritage Expeditions Limited, 1995, pp4, 5).

37 Although Rodney Russ (21 January 1996) suggested that this result might be partially because I administered the questionnaire just after we visited Macquarie Island.

38 The digesters, to boil penguins down into oil, were built by Joseph Hatch and his wife, their story told in *Joseph Hatch or the Wreck of the Kakanui*, Rodney Russ informed us.

39 Russ provides bed nights on his vessel for Department of Conservation personnel and scientists and carries expedition gear to various bases (Southern Heritage Expeditions, 1997, p1). One such scientist on our trip, Nick Gales, was researching the dive depth of the rarest sea lion, Hooker sea lions, which were getting caught in squid trawl nets.

40 Although one guide, Steven, describes the sub-adult males as 'teenage lads' roaming the beach and harassing the females.

Chapter 3: So Long and Thanks For All the Fish

1 The dolphins' farewell to humans in *The Hitchhiker's Guide to the Galaxy* by Douglas Adams (1995), originally a radio serial in the 1980s.

2 Reputedly, 'sharks are no match for the dolphin kind' and leave when dolphins arrive (Montagu, 1963, p17). Richard Connor (interview with Sue Doye, July 1994, courtesy of Sue Doye), who researches the Monkey Mia dolphins, claims dolphins are sometimes unaware that a shark has entered their waters.

3 In *Dolphins into the Future* (1997), Joan Ocean describes swimming daily with the wild spinner dolphins for eight years, imitating their sounds and thus being child to their parent. One day, 'a ring of light around the dolphins' signalled that 'we were no longer different species, our thoughts merged together' (in Bryld and Lykke, 2000, pp210–211; see also Nollman, 1987, p187).

4   As a result of the World Trade Organization (WTO), the US Marine Mammal Protection Act has been struck down because it banned the importation of tuna caught in Mexican and European drift nets that slaughter dolphins at an estimated annual rate of 150,000 each year. The WTO was also used to override the US Endangered Species Act, which made shrimp farmers equip their nets with inexpensive turtle excluder devices to protect endangered Asian sea turtles (Barlow and Clarke, 2001, p79). Purse seine tuna fishing nets with dolphin escape hatches have also been devised and are used by some fishing vessels. Pelagic spotted dolphin appear knowledgeable concerning purse seine nets. They no longer thrash about but wait for the net to be lowered below the water level so they can escape. Dolphins avoid the right hand side of boats, the usual location for the cranes and machinery which handle the nets (Griffin, 1992, p214).

5   Richard Connor refers in particular to Lilly's search for meaning via experiments with LSD for which Lilly built himself a special flotation tank. At this juncture, Lilly had left others to carry on his dolphin research, but his later writing (e.g. see Lilly, 1972) influenced the scientific community's evaluation of his research.

6   Similarly, Davis (1997, p143) is critical of San Diego's Sea World education programmes for school children as 'first and foremost marketing and public relations tools'.

7   This story has come full circle with the recent announcement that the Monkey Mia resort will become a joint venture with the local Aboriginal Yadgalah Corporation, investing $3.2 million (about US$2 million) (half of it a loan from the Aboriginal and Torres Strait Islander Commission) to buy 23 per cent. Indigenous Business Australia has also bought a quarter share. It is envisaged that Aboriginal people will be employed at the resort where they will promote their local culture (Egan, 2002, p2; my thanks to Michael Koorndyk for alerting me to this news item).

8   Holy Fin died in 1995, probably aged 35 to 37 years old. 'Her skeleton will be exhibited in the new centre, which is due to be built mid next year' (Charles, 1999, pp13–14).

9   When I visited the Grassy Key Dolphin Research Centre, Barb ('host' of DolphInsight, Dolphin Research Centre, 17 May 1992) said the Monkey Mia bay was polluted with effluent and condemned feeding dead fish to the dolphins. She felt that visitors should just play with the dolphins and described Monkey Mia as a 'herded' experience, like a 'zoo'.

10 Over the previous 20 years, only 5 of 17 calves born to provisioned dolphins had survived, 36 per cent compared with 67 per cent for non-provisioned dolphins. The four original dolphins each had nine, five, two and one infant, of which only one born since regular provisioning had survived. For example, Hobbitt was killed by a shark, when his mother and other adult females were interacting with people (Wilson, 1994, pp9–10, 8).

11 Edwards (1989, p24–25, 45–46) notes how the dolphins deliberately splash people, herd in snapper to 'feed' to the people on the beach or mimic human beach clean-ups by bringing in cigarette butts from the water. 'Some of them are likely to bring seaweed for dolphin–human games of tug-of-war' (Horne, 1992, p10).

12 In mid 1987, 30–40 kilograms of fish a day was sold to the public: it was decided to reduce this amount by about 30 per cent (Edwards, 1989, p98). By mid 1995, feeding was restricted to 2 kilograms per day per dolphin (Doye, 1995, p16).

13 In the mid 1960s, Evelyn Smith began feeding dolphins in the Leschenault Estuary (Edwards, 1989, p99). In time, she could summon the dolphins by slapping the water with a rake. Gradually the dolphins accepted fish from Smith's hand and she became a tourist attraction, 3500 people signing her visitors' book from February

to September 1969 (Edwards, 1989, p100). Mrs Smith died in 1974, it being a Bunbury legend that on the day of her death the dolphins came back to her jetty for the last time. Some years after Smith's death dolphins have returned to the shallows (Edwards, 1989, p101).

14 Citations to the *Portside Messenger* in this section are based on a content analysis of the newspaper between 1950 and 2001. Only where specific text is cited are full references given.

15 Adopting a dolphin lends support to campaigns opposing deliberate killing of dolphins: dolphins caught in tuna nets, dolphin hunting in the Faroe Islands, death by pollution, and capture for entertainment purposes (Whale and Dolphin Conservation Society, 1997). Adopt a dolphin projects are also offered by WWF-Denmark and Grassy Key in Florida.

16 In 1994, Mike Bossley could recognize about 140 individual dolphins; by 1998 he had identified 250 dolphins over the years (Gunther, 1994, p1; Bossley, 1998, p32). The unique nature of the Port Adelaide dolphins is debatable. Dolphins are sometimes spotted in the Swan River estuary in another Australian city, Perth, as well as off the beach, for example at Cottesloe, although I know of no one studying them or claiming that pods live in the estuary.

17 Billy's relationship with Sandford and his horses was told in a children's picture book (Rockley, 1990, p4) and the 1990 heritage parade (*Portside Messenger*, 1990, p9).

18 Prideaux and Bossley (2000, pp2, 4, 6) outline the hazards faced by dolphins in waters around Australia. They argue that the bottlenose dolphins in South Australia's Gulf St Vincent have been recorded with the highest mercury levels in the world. The noise of seismic testing threatens dolphins' auditory communication capacities in Western Australia and Victoria. Dolphins in the Gippsland Lakes on the east Victorian coast are threatened by toxic algal blooms, caused by nutrients leaching from contaminated ground water and agricultural runoff. Packaging straps, plastic bags and fishing line pose hazards of ingestion and entanglement, as does global warming, particularly to whales travelling to the Antarctic waters. Vying with the Port River dolphins for the title of slum dolphins are the estimated 250 Indo-Pacific hump back dolphins (*sousa chinensis*) who live in the polluted waters of Hong Kong Harbour, and are visited through Hong Kong Dolphinwatch tours (Newton, 2001, pp10–11).

19 Patrica Irvine (interview 20 December 2000) is critical of this claim, noting that the Torrens Island Power Station, already in operation, heats the water more than the Pelican Point Power Station was projected to do. Bottlenose dolphins are 'cosmopolitan', able to live in a great range of water temperatures. The power station was a good distance from the mangroves and was unlikely to affect fish breeding grounds. Certainly the dolphins were not going to 'boil' to death, as some claimed.

20 Similarly, subjects responding to slides of the same animals in a naturalistic zoo, caged zoo and wild environment rated the zoo animals as more restricted, tame and passive compared with both the naturalistic zoo and the wild animal slides (Finlay et al, 1988, p520).

21 Used by both the US (from 1959) and Russian defence forces, dolphins blew up submarines with explosives strapped to their bodies; they carried bombs and hypodermic syringes with carbon dioxide to kill Vietcong divers in the Vietnam War (May, 1990, pp125–127; Bryld and Lykke, 2000, p180). Dolphins clamped markers on frogmen to be killed. There is some suggestion the dolphins were coerced, food withheld or the dolphins physically abused if they did not perform correctly (May,

1990, pp125–127). By contrast, journalist Carson Creagh describes these claims as 'a total urban myth', claiming that dolphins were willing to attack dummies but not enemy divers (Leser, 1988, p36). In the Ukraine, the 70 members of the dolphin squadron have been sold to the Red Sea swim-with-the-dolphins therapy centre in Israel (Bryld and Lykke, 2000, p181).

22 Gould (1999, p3) and Woodford (1999, p4) report on Scottish research that suggests that dolphins are capable of infanticide and notes the increasing frequency of violent incidents against tourists. Ricou Browning, who also worked as trainer and producer of Flipper, says 'Most people want to believe that dolphins love people ... Well, I don't think this is true', although they can be 'affectionate' (in Rothel, 1980, p47).

Introduction – Part 2: The Nature of Modern Society

1 The percentage of people in the categories add up to more than 100 as many people in Kellert's survey expressed more than one orientation.

2 '(H)umans are characterized by a tendency to respond positively to nature ... this disposition has a partly genetic basis' (Ulrich, 1993, p120; see also Kellert, 1993a, pp20, 32–33).

3 See Appendix 1 for research methods and Appendix 2 for the questionnaire.

4 The Australian Conservation Foundation suggests that, with vast tracts of land unsuitable for agriculture, 'free ranging or wild harvesting of animals makes sense'. They realize, however, that 'harvesting roos for human consumption has been one of the more controversial issues for both the conservation movement and the animal rights movement' (Sampson, 2001, p24).

5 'Of all demographic variables, education was the most sensitive indicator of appreciation, concern, affection, knowledge and respect for animals' (Kellert and Berry, 1978, p71).

6 Research is now uncovering the link between the physical and sexual abuse of women in the home and the abuse of their companion animals (Ascione et al, 1997, pp205, 208; Hutton ,1983).

Chapter 4: Recapturing Lost Meanings

1 *Primate Visions* argues that, in their liminal role at the border between the human and natural worlds, primates are invested with shifting interpretations of the human/nature divide, including the impact of imperialism and sexism (Haraway, 1992).

2 A study of visitors to Perth's UnderWater World marine park and Bunbury Dolphin Discovery Centre found that those who swam with dolphins had greater physiological and psychological wellbeing, as measured by a self-administered questionnaire, both before (when they anticipated swimming with dolphins) and after swimming with dolphins than those who swam without anticipating or experiencing dolphins. There were no gender differences (Webb and Drummond, 2001, pp81, 83).

3 Shari Huhndorf (2001, pp21, 158), in tracing the representation of the Indian across three centuries of white settlement in the US, argues that the romanticism of native life only really emerges once the military conquest of Native America is complete. Furthermore, the Native Americans conveniently vanish at the end of these narratives, leaving behind what is most valuable to non-indigenous people, native culture.

4   'Ecofeminism' was coined by the French writer Françoise d'Eaubonne in 1974 (Merchant, 1990, p100).

5   I am grateful to Robin Webb-Jones for drawing my attention to this article.

6   With its slogan 'the personal is political is spiritual', nature religion is at the forefront of protests against road construction, pressure groups to accept sacred sites and animal rights, campaigns against pollution (Puttock, 1997, p230). In Australia, 'ferals' draw on hippy, punk, pagan and anarchist philosophies to defend wilderness areas or locations considered sacred by indigenous people (St John, 2000, pp210, 213, 214)

7   A group of tourists in Carnarvon Gorge were profoundly unsettled to see Jackie Huggins and members of her family as visitors to the site. Jackie Huggins' mother, Rita Huggins, told the white tourists that she 'was born here, this is my country' (Huggins et al, 1997, p237).

8   Aboriginal people were invited to the Second International Whale and Dolphin Conference at Nambucca Heads in 1990 and performed their dolphin dreaming to the audience, after all the women had been asked to leave the room (Dobbs, 1992, p120). Jarvis (2000, p182) refers to a popular book that claims the Wurunjeri are known as the 'Dolphin People' because they communicated with dolphins when they required advice on important tribal matters.

9   Possibly 40–50 per cent of the population have spiritual or mystical experiences which cause ontic shifts, and usually involve a vision or, at least, a significantly altered mental state, if only temporarily. However, it is one of the 'great cultural conspiracies of the West' that these experiences are rarely discussed (Lewis, 1989, p26).

10   Accounts of the origin of the term landscape differ, one claiming it was first used in 1603 to characterize an 'inland area that can be taken in at a glance' (Fuller, 1988, p17). By contrast, Martin Woollacott (2001, p14, citing *Jorwerd* by Geert Mak) notes that landscape comes from the Dutch word '*lanschap*, implying something shaped but not made by man'. There is also some dispute over the claim that landscape painting was reconfigured by the Romantic tradition (Soper, 1995, pp235–236).

11   In the debate over opening a mining exploration zone in Stage II of Kakadu, which included Coronation Hill, the Australian Conservation Foundation in 1989 used the term 'sacred' in its submission to the government (Kelly, 1992, p538).

12   Such views expressed by men who are immersed every day in the wildness of Macquarie Island might appear to undermine the line of my argument. Perhaps our tour guide was performing masculinity for us. Australian Antarctica is well known for its masculine culture, particularly before the advent of female scientists or female base leaders. Only 6 of the 19 countries that had wintering communities in 1992 had any women at all in those communities over the previous ten years (Bowden, 1997, p447). In 1979, Diana Paterson applied for the position of station leader and was told she would be welcome as a radio operator or a cook (Bowden, 1997, p457). In 1989, she was appointed officer in charge of the Australian base, Mawson, the first continental woman station leader. She was dubbed 'Lady Di' because of 'her perceived authoritarian behaviour' (Bowden, 1997, p458). Male Antarctic expeditioners are famous for indulging in that peculiarly widespread male Australian idea of a good joke, cross-dressing and putting on 'impromptu' shows (Bowden, 1997, p467). Female station leaders, like Joan Russell, grappled with issues such as girlie posters in the work areas, and bullying within as well as across genders (Bowden, 1997, p466). However, in their more private registers, many over-winterers are caught by the majesty of their experience. They 'refer, time and again, to the constant renewal they get from the physical beauties of Antarctica'. "Every

morning when I look out," Sheryl White says, "I think there's no other place in the world like it" (Murray-Smith, 1988, p221).

13 Most tourists to famous sites will have seen models or photographs of the site before they visit, thus framing what they see when they arrive (MacCannell, 1976, pp44–45; Pearce, 1988, p144). Some places, like Niagara Falls, become so structured by pre-existing cultural images that the physical object is barely 'seen' at all (Urry, 1990, p66).

14 Many ecofeminists use the concept of 'Gaia', James Lovelock's hypothesis of the total interconnectedness of all things on the planet (Allen, 1990, p54).

Chapter 5: Loving Knowing

1 Independently, both the Spanish physician Gomez Pereira in 1554 and Descartes in the 1630s argued that animals were automata (Thomas, 1983, p33).

2 For example cormorants used by Chinese fishermen are given every seventh fish that they catch, rather than the fish caught on the seventh dive. Sometimes the fisherman loses count and fails to untie the string around the cormorant's neck so it can swallow its fish. The cormorant refuses to dive again until given its fish, the cormorant distinguishing between the number of dives and fish caught (Hauser, 1999, p43). For a discussion of animal intelligence see Griffin (1976; 1982; 1992).

3 My thanks to Shannon Dowling for supplying this article.

4 My thanks to Christine Nicholls for sending me a copy of this book: she was correct to say that it is an important contribution to untangling the ethical dilemmas of human–animal relations.

5 Sea World's public relations director refused to be associated with research on whether animals have emotions because it 'smacked of anthropomorphism'. Yet Sea World train their dolphins to shake hands and splash water at spectators (Masson and McCarthy, 1996, p13).

6 The impact of gender on animal observations has now been widely researched. Women primatologists discover cooperative primate troops or notice baboon mothers 'juggling time' just like human mothers (Haraway, 1992, p313). Males, like Robert Ardrey and Desmond Morris, focused on human territoriality and aggression (Soper, 1995, p57; see critique in Sperling, 1991, p20). Similarly, as Western society became more open to discussions of sex, the maintenance of social connections through heterosexual play (de Waal, 1991, pp200–219) and homosexual relationships have also been 'discovered' (Bagemihl, 1999).

7 My thanks to Lenore Layman for alerting me to this important book.

8 By contrast, The Sierra Club was founded in 1892 under the leadership of John Muir, who described it as something 'for wildness and [to] make the mountains glad'. The Ecological Society of America was founded in 1915 (Nash, 1973, pp132, 198).

9 Similarly, a survey asking Australians in which organizations they were active members, found that 33 per cent said sport, 25 per cent arts, 21 per cent church, 12 per cent trade unions and only 7 per cent environmental (with 3 per cent saying political parties) (Marsh, 2000, p131). A 1996 survey found environmental organization membership for only 4.5 per cent of the sample, although 70 per cent said environmental protection was as important as economic growth (Smith, 1999, p290).

10 Letter bombs in Kent, injuring young girls and farmers, have been attributed to the Animal Liberation Front. Although they have not claimed responsibility, 'animal issues are common to each target' (Wainwright, 2001, p8).

11 Low (2002, pp275–280) notes that the campaign to build ponds and save green tree frogs and other species, started by Martin and Hillary Boscott in 1981 in Brisbane, was largely successful only for the marsh-frog, which was hardy and would have survived without human assistance. Wattle birds lured to stay south by native shrubs planted in gardens may be missing the thiamine they formerly gained from eating insects when they migrated north in winter (Low, 2002, p281).

12 Richard Ogust and three full-time workers rehabiliate turtles saved from Chinese restaurants. They are responding to the problem that two-thirds of the world's remaining freshwater turtles and tortoises are threatened, according to the Turtle Conservation Fund (Haughney, 2003, p33).

13 As suggested by a US content analysis of newspapers in which city newspapers developed a more humanistic and ecological content during the 1960s, but rural newspapers retained their utilitarian emphasis (Kellert and Westervelt, 1985).

14 The research on the therapeutic effects of wilderness is inconclusive, especially concerning whether it is the exercises (like trust building) or the impact of the natural environment which most contribute to improved self-esteem (Mitten, 1994, p55; see also Powch, 1994 and Levine, 1994, p183 for discussions of 'feminist spirituality wilderness therapy'; Angell, 1994, pp85–89 and Gracen, 1994, p154 on abuse survivors). Hammitt's survey of university students enrolled in outdoor recreation revealed that the major function of wilderness solitude was emotional release from the anxiety and fatigue of everyday life, a disengagement from social roles (Hammitt, 1982, pp57–58). Lynn Levitt (1982, p82) reviews 100 studies of the therapeutic effects of camping on emotionally disturbed children and adolescents. The studies report enhanced self-concept, improved social attitudes and behaviour, improved physical health, fewer emotional problems and pathological symptoms. She notes problems with experimental design and methodology in a number of them, perhaps reflecting, along with companion animal research, 'I like this so thus must my charges'.

15 That women are more likely to have been helped by an animal may be an effect of one of the few animal-related activities which were significantly influenced by gender, pet-ownership (see Table 3.13 in Appendix 3).

16 In Xishuangbanna, Yunnan Province, adjacent to the Sanchale Primeval Forest Reserve, described as 'Wild Elephant Heaven'. In one photograph 'A girl plays with a baby elephant that her family is taking care of' (CD News, 1993, p6).

17 Kunming City has provided 50,000 yuan ($8,620) to animal protection organizations to feed about 25,000 red-billed petrels that flew from Siberia to Kunming, capital city of southwest China's Yunnan Province, to escape the harsh winter (Wang, 1993, p1).

18 'While health care remains scarce in the rest of China, a team of 16 doctors was available around the clock to look after Dudu [the oldest panda in captivity], who was put on a life support machine' (August, 1999, p10).

19 Pandas also appear to be ungrateful in their reluctance to breed, this article noting the panda is an 'archaic' animal with a very inefficient reproductive system. Scientists turned to Viagra after traditional Chinese herbal medicines failed (Hill, 2001, p23).

20 Australia now has a Field Station exploring ways to reduce road-kill, for example reflectors (of headlights) or scents to deter kangaroos on roadside hotspots (Young, 2003, p21).

21 Some 50 cases of feral children have been recorded over the last 600 years, involving adoption by wolves, bears, leopards, monkeys, sheep and a gazelle. While adopted children learn an animal's language, some animals also learn human

versions of their own language. The gazelle boy replaced some gazelle signs he could not make (because his ears were covered) with facial expressions and the gazelles added these to their repertoire of communication (Noske, 1989, p166).

22 Discussing results from a suspect experiment (which involved comparing 'hooking' a fish and a dog for example), the authors conclude that dolphins, dogs and cats are 'our' kinds of animals, and 'native species are definitely "ours"' (Rajecki et al, 1993, p57).

23 Tim Low (1999, pp192–193) is less convinced that feral cats are to blame for wildlife extinction, suggesting that foxes or exotic viruses brought in with mice might be more significant culprits.

24 Although most of the city groups located in Canberra and Melbourne also described urban wildlife (Aslin, 1996, p 306). Most of the representatives of animal associations saw wildlife as all wild animals, including marine animals, while some even included micro-organisms. Among the focus groups, some used size to define wildlife, while others worked with the native/exotic distinction (Aslin, 1996, pp176, 240–241).

25 Today global capitalism threatens indigenous ecosystems. For example 3000 marine species travel the world's oceans as unsought passengers on ships (Williams, 2000, p13).

26 By contrast, China ordered the mass destruction of civet cats, a delicacy in southern China accused of spreading the SARS virus. Many cats were clubbed to death rather than killed via the officially sanctioned method of drowning in disinfectant (Correspondents in Beijing, 2004, p11).

27 As evidence of these shifts in understanding human obligations to nature are the Endangered Species Act of 1973 'which granted nonhuman organisms a near-absolute right to exist regardless of economic costs'; the Greenpeace slogan 'Humankind is not the center of life on the planet' and Earth First!'s slogan 'No compromise in Defense of Mother Earth' (Baron, 2004, p156); '$20 billion in public spending committed between 1998 and 2002 to preserve open space' (Baron, 2004, p9).

Chapter 6: Respectful Stewardship of a Hybrid Nature

1 The general argument in relation to animal rights is that they should run in accordance with animals' needs or interests. For example Peter Singer's (1977) classic argument in *Animal Liberation* is based largely on claims that the suffering of all sentient beings should be minimized. Peter Singer's (2001, ppxiv–xvi) four propositions are as follows. (1) 'Pain is bad, and similar amounts of pain are equally bad, no matter whose pain it might be.' Pain includes 'suffering or distress of all kinds'. Conversely, 'pleasure and happiness are good'. (2) Most nonhuman animals are capable of feeling pain and suffering. (3) 'When we consider how serious it is to take a life, we should look, not at the race, sex or species to which that being belongs, but at the characteristics of the individual being killed, for example its own desires about continuing to live, or the kind of life it is capable of leading.' (4) We are responsible both for what we do and 'what we could have prevented', including saving the lives of strangers in a distant country (Singer, 2001, pxvi). Singer's controversial support for euthanasia and infanticide in particular cases arises from his claim that inflicting pain and killing are not in the same calculus (Singer, 2001, p42).

2 Pearce and Caltabiano (1983) found that well travelled tourists were more likely to experience self-actualization (reflection on 'profound issues' and 'life's mysteries')

and love and belongingness (family ties or 'worthwhile contacts with the host community'). Those with little travel experience were more likely to record a physiological experience: good food, sun and relaxation.

3   Many northern Protestant states passed animal protection legislation around the same time, for example Saxony, Prussia and Württemberg in the 1830s, Switzerland and Norway in 1842, Sweden in 1857 (Ryder, 1989, pp167–168). France passed a law in 1850 that made it illegal to beat animals in public (Corbin, 1990, p538). In 1876 a British Act to Amend the Law relating to Cruelty to Animals was the only legal restriction in the world against the experimental use of animals (Lansbury, 1985, pp9–10) while the Protection of Animals Act was passed in 1911 (Ryder, 1989, p130). General Franco suppressed the humane movement in Spain, dictator and church alike condemning animal protection for pit-ponies, birds, horses in bullfights as 'foreign ideas and Protestant influence' (Ryder, 1989, pp170–171).

4   The concept 'ecological footprint' calculates how much land is required to support people's lifestyle. It requires 4.5 hectares for each person living in Sydney. If all the world's population used the same amount of resources, it would require three times the present area of productive land on earth (Gaynor, 1999, p39).

5   The top holding companies in 1996 being Pepsi, Marriott, McDonald's Corporation and Disney (McLaren, 1998, p14).

6   An 18-hole golf course in a dry country can consume as much water as a town of 10,000 inhabitants. In some places, 55 tourist days expend enough water to grow rice to feed 100 villagers for 15 years (Addley, 2001, p22). In Nepal, a typical two-month climbing expedition will use 150 per cent of the fuel wood that a traditional hearth burns in one year (Whelan, 1991, p12).

7   Tourists demand inauthentic encounters, encounters that presume they are not tourists but friend and equal, guests of a host. The locals treat strangers as either nuisances or walking moneybags (Crick, 1989, p321). Tourists' culture and money sows prostitution, homosexuality, crime, liquor consumption and begging (see discussions in Urbanowicz, 1978, p90; 'Akau'ola et al, 1980, p12; Meleisea and Meleisea, 1980, p45; Johnston, 1991, p405; McLaren, 1998, p83).

8   Not quite what Wildscreen@Bristol promises to be, but close. This electronic zoo, which hosts the leading film festival of wildlife filmmakers, substitutes real animal encounters with wildlife films and an ARKive, or 'digital Noah's ark' consisting of 'a storehouse of knowledge about the world's endangered species' (www.arkive.org.uk) (Davies, 2000, p254).

9   Of Jarvis' (2000, pp232–233) respondents who went dolphin watching in Port Phillip Bay, 13 per cent were drawn by the marine environment or other animals more generally.

10   Plumwood (2002, pp143–166) suggests that the focus on individual behaviour recommended by well-meaning animal liberationists, for example that we become vegetarian, is limited and contradictory. It does not attack systems of exploitation, or acknowledge the need for alliances with workers, small farmers and so on. It cannot readily be sustained, for example, animals eat other animals. Instead we must work out ways to deal with the natural world respectfully for meat and the other materials we need.

11   By contrast, in Taiwan, a bill to ban people from eating dog meat has been passed (Guardian, 2001, p14).

12   Paul Waley (2000, pp168–169) suggests that the 'Japanese ontological world is free of the opposed dualities of moral absolutes' by which Western philosophy understands the world. This approach 'encourages a sort of animal anthropomorphism that has been identified as a particularly strong feature of Japanese attitudes towards animals'.

13 Indeed, tourists enslaved by the fetishism of commodities are probably the more numerous. West Edmonton Mall is 'Disneyland, Malibu Beach, Bourbon Street, the San Diego Zoo, Rodeo Drive in Beverley Hills and Australia's Great Barrier Reef ... in one weekend – and under one roof'. In 1987 it attracted over 9 million tourists, the third most popular tourist attraction after Walt Disney World and Disneyland (Urry, 1990, p147).

14 Another suggestion was to use feral and other culled animals in animal experimentation, innovative if not entirely responsive to the moral issues raised by animal experimentation.

15 Rupert Ormond, director of the marine biological station at Millport in Scotland, believes that most coral reefs will disappear within 30–50 years, due to global warming. The disappearance of up to 90 per cent of coral in the tropical Indian Ocean at the height of the last el Niño, in 1998, presaged things to come. He believes the situation is hopeless, given 'a 50-year time lag between us trying to control carbon dioxide emissions and the temperature in the oceans beginning to drop' (Radford, 2001, p23).

16 While the number of hunters in the US has declined by 8 per cent in the past decade, the US population has increased by 13 per cent. 'Since 1990, voters in California, Colorado, Arizona, Oregon, Alaska, Massachusetts, Michigan, and Washington have passed ballot measures that restrict the hunting and trapping of bears, beavers, bobcats, wolves, wolverines, foxes, lynx, and cougars' (Baron, 2004, p10).

17 Aslin (1996, p321) describes her approach in terms of Morris Berman's (1981, p71) notion of 'participating consciousness'. Rather than yearning for an impossible return to the past, one should seek to refigure reality in a way that combines fact and value, self and society (Berman, 1981, p195). We should look for 'rational re-enchantment' (King, 1990, p121; see also Wolff, 1991, p209 who suggests we need to surrender to the experience at the same time as we catch or harvest it).

18 Clearly, humans cannot let all animals live out their full population potential as long as we wish some humans to live, some animals to be pets, some animals to be kept for milk, meat or clothing, some animals to prey on others. We must make choices (Stone and Stone, 1986, pp8–9).

19 To purchase this silence, BHP and Esso have donated only $300,000 between them over three years (Jarvis, 2000, p134). The other more 'controversial' issue that the Visitor Centre fails to address is over-harvesting of penguins' food, pilchards and anchovies, by the commercial fishing industry (Jarvis, 2000, p135).

20 And yet this is reversible: 'With $200 or $300 million, we could stop most of the habitat loss in this country', says Hugh Possingham, recently appointed director of Queensland University's Ecology Centre (Powell, 2003, p29).

21 Zoo research still 'tends to objectify nature, positions people as separate from nature, assumes a value-free stance, attempts to predict with accuracy, and privileges quantitative knowledge and methods over other ways of knowing and problem-solving' (Mazur, 2001, p84).

22 'People aren't going to save quolls or potoroos if they don't know what they are'. A 'team of South Australians who had hand-reared endangered southern hairy-nosed wombats are providing crucial advice to the Queensland recovery program for the critically endangered northern hairy-nosed wombat' (Hodge, 2003, p19).

23 In UK surveys, despite evidence of young people's concern with animals and the environment (Wilkinson and Mulgan, 1995, pp16, 96, 106), there is also evidence of a retreat from international concerns to 'a distinctly personal world view, directing ... energies inwards rather than into changing the world' (Wilkinson and Howard, 1997, p72).

24 Activities can also work against each other, the NHT seeking to reverse land clearing with its Bushcare project, involving the active participation of up to 53,000 people in some projects, while continued land clearing policies have meant a net loss in bush and forest land in most States over the life of the NHT (Australian Conservation Foundation, 2000).

25 Some research suggests that 81 per cent retention occurs with sight-based information, 11 per cent from hearing and 8 per cent from the other senses (Oliver, 1992, p56).

26 Some zoo environmental educators enhance the skills visitors can take away with them, e.g. how to observe and read animal behaviour more effectively (Hopgood, 1999, pp6–7; see also Bell, 1990, p51).

Appendices

1 Visitor behaviour is most reliably assessed by observation at the visitor site, where immediate and untutored responses to the experience can also be recorded (Gale and Jacobs, 1987, pp22–27).

2 Of the 25 focus group members, half were male (13) and half female (12); 19 were aged 20–40 and 6 were aged 40–55; 10 had not completed high school, 6 had completed high school and 8 had university degrees; all but three were born in Australia, two being born in England and one in Italy. Ten had grown up in the suburbs of a capital city and seven in a central capital city, while three had grown up in a rural area and two in a provincial city.

3 Besides being asked for their reactions to the animal encounter sites they had visited, focus group participants were asked for their feelings about different kinds of animals, about being out in the bush, attitudes to various activities such as conservation, vegetarianism, experimentation on animals, watching wildlife films, hunting animals, and any unplanned authentic animal encounters they had experienced (which ranged from a tree snake in Brisbane's botanic gardens to finding their own koala in a roadside tree).

4 These are in no way representative of visitation rates, given the basis for selecting focus group members.

5 2.3 per cent for Australia as a whole, but only 1.6 per cent in South Australia, although higher in Queensland and Western Australia (Maunders, 2001, p70).

6 Siobhan Brooks (2002, p115) suggests that urban women of colour, at any rate, are disinclined to 'love nature', having been warned by their mothers not to go to parks alone 'for fear of being raped'.

References

Accoom, R (1992) 'Aboriginal environment in national parks: Aboriginal rangers' perspectives' in J Birckhead, T de Lacy and L Smith (eds) *Aboriginal Involvement in Parks and Protected Areas*, Aboriginal Studies Press, Canberra

Ackerman, P (1997) 'The four seasons: one of Japanese culture's most central concepts' in P J Asquith and A Kalland (eds) *Japanese Images of Nature: Cultural perspectives*, Nordic Institute of Asian Studies and Curzon, Richmond, Surrey

Adams, C J (1990) *The Sexual Politics of Meat*, Basil Blackwell, Oxford

Adams, C J (1994) *Neither Man nor Beast: Feminism and the Defense of Animals*, Continuum, New York

Adams, D (1995) *The Hitchhiker's Guide to the Galaxy: A Trilogy in Five Parts,* Heinemann, London

Adams, R (1987) 'Some thoughts on animals in religious imagery' in V McKenna, W Travers and J Wray (eds) *Behind the Bars: The Zoo Dilemma*, Thorsons Publishing, Rochester, Vermont

Addley, E (2001) 'Tourists bleed resorts dry', *Guardian Weekly*, 31 May–6 June, p22

Advertiser (1998) 'Quick response to appeal', *The Advertiser*, 25 August, p13

Advertiser (1999) 'Mum's first kiss for her baby', *The Advertiser*, 9 December, p1

Agarwal, B (1992) 'The gender and environment debate: lessons from India', *Feminist Studies*, vol 18, no 1, pp119–158

Agarwal, B (1998) 'Environmental management, equity and ecofeminism: debating India's experience', *The Journal of Peasant Studies,* vol 25, no 4, pp55–95

Agence France Presse (2002) 'Porn panders to lazy blokes', *The Australian* 'Magazine', 28 June, p7

Ahmed, S, Kilby, J, Lury, C, McNeil, M and Skeggs, B (2000) 'Introduction: thinking through feminism' in S Ahmed, J Kilby, C Lury, M McNeil and B Skeggs (eds) *Transformations: Thinking Through Feminism*, Routledge, London and New York

'Akau'ola, Lata, 'Ilaiu, Lupe, and Samate, 'Asinate (1980) 'The social and cultural impact of tourism in Tonga' in F Rajotte and R Crocombe (eds) *Pacific Tourism as Islanders See It*, Institute of Pacific Studies of the University of the South Pacific, Suva

Albert, D M and Bowyer, R T (1991) 'Factors related to grizzly bear–human interactions in Denali National Park', *Wildife Society Bulletin*, vol 19, pp339–349

Allen, C (2001) 'The scholars and the goddess', *Atlantic Monthly*, vol 287, no 1, pp19–22

Allen, P G (1986) *The Sacred Hoop: Recovering the Feminine in American Indian Traditions*, Beacon Press, Boston

Allen, P G (1990) 'The woman I love is a planet; The planet I love is a tree' in I Diamond and G Feman Orenstein, *Reweaving the World: The Emergence of Ecofeminism*, Sierra Club Books, San Francisco

Allin, M (1998) *Zarafa: The True Story of a Giraffe's Journey from the Plains of Africa to the Heart of Post-Napoleonic France*, Headline, London

Almagor, U (1985) 'A tourist's "vision quest" in an African game reserve', *Annals of Tourism Research*, vol 12, pp31–47

Alpers, A (1960) *Dolphins: The Myth and the Mammal*, Houghton Mifflin Company and Riverside Press, Boston and Cambridge

Amalfi, C (2000) 'Students seek lure of Bunbury dolphins', *The West Australian*, 22 January, p53

Ammer, C (1989) *It's Raining Cats and Dogs ... and Other Beastly Expressions*, Random House, New York

Ananthaswamy, A (2003) 'Has this chimp taught himself to talk?' *New Scientist*, 4 January, p12

Anderson, C (1994) 'Black, green and white politics', *The Independent Monthly*, April, pp44–45

Anderson, K (1998) 'Animals, science and spectacle in the city' in J Wolch and J Emel (eds) *Animal Geographies: Place, Politics, and Identity in the Nature–Culture Borderlands*, Verso, London

Anderson, K J (1994) 'Behind bars – The meaning of zoos' in D Headon et al (eds) *The Abundant Culture: Meaning and Significance in Everyday Australia*, Allen and Unwin, St Leonards

Andrews, M and Whorlow, R (2000) 'Girl power and the post-modern fan' in M Andrews and M M Talbot (eds) *All the World and Her Husband: Women in Twentieth Century Consumer Culture*, Cassell, London

Angell, J (1994) 'The wilderness solo: An empowering growth experience for women' in E Cole, E Erdman and E D Rothblum (eds) *Wilderness Therapy for Women: The Power of Adventure*, Haworth Press, New York

Appleyard, B (1993) *Understanding the Present*, Pan Macmillan, London

Aquarium of Western Australia (2001) 'Visitor guide', Aquarium of Western Australia, Perth

Arluke, A (1993) 'Associate editor's introduction: Bringing animals into scientific research', *Society and Animals*, vol 1, no 1, pp5–7

Arluke, A and Carter, L (1997) 'Physical cruelty toward animals in Masachusetts', *Society and Animals,* vol 5, no 3, pp195–204

Armstrong, E A (1973) *Saint Francis: Nature Mystic. The Derivation and Significance of the Nature Stories in the Franciscan Legend*, University of California Press, Berkeley

Armstrong, M (1992) 'Wintering with the whales', *The Australian Way* (in-flight magazine of Australian Airlines which later became Qantas), May, pp44–45

Aron, C S (1999) *Working at Play: A History of Vacations in the United States*, Oxford University Press, New York and Oxford

Ascione, F R, Weber, C V, and Wood, D S (1997) 'The abuse of animals and domestic violence: a national survey of shelters for women who are battered', *Society and Animals*, vol 5, no 3, pp205–218

Aslin, H (1996) 'Speaking of the wild: Australian attitudes to wildlife', thesis submitted for the degree of Doctor of Philosophy of the Australian National University, Australian National University, Canberra

Aslin, H J and Norton, T W (1995) 'No one answer – Sustainable use of wildlife in a multicultural society' in G C Grig et al (eds) *Conservation Through Sustainable Use of Wildlife*, Centre for Conservation Biology, University of Queensland, St Lucia

Associated Press (2001) 'Hail the Ig Nobel Laureate', *The Australian* 'Magazine', 10 October, p41

Attenborough, D (1990) *The Trials of Life: A Natural History of Animal Behavior*, Little Brown, Boston

Auckland City (2003) '2002 Annual Report', Auckland City, Auckland, http://www.aucklandcity.govt.nz/council/documents/annualreport/report2002/events.asp

August, O (1999) 'China mourns as Dudu succumbs to heat', *The Australian* 'Magazine', 28 July, p10

Austin, N (2004) 'Even better way to watch Bight whales', *The Advertiser*, 10 March, p29

Australian Bureau of Statistics (2003) *Tourism Indicators Australia*, Australian Government Publishing Service, Canberra

Australian Conservation Foundation (2000) 'ACF's Assessment of the Natural Heritage Trust: An analysis of mid-term performance and recommendations for reform', Australian Conservation Foundation, Melbourne, http://www.acfonline.org.au/

Bagemihl, B (1999) *Biological Exuberance*, St Martin's Press, New York

Baird, A (1992) 'Aboriginal environment in national parks: Aboriginal rangers' perspectives' in J Birckhead, T de Lacy and L Smith (eds) *Aboriginal Involvement in Parks and Protected Areas*, Aboriginal Studies Press, Canberra

Baker, P (2001) 'Tourist makes history in space', *The Guardian Weekly*, 3–9 May, p32

Baker, S (1993) *Picturing the Beast: Animals Identity and Representation*, Manchester University Press, Manchester and New York

Barber, L (1980) *The Heyday of Natural History*, Jonathan Cape, London

Barber, T X (1993) *The Human Nature of Birds*, St Martin's Press, New York

Barlow, M and Clarke, T (2001) *Global Showdown: How the New Activists are Fighting Global Corporate Rule*, Stoddart, Toronto

Baron, D (2004) *The Beast in the Garden: A Modern Parable of Man and Nature*, W.W. Norton and Company, New York and London

Barsh, R (1990) 'Indigenous peoples, racism and the environment', *Meanjin*, vol 49, no 4, pp723–731

Bateson, G (1966) 'Problems in cetacean and other mammalian communication' in K S Norris (ed) *Whales, Dolphins and Porpoises*, University of California Press, Berkeley and Los Angeles

Bateson, G (1972) *Steps to an Ecology of Mind: Collected Essays in Anthropology, Psychiatry, Evolution, and Epistemology*, Chandler, San Francisco

Bauman, Z (2003) *Liquid Love: On the Frailty of Human Bonds*, Polity, Cambridge

Baxter, C and Halstead, C (1989) 'Koalas on Kangaroo Island', *Australian Ranger Bulletin*, vol 5, no 2, pp6–7

Bayet, F (1994) 'Overturning the doctrine: Indigenous people and wilderness – being Aboriginal in the environmental movement', *Social Alternatives*, vol 13, no 2, pp27–32

Beal, Diuana (1998) 'Earth Sanctuary shareholders are amazing!', 'Earth News', no 24, May, pp1–2

Beck, U (1992) *Risk Society: Towards a New Modernity*, translated by Mark Ritter, Sage, London

Beer, G (1986) '"The face of nature": The language of *On The Origin of Species*' in L J Jordanova (ed) *Languages of Nature*, Rutgers University Press, New Brunswick

Beirnes, P (1994) 'The Law is an ass: Reading E.P. Evans' *The Medieval Prosecution and Capital Punishment of Animals*', *Society & Animals* vol 2, no 1, pp27–46

Bell, G (1990) 'Are zoos for animals or people?', *Bulletin*, 4 September, pp44–52

Bell, L (2001) 'The devil made me do it', *The Weekend Australian* 'Magazine', 31 March–1 April, pR30

Bellos, A (2001) 'Galapagos fishermen threaten marine life', *Guardian Weekly*, 4–10 January, p5

Bennett, T, Bulbeck, C and Finnane, M (1991) *Accessing the Past*, Institute of Cultural Policy Studies, Faculty of Humanities, Griffith University, Nathan, Brisbane

Benson, T L (1983) 'The clouded mirror: Animal stereotypes and human cruelty' in H B Miller and W H Williams (eds) *Ethics and Animals*, Humana Press, Clifton, New Jersey

Benton, T (1993) *Natural Relations: Ecology, Animal Rights and Social Justice*, London, Verso

Berger, J (1980) *About Looking*, Pantheon, New York

Berman, M (1981) *The Reenchantment of the World*, Cornell University Press, New York

Bilger, B (2001) 'A shot in the dark', *The New Yorker*, 5 March, pp74–83

Birke, L (1994) *Feminism, Animals and Science: The Naming of the Shrew*, Open University Press, Buckingham and Philadelphia

Bolt, A (1998) 'Their lives will end in terror', *The Advertiser*, 20 January, p23

Bolton, G (1981) *Spoils and spoilers: Australians Make Their Environment 1788–1980*, George Allen and Unwin, Sydney

Boo, E (1990) *Ecotourism: The Potentials and Pitfalls*, Vol 1, World Wildlife Fund, Washington DC

Booth, M (2000) 'Prospectus that offers wild returns', *The Advertiser*, 1 February, p25

Bosselman, F P (1978) *In the Wake of the Tourist: Managing Special Places in Eight Countries*, The Conservation Foundation, Washington DC

Bossley, M (1998) 'Dolphin park', *The Advertiser*, 27 August, p32

Bourdieu, P (1984) *Distinction*, Routledge and Kegan Paul, London

Bowden, T (1997) *The Silence Calling: Australians in Antarctica 1947–97*, Allen and Unwin, Sydney

Bowdler, S (1999) 'Research at Shark Bay, WA, and the nature of coastal adaptations in Australia' in J Hall and I McNiven (eds) *Australian Coastal Archaeology*, ANH Publications, R.S.P.A.S., Australian National University, Canberra

Brabant, S and Mooney, L A (1989) 'When "critters" act like people: anthropomorphism in greeting cards', *Sociological Spectrum*, vol 9, pp477–494

Bradford, G (1993) 'Toward a deep social ecology' in M E Zimmerman, J B Callicott, G Sessions, K J Warren and J Clark (eds) *Environmental Philosophy: From Animal Rights to Radical Ecology*, Prentice Hall, Englewood Cliffs, New Jersey

Breckwoldt, R (1989) 'The dingo: Time to make peace with an elegant survivor', *Habitat, Australia*, vol 17, no 3, pp17–19

Brennan, E J, Else, J G and Altman, J (1985) 'Ecology and behaviour of a pest primate: Vervet monkeys in a tourist-lodge habitat', *African Journal of Ecology*, vol 23, no 1, pp35–44

Brisbane City Council (1993) 'Keeping Brisbane green', Brisbane City Council, Brisbane

Brockelman, W Y and Dearden, P (1990) 'The role of nature trekking in conservation: A case study in Thailand', *Environmental Conservation*, vol 17, no 2, pp141–148

Brockes, E (1999) 'Meet the men who motivate with metaphor', *The Guardian Weekly*, 20 June, p25

Brook, S (2001) 'Breaking down the whaling wall', *The Weekend Australian* 'Magazine', 28–29 July, p21

Brooks, D (2000) *Bobos in Paradise. The New Upper Class and How they Got There*, Simon and Schuster, New York

Brooks, S (2002) 'Black feminism in everyday life' in D Hernández and B Rehman (eds) *Colonize This!: Young Women of Color on Today's Feminism*, Seal Press, New York

Brown, P (1999) 'Sweet little monsters', *The West Australian*, 'Today', 26 July, pp12–13

Brumbaugh, R S (1978) 'Of man, animals, and morals: A brief history' in R K Morris and M W Fox (eds) *On the Fifth Day: Animal Rights and Human Ethics*, Acropolis, Washington DC

Bryld, M and Lykke, N (2000) *Cosmodolphins: Feminist Cultural Studies of Technology, Animals and the Sacred*, Zed, London

Budiansky, S (1992) *The Covenant of the Wild: Why Animals Chose Domestication*, William Morrow, New York

Bulbeck, C (1999) 'The nature dispositions of visitors to animal encounter sites in Australia and New Zealand', *The Journal of Sociology*, vol 35, no 2, pp129–148

Burawoy, M (2000) 'Conclusion' in M Burawoy, J A Blum, S George, Z Gille, T Gowan, L Haney, M Klawiter, S H Lopez, Seán Ó Riain and M Thayer, *Global Ethnography: Forces, Connections and Imaginations in a Postmodern World*, University of California Press, Berkeley and Los Angeles

Bureau of Tourism Research and David H. Jacobs Consultants (1992) *Japanese Tourism in Australia. Market Segmentation: A Key to New Opportunities*, Bureau of Tourism Research, Canberra

Bureau of Tourism Research (1991a) *International Visitor Survey*, Bureau of Tourism Research, Canberra

Bureau of Tourism Research (1991b) *Japanese Visitors and the Australian Environment*, Bureau of Tourism Research, Canberra

Bureau of Tourism Research (2004) 'Nights in states and territories, 1999', www.btr.gov.au/service/datacard, Bureau of Tourism Research, Canberra

Burger, J and Gochfield, M (1993) 'Tourism and short term behavioural responses of nesting masked, red-footed, and blue-footed boobies in the Galápagos', *Environmental Conservation*, vol 20, pp255–259

Burney, L (1994) 'An Aboriginal way of being Australian', *Australian Feminist Studies*, no 19, pp17–24

Caldwell, M C and Caldwell, D K (1966) 'Epimeletic caregiving behavior in cetacea' in K S Norris (ed) *Whales, Dolphins and Porpoises*, University of California Press, Berkeley and Los Angeles

Candland, D K (1993) *Feral Children and Clever Animals: Reflections on Human Nature*, Oxford University Press, New York

Canfield, P (1987a) 'A study of koala deaths', *Australian Science Magazine*, no 4, pp24–25

Canfield, P (1987b) 'Koalas abroad', *Australian Science Magazine*, no 4, p36

Carroll, P (1991a) 'Tourism as a focus for study: concepts, approaches and data' in P Carroll et al (ed) *Tourism in Australia*, Harcourt Brace Jovanovich, Marrickville

Carroll, P (1991b) 'Policy issues and tourism' in P Carroll et al (ed) *Tourism in Australia*, Harcourt Brace Jovanovich, Marrickville

Carruthers, F (2000) 'Wanted dead and alive', *The Australian* 'Magazine', 9–10 December, p18–25

Carson, R (1962) *Silent Spring*, Hamilton, London

Carsten, J (2000) 'Introduction: cultures of relatedness' in J Carsten (ed) *Cultures of Relatedness: New Approaches to the Study of Kinship*, Cambridge University Press, Cambridge

Carter, P (1992) 'Lines of communication: Meaning in the migrant environment' in S Gunew amnd K O Langley (eds) *Striking Chords: Multicultural Literary Interpretations*, Allen and Unwin, Sydney

CD News (1993) 'Wild elephant heaven', *China Daily*, 10 December, p6

Central Land Council, Pitjantjatjara Land Council and Mutitjulu Community (1987) *Sharing the Park: Anangu Initiatives in Ayers Rock Tourism*, Institute for Aboriginal Development, Canberra

Cesaresco, Countess Evelyn Mertinengo (1909) *The Place of Animals in Human Thought*, Charles Scribner's Sons, New York

Charbonneau-Lassay, L (1991) *The Bestiary of Christ*, translated and abridged by D M Dooling, Parabola Books, New York

Charles, D (1999) 'Life lines', *The Australian* 'Magazine', 27–28 November, pp13–14

Cherfas, J (1984) *Zoo 2000: A Look Beyond the Bars*, BBC, London

Chodorow, N (1978) *The Reproduction of Mothering: Psychoanalysis and the Sociology of Gender*, University of California Press, Berkeley, California

Chow, R (1991) 'Violence in the other country: China as crisis, spectacle, and woman' in C T Mohanty (ed) *Third World Women and the Politics of Feminism*, Indiana University Press, Bloomington and Indianapolis

Christoff, P (1999) "Ecosystems" a review of D Hutton and L Connors, *A History of the Australian Environment Movement'*, *Australian Book Review*, June, pp 20–21

Chryssides, H (2001) 'Call of the wild', *Reader's Digest*, May, vol 158, no 949, pp41–46

Cimino, R and Lattin, D (1998) *Shopping for Faith: American Religion in the New Millenium*, Jossey-Bass, San Francisco

Cixous, H (1994) 'The newly born woman', in Susan Sellers (ed) *The Hélène Cixous Reader*, Cambridge, Routledge

Clark, E (1990) 'Recreation in the high country' in D Rowe and G Lawrence (eds) *Sport and Leisure: Trends in Australian Popular Culture*, Harcourt Brace Jovanovich, Marrickville

Clark, S R L (1977) *The Moral Status of Animals*, Clarendon, Oxford

Clark, W B and McMunn, M T (1989) 'Introduction' in W B Clark and M T McMunn (eds) *Beasts and Birds of the Middle Ages*, University of Pennsylvania Press, Philadelphia

Clery, D (2001) 'Life's a struggle for rare gibbon', *West Australian*, 3 March, p4

Clutton-Brock, J (1981) *Domesticated Animals from Early Times*, Heinemann and British Museum, London

Clutton-Brock, J (1999) *A Natural History of Domesticated Mammals*, Cambridge University Press, Cambridge (2nd edition of *Domesticated Animals from Early Times*)

Coates, P (1998) *Nature: Western Attitudes Since Ancient Times*, Polity, Cambridge Press

Coetzee, J M (1999) *The Lives of Animals*, Profile Books, London

Cohen, L (2003) *A Consumers' Republic: The Politics of Mass Consumption in Postwar America*, Alfred A. Knopf, New York

Colin, S (1987) 'The wild man and the Indian in early 16th century book illustrations' in Christian Feest (ed) *Indians and Europe: An Interdisciplinary Collection of Essays*, Herdot Alano Verlag, Aachen

Collard, A (1989) *The Rape of the Wild: Man's Violence Against Animals and Earth*, Women's Press, London

Connell, R W (1995) *Masculinities*, Allen and Unwin, Sydney

Connell, R W (1997) 'Masculinities and globalization', revised from address 'Men in the world: Masculinities and globalization' given at the colloquium on 'Masculinities in Southern Africa', University of Natal-Durban, July

Connor, R C, Heithaus, M R and Barre, L M (1999) 'Superalliance of bottlenose dolphins', *Nature*, vol 397, pp571–572

Connor, R C and Peterson, M D (1994) *The Lives of Whales and Dolphins*, Henry Holt and Company, New York

Connor, R C, Richards, A, Smolker, R and Mann, J (1993) 'As the tide turns: The social lives of bottlenose dolphins', *Australian Natural History Magazine* vol 24, no 4, pp23–29

Connor, S (2001) 'Sheep cannot be accused of woolly thinking, say scientists', *The Independent*, 8 November, p13

Constantine, D (1983) *Watching For Dolphins*, Bloodaxe Books, Newcastle Upon Tyne

Cook, A (1998) 'Fury as birds shot', *The Advertiser*, 13 August, p5

Cooper, C (1995a) 'Randy Jock liked it boat ways', *Portside Messenger*, 8 February, p3

Cooper, C (1995b) 'Dirty river becomes a minefield for dolphins, sea birds', *Portside Messenger*, 28 June, p4

Corben, R (1994) 'Conservationists fight profits to save animals from torture', *Weekend Australian*, 19–20 February, p14

Corbin, A (1990) 'Backstage', in M Perrott (ed) *A History of Private Life: IV. From the Fires of Revolution to the Great War*, translated by A Goldhammer, Belknap Press and Harvard University Press, Cambridge

Correspondents in Beijing (2004) 'Cat-clubbing may boost China's SARS risk', *The Weekend Australian*, 10–11 January, p11

Cowan, J (1993) *Messengers of the Gods: Tribal Elders Reveal the Ancient Wisdom of the Earth*, Vintage, Random House, Sydney

Craik, J (1991) *Resorting to Tourism: Cultural Policies for Tourist Development in Australia*, Allen and Unwin, Sydney

Crane, J (2000) 'Review of Gordon L. Miller (ed.) *Nature's Fading Chorus: Classic and Contemporary Writings on Amphibians* Washington DC: Island Press', H–Net Reviews, H-REVIEW@H-NET.MSU.EDU, 11 October 2000

Crawford, M (1999) 'Balloon goes up on Alexandra', *The Weekend Australian* 'Magazine', 4–5 September, p3

Crawshaw, C and Urry, J (1997) 'Tourism and the photographic eye' in C Rojek and J Urry (eds) *Touring Cultures: Transformation of Travel and Theory*, Routledge, London and New York

Cribb, J (1988) 'The animals that ate Australia', *The Australian* 'Magazine', Supplement 4, 10–11 December, p4

Crick, M (1989) 'Representations of international tourism in the social sciences: Sun, sex, sights and servility', *The Annual Review of Anthropology*, vol 18, pp307–344

Crossley, L (1995) *Explore Antarctica*, Cambridge University Press in association with the Australian Antarctic Foundation, Australian Surveying and Land Information Group, Cambridge

Crosweller, A (1999) 'Healthy zoo animals killed to be kind', *The Australian* 'Magazine', 30 November, p6

Crosweller, A (2003) 'Boost for Murray aimed at key sites', *The Weekend Australian* 'Magazine', 15–16 November, p5

Cuthbert, D and Grossman, M (1997) 'Crossing cultures: an interview with Helena Gulash', *Hecate*, vol 23, no 2, pp48–66

Daltabuit, M and Oriol, P-S (1990) 'Tourism development in Quntiana Roo, Mexico', *Cultural Studies Quarterly*, vol 14, no 1, pp9–13

Dann, C (1991) 'Ecofeminism, women and nature' in R du Plessis (ed) *Feminist Voices: Women's Studies Texts for Aotearoa/New Zealand*, Oxford University Press, Auckland

Darby, A (1991) 'Dead in the water', *Sydney Morning Herald*: 'Good Weekend', 5 January, pp12–15

Davallon, F C and Davallon, J (1987) 'Du Musée au Parc: Exposer le vivant', *Society and Leisure*, vol 10, no 1, pp23–43

David Suzuki Foundation (1992) 'Declaration of interdependence', David Suzuki Foundation, Vancouver

Davidson, A I (1991) 'The horror of monsters' in J J Sheehan and M Sosna (eds) *The Boundaries of Humanity: Humans, Animals, Machines*, University of California Press, Berkeley

Davidson, J and Spearritt, P (2000) *Holiday Business: Tourism in Australia Since 1870*, Melbourne University Press and Miegenyah Press, Melbourne

Davies, G (2000) 'Virtual animals in electronic zoos: the changing geographies of animal capture and display' in C Philo and C Wilbert (eds) *Animal Spaces,*

Beastly Places: New Geographies of Human–Animal Relations, Routledge, London and New York

Davies, M (1990) 'Wildlife as a tourism attraction', *Environment*, vol 20, no 3, pp74–77

Davis, B (1989) 'The wild environment: Description and definition' in J Vulkner and G McDonald (eds) *Architecture in the Wild: The Issues of Tourist Development in Remote and Sensitive Environments*, Royal Australian Institute of Architects National Education Division, Red Hill, A.C.T.

Davis, F (1979) *Yearning for Yesterday: A Sociology of Nostalgia*, Free Press, New York

Davis, S (1997) *Specular Nature: Corporate Culture and the Sea World Experience*, University of California Press, Berkeley and Los Angeles

Dawson, N (1992) 'Access to Nature in Queensland: A Legislative Framework' in B Weir (ed) *Ecotourism Incorporating the Global Classroom,* Bureau of Tourism Research, Canberra

de Gryse, T (1989) 'Landscape at the edge of wilderness' in J Vulkner and G McDonald (eds) *Architecture in the Wild: The Issues of Tourist Development in Remote and Sensitive Environments*, Royal Australian Institute of Architects National Education Division, Red Hill, A.C.T.

Dekkers, M (1994) *Dearest Pet: On Bestiality*, Verso, London

Dennis, T (1989) 'The Australian Sea-Lion in South Australia', *Australian Ranger Bulletin*, vol 5, no 2, pp16–17

Department of Environment and Planning (1983) *Cleland Conservation Park Management Plan Mount Lofty Ranges, South Australia*, National Parks and Wildlife Service, Department of Environment and Planning, Adelaide

Department of Environment and Planning (1985) *The Nature of Cleland*, National Parks and Wildlife Service, Department of Environment and Planning, Adelaide

Department of Environment, Heritage and Aboriginal Affairs (1998) *Great Australian Bight Marine Park Management Plan, Part A*, Department of Environment, Heritage and Aboriginal Affairs, Adelaide

de Waal, F (1991) *Peacemaking Among Primates*, Penguin, Harmondsworth

de Waal, F (1999) 'Apeing art', *The Australian* 'Magazine', 8 December, pp40–1

Dexter, Brian (2001) 'Walk among wolves in Haliburton', *The Toronto Star*, 12 May, pL12

Digirolamo, R (1998) 'Foundation's decade of tracking our dolphins', *Portside Messenger*, 26 August, p4

Digirolamo, R (1999) 'Crusading for dolphins' *Portside Messenger*, 14 May, p7

Dillard, A (1988) 'The Muskrat' in Irene Zahava (ed) *Through Other Eyes*, The Crossing Press, Freedom, California

Dobbs, H (1992) *Journey into Dolphin Dreamtime*, Jonathan Cape, London

Dombrovskis, P, Brown, B (1983) *Wild Rivers*, West Wind Press, Hobart, Tasmania

Domm, S (1988) 'National parks: Some basic concepts', *Australian Ranger Bulletin*, vol 4, no 4, pp7–8

Donaldson, L E (1999) 'On medicine women and white shame-ans: new age Native Americanism and commodity fetishism as pop culture feminism', *Signs: Journal of Women in Culture and Society*, vol 24, pp677–696

Douglas, K (1999) 'Unusual suspects', *New Scientist*, 31 July, p3636

Douglas, M (1970) *Purity and Danger: An Analysis of the Concepts of Pollution and Taboo*, Penguin, Harmondsworth

Dowling, R K (1992) 'An ecotourism planning model' in B Weir (ed) *Ecotourism incorporating the Global Classroom*, Bureau of Tourism Research, Canberra

Doye, S (1995) 'To touch the magic', Draft of a thesis submitted for degree of Master of Arts, Australian National University, Canberra

Drengson, A R (1980) 'Social and psychological implications of human attitudes toward animals', *The Journal of Transpersonal Psychology*, vol 12, no 1, pp63–74

Drewe, R (2001) 'Echo beach', *The Australian* 'Magazine', 6–7 January, pp17–19

Duffus, D A and Dearden, P (1990) 'Non-consumptive wildlife-oriented recreation: A conceptual framework', *Biological Conservation*, vol 53, no 3, pp213–231

Dunlap, T R (1999) *Nature and the English Diaspora: Environment and History in the United States, Canada, Australia, and New Zealand*, Cambridge University Press, Cambridge

Dunn, R (1989) 'Christmas Island casino expected to lure Indonesians', *Australian Financial Review*, 16 February, p5

During, S (1991) 'Waiting for the post: Some relations between modernity, colonization and writing' in I Adam and H Tiffin (eds) *Past the Last Post: Theorizing Post-Colonialism and Post-Modernism*, Harvester Wheatsheaf, New York

Durrell, G (1976) *The Stationary Ark*, Collins, London

Eagles, P F J (1992) 'The motivations of Canadian ecotourists' in B Weir (ed) *Ecotourism Incorporating the Global Classroom*, Bureau of Tourism Research, Canberra

Earth Sanctuaries (1993) 'Yookamurra', Earth Sanctuaries Limited, Adelaide

Earth Sanctuaries (1995) Annual Report, Earth Sanctuaries Limited, Adelaide

Earth Sanctuaries (1996) 'Prospectus 1st April 1995–31st March 1996', Earth Sanctuaries Limited, Adelaide

Earth Sanctuaries (2000a) 'Get back to nature, as it was over 200 years ago', advertisement, *The Australian Magazine*, 23–24 September, pp30–31

Earth Sanctuaries (2000b) 'Prospectus', Earth Sanctuaries Ltd, Adelaide

Earth Sanctuaries, (2002) 'Notice of general meeting and explanatory memorandum in relation to the proposed sale of five sanctuaries and buy-back authorisation', distributed to shareholders, June, Earth Sanctuaries Ltd, Adelaide

Earth Sanctuaries (2003) 'Annual Report', Earth Sanctuaries Ltd, Adelaide

Easlea, B (1980) *Witch Hunting, Magic and the New Philosophy: An Introduction to Debates of the Scientific Revolution 1450–1750*, Harvester Press, Sussex

Eastwood, H (2000) 'Why are Australian GPs using alternative medicine? Postmodernisation, consumerism and the shift towards holistic health', *Journal of Sociology*, vol 36, no 2, pp133–156

Eco, U (1986) *Travels in Hyperreality: Essays*, translated by William Weaver, Harcourt Brace Jovanovich, San Diego.

Edensor, T (2000) 'Walking in the British countryside: reflexivity, embodied practices and ways to escape', *Body & Society*, vol 6, nos 3–4, pp81–106

Eder, K (1996) *The Social Construction of Nature: A Sociology of Ecological Enlightenment*, Sage, London, enlarged and revised version of work originally published in German in 1988

Edington, J M and Edington, M A (1986) *Ecology, Recreation and Tourism*, Cambridge University Press, New York

Edwards, H (1989) *The Remarkable Dolphins of Monkey Mia: Wild Dolphins Meet People at the Shark Bay Shore*, Hugh Edwards, Swanbourne

Egan, C (2002) 'Resort deal seen as native title coup', *The Australian 'Magazine'*, 10 June, p2

Ehrlich, P R (1971) *The Population Bomb*, Ballantine Books, New York, first published 1968

Eisler, R (1988) *The Chalice and the Blade: Our History, Our Future*, Harper and Row, San Francisco

Elder, G, Wolch, J and Emel, J (1998) *'Le pratique sauvage*: race, place, and the human–animal divide' in J Wolch and J Emel (eds) *Animal Geographies: Place, Politics, and Identity in the Nature–Culture Borderlands*, Verso, London

Eller, C (1993) *Living in the Lap of the Goddess: The Feminist Spirituality Movement in America*, Crossroad, New York

Emel, J (1998) 'Are you man enough, big and bad enough? Wolf eradication in the US' in J Wolch and J Emel (eds) *Animal Geographies: Place, Politics, and Identity in the Nature–Culture Borderlands*, Verso, London

Environment Canada Parks Service (1989) 'You are in bear country', Minister of the Environment and Minister of Supply and Services, Ottawa

Evans, E P (1906) *The Criminal Prosecution and Capital Punishment of Animals. The Lost History of Europe's Animal Trials*, William Heinemann, London, reprinted by Faber and Faber, London, 1987

Evans, G (1997) 'Coming together: Green and black views on the land', *Habitat Australia*, vol 125, no 2, pp10–13

Fackham, M (1978) *Wild Animals, Gentle Women*, Harcourt Brace Jovanovich, New York

Farmer, B (1992) *The Seal Woman*, University of Queensland Press, St Lucia

Featherdale Wildlife Park (c1988) 'Nature's gift to the world', Featherdale Wildlife Park, Sydney

Fergie, D (1994) 'Unsettled visions: A Mudmap for exploring Australia's interiors', *Free for All Broadsheet*, vol 23, no 4, pp3–7

Ferguson, P (1995) 'Researching the role of "slum" dolphins', *Portside Messenger*, 4 October, p5

Fichtelius, K-E and Sjölander, S (1973) *Man's Place: Intelligence in Whales, Dolphins and Humans*, translated by Thomas Teal, Victor Gollancz, London

Field, K (1995) 'The gift of Tuwharetoa', *Pacific Way*, April, pp47–51

Fincke, M (1992) 'Wild things', *The Australian Way*, July, pp12–14

Finlay, T, James, L R and Maple, T L (1988) 'People's perceptions of animals: the influence of zoo environment', *Environment and Behavior*, vol 20, pp508–528

Fisher, S (2001) 'Traditional fare or mean cuisine?', *Sunday Telegraph*, 28 January, pp20–23

Flannery, T I (1994) *The Future Eaters: An Ecological History of the Australasian Lands and People*, Reed, Chatswood, Sydney

Fletcher Challenge Canada (1991) 'What's happening in our forests?', Fletcher Challenge Canada, Vancouver

Flyvbjerg, B (2001) *Making Social Science Matter: Why Social Inquiry Fails and How it Can Succeed Again*, Cambridge University Press, Cambridge

Fortescue, M (1992) 'Breeding biology and management of the Little Penguin *Eudyptala Minor* (Forster), 1780, on Bowen Island, Jervis Bay', ACT Parks and Wildlife Service, Canberra

Fossey, D (1985) *Gorillas in the Mist*, Penguin, Harmondsworth, first published 1983

Foster, B (1999) 'The Gift of the GAB', *Habitat Australia*, vol 23, no 6, p23

Foucault, M (1973) *The Order of Things: An Archaeology of the Human Sciences*, Vintage, New York

Fouts, R (1997) *Next of Kin: What Chimpanzees Have Taught Me About Who We Are*, William Morrow and Company, New York

Frankfurt Zoological Gardens (no date) 'Zoo Frankfurt', Frankfurt Zoological Gardens, Frankfurt

Franklin, A (1999) *Animals and Modern Cultures: A Sociology of Human–Animal Relations in Modernity*, Sage, London

Franklin, A (2001) 'Neo-Darwinian leisures, the body and nature: hunting and angling in modernity', *Body and Society*, vol 7, no 2, pp57–76

Franklin, A (2002) *Nature and Social Theory*, Sage, London

Franklin, A and White, R (2001) 'Animals and modernity: changing human–animal relations, 1949–1998', *Journal of Sociology*, vol 37, pp219–238

Franklin, S, Lurie, C and Stacey, J (2000) *Global Nature, Global Culture*, Sage, London

Fraser, N (1997) *Justice Interruptus: Critical Reflections on the "Postsocialist" Condition*, Routledge, New York

Freeman, M R (1994) 'Science and trans-science in the whaling debate' in

M R Freeman and U P Kreuter (eds) *Elephants and Whales: Resources for Whom?*, Gordon and Breach Science Publishers, Reading

Freeman, M R and Kellert, S R (1994) 'International attitudes to whales, whaling and the use of whale products: a six-country survey' in M R Freeman and U P Kreuter (eds) *Elephants and Whales: Resources for Whom?*, Gordon and Breach Science Publishers, Reading

French, M (1987) *Her Mother's Daughter*, Pan Heinemann, London

Frey, R G (1980) *Interests and Rights: The Case Against Animals*, Clarendon, Oxford

Fudge, E (2000) *Perceiving Animals: Humans and Beasts in Early Modern English Culture*, Macmillan and St Martin's Press, Houndmills, Basingstoke and New York

Fukuyama, F (1992) *The End of History and the Last Man*, Hamish Hamilton, London

Fuller, P (1988) 'The geography of mother nature' in D Cosgrove and S Daniels (eds) *The Iconography of Landscape: Essays on the Symbolic Representation, Design and Use of Past Environments*, Cambridge University Press, Cambridge

Gaard, G (1993) 'Ecofeminism and Native American cultures: Pushing the limits of cultural imperialism' in G Gaard (ed) *Ecofeminism: Women, Animals, Nature*, Temple University Press, Philadelphia

Gaita, R (2002) *The Philosopher's Dog*, Text Publishing, Melbourne

Galdikas, B (1995) *Reflections of Eden: My Life with the Orangutans of Borneo*, Victor Gollancz, London

Gale, F and Jacobs, J M (1987) *Tourists and the National Estate: Procedures to Protect Australia's Heritage*, Australian Government Publishing Service, Canberra

Ganguly, I (1992) 'Cross–cultural body image', *MediaMatters*, vol 2, no 3, pp2–3, newsheet of MediaSwitch Queensland

Gateway Antarctica (c2000) 'Tourism in Antarctica', Gateway Antarctica, University of Canterbury, Christchurch, NZ, http://www.anta.canterbury. ac.nz/frame.htm?resources/general/tourism.html~mainpb

Gauntlett, K (2002) 'Aboriginals in Monkey Mia venture', *The West Australian,* 10 June, http://www.thewest.com.au, accessed 11 June 2002

Gawain, E (1981) *The Dolphin's Gift*, Boobook Publications, Sydney

Gaynor, A (1999) 'From chook run to chicken treat: speculation on changes in human–animal relationships in twentieth-century Perth, Western Australia', *Limina*, vol 5, pp26–39

Gelder, K and Jacobs, J M (1998) *Uncanny Australia: Sacredness and Identity in a Postcolonial Nation*, Melbourne University Press, Melbourne

Gilling, T (1999) *The Sooterkin*, Text Publishing, Melbourne

Gilmore, M (1934) *Old Days, Old Ways*, Angus & Robertson, Sydney

Gimbutas, M (1989) *The Language of the Goddess*, Harper, San Francisco

Goldberg, E (2000) *Jane Goodall: Reason for Hope*, KJCA–TV, London

Goodall, J (1993) 'Chimpanzees – bridging the gap' in P Cavalieri and P Singer (eds) *The Great Ape Project: Equality Beyond Humanity*, Fourth Estate, London

Goodison, L (1990) *Moving Heaven and Earth: Sexuality, Spirituality and Social Change*, The Women's Press, London

Goodman, D (1990) 'Fear of circuses: Founding the National Museum of Victoria', *Continuum*, vol 3, no 1, pp18–34

Gough, K (2000) 'Slick new penguin suits in vogue', *The Australian* 'Magazine', 5 January, p3

Gould, V (1999) 'Dolphins are anything but cute', *The West Australian* 'Big Weekend', 30 October, p3

Gracen, D (1994) 'Two bears, dancing: A mid–life vision quest', in E Cole, E Erdman and E D Rothblum (eds) *Wilderness Therapy for Women: The Power of Adventure*, Haworth Press, New York

Green Groups (1993) 'Sharing the land – healing the land native title and reconciliation, joint statement September' *WilderNews*, October/November

Greer, G (1991) *The Change: Women, Ageing and the Menopause*, Hamish Hamilton, London

Griffin, D R (1976) *The Question of Animal Awareness: Evolutionary Continuity of Mental Experience*, Rockefeller University Press, New York

Griffin, D R (ed) (1982) *Animal Mind – Human Mind*, Springer-Verlag, Berlin

Griffin, D R (1992) *Animal Minds*, University of Chicago Press, Chicago and London

Griffin, S (1978) *Woman and Nature: The Roaring Inside Her*, Harper and Row, New York

Griffiths, T (1996) *Hunters and Collectors: The Antiquarian Imagination in Australia*, Cambridge University Press, Cambridge

Grimwood, K (1996) *Into the Deep,* Morrow, New York

Grove, R H (1995) *Green Imperialism: Colonial Expansion, Tropical Island Edens and the Origins of Environmentalism, 1600–1860*, Cambridge University Press, Cambridge

Guardian (2001) 'In brief: Taiwan diners lose dog dinner', *The Guardian*, 'Foreign Pages', 4 January, p14

Guardian Weekly (2000) 'Oversized, over here: crackdown on exotic invader', *The Guardian Weekly*, 14–20 September, p10

Gunther, K (1994) 'Researcher's warning: pollution killing baby dolphins', *Portside Messenger*, 29 June, p1

Hadley, C (1997) 'Sealed fate', *The Guardian*, 8 July, pp4–5

Hahn, E (1990) *Animal Gardens or Zoos Around the World*, Begos and Rosenberg, New York, 1967

Hains, B (2002) *The Ice and the Inland: Mawson, Flynn and the Myth of the Frontier*, Melbourne University Press, Melbourne

Hamilton-Smith, E (1988) 'Volunteerism or localism?', *Australian Ranger Bulletin*, vol 5, no 1, p31

Hammitt, W E (1982) 'Psychological dimensions and functions of wilderness solitude' in F E Boteler (ed) *Wilderness Psychology Group: Third Annual Conference Proceedings*, Division of Forestry, West Virginia University, Morgantow, West Virginia

Hancocks, D (2001) *A Different Nature: The Paradoxical World of Zoos and Their Uncertain Future*, University of California Press, Berkeley

Hanes, A (2001) 'Granby Zoo's dolphin plan makes waves with activists', *The Gazette*, Montreal, 29 May, A10

Haraway, D (1991) *Simians, Cyborgs, and Women*, Freis Association Books, London

Haraway, D (1992) *Primate Visions: Gender, Race and Nature in the World of Modern Science*, Verso, London

Hardin, G (1974) 'Foreword' in C D Stone, *Should Trees Have Standing? Toward Legal Rights for Natural Objects*, William Kaufmann, Los Altos, California

Harding, R (1990) 'Koala politics: Good and bad for nature conservation?' in K Dyer and J Young (eds) *Changing Directions: The Proceedings of the Conference Ecopolitics IV*, University of Adelaide, Adelaide

Harper, P and Allen, G (1999) 'Do you like seeing active animals?', *Zoo Times*, vol 16, no2, p4

Haughney, C (2003) 'Saving turtles from the soup kettle', *Guardian Weekly*, 17–23 July, p33

Hauser, M (1999) 'Maths in the wild could be a matter of survival', *The Australian*, 5 May, p43

Hazleden, R (2003) 'Love yourself: the relationship of the self with itself in popular self-help texts', *Journal of Sociology*, vol 39, pp413–428

Healey, K (1992) *Animal Rights: Issues for the Nineties Volume 4*, Spinney Press Australia, Wentworth Falls

Healy, G (1999) 'Whale may seek harbour birth', *The Weekend Australian*, 21–22 August, p4

Hearne, V (1987) *Adam's Task: Calling Animals By Name*, Random House, New York

Hearne, V (1994) *Animal Happiness*, HarperCollins, New York

Heller, C (1993) 'For love of nature: Ecology and the cult of the romantic' in G Gaard (ed) *Ecofeminism: Women, Animals, Nature*, Temple University Press, Philadelphia

Henderson, M (2003) 'Gaping but not dumb', *The Australian* 'Magazine', 8 October, p29

Hendry, J (1997) 'Nature tamed: gardens as a microcosm of Japan's view of the world' in P J Asquith and A Kalland (eds) *Japanese Images of Nature: Cultural Perspectives*, Nordic Institute of Asian Studies and Curzon, Richmond, Surrey

Herr, R (1989) 'The Antarctic experience: Tourism's final frontier?' in J Vulkner and G McDonald (eds) *Architecture in the Wild: The Issues of Tourist*

Development in Remote and Sensitive Environments, Royal Australian Institute of Architects National Education Division, Red Hill, A.C.T.

Highwater, J (1981) *The Primal Mind: Vision and Reality in Indian America*, Meridian, New York

Hill, D (2001) 'The hard sell', *The Weekend Australian* 'Magazine', 23–26 August, p23–25

Hill, R (1992) 'Models for Aboriginal involvement in natural resource management on Cape York' in J Birckhead, T de Lacy and L Smith (eds) *Aboriginal Involvement in Parks and Protected Areas*, Aboriginal Studies Press, Canberra

Hills, A M (1993) 'The motivational bases of attitudes toward animals', *Society and Animals*, vol 1, pp111–128

Hochschild, A R (2003) *The Commercialization of Intimate Life: Notes from Home and Work*, University of California Press, Berkeley

Hodge, A (2002) 'Ecotourist trap', *The Weekend Australian* 'Magazine', 16–17 November, pp38–42

Hodge, A (2003) 'Pet theory', *The Weekend Australian* 'Magazine', 26–27 April, p19

Hooper, B (2000) 'Icon faces cash crisis: receiver takes over Balfours', *The Advertiser*, 17 October, pp1, 4

Hopgood, J (1999) 'Zoo education 2010 AD: part 2', *Zoo Times*, vol 16, no 1, pp6–7

Horne, D (1992) *The Intelligent Tourist*, Margaret Gee, McMahons Point

Horne, J (1991) 'Travelling through the romantic landscapes of the Blue Mountains', *Australian Cultural History*, no 10, pp84–98

Huggins, J, Huggins, R and Jacobs, J M (1997) 'Kooramindanjie: place and the postcolonial' in R White and P Russell (eds) *Memories and Dreams: Reflections on 20th Century Australia*, Allen and Unwin, St Leonards

Hughes, P (2001) 'Animals, values and tourism – structural shifts in UK dolphin tourism provision', *Tourism Management*, vol 22, pp321–330

Huhndorf, S M (2001) *Going Native: Indians in the American Cultural Imagination*, Cornell University Press, Ithica and London

Hullick, J (1998) 'New call for dolphin sanctuary', *Portside Messenger*, 16 September, p9

Hume, I (1987) 'Diets for koalas – natural and artificial', *Australian Science Magazine*, no 4, pp34–35

Humphrey, N K (1988) 'The social function of intellect' in R Byrne and A Whiten (eds) *Machiavellian Intelligence: Social Expertise and the Evolution of Intellect in Monkeys, Apes and Humans*, Clarendon, Oxford

Huppatz, B (1999) 'Code to prevent shark-viewing "circus"', *The Advertiser*, 9 February, p14

Hurrell, B (1997) 'Kill koalas and save an island', *The Advertiser*, 17 March, p3

Hurrell, B (1998) 'Dob in the killer', *The Advertiser*, 20 August 1998, p3

Hurrell, B (1999a) '60 years on, stick-nest rats come home', *The Advertiser*, 15 April, p27

Hurrell, B (1999b) 'First lead in hunt for dolphin killer', *The Advertiser*, 8 April, p6

Hurrell, B (1999c) 'Rescue success for dolphins in distress', *The Advertiser*, 23 March, p3

Hutton, D and Connors, L (1999) *A History of the Australian Environment Movement*, Cambridge University Press, Cambridge

Hutton, J S (1983) 'Animal abuse as a diagnostic approach in social work: A pilot study' in A H Katcher and A M Beck (eds) *New Perspectives on Our Lives With Companion Animals*, University of Pennsylvania Press, Philadelphia

Huxley, E (1981) *Whipsnade: Captive Breeding for Survival*, Collins, London

Hvenegaard, G T (1994) 'Ecotourism: A status report and conceptual framework', *Journal of Tourism Studies*, vol 5, no 2, pp24–35

Hyde, G and King, B (eds) (1987) 'A survey of visitor and community attitudes to the Melbourne Zoo', Tourism and Marketing Studies, Footscray Institute of Technology, Footscray

Illing, D (1994) 'Spirit of explorers lives on in the name of science', *Campus Review*, 27 January–2 February, p16

Innes, S (1992) 'The last continent', *The Advertiser*, 'Travel', 22 August 1992, p1

Innes, S (2000) 'Life gets a little sweeter for bilbies', *The Advertiser*, 25 May, p24

Jackson, J (1998) 'What, if anything, is sustainable on coral reefs', address to the IX Pacific Science Inter-Congress, Academia Sinica, Taipei, November

Jaeckel, H (2000) 'The closure of Cheynes Beach Whaling Company, Albany, Western Australia, 1978: the environmental issues', honours thesis presented for degree of Bachelor of Arts, Murdoch University, Perth

Jakob-Hoff, R (1992) 'Recent developments in the Australasian species management program', *International Zoo Yearbook*, vol 31, pp12–19

Jakob-Hoff, R (1993) 'Zoos as conservation tool', paper presented to the Department of Conservation Management Techniques Training Course, Pirongia, New Zealand, 27 May 1993

Janzen, D (1998) 'Gardenification of wildland nature and the human footprint', *Science*, vol 279, pp1312–1313

Jarvis, C H (2000) 'If Descartes swam with dolphins: The framing and consumption of marine animals in contemporary Australian tourism', doctoral dissertation, Department of Geography and Environmental Studies, University of Melbourne, Melbourne

Jasen, P (1995) *Wild Things: Nature, Culture and Tourism in Ontario 1790–1914*, University of Toronto Press, Toronto, Buffalo and London

Jasper, J M and Nelkin, D (1992) *The Animal Rights Crusade: The Growth of a Moral Protest*, Free Press, New York

Jiggins, J and Röling, N (2000) 'Adaptive management: Potential and limitations for ecological governance', *International Journal of Agricultural Resources, Governance and Ecology*, vol 1, no 1, pp28–42

JijiPress (2003) 'Humpback jump-starts season for whale watchers', *The Asahi Shimbun*, 25–26 January, p1

Johnson, W (1990) *The Rose-Tinted Menagerie*, Heretic, London

Johnston, E (1991) *Royal Commission into Aboriginal Deaths in Custody: National Report*, vol 4, Australian Government Publishing Service, Canberra

Jope, K L (1985) 'Implications of grizzly bear habituation to hikers', *Wildlife Society Bulletin*, no 13, pp32–37

Jory, R (1998) 'A natural gem in our midst', *The Advertiser*, 30 July, p18

Joyce, T (c1992) 'Antarctica', *Club Marine*, vol 7, no 3, pp51–62

Kadri, F (2003) 'Stray seal reveals more about Japan's problems than natural history', *Japan Times*, 2 February, p2

Kafka, F (1952) 'A Report to an academy' in *Selected Short Stories of Franz Kafka*, translated by Willa and Edwin Muir, Modern Library, New York, first published in 1917

Kalland, A (1994) 'Whose whale is that? Diverting the commodity path' in M R Freeman and U P Kreuter (eds) *Elephants and Whales: Resources for Whom?*, Gordon and Breach Science Publishers, Reading

Kalland, A and Asquith, P J (1997) 'Japanese perceptions of nature: ideals and illusions' in P J Asquith and A Kalland (eds) *Japanese Images of Nature: Cultural Perspectives*, Nordic Institute of Asian Studies and Curzon, Richmond, Surrey

Kamilia Council and its Chair, Paddy Neowarra (1997) 'Ngarinyin response to the *Wik* decision', *Indigenous Law Bulletin*, vol 4, no 1, p16

Kangaroo Island Tourism Working Party (1991) 'Kangaroo Island Tourism Policy', Tourism South Australia, Adelaide

Kaplan, S and Talbot, J F (1983) 'Psychological benefits of a wilderness experience' in I Altman and J Wohlwill (eds) *Behavior and the Natural Environment*, Plenum Press, New York and London

Keller, E F (1985) *Reflections in Gender and Science*, Yale University Press, New Haven, Connecticut and London

Kellert, S R (1978a) *Policy Implications of a National Study of American Attitudes and Behavioral Relations to Animals*, Department of the Interior, United States Fish and Wildlife Service, Washington

Kellert, S R with the assistance of Berry, J K (1978b) *Activities of the American Public Relating to Animals*, Department of the Interior, United States Fish and Wildlife Service, Washington

Kellert, S R (1983) 'Affective, cognitive, and evaluative perceptions of animals' in I Altman and J Wohlwill (eds) *Behavior and the Natural Environment*, Plenum Press, New York and London

Kellert, S R (1989) 'Perceptions of animals in America' in R J Hoage (ed) *Perceptions of Animals in American Culture*, Smithsonian Institution Press, Washington DC

Kellert, S R (1993a) 'Introduction' in S R Kellert and E O Wilson (eds) *The Biophilia Hypothesis*, Island Press and Shearwater Books, Washington DC and Covelo, California

Kellert, S R (1993b) 'The biological basis for human values of nature' in S R Kellert and E O Wilson (eds) *The Biophilia Hypothesis*, Island Press and Shearwater Books, Washington DC and Covelo, California

Kellert, S R and Berry, J K (1978) *Knowledge, Affection and Basic Attitudes Toward Animals in American Society*, Department of the Interior, United States Fish and Wildlife Service, Washington

Kellert, S R and Westervelt, M O (1985) 'Historical trends in American animal use and perception', *International Journal for the Study of Animal Problems*, vol 4, no 2, pp133–145

Kellert, S R and Dunlap, J (1989) 'Informal learning at the zoo: A study of attitudes and knowledge impacts', A Report to the Zoological Society of Philadelphia of a Study Funded by the G.R. Dodge Foundation, Philadelphia

Kelly, P (1992) *The End of Certainty: The Story of the 1980s*, Allen and Unwin, St Leonards, Sydney

Kemp, M (1998) 'Jail or $40,000 fine', *The Advertiser*, 25 August, p13

Kennedy, F (1997) 'Message from the dugongs', *The Weekend Australian* 'Review', 1–2 March, p4

Kent, D (1990) 'Tourism, development and national parks on Kangaroo Island' in K Dyer and J Young (eds) *Changing Directions: The Proceedings of the Conference Ecopolitics IV*, University of Adelaide, Adelaide

Kershaw, J (1998) *In the Wild: Lemurs with John Cleese*, Tigress Production, Thirteen/WNET and the BBC, New York and London

Kierchhoff, H-W (1986) *Deutsch Down Under: An Analysis of the German Travel Market for Australia*, Bureau of Tourism Research, Canberra

Kiernan, K (1990) 'I saw my temple ransacked' in C Pybus and R Flanagan (eds) *The Rest of the World is Watching: Tasmania and the Greens*, Pan Macmillan, Sydney

Kilbourne, J (2003) 'Exploitation as cool', review of Alissa Quart *Branded: The Buying and Selling of Teenagers*, *The Women's Review of Books*, vol 20, no 8, pp7–8

Kinder, M (1991) *Playing with Power in Movies, Television and Video Games: From Muppet Babies to Teenage Mutant Ninja Turtles*, University of California Press, Berkeley

King, M (1999) 'No place for a dog on the streets of Korea', *The Advertiser*, 27 May, p26

King, M (2000) 'The archbishop takes his flock to the zoo', *The Advertiser*, 16 March, p15

King, M (ed) (1991) *Pakeha: The Quest for Identity in New Zealand*, Penguin, Auckland

King, Y (1990) 'Healing the wounds: Feminism, ecology, and the nature/culture dualism' in I Diamond and G F Orenstein (eds) *Reweaving the World: The Emergence of Ecofeminism*, Sierra Club Books, San Francisco

Kirschenblatt-Gimblett, B (1998) *Destination Culture: Tourism, Museums and Heritage*, University of California Press, Berkeley and Los Angeles

Klein, N (2000) *No Logo*, Flamingo, London

Klingender, F (1971) *Animals in Art and Thought to the End of the Middle Ages*, edited by E Antal and J Harthan, Routledge Kegan Paul, London

Knight, J (2000a) 'Culling demons: The problem of bears in Japan' in J Knight (ed) *Natural Enemies: People–Wildlife Conflicts in Anthropological Perspective*, Routledge, London and New York

Knight, J (2000b) 'Afterword: Enclosure' in J Knight (ed) *Natural Enemies: People–Wildlife Conflicts in Anthropological Perspective*, Routledge, London and New York

Knudtson, P and Suzuki, D (1992) *Wisdom of the Elders*, Stoddart, Toronto

Komar, V and Melamid, A (2000) 'Brush with death', *The Weekend Australian* 'Magazine', 25–26 November, pp2–3

Komatsu, M and Misaki, S (2001) *The Truth Behind the Whaling Dispute*, Japan Whaling Association, Tokyo

Labor South Australia (2001) 'New directions to protect our environment', Australian Labor Party, Adelaide

Langton, M (1995) 'The European construction of wilderness', *Wilderness News*, no 143, pp16–17

Lansbury, C (1985) *The Old Brown Dog: Women, Workers, and Vivisection in Edwardian England*, University of Wisconsin Press, Wisconsin

Lattas, A (1992) 'Primitivism, nationalism and individualism in Australian popular culture' in B Attwood and J Arnold (eds) *Power, Knowledge and Aborigines: Special Issue of Journal of Australian Studies,* La Trobe University Press in association with the National Centre for Australian Studies, Monash University, Melbourne

Laurie, V (1994) 'Creature Comforts' *The Australian* 'Magazine', 26–27 November 1994, pp62–66

Laurie, V (1999a) 'The arks and the covenants', *The Australian* 'Magazine', 18–19 September, pp38–41

Laurie, V (1999b) "Froggies go a-wooing", *The Weekend Australian*, 'Review', 27–28 November, pp6–8

Lawlor, R (1991) *Voices of the First Day: Awakening in the Aboriginal Dreaming*, Inner Traditions International, Rochester, Vermont

Lawrence, E A (1994) 'Conflicting ideologies: Views of animal rights advocates and their opponents', *Society and Animals*, vol 2, pp175–190

Leach, E (1964) 'Anthropological aspects of language: animal categories and verbal abuse' in E H Lenneberg (ed) *New Directions in the Study of Language*, MIT Press, Cambridge, Massachusetts

Leach, E (1970) *Lévi–Strauss*, William Collins, London

Lee Geok Boi (1994) 'Hot & Wild', *Her World*, October, pp258–261

Lee, R (1970) *Not So Dumb: The Life and Times of the Animal Actors*, Barnes and Company, New Jersey

Lee-Johnson, E and Lee-Johnson, E (1994) *Opo: The Hokianga Dolphin*, David Ling Publishing, Auckland

Leimbach, C (1984) 'The road to Monkey Mia', *Australian Wellbeing*, June, pp8–13

Lennon, J and Foley, M (2000) *Dark Tourism: The Attraction of Death and Disaster*, Continuum, London

Leopold, A (1949) *A Sand Country Almanac and Sketches Here and There*, Oxford University Press, London

Leser, D (1988) 'The dolphin mystique', *The Australian* 'Magazine', 12–13 November, pp32–42

Levine, D (1994) 'Breaking through barriers: Wilderness therapy for sexual assault survivors' in E Cole, E Erdman and E D Rothblum (eds) *Wilderness Therapy for Women: The Power of Adventure*, Haworth Press, New York

Levinson, B M (1972) *Pets and Human Development*, Charles C. Thomas, Springfield, Illinois

Levitt, L (1982) 'How effective is wilderness therapy?: A critical review' in F E Boteler (ed) *Wilderness Psychology Group: Third Annual Conference Proceedings*, Division of Forestry, West Virginia University, Morgantown, West Virginia

Levy, A, Scott-Clark, C and Harrison, D (1997) 'Save the rhino, but kill the people', *Guardian Weekly*, 30 March, p5

Lewis, I M (1989) *Ecstatic Religion: A Study of Shamanism and Spirit Possession*, Routledge, London and New York

Lilly, J C (1962) *Man and Dolphin*, Victor Gollancz, London

Lilly, J C (1972) *Center of the Cyclone: An Autobiography of Inner Space*, Paladin, London

Lines, W J. (1991) *Taming the Great South Land: A History of the Conquest of Nature in Australia*, Allen and Unwin, Sydney

Littleton, C (1995) 'Cleanup strategy wins Port praise', *Portside Messenger*, 25 October, p3

Lodge, D (1992) *Paradise News*, Penguin, London

Loechel, K (2001) 'Monarto's captive breeding programme', 'Zoo Times', Newsletter of the Royal Zoological Society of South Australia Incorporated, vol 17, no 2, p10

Lopez, B (1986) *Arctic Dreams: Imagination and Desire in a Northern Landscape*, Macmillan, London

Lorenz, K (1954) *Man Meets Dog*, Methuen and Company, London, translated by Marjorie Kerr Wilson

Lott, D F (1988) 'Feeding wild animals: The urge, the interaction, and the consequences', *Anthrozoos*, vol 1, pp255–256

Lourandos, H (1997) *Continent of Hunter-Gatherers: New Perspectives in Australian Prehistory*, Cambridge University Press, Cambridge

Love, R (2000) 'The unbearable lightness of micro-gravity', *Meanjin*, vol 59, pp211–219

Low, T (1988) 'International terrorist masquerades as true-blue Aussie', *Australian Geographic*, no 10, April–June, p22

Low, T (1999) *Feral Future: The Untold Story of Australia's Exotic Invaders*, Viking, Camberwell, Victoria

Low, T (2002) *The New Nature*, Viking, Camberwell, Victoria

Lynn, W S (1998) 'Animals, ethics and geography' in J Wolch and J Emel (eds) *Animal Geographies: Place, Politics, and Identity in the Nature–Culture Borderlands*, Verso, London

MacCannell, D (1976) *The Tourist: A New Theory of the Leisure Class*, Schocken Books, New York

McClelland, L F (1998) *Building the National Parks: Historic Landscape Design and Construction*, Johns Hopkins University Press, Baltimore and London

McCormack, G (1996) *The Emptiness of Japanese Affluence*, Allen and Unwin, St Leonards

McDonough, M H (1982) 'Visitor centres – A planned approach', *Australian Ranger Bulletin*, vol 1, no 4, pp79–84

McGarry, A (1998) 'Shotgun blasts turn tide against lonely orphan Miki', *The Weekend Australian* 'Magazine', 22–23 August, p5

McGrath, A (1991) 'Travels to a distant past: the mythology of the outback', *Australian Cultural History*, no 10, pp113–124

McGrath, S (1978) 'Life behind bars – sentence or sanctuary', *The Australian* 'Magazine', 19–20 August, p11

McIntosh, P (1992) 'White privilege and male privilege: A personal account of coming to see correspondences through work in women's studies' in M L Anderson and P H Collins (eds) *Race, Class and Gender*, Wadsworth, Belmont, California

McKenna, V (1987) 'Past, present – future indicative' in V McKenna, W Travers and J Wray (eds) *Behind the Bars: The Zoo Dilemma*, Vermont, Thorsons Publishing, Rochester

McLaren, D (1998) *Rethinking Tourism and Ecotravel: The Paving of Paradise and What You Can Do to Stop It*, Kumarian Press, West Hartford, Connecticut

McNair (1990) 'An investigation of the target market for Currumbin Sanctuary', McNair, Sydney

McNaught, P (compiler) (1991) *Directory of Queensland Museum*, Queensland Museum and Museums Association of Australia (Queensland Branch), Townsville

Macnaghten, P and Urry, J (1998) *Contested Natures*, Sage, London

Macnaghten, P and Urry, J (2000a) 'Bodies of nature: introduction', *Body & Society*, vol 6, nos 3–4, pp1–11

Macnaghten, P and Urry, J (2000b) 'Bodies in the woods', *Body & Society*, vol 6, nos 3–4, pp166–182

McNeely, J A and Wachtel, P S (1988) *Soul of the Tiger: Searching for Nature's Answers in Exotic Southeast Asia*, Doubleday, New York

Macpherson, J (1993) 'Koala farmer breeds his furry friends minus pats or stress', *Sunday Mail*, 7 March, p31

McQueen, H (1991) *Tokyo World: An Australian Diary*, William Heinemann, Melbourne

Mabey, R (ed) (1997) *The Oxford Book of Nature Writing*, Oxford University Press, Oxford

Marcus, J (1997) 'The journey out to the centre' in G Cowlishaw and B Morris (eds) *Race Matters: Indigenous Australians and 'Our' Society*, Australian Institute of Aboriginal and Torres Strait Islander Studies, Canberra

Marsh, I (2000) 'Political integration and the outlook for the Australian party system: party adaptation or system mutation?' in P Boreham, G Stokes and R Hall (eds) *The Politics of Australian Society: Political Issues for a New Century*, Pearson Education, Frenchs Forest

Marsh, J S (1987) 'National parks and tourism in small developing countries' in S Britton and W C Clarke (eds) *Ambiguous Alternatives: Tourism in Small Developing Countries*, University of South Pacific, Suva

Martin, C (1978) *Keepers of the Game: Indian–Animal Relationships and the Fur Trade*, University of California Press, Berkeley

Martinsen, P N (1985) 'The future direction of the native wildlife zone of Cleland Conservation Park', Cleland, Adelaide

Marx, K (1965) *Capital Volume I*, Progress Publishers, Moscow

Masson, J and McCarthy, S (1996) *When Elephants Weep: The Emotional Lives of Animals*, Vintage, London

Masri, Al-Hafiz B A (1987) *Islamic Concern for Animals*, Athene Trust, Petersfield, Hants

Masri, Al-Hafiz B A (1989) *Animals in Islam*, Athene Trust, Petersfield Hants

Masterson, A (1994) 'Island of turtles and tears', *The Australian Way*, April, pp72–75

Maunders, D (2001) 'Excluded or ignored? Issues for young people in Australia', *Development Bulletin*, no 56, pp70–73

May, J (1990) *The Greenpeace Book of Dolphins*, Slerting, New York

Maybury-Lewis, D (1992) *Millenium: Tribal Wisdom and the Modern World*, Viking, New York

Mazur, N A (1994) 'Zoos, government wildlife agencies and conservation organizations: Partners? Colleagues? or Adversaries?', paper presented to the ARAZPA/ASZK Annual Conference, Darwin, 17–22 April

Mazur, N (2001) *After the Ark? Environmental Policy Making and the Zoo*, Melbourne University Press, Melbourne

Mee, B (2000) 'A law unto themselves', *The Weekend Australian* 'Review', 5–6 August, pp4–6

Melba (1999) 'Melba's column', *The Weekend Australian* 'Magazine', 27–28 November, p2

Meleisea, M and Meleisea, P (1980) '"The best kept secret": Tourism in Western Samoa' in F Rajotte and R Crocombe (eds) *Pacific Tourism as Islanders See It*, Institute of Pacific Studies of the University of the South Pacific, Suva

Merchant, C (1990) 'Ecofeminism and Feminist Theory' in I Diamond and G F Orenstein, *Reweaving the World: The Emergence of Ecofeminism*, Sierra Club Books, San Francisco

Messenger Press (2000) 'Environment cause lures most volunteers', *The City Messenger*, 21 June, p15

Michel, S M (1998) 'Golden eagles and the environmental politics of care' in J Wolch and J Emel (eds) *Animal Geographies: Place, Politics, and Identity in the Nature–Culture Borderlands*, Verso, London

Midgley, M (1978) *Beast and Man: The Roots of Human Nature*, Harvester, Hassocks

Midgley, M (1983) *Animals and Why They Matter*, Penguin, Harmondsworth

Midgley, M (1993) 'The four-leggeds, the two-leggeds, and the wingeds: An overview of *Society and Animals*, vol 1', *Society and Animals*, vol 1, pp9–15

Mies, M (1993) 'White man's dilemma: his search for what he has destroyed' in M Mies and V Shiva, *Ecofeminism*, Zed, London

Millar, M S (1998) *Cracking the Gender Code: Who Rules the Wired World?* Second Story Press, Toronto

Miller, M L and Kaae, B C (1993) 'Coastal and marine ecotourism: A formula for sustainable development?', *Trends*, vol 30, no 2, pp35–41

Milling, H (1987) 'No close encounters', *G.O. (Government Officers' Magazine)*, vol 4, no 3, pp18–19

Milton, K (2000) 'Ducks out of water: Nature conservation as boundary maintenance' in J Knight (ed) *Natural Enemies: People–Wildlife Conflicts in Anthropological Perspective*, Routledge, London and New York, pp229–246

Minister of the Environment and Minister of Supply and Services (1990) 'Yoho National Park Highline', Minister of the Environment and Minister of Supply and Services, Ottawa

Mitchell, J (1992) 'Survey of Cleland Visitors', John Mitchell Public Relations, Hyde Park, Adelaide

Mitchell, R (1993) 'Humans, nonhumans and personhood' in P Cavalieri and P Singer (eds) *The Great Ape Project: Equality Beyond Humanity*, Fourth Estate, London

Mitten, D (1994) 'Ethical considerations in adventure therapy: A feminist critique' in E Cole, E Erdman and E D Rothblum (eds) *Wilderness Therapy for Women: The Power of Adventure*, Haworth Press, New York

Moar, K (1987) 'Determination of visitors' perceptions of the Adelaide Zoo', honours thesis submitted for Bachelor of Science, Department of Psychology, University of Adelaide

Monk, S (1998) '"White thugs" killing their cocky cousins', *The Advertiser*, 14 July, p5

Montagu, A (1963) 'The history of the dolphin' in A Montagu and J C Lilly (eds) *The Dolphin in History*, William Andrews Clark Memorial Library, University of California, Los Angeles

Montgomery, B (1997) 'More valuable alive than they are dead', *The Weekend Australian* 'Magazine', 13–14 September, p3

Montgomery, S (1991) *Walking with the Great Apes: Jane Goodall, Dian Fossey, Biruté Galdikas*, Houghton Mifflin, Boston

Moon, O (1997) 'Marketing nature in rural Japan' in P J Asquith and A Kalland (eds) *Japanese Images of Nature: Cultural Perspectives*, Nordic Institute of Asian Studies and Curzon, Richmond, Surrey

Moore, M (1999) 'Counting the cost of whale watching', *Guardian Weekly*, 25 April, p20

Morton, J (1993) 'Romancing the stones', *Arena Magazine*, no 4, pp39–40

Moss, S and Mills, M (2001) 'Is it closing time for the big game attractions?', *Guardian Weekly*, 8–14 November, p21

Muir, J (2000) 'Swimming with seals is the fun part of saving Port Phillip Bay', *The Australian* 'Magazine', 4–5 March, p14

Muir, K (2001) 'World heritage achieved', *Habitat Australia*, August, p14

Mullan, B and Marvin, G (1987) *Zoo Culture*, Weidenfeld and Nicolson, London

Mulligan, L (2000) 'A painted forest for baby gorilla in its midst', *The Australian* 'Magazine', 23 February, p3

Mullin, M H (1999) 'Mirrors and windows: sociocultural studies of human–animal relationships', *Annual Review of Anthropology*, vol 28, pp201–224

Mullins, J (1992) 'My own cannibal paradise', *The Australian*, 'Weekend Review', 22–23 August, p8

Mulvey, C (1987) 'Among the Sag-a-Noshes: Ojibwa and Iowa Indians with George Catlin in Europe, 1843–1848' in C Feest (ed) *Indians and Europe: An Interdisciplinary Collection of Essays*, Herdot Alano Verlag, Aachen

Murray, A J (1991) *No Money, No Honey: A Study of Street Traders and Prostitutes in Jakarta*, Oxford University Press, Oxford

Murray-Smith, S (1988) *Sitting on Penguins: People and Politics in Australian Antarctica*, Hutchinson Australia, Sydney

Nakajima, K (2000) 'Whaling: The facts', Japan Whaling Association, Tokyo

Nash, H (1982) *How Preschool Children View Mythological Hybrid Figures: A Study of Human/Animal Body Imagery*, University Press of America, Washington

Nash, R (1973) *Wilderness and the American Mind*, Yale University Press, New Haven and London, first published 1967

Nash, R F (1990) *The Rights of Nature: A History of Environmental Ethics*, Primavera Press, Leichhardt

Nathanson, D E (1989) 'Using Atlantic Bottlenose Dolphins to increase cognition of mentally retarded children' in P F Lovibond and P H Wilson (eds) *Clinical and Abnormal Psychology*, Elsevier Science Publishers, North Holland

National Parks and Wildlife SA (1992) 'Discovering penguins', Department of Environment and Heritage, Adelaide

Nationwide News (1992) 'John King, 8, cries over whales beached at Seal Rocks', *Weekend Australian*, 18–19 July, p23

Nationwide News Pty Ltd (1993) '"Echidna was good tucker": Edward Mailman was charged with eating echidna in Roma, Queensland', *The Advertiser*, 23 July, p2

Nationwide News Pty Ltd (2003) 'Return of the giants', *The Sunday Mail*, 1 June, p46

Nelson, S M (1993) 'Diversity of the Upper Paleolithic "Venus" figurines and archaeological mythology' in C B Brettel and C F Sargent (eds) *Gender in Cross-Cultural Perspective*, Prentice Hall, Englewood Cliffs, New Jersey

New South Wales Tourism Commission (1989a) 'The domestic holiday market', New South Wales Tourism Commission, Sydney

Newton, J (2001) 'On the dolphin watch', *The West Australian*, 'Today', 19 July, pp10–11

New York Zoological Society (c1991) 'Bronx Zoo', New York Zoological Society, New York

New Zealand Antarctic Institute (2000) 'Information Sheets – Tourism in Antarctica', The New Zealand Antarctic Institute, Christchurch, New Zealand, http://www.antarcticanz.govt.nz/Pages/InfoEducation/ISTourism.msa

Nicoll, F (1993) 'The art of reconciliation: Art, aboriginality and the state', *Meanjin*, vol 52, pp705–718

Nollman, J (1987) *Animal Dreaming: The Art and Science of Interspecies Communication*, Bantam, New York

Norris, K S (1991b) 'Essay: Looking at captive dolphins' in K Pryor and K S Norris (eds) *Dolphin Societies: Discoveries and Puzzles*, University of California Press, Berkeley and Los Angeles

Northern Territory Tourist Commission (1993) 'Come share our culture: A guide to Northern Territory Aboriginal tours, arts and crafts', Northern Territory Tourist Commission, Darwin

Noske, B (1989) *Humans and Other Animals*, Pluto, London

O'Barry, R (1991) *Behind the Dolphin Smile*, Berkley Books, New York

O'Brien, P (1990) 'Managing Australian wildlife', *Search*, vol 21, pp24–27

O'Brien, S (2000a) 'Zambesi junior earns his stripes', *The Advertiser*, 18 October, p3

O'Brien, S (2000b) 'Young lifesaver visits a sick mate', *The Advertiser*, 10 October, p9

O'Donnell, L (2000a) 'Rent-a-panda hard to bear', *The Weekend Australian* 'Magazine', 9–10 December, p12

O'Donnell, L (2000b) 'Race to save "milked" bears', *The Weekend Australian* 'Magazine', 19–20 August, p14

O'Donnell, L (2001) 'A taste of freedom', *The Australian* 'Magazine', 10–11 February, pp22–25

Ocean, J (1997) *Dolphins into the Future*, Dolphin Connection, Hawaii

Oelschlaeger, M (1991) *The Idea of Wilderness from Prehistory to the Age of Ecology*, Yale University Press, New Haven and London

O'Grady, R (1982) *Tourism in the Third World: Christian Reflections*, Orbis, New York

Ohnuki-Tierney, E (1987) *The Monkey as Mirror: Symbolic Transformations in Japanese History and Ritual*, Princeton University Press, Princeton

Ohnuki-Tierney, E (1993) *Rice as Self: Japanese Identities Through Time*, Princeton University Press, Princeton, New Jersey

Oliver, J (1992) 'All Things Bright and Beautiful: Are Tourists Getting Responsible Adult Environmental Education Programs?' in B Weir (ed) *Ecotourism Incorporating the Global Classroom*, Bureau of Tourism Research, Canberra

Omeenyo, A (1992) 'Aboriginal Environment in National Parks: Aboriginal rangers' perspectives' in J Birckhead, T de Lacy and L Smith (eds) *Aboriginal Involvement in Parks and Protected Areas*, Aboriginal Studies Press, Canberra

Orams, M B (1995). 'Managing interaction between wild dolphins and tourists at a dolphin feeding program, Tangalooma, Australia: the development and application of an education program for tourists, and an assessment of "pushy" dolphin behaviour', Doctor of Philosophy thesis submitted to University of Queensland, St Lucia, Brisbane

Ortega y Gasset, J (1972) *Meditations on Hunting*, Charles Scribner's Sons, New York, translated by Howard B. Wescott and introduced by Paul Shepard

Osborne, E (2000) 'Zoo's big draw macaws', *The Advertiser*, 1 June, p15

Osburne, B S (1988) 'The iconography of nationhood in Canadian art' in D Cosgrove and S Daniels (eds) *The Iconography of Landscape: Essays on the Symbolic Representation, Design and Use of Past Environments*, Cambridge University Press, Cambridge

Osprey Wildlife Expeditions (1994) 'Wintering with whales/songlines of Undiri', Osprey Wildlife Expeditions, Adelaide

Packard, J M, Babbitt, K J, Hannon, P G and Grant, W E (1990) 'Infanticide in Captive Collared Peccaries (*Tayassu tajacu*)', *Zoo Biology*, vol 9, pp49–53

Paddle, R (2000) *The Last Tasmanian Tiger: The History and Extinction of the Thylacine*, Cambridge University Press, Cambridge

Papps, D (1988) 'Wilderness: New Legislation for NSW', *Australian Ranger Bulletin*, vol 4, no 4, pp9–14

Parry, R L (2004) 'Blood boils over dolphin slaughter', *The Weekend Australian* 'Magazine', 7–8 February, p12

Pattullo, P (1996) *Last Resorts: The Cost of Tourism in the Caribbean*, Monthly Review Press, New York

Paul, E S (1995) 'Us and Them: Scientists' and Animal Rights Campaigners'

Views of the Animal Experimentation Debate', *Society and Animals*, vol 3, pp1–21

Payne, W and Brown, P (1999) 'Sweet little monsters', *The West Australian* 25 July, p12

Pearce, A (2001) 'Dingo discourse: constructions of nature and contradictions of capital in an Australian eco-tourist location', *Anthropological Forum*, vol 11, pp175–194

Pearce, P L (1988) *The Ulysses Factor: Evaluating Visitors in Tourist Settings*, Springer-Verlag, New York

Pearce, P L and Caltabiano, M L (1983) 'Inferring travel motivation from travelers' experiences', *Journal of Travel Research*, vol 22, pp16–20

Pearson, M (1991) 'Travellers, Journeys, Tourists: the meanings of journeys', *Australian Cultural History*, no 10, pp113–124

Pengelley, J (2000) 'Nature sets the scene for a battle of the species', *The Advertiser*, 18 April, p13

Peretti, P O (1990) 'Elderly–Animal Friendship Bonds', *Social Behavior and Personality*, vol 18, pp151–156

Peterson, D and Goodall, J (1993) *Visions of Caliban: On Chimpanzees and People*, Houghton Mifflin, Boston

Peterson, J H Jr (1994) 'Sustainable wildlife use for community development in Zimbabwe' in M Freeman and U P Kreuter *Elephants and Whales: Resources for Whom?*, Gordon and Breach Science Publishers, Reading

Phelps, B (2001) 'Genetic engineering – into law and into the environment?', *Habitat Australia*, 39(1), p26

Phillips, P (1992) 'Nature Travel Spring Tours' (brochure), Nature Travel, Brisbane

Pitt, D B (1998) 'Creature feature', *The Weekend Australian* 'Magazine', 7–8 March, pp15–17

Plane, T (1997) 'Kind cut for koalas', *The Weekend Australian* 'Magazine', 1–2 March, p4

Plane, T (2000) 'Birds in the hand, but few in the bush', *The Weekend Australian* 'Magazine', 28–29 October, p7

Plumwood, V (1990) 'Gaia and greenhouse; how helpful is the use of feminine imagery for nature?' in K Dyer and J Young (eds) *Changing Directions: The Proceedings of the Conference Ecopolitics IV*, University of Adelaide, Adelaide

Plumwood, V (1992) 'SealsKin', *Meanjin*, vol 51, pp45–57

Plumwood, V (1993) *Feminism and the Mastery of Nature*, Routledge, London and New York

Plumwood, V (2002) *Environmental Culture: The Ecological Crisis of Reason*, Routledge, London and New York

Poutney, M (1999b) 'Oh doctor, take pity on a poor baby', *The Advertiser*, 2 December, p7

Poppenbeek, P (1994) 'Inside images by outsiders: stereotypes of and by both black and white Australians' in Curtin University of Technology (ed) *Australia in the World: Perceptions and Possibilities*, Black Swan Press, Perth

Porter, D (1988) 'The Feral Peril', *Sydney Morning Herald*, 'Good Weekend', 30 January, pp12–13, 15

Portside Messenger (1990) 'Streets about to come alive in heritage parade', *Portside Messenger*, 28 November, p9.

Portside Messenger (1992) 'First glimpse of ocean delights kids', *Portside Messenger*, 22 July, p1

Portside Messenger (1995) 'Sponsorships to aid dolphin study', *Portside Messenger*, 22 March, p7

Portside Messenger (1996) 'Melody lingers to study the special mystery of dolphins in the Port River', *Portside Messenger*, 3 July, p4

Portside Messenger (1997) 'EPA to help fund Port River chemical testing', *Portside Messenger*, 27 August, p6

Portside Messenger (1998a) 'Dolphin detective', *Portside Messenger*, 1 September, p13

Portside Messenger (1998b) 'Marine shock', *Portside Messenger*, 19 August, p7

Possamaï, Adam (2000) 'A profile of New Agers: social and spiritual aspects', *Journal of Sociology*, vol 36, pp364–377

Poutney, M (1999a) 'Medical experts rally to save zoo's new baby', *The Advertiser*, 30 November, p3

Powch, I G (1994) 'Wilderness therapy: What makes it empowering for women?' in E Cole, E Erdman and E D Rothblum (eds) *Wilderness Therapy for Women: The Power of Adventure*, Haworth Press, New York

Powell, S (1999) 'Flying foxes are eaten, despised, adored, feared', *The Weekend Australian*, 'Review', 17–18 April, pp6–8

Powell, S (2003) 'The new zoo', *The Weekend Australian* 'Magazine', 22–23 February, pp27–31

PPK Consultants in Association with KPMG (1991) *Kangaroo Island Tourism Road Evaluation: Final Report*, Tourism South Australia, Adelaide

Price, J (1999) *Flight Maps: Adventures with Nature in Modern America*, Basic Books, New York

Prideaux, M (2000) 'The complex game of protecting whales', *Habitat Australia*, vol 24, number 4, pp8–10

Prideaux, M and Bossley, M (2000) 'Lethal waters: the assault on our marine mammals', Special Habitat Supplement, *Habitat*, vol 28, no 2, p3

Putnam, R D (2000) *Bowling Alone: The Collapse and Revival of American Community*, Simon and Schuster, New York

Puttick, E (1997) *Women in New Religions: In Search of Community, Sexuality and Spiritual Power*, Macmillan, Houndmills

Pybus, C and Flanagan, R (1990) *The Rest of the World is Watching*, Macmillan, Sydney

Qantas (1994) 'Airtime: news and views from Qantas', *The Australian Way –* (Inflight Magazine), October, p8

Quart, A (2003) *Branded: The Buying and Selling of Teenagers*, Perseus, New York

Radford, T (2001) 'Coral reefs "face total destruction"', *The Guardian Weekly*, 13–19 September, p23

Radford, T (2002) 'Elephants die young in zoos', *The Guardian Weekly*, 31 October–6 November, p11

Rajecki, D W, Rasmussen, J L, and Craft, H D (1993) 'Labels and the treatment of animals: Archival and experimental cases', *Society and Animals*, vol 1, pp45–60

Regan, T (1982) *All That Dwell Therein: Animal Rights and Environmental Ethics*, University of California Press, Berkeley and Los Angeles

Regan, T (1991) *The Thee Generation: Reflections on the Coming Revolution*, Temple University Press, Philadelphia

Reid, E (1996) 'Whale watchers of the Head of the Bight: A 1995 visitor profile and implications for management', Occasional paper no 11, Adelaide: Mawson Graduate Centre for Environmental Studies, University of Adelaide, Adelaide

Rice, E (2000) 'Charlie and Madidid as free as the air', *The Advertiser*, 12 December, p10

Richardson, J (1993) *Ecotourism and Nature-based Holidays*, Simon and Schuster, Marrickville

Ritvo, H (1987) *The Animal Estate: The English and Other Creatures in the Victorian Age*, Penguin, Harmondsworth

Ritzer, G and Liska, A (1997) '"McDisneyization" and "post-tourism": complementary perspectives on contemporary tourism' in C Rojek and J Urry (eds) *Touring Cultures: Transformation of Travel and Theory*, Routledge, London and New York

Robinson, A C and Heard, L M B (1985) 'National Parks' in C R Twidale, M J Tyler and M Davies (eds) *Natural History of Eyre Peninsula*, Royal Society of South Australia (Inc), Adelaide

Robson, F (1988) *Pictures in the Dolphin Mind*, Angus and Robertson, North Ryde

Robson, F (2001), 'A monster of our own making …' *The West Australian*, 'Big Weekend', 17 February, pp1–2

Rockley, T (1990) 'Frolicking dolphins captured in Martin's book', *Portside Messenger*, 15 August, p4

Roe, J (1998) 'Dayspring: Australia and New Zealand as a setting for the "New Age" from the 1890s to Nimbin' in D Walker and M Bennett (eds), *Australian Cultural History*, no 16, pp170–187

Rojek, C (1997) 'Indexing, dragging and the social construction of tourist sites' in C Rojek and J Urry (eds) *Touring Cultures: Transformation of Travel and Theory*, Routledge, London and New York

Rollin, B E (1990) *The Unheeded Cry: Animal Consciousness, Animal Pain and Science*, Oxford University Press, Oxford

Rolls, E (1981) *A Million Wild Acres: 200 Years of Man and an Australian Forest*, Thomas Nelson, Melbourne

Rolls, E (1992) *Sojourners: The Epic Story of China's Centuries-Old Relationship with Australia*, University of Queensland Press, Brisbane

Ross, G E (1988) 'Destination attraction and Kakadu: An exploration of factors associated with the touristic attractiveness of Kakadu National park' in B Faulker and M Fagence (eds) *Frontiers in Australian Tourism: The Search for New Perspectives in Policy Development and Research*, Bureau of Tourism Research, Canberra

Rothel, D (1980) *The Great Show Business Animals*, Barnes and Company, San Diego

Rothfels, N (2002) *Savages and Beasts: The Birth of the Modern Zoo*, John Hopkins University Press, Baltimore and London

Rothman, H (1989) *Preserving Different Pasts: The American National Monuments*, University of Illinois Press, Urbana and Chicago

Rothschild, M (1986) *Animals and Man: the Romanes Lecture for 1984–5*, Oxford Press, Clarendon

Rowe, D (1993) 'The Tourism Mirage', *Arena Magazine*, no 2, pp7–8

Rowell, G (1976) 'How Yosemite is Solving the Bear Problem', *National Wildlife*, vol 44, no 30, pp24–28

Rowland, B (1971) *Blind Beasts: Chaucer's Animal World*, Kent State University, Kent, Ohio

Royal Zoological Society of South Australia (1992) 'Introduction to Monarto Zoological Park', Royal Zoological Society of South Australia, Adelaide

Royal Zoological Society of South Australia (1992) *114th Annual Report 1991–1992*, Royal Zoological Society of South Australia, Adelaide

Royal Zoological Society of South Australia Incorporated (1998) 'Zoo Times', the newsletter of the Royal Zoological Society of South Australia Incorporated, Adelaide, vol 15

Royal Zoological Society of South Australia Incorporated (1999) 'Zoo Times', the newsletter of the Royal Zoological Society of South Australia Incorporated, Adelaide, vol 16

Russell, A (1984) *Memoirs of a Mountain Man*, Macmillan of Canada, Toronto

Russell, P (1993) 'The Paeolithic mother–goddess: Fact or fiction?' in H du Cros and L Smith (eds) *Women in Archaeology: A Feminist Critique*, Department of Prehistory, Research School of Pacific Studies, The Australian National University, Canberra

Ryder, R D (1989) *Animal Revolution: Changing Attitudes Towards Speciesism*, Basil Blackwell, Oxford

Ryel, R and Grasse, T (1991) 'Marketing ecotourism: Attracting the elusive ecotourist' in T Whelan (ed) *Nature Tourism: Managing for the Environment*, Island Press, Washington DC

Sackett, L (1991) 'Promoting primitivism: Conservationist depictions of Aboriginal Australians', *The Australian Journal of Anthropology*, vol 2, pp233–245

Safe, M (1998) 'Prince of whales', *The Australian* 'Magazine', 15–16 August, pp19–21

Safe, M (1999) 'The wrong stuff', *The Australian* 'Magazine', 11–12 September, pp22–26

Sagan, C and Druyan, A (1992) *Shadows of Forgotten Ancestors: A Search for Who We Are*, Random House, New York

St John, G (2000) 'Ferals: Terra-ism and radical ecologism in Australia', *Journal of Australian Sudies*, no 64, pp208–216, 289–291

Salisbury, J E (1994) *The Beast Within: Animals in the Middle Ages*, New York and Routledge, London

Salleh, A (1996a) 'Politics in/of the wilderness', *Arena Magazine*, no 23, pp26–30

Salmon, P W and Salmon, I M (1983) 'Who owns who? Psychological research into the human–pet bond in Australia' in A H Katcher and A M Beck (eds) *New Perspectives on Our Lives With Companion Animals*, University of Pennsylvania Press, Philadelphia

Salt, H B (1980) *Animals' Rights Considered in Relation to Social Progress*, Society for Animal Rights, Clarks Summit, Pennsylvania

Sama, A (1992) 'Rain forests are a growing feature at U.S. zoos', *USA Today*, 19 May, p5D

Sampson, A (2001) 'Is that you, Skippy?', *Habitat Australia*, August, p24

Sandall, R (2001) *The Culture Cult: Designer Tribalism and Other Essays*, Westview Press, Boulder, Colorado

Sanders, C R and Arluke, A (1993) 'If lions could speak: investigating the human–animal relationship and the perspectives of nonhuman others', *The Sociological Quarterly*, vol 34, pp377–390

Sanderson, K (1994) '*Grind*: ambiguity and pressure to conform: Faroese whaling and the anti-whaling protest' in M R Freeman and U P Kreuter (eds) *Elephants and Whales: Resources for Whom?*, Gordon and Breach Science Publishers, Reading

Savage, M, Barlow, J, Dickens, P and Fielding, T (1992) *Property, Bureaucracy and Culture*, Routledge, London

Savage, R (1997) 'New look at the zoo', *The Advertiser*, 27 December, p59

Sax, B (1998) *The Serpent and the Swan: The Animal Bride in Folklore and Literature*, McDonald and Woodward Publishing, Blacksburg, Virginia

Schoenfeld, D (1989) 'Effects of environmental impoverishment on the social behavior of marmosets *(callithrix jacchus)*,' *American Journal of Primatology Supplement*, vol 1, pp45–51

Scott, A (2001) 'Trafficking in monstrosity: conceptualizations of "nature" within feminist cyborg discourses', *Feminist Theory*, vol 2, pp367–379

Scott, J W (1997) 'Women's studies on the edge: introduction', *Differences: A Journal of Feminist Cultural Studies*, vol 9, ppi–v

Scourfield, S (2001) 'The eve of destruction', *The West Australian*, 'Big Weekend', 10 November, p1

Seager, J (1993) *Earth Follies: Coming to Feminist Terms with the Global Environmental Crisis*, Routledge, New York

Seebeck, J (1995) 'The Conservation of Mammals in Victoria – Development of Legislative Controls', *Journal of Australian Studies*, vol 45, pp3–65

Seidman, S (1997) 'Revitalizing sociology: the challenge of cultural studies' in E Long (ed) *From Sociology to Cultural Studies*, Blackwell, Malden, Massachusetts and Oxford, England

Serpell, J (1986) *In the Company of Animals: A Study of Human–Animal Relationships*, Basil Blackwell, Oxford

Shapiro, K (1993) 'Editor's introduction to *Society and Animals*', *Society and Animals*, vol 1, no 1, pp1–4

Shark Bay Visitor and Travel Centre (c1991) 'Shark Bay – Western Australia', Shark Bay Visitor and Travel Centre, Denham

Shears, R (1993) 'The Tree Ceremony', *Australian Way*, August, pp57–60

Shepard, P Jr (1973) *The Tender Carnivore and the Sacred Game*, Charles Scribner's Sons, New York

Singer, P (1977) *Animal Liberation: Towards an End to Man's Inhumanity to Animals*, Discus/Avon, New York, first published 1975

Singer, P (2001) *Writings on an Ethical Life*, Fourth Estate (HarperCollins), London

Smith, N (1999) 'The howl and the pussy: Feral cats and wild dogs in the Australian imagination', *Australian Journal of Anthropology*, vol 10, pp288–305

Smith, S L (1983) 'Interactions between pet dog and family members: An ethological study' in A H Katcher and A M Beck (eds) *New Perspectives on Our Lives With Companion Animals*, University of Pennsylvania Press, Philadelphia

Smolker, R (2001) *To Touch a Wild Dolphin: The Lives and Minds of the Dolphins of Monkey Mia*, Random House Australia, Milsons Point

Smolker, R, Richards, A, Connor, R, Mann, J and Berggren, P (1997) 'Sponge carrying dolphins (Delphinidae, *Tursiops* sp.): A foraging specialization involving tool use?', *Ethology*, vol 103, pp454–465

Snowdon, C T (1989) 'The criteria for successful captive propagation of endangered primates', *Zoo Biology Supplement*, vol 1, pp149–161

Sofield, T H B (1991) 'Sustainable ethnic tourism in the South Pacific: Some principles', *The Journal of Tourism Studies*, vol 2, pp56–71

Soper, K (1990) *Troubled Pleasures: Writings on Politics, Gender and Hedonism*, Verso, London

Soper, K (1995) *What is Nature? Culture, Politics and the Non-Human*, Blackwell, Oxford and Cambridge

Soulsby, L (1988) *Companion Animals in Society*, Oxford University Press, Oxford

South Australian Department of Tourism (1984) *Tourism Development and Management on Kangaroo Island: Working Party Report*, South Australian Department of Tourism, Adelaide

Southern Heritage Expeditions Limited (1995) *Initial Environmental Evaluation*, SHEL, Christchurch

Southern Heritage Expeditions Limited (1997) 'Heritage Expedition News', Autumn, SHEL, Christchurch

Southern Heritage Expeditions Limited (2000) 'Plan a wild Christmas or New Year', 'Heritage News', newsletter of Southern Heritage Expeditions, June, p3

Spence, M D (1999) *Dispossessing the Wilderness: Indian Removal and the Making of the National Parks*, Oxford University Press, New York and Oxford

Sperling, S (1991) 'Baboons with briefcases: Feminism, functionalism, and sociobiology in the evolution of primate gender', *Signs*, vol 17, pp1–27

Spretnak, C (1990) 'Ecofeminism: Our Roots and Flowering' in I Diamond and G F Orenstein, *Reweaving the World: The Emergence of Ecofeminism*, Sierra Club Books, San Francisco

Stacker, L (1985) 'Greenpeace – Waging Peace on Behalf of Mother Nature', *NSW Animal Welfare League News*, no 33, pp6–7

Stange, M Z (1997) *Woman the Hunter*, Beacon Press, Boston

Starick, P (1993) 'Lonely river journey for long-distance oarsman', *Portside Messenger*, 14 April, p8

Steinhart, P (1980) 'Essay: The Need to Feed', *Audubon Journal*, vol 82, pp126–127

Stone, M and Stone, J (1986) 'Principles and Animals', *Current Affairs Bulletin*, vol 63, no 3, pp4–13

Stratford, E (1994) 'Thoughts on the place of the home in environmental studies', *Social Alternatives*, vol 13, no 2, pp9–23

Sturgeon, N (1997) *Ecofeminist Natures: Race, Gender, Feminist Theory, and Political Action*, Routledge, New York

Summers, C (2002) 'A clash of culinary cultures', BBC News, 17 July, accessed at http://news.bbc.co.uk/2/hi/science/nature/2051091.stm

Suzuki, D (1992) 'Wisdom of the Elders', public lecture, Adelaide, 16 May

Swart, B (1993) 'The chimp farm' in P Cavalieri and P Singer (eds) *The Great Ape Project: Equality Beyond Humanity*, Fourth Estate, London

Szasz, K (1968) *Petishism: Pets and their People in the Western World*, Hutchinson, London

Tacey, D J (1995) *Edge of the Sacred: Transformation in Australia*, HarperCollins, Melbourne

Tangalooma (1997) 'Dolphin feeding', Tangalooma, Moreton Bay

Tapper, R L (1988) 'Animality, Humanity, Morality, Society' in T Ingold (ed) *What is an Animal?*, Unwin Hyman, London

Taylor, C (1989) *Sources of the Self: The Making of the Modern Identity*, Harvard University Press, Cambridge, Massachusetts

Te Awekotuku, N (1991) *Mana Wahine Maori: Selected Writings on Maori Women's Art, Culture and Politics*, New Women's Press, Auckland

Telegraph Group (2001a) 'On reflection, dolphins are smart', *The West Australian*, 7 May, p8

Telegraph Group (2001b) 'Dolphin studies stun boffins', *The West Australian*, 2 February, p3

Temple, L (1992) *Where Would We Sleep?: Children on the Environment*, Unicef Australia and Random House, Milsons Point, NSW

Tester, K (1991) *Animals & Society: The Humanity of Animal Rights*, Routledge, London

Thacker, C (1983) *The Wildness Pleases: the Origins of Romanticism*, Croom Helm, London

The Australian (2000) 'Torch to the animals: John Bertrand carries the Olympic flame past the elephant enclosure at Taronga Zoo', 'The Olympics', *The Australian* 'Magazine', 16 September, p11.

Thomas, K (1983) *Man and the Natural World: Changing Attitudes in England 1500–1800*, Allen Lane, London

Thrift, N (2000) 'Still life in nearly present time: the object of nature', *Body & Society*, vol 6, nos 3–4, pp34–57

Thubron, C (1987) *Behind the Wall: A Journey Through China*, Heinemann, London

Tilbrook, K (1989) 'The Sea Lions of Seal Bay', *Australia Now*, vol 13, no 4, pp12–15

Tilbrook, K (2002) 'Kill Port dolphins and face fine of $10,000', *The Advertiser*, 7 February, p12

Tilden, F (1977) *Interpreting Our Heritage*, University of North Carolina Press, Chapel Hill, first published 1957

Torgovnick, M (1990) *Gone Primitive: Savage Intellects, Modern Lives*, University of Chicago Press, Chicago and London

Torgovnick, M (1998) *Primitive Passions: Men, Women, and the Quest for Ecstasy*, University of Chicago Press, Chicago and London

Tourism South Australia (1991a) *Making South Australia Special: South Australian Tourism Plan 1991–1993*, Planning and Development Division, South Australian Tourism Board, Adelaide

Tourism South Australia and Kangaroo Island Tourist Association (1988) *Kangaroo Island Visitor Survey 1987/88 Research Report*, Tourism South Australia, Adelaide

Townsend, Amanda (1988) 'Attitudes, Perceptions and Behaviour Among Visitors at the Adelaide Zoo', Honours Thesis submitted for Bachelor of Arts, Department of Psychology, University of Adelaide, Adelaide

Traynor, S (1992) 'Appealing to the Heart as Well as the Head: The Northern Territory Junior Ranger Program', *Australian Ranger*, no 25, pp23–25

Tuan, Yi–Fu (1984) *Dominance and Affection: The Making of Pets*, Yale University Press, New Haven and London

Turkle, S (1991) 'Romantic reactions: paradoxical responses to the computer prescene' in J J Sheehan and M Sosna (eds) *The Boundaries of Humanity: Humans, Animals, Machines*, University of California Press, Berkeley

Turner, J (1980) *Reckoning with the Beast: Animals, Pain, and Humanity in the Victorian Mind*, John Hopkins University Press, Baltimore, Maryland

Turner, J (1996) *The Abstract Wild*, The University of Arizona Press, Tucson

Ulrich, R S (1993) 'Biophilia, biophobia and natural landscapes' in S R Kellert and E O Wilson (eds) *The Biophilia Hypothesis*, Island Press and Shearwater Books, Washington DC and Covelo, California

Urbanowicz, C F (1978) 'Tourism in Tonga: Troubled times' in V L Smith (ed) *Hosts and Guests: The Anthropology of Tourism*, Basil Blackwell, Oxford

Urry, J (1990) *The Tourist Gaze: Leisure and Travel in Contemporary Societies*, Sage, London

Urry, J (1992) 'The Tourist Gaze and the "Environment"', *Theory, Culture and Society*, vol 9, no 3, pp1–26

Valentine, P S (1992a) 'Ecotourism and nature conservation: A definition with some recent developments in Micronesia' in B Weir (ed) *Ecotourism Incorporating the Global Classroom*, Bureau of Tourism Research, Canberra

Varcoe, T (1988) 'Cultural tourism: A new approach to tourism in Victoria', *Australian Ranger Bulletin*, vol 4, no 4, pp26–28

Vest, J H C. (1987) 'The philosophical significance of wilderness solitude', *Environmental Ethics*, vol 9, pp303–330

Vialles, N (1994) *Animal to Edible*, Cambridge University Press, Cambridge, translated by J A Underwood

Vidal, J (2003) 'Unruly gulls put humans in the firing line', *The Guardian Weekly*, 22–28 May, p21

Wainwright, M (2001) 'Letter bombs linked to animal rights terror', *The Guardian Weekly*, 11–17 January, p8

Wakelin, J (2000a) 'Twilight time: a new dawn for desert bilby', *The Advertiser*, 20 April, p3

Wakelin, J (2000b) 'Shooting koalas the best answer', *The Advertiser*, 19 February, p12.

Waley, P (2000) 'What's a river without fish? Symbol, space and ecosystem in the waterways of Japan' in C Philo and C Wilbert (eds) *Animal Spaces, Beastly Places: New Geographies of Human–Animal Relations*, Routledge, London and New York

Walker, D (1991) 'Fauna and Flora Protection in New South Wales, 1866–1948', *Journal of Australian Studies*, no 28, pp17–28

Walker, S (1983) *Animal Thought*, Routledge and Kegan Paul, London

Wamsley, J (1994) 'The sanctuary movement: preserving Australia's mammals', *Policy*, vol 10, pp20–22

Wamsley, J (1995) 'Boodies Return to South Australia', *Earth Sanctuaries News*, no 10, p1

Wamsley, J (1999a) 'The mala, spinifex and Scotia', *Earth News*, no 30, May 1999, p4

Wamsley, J (1999b) 'Self generating and regenerating assets – a new look at living organisms', *Earth Sanctuaries News* no 32, October, pp2–3

Wamsley, J (1999c) 'A sanctuary for the endangered Bush Stone Curlew, restoring the balance, Newsletter of Earth Sanctuaries Foundation, no 2, p4

Wang, Chih-Yung and P S Miko (1997) 'Environmental impacts of tourism on U.S. national parks', *Journal of Travel Research*, vol 35, no 4, pp31–37

Wang, Yonghong (1993) 'Forests greening, but mature stands few', *China Daily*, 15 December, p1

Wanke, D (1989) 'Bandicoots at Belair', *Australian Ranger Bulletin*, vol 5, no 2, p6

Ward, P (1992) 'A matter of survival', *The Australian*, 'Weekend Review', 8–9 August, p3

Webb, N L and Drummond, P D (2001) 'The effect of swimming with dolphins on human well-being and anxiety', *Anthrozoös*, vol 14, no 2, pp81–85

Weir, L (1996) 'Whale park pleads for facilities', *The Advertiser*, 4 May, p12

Weir, S (1998) 'Declare estuary dolphin haven', *The Advertiser*, 15 September, p11

Weisman, A D (1991) 'Bereavement and Companion Animals', *Omega*, vol 22, pp241–8

Wescoat, J L Jr (1998) 'The "right of thirst" for animals in Islamic law: a comparative approach' in J Wolch and J Emel (eds) *Animal Geographies: Place, Politics, and Identity in the Nature–Culture Borderlands*, Verso, London

Wesolwoski, D (1998) 'Troubled waters', *Portside Messenger*, 25 March, p3

West Australian, 'Television programme' (2001) *The West Australian*, 'The West Magazine', 22 December, p32

Weston, D (1989) 'Satisfying the Demand' in J Vulkner and G McDonald (eds) *Architecture in the Wild: The Issues of Tourist Development in Remote and Sensitive Environments*, Royal Australian Institute of Architects National Education Division, Red Hill, ACT

Wexham, Brian (publisher) (1995) 'Antarctic tourism must tread with care as worried world watches', *Campus Review*, vol 5, no 7, p10

Whale and Dolphin Conservation Society (1997) 'Adopt a dolphin from only £12.50', Whale and Dolphin Conservation Society, Bath

Wheater, R J (1986) 'Advances in animal conservation: zoos of the future', *Current Affairs Bulletin*, vol 62, no 4, pp26–31

Whelan, T (1991) 'Ecotourism and its role in sustainable development' in T Whelan (ed) *Nature Tourism: Managing for the Environment*, Island Press, Washington DC

Wijers-Hasegawa, Y (2003) 'Sumatra islander tells court how aid project destroyed lives', *The Japan Times*, 4 July, p3

Wilkinson, H and Howard, M with Gregory, S, Hayes, H and Young, R (1997) *Tomorrow's Women*, Demos, London

Wilkinson, H and Mulgan, G 1995 *Freedom's Children: Work, Relationships and Politics for 18–34 Year Olds in Britain Today*, Demos, London

Williams, R (1993) 'Out of Perth', *The Australian Way*, December, p94

Williams, T (2000) 'Exotic pests a threat', *The Advertiser*, 10 October, p13

Willis, R (1990) 'Introduction' in R Willis (ed) *Signifying Animals: Human Meaning in the Natural World*, Unwin Hyman, London

Wilson, A (1992) *The Culture of Nature: North American Landscape from Disney to the Exxon Valdez*, Blackwell, Cambridge, Massachusetts

Wilson, B (1994) 'Review of Dolphin Management at Monkey Mia', unpublished report to executive director, State of WA, Department of Conservation and Land Management, Perth, Western Australia

Wilson, E O (1993) 'Biophilia and the conservation ethic', in S R Kellert and E O Wilson (eds) *The Biophilia Hypothesis*, Island Press and Shearwater Books, Washington DC and Covelo, California

Wilson, G, McNee, A and Platts, P (1992) *Wild Animal Resources: Their Use by Aboriginal Communities*, Bureau of Rural Resources, Australian Government Publishing Services, Canberra

Wiltsie, G (1990) 'Journey to the Bottom of the World', *National Parks*, vol 64, nos 5–6, pp18–25

Winnipeg Tourist Brochure (2001) 'What's on Winnipeg', *Where Winnipeg*, May/June, pp6–7

Wise, S M (2000) *Rattling the Cage: Toward Legal Rights for Animals*, Perseus Books, Cambridge, Massachusetts

Wolch, J (1998) 'Zoöpolis' in J Wolch and J Emel (eds) *Animal Geographies: Place, Politics, and Identity in the Nature–Culture Borderlands*, Verso, London

Wolff, K H (1991) '"Surrender-and-catch" and sociology' in H Etkowitz and R M Glassman (eds) *The Renaissance of Sociological Theory: Classical and Contemporary*, Peacock, Itasca, Illinois

Wood, D, with R Mannion (1992) *A Tiger By the Tail: A History of Auckland Zoo 1922–1992*, Auckland City, Auckland

Woodford, J (1999) 'Beware Flipper's dark side, warn researchers', *Sydney Morning Herald*, 8 July, p4

Woollacott, M (2001) 'Farmers learn lie of the land', *Guardian Weekly*, 8–14 March, p14

World Heritage Unit (1996) 'World Heritage listing: What does it really mean?', Department of the Environment, Sport and Territories, Canberra

Worster, D (1977) *Nature's Economy: A History of Ecological Ideas*, Cambridge University Press, Cambridge

Wuthnow, R (1998) *After Heaven: Spirituality in American Since the 1950s*, University of California Press, Berkeley

Wyatt, M (2000) 'The good, the bad and the ugly', *ZooTimes: Newsletter of the Royal Zoological Society of South Australia* 17(3), p5

Wyllie, T (1984) *Dolphins, Extraterrestrials and Angels: Adventures Among Spiritual Intelligence*, Bozon Enterprises, Fort Wayne

Yang Yi and Li Shuo (1993) 'Project for Panda Protection', *China Daily*, 11 October, p5

Young, E (1995) *Third World in the First: Development and Indigenous Peoples*, Routledge, London and New York

Young, E (2003) 'Slaughter in the outback', *The Guardian Weekly*, 18–24 December, p21

Young, V (1997) 'Survey says: conserve our wilderness', *Wilderness News*, Summer, p2

Zeppel, H (2000) 'Selling the dreamtime: Aboriginal culture in Australian tourism' in D Rowe and G Lawrence (eds) *Tourism, Leisure, Sport: Critical Perspectives*, Cambridge University Press, Cambridge

Index